Resilient Infrastructure: Mathematical Modeling, Assessment and Smart Sensing

Resilient Infrastructure: Mathematical Modeling, Assessment and Smart Sensing

Guest Editors

Zhongkai Huang
Dongming Zhang
Xingtao Lin
Dianchun Du
Jinzhang Zhang

Basel • Beijing • Wuhan • Barcelona • Belgrade • Novi Sad • Cluj • Manchester

Guest Editors

Zhongkai Huang
Department of Geotechnical Engineering
Tongji University
Shanghai
China

Dongming Zhang
Department of Geotechnical Engineering
Tongji University
Shanghai
China

Xingtao Lin
College of Civil and Transportation Engineering
Shenzhen University
Shenzhen
China

Dianchun Du
School of Civil Engineering
Southeast University
Nanjing
China

Jinzhang Zhang
Department of Geotechnical Engineering
Tongji University
Shanghai
China

Editorial Office
MDPI AG
Grosspeteranlage 5
4052 Basel, Switzerland

This is a reprint of the Special Issue, published open access by the journal *Mathematics* (ISSN 2227-7390), freely accessible at: https://www.mdpi.com/si/mathematics/Res_Infrastruct_Modeling_Assess_Smart.

For citation purposes, cite each article independently as indicated on the article page online and as indicated below:

Lastname, A.A.; Lastname, B.B. Article Title. *Journal Name* **Year**, *Volume Number*, Page Range.

ISBN 978-3-7258-4153-0 (Hbk)
ISBN 978-3-7258-4154-7 (PDF)
https://doi.org/10.3390/books978-3-7258-4154-7

© 2025 by the authors. Articles in this book are Open Access and distributed under the Creative Commons Attribution (CC BY) license. The book as a whole is distributed by MDPI under the terms and conditions of the Creative Commons Attribution-NonCommercial-NoDerivs (CC BY-NC-ND) license (https://creativecommons.org/licenses/by-nc-nd/4.0/).

Contents

Zhongkai Huang, Dongming Zhang, Xingtao Lin, Dianchun Du and Jinzhang Zhang
Resilient Infrastructure: Mathematical Modeling, Assessment, and Smart Sensing
Reprinted from: *Mathematics* 2023, 11, 4816, https://doi.org/10.3390/math11234816 1

Jianhong Zhang, Aixia Wang, Limin Zhang and Xiangsheng Chen
Coupling Failure Mechanism of Underground Structures Induced by Construction Disturbances
Reprinted from: *Mathematics* 2023, 11, 615, https://doi.org/10.3390/math11030615 3

Xu-Yang Cao
An Iterative PSD-Based Procedure for the Gaussian Stochastic Earthquake Model with Combined Intensity and Frequency Nonstationarities: Its Application into Precast Concrete Structures
Reprinted from: *Mathematics* 2023, 11, 1294, https://doi.org/10.3390/math11061294 20

Xiaomu Ye, Pengfei Ding, Dawei Jin, Chuanyue Zhou, Yi Li and Jin Zhang
Intelligent Analysis of Construction Costs of Shield Tunneling in Complex Geological Conditions by Machine Learning Method
Reprinted from: *Mathematics* 2023, 11, 1423, https://doi.org/10.3390/math11061423 39

Caixia Guo, Yingying Tao, Fanchao Kong, Leilei Shi, Dechun Lu and Xiuli Du
Analytical Predictions on the Ground Responses Induced by Shallow Tunneling Adjacent to a Pile Group
Reprinted from: *Mathematics* 2023, 11, 1608, https://doi.org/10.3390/math11071608 61

Qingtao Lin, Caixia Guo, Xu Meng, Hongyu Dong and Fanchao Kong
Experimental Research on the Settlement Feature of Two Ground Deformation Modes Induced by Tunnelling
Reprinted from: *Mathematics* 2023, 11, 2351, https://doi.org/10.3390/math11102351 80

Yiwei Sun, Kan Huang, Xiangsheng Chen, Dongmei Zhang, Xiaoming Lou, Zhongkai Huang, et al.
Study on the Reinforcement Mechanism of High-Energy-Level Dynamic Compaction Based on FDM–DEM Coupling
Reprinted from: *Mathematics* 2023, 11, 2807, https://doi.org/10.3390/math11132807 104

Yimin Wu, Haiping Wu, Chenjie Gong and Le Huang
Numerical Investigation of Key Structural Parameters for Middle-Buried Rubber Waterstops
Reprinted from: *Mathematics* 2023, 11, 3546, https://doi.org/10.3390/math11163546 123

Minglei Ma, Wei Wang, Jianqiu Wu, Lei Han, Min Sun and Yonggang Zhang
Numerical Computing Research on Tunnel Structure Cracking Risk under the Influence of Multiple Factors in Urban Deep Aquifer Zones
Reprinted from: *Mathematics* 2023, 11, 3600, https://doi.org/10.3390/math11163600 145

Chen Wang, Ming Song, Min Zhu, Xiangsheng Chen and Xiaohua Bao
The Effect of Asynchronous Grouting Pressure Distribution on Ultra-Large-Diameter Shield Tunnel Segmental Response
Reprinted from: *Mathematics* 2023, 11, 4502, https://doi.org/10.3390/math11214502 164

Editorial

Resilient Infrastructure: Mathematical Modeling, Assessment, and Smart Sensing

Zhongkai Huang [1,2,*], Dongming Zhang [1,2], Xingtao Lin [3], Dianchun Du [4] and Jinzhang Zhang [1,2]

1. Key Laboratory of Geotechnical and Underground Engineering of the Ministry of Education, Tongji University, Shanghai 200092, China; 09zhang@tongji.edu.cn (D.Z.); zhangjz@tongji.edu.cn (J.Z.)
2. Department of Geotechnical Engineering, College of Civil Engineering, Tongji University, Shanghai 200092, China
3. College of Civil and Transportation Engineering, Shenzhen University, Shenzhen 518061, China; xtlin@szu.edu.cn
4. School of Civil Engineering, Southeast University, No.2, Southeast University Road, Jiangning District, Nanjing 211189, China; dudianchun@seu.edu.cn
* Correspondence: 5huangzhongkai@tongji.edu.cn

MSC: 74S05; 65Z05; 00A06

As big cities become more dense, there is a growing demand for infrastructures, i.e., buildings, bridges, rail transit, pipelines, and utility tunnels. These facilities function as cross-scale complex network systems [1–3], and their serviceability is closely related to human life in terms of transportation, water conveyance, and energy supply. However, coupled with unseen strata and uncertain environments, even small variations in the system could lead to failure under extreme situations [4,5]. Such accidents have been reported repeatedly around the world, resulting in tremendous economic and social losses. Therefore, it is essential to enhance the resilience of infrastructures using multiple modern mathematical technologies. The National Academy of Sciences of the United States defines resilience as the ability to prevent, bear, recover, and adapt to adverse events. Thus, resilient infrastructures must be capable of avoiding catastrophic engineering failures and rapidly recovering its serviceability [6]. We proposed this Special Issue to build a stage for communicating the most recent progress in achieving resilient infrastructure via advanced mathematical modeling, risk assessment, and smart sensing technologies. It is believed that building resilient infrastructures will establish a more resilient and sustainable city.

Resilient infrastructure is crucial for ensuring the sustained functionality of essential systems in the face of various challenges, including natural disasters, climate change, and other unforeseen events [7]. The purpose of this Special Issue is to introduce advanced methods in the mathematical modeling of engineering problems, assessment, and smart sensing of essential infrastructures to address practical challenges in related fields. This Special Issue will provide a platform for researchers to share their insights, methodologies, and innovations in enhancing the resilience of critical infrastructure.

The response of the scientific community was significant, with a total of twenty-three papers being submitted for consideration, of which ten were accepted for publication after attentive peer review by respected reviewers in the fields of the papers.

As the Guest Editors for this Special Issue, we are delighted to bring the "Resilient Infrastructure: Mathematical Modeling, Assessment, and Smart Sensing" Special Issue to a close. This collection of articles has provided an insightful and comprehensive exploration of the multifaceted aspects involved in enhancing the resilience of critical infrastructure. The contributions to this Special Issue have been diverse, covering a wide range of topics within the overarching theme. From advanced mathematical modeling techniques to innovative smart sensing technologies, the articles collectively showcase the depth and breadth of research being conducted in the field.

One of the key takeaways from this Special Issue is the importance of adopting a holistic approach to resilient infrastructure. The integration of mathematical models, robust assessment methodologies, and smart sensing technologies has emerged as a powerful strategy for fortifying infrastructure against various challenges, including natural disasters, climate change, and unforeseen disruptions.

The inclusion of original research articles, review papers, and practical case studies has enriched the content, providing readers with a well-rounded understanding of the current state of resilient infrastructure research. The success stories shared in the case studies, along with the lessons learned from past failures, contribute valuable insights that can guide future research and real-world applications.

In conclusion, we extend our sincere appreciation to all the authors who have contributed their research to this Special Issue, the peer reviewers who dedicated their time and expertise, and the editorial team for their support throughout the process. We hope that this Special Issue serves as a catalyst for continued advancements in the field of resilient infrastructure and inspires further research and innovation.

Author Contributions: Conceptualization, Z.H., D.Z., X.L., D.D. and J.Z.; methodology, Z.H., D.Z., X.L., D.D. and J.Z.; writing—original draft preparation, Z.H.; writing—review and editing, Z.H., D.Z., X.L., D.D. and J.Z.; project administration, Z.H. All authors have read and agreed to the published version of the manuscript.

Funding: The first author was supported by the National Natural Science Foundation of China (grant No. 52108381, 52238010, and 52090082), the Shanghai Science and Technology Committee Program (grant No. 22dz1201202, 21dz1200601, 20dz1201404, and 22XD1430200), and the Natural Science Foundation of Chongqing, China (No. CSTB2023NSCQ-MSX0808).

Conflicts of Interest: The authors declare no conflict of interest.

References

1. Joyner, M.D.; Sasani, M. Building performance for earthquake resilience. *Eng. Struct.* **2020**, *210*, 110371. [CrossRef]
2. Decò, A.; Bocchini, P.; Frangopol, D.M. A probabilistic approach for the prediction of seismic resilience of bridges. *Earthq. Eng. Struct. Dyn.* **2013**, *42*, 1469–1487. [CrossRef]
3. Feng, Z.H.; Ma, Q.; An, Z.; Ma, H.; Bai, X. New Fatigue Life Prediction Model for Composite Materials Considering Load Interaction Effects. *Int. J. Appl. Mech.* **2023**, *15*, 2350076. [CrossRef]
4. Compton, P.; Dehkordi, N.R.; Sarrouf, S.; Ehsan, M.F.; Alshawabkeh, A.N. In-situ Electrochemical Synthesis of H_2O_2 for P-nitrophenol Degradation Utilizing a Flow-through Three-dimensional Activated Carbon Cathode with Regeneration Capabilities. *Electrochim. Acta* **2023**, *441*, 141798. [CrossRef]
5. Fathianpour, A.; Jelodar, M.B.; Wilkinson, S.; Evans, B. Resilient Evacuation Infrastructure; an Assessment of Resilience toward Natural Hazards. *Int. J. Disaster Resil. Built Environ.* **2023**, *14*, 536–552. [CrossRef]
6. Huang, Z.K.; Ning, C.L.; Zhang, D.M.; Huang, H.W.; Zhang, D.M.; Argyroudis, S. PDEM-based Seismic Performance Evaluation of Circular Tunnels under Stochastic Earthquake Excitation. *Georisk Assess. Manag. Risk Eng. Syst. Geohazards* **2023**, *18*, 1–13. [CrossRef]
7. Xu, M.; Pang, R.; Zhou, Y.; Xu, B. Seepage Safety Evaluation of High Earth-rockfill Dams Considering Spatial Variability of Hydraulic Parameters Via Subset Simulation. *J. Hydrol.* **2023**, *626*, 130261. [CrossRef]

Disclaimer/Publisher's Note: The statements, opinions and data contained in all publications are solely those of the individual author(s) and contributor(s) and not of MDPI and/or the editor(s). MDPI and/or the editor(s) disclaim responsibility for any injury to people or property resulting from any ideas, methods, instructions or products referred to in the content.

Article

Coupling Failure Mechanism of Underground Structures Induced by Construction Disturbances

Jianhong Zhang [1,*], Aixia Wang [1], Limin Zhang [2] and Xiangsheng Chen [3]

1. Department of Hydraulic Engineering, State Key Laboratory of Hydroscience and Engineering, Tsinghua University, Beijing 100084, China
2. Department of Civil and Environmental Engineering, The Hong Kong University of Science and Technology, Hong Kong, China
3. College of Civil and Transportation Engineering, Shenzhen University, Shenzhen 518060, China
* Correspondence: cezhangjh@tsinghua.edu.cn; Tel.: +86-10-62785593

Abstract: The development of cities often involves the construction of new tunnels buried underneath densely distributed existing structures. When tunnels experience complicated and difficult conditions, coupling failure mechanisms often develop, in which the failure of one structure results in the failures of adjacent structures caused by soil failure initiated from the excavation of the new tunnel. Four centrifuge tests were performed in this study to reveal three major mechanisms, i.e., rapid sand flow, partial failure and overall collapse induced by the instability of a tunnel face and the effects of soil types and buried existing structures. Data are presented about the deformation and the failure mechanisms. Effects of soil properties and groundwater are discussed. The tests indicate that rapid sand flow can be easily triggered by tunnel face instability, a chimney-like mechanism creating gaps underneath existing structures. In cohesive soil, failure may be limited in front of the tunnel face due to the formation of arching, rendering a partial collapse. An overall collapse may occur in less cohesive soil when involving changes in underground water, which is a failure mode of a ground block bounded by two single shear planes extending from the tunnel face to the surface. It was observed that the bending deformation of the existing tunnel is well correlated with the failure mode, and a limited partial collapse had the smallest impact on the tunnel. The magnitude of the deformation of the structures depended not only on the failure mode but also on the scope and orientation of the failure.

Keywords: coupling failure mechanism; tunnel face; underground structures; sand flow; partial collapse; overall collapse

MSC: 70; 74

1. Introduction

The development of cities often involves the construction of new tunnels buried underneath existing surface buildings and underground structures. When tunnels experience complicated and difficult conditions, devastating destruction can be induced by construction disturbances. For instance, in 2018, as shown in Figure 1, an over 40 m long tunnel failed at Guangdong Foshan Metro Line 2 in a water-rich interbed of muddy silt, silt and fine and medium sand. An earth pressure balance shield machine was being driven from east to west. During the assembly of segments, leakage occurred at the tail of the shield. Grease was injected immediately, trying to plug the leakage point. Within two or three hours, the leakage intensified to quick sand flow. Water and sand kept gushed out, flooded the tunnel and eventually caused the failure of the tunnel. The failure claimed 11 lives, and the overall collapse of the ground extended to the surface, damaged unground gas pipelines and created 6–8 m deep ground subsidence.

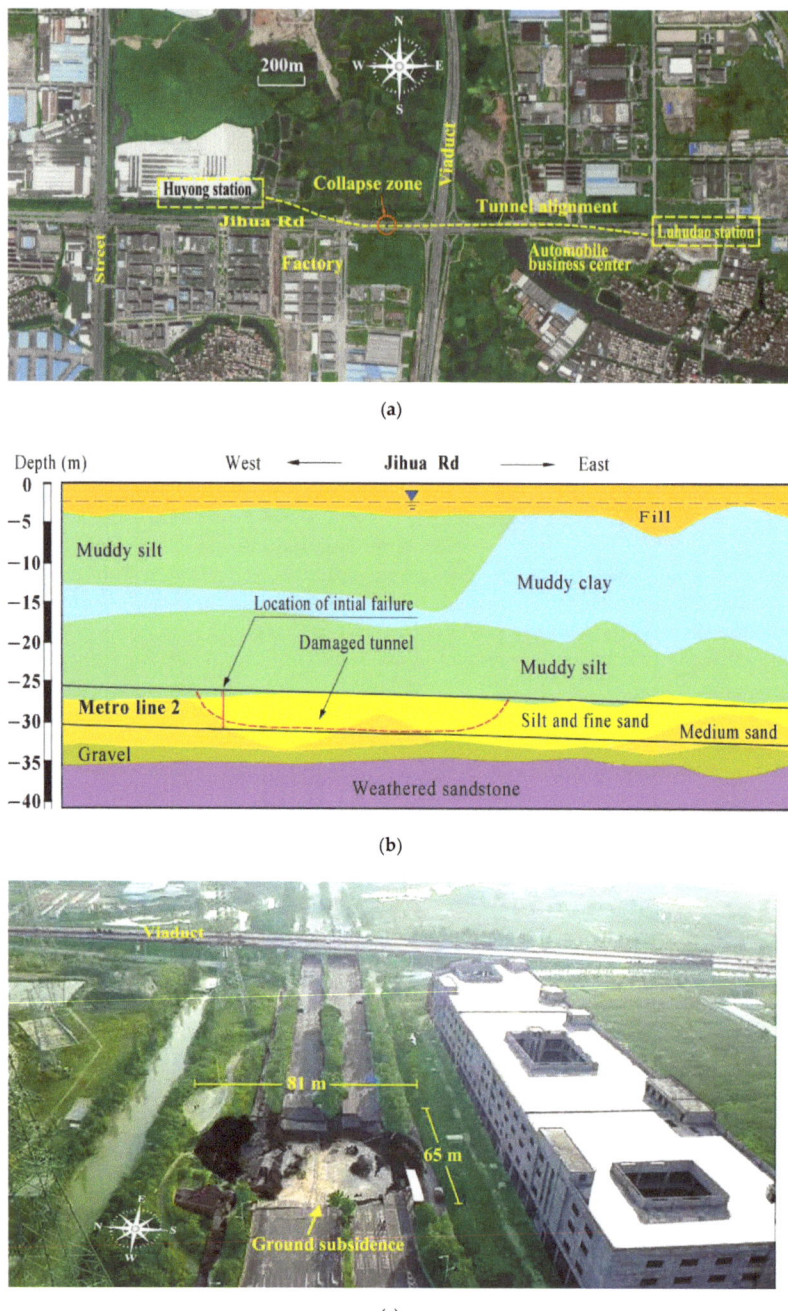

Figure 1. Failure of shield−driven tunnel at Guangdong Foshan Metro Line 2: (**a**) Aerial view of collapse zone; (**b**) Location of initial failure and damaged tunnel; (**c**) Ground subsidence measuring 81 m × 65 m × 8 m (depth).

Tan et al. (2021) [1] reported a 238 m long tunnel damaged at Shanghai Metro Line 4, as shown in Figure 2. The initial failure was located at a cross passage connecting two tunnels. The main reason of the failure lies in three aspects: the excavation sequence of the air shaft and the cross passage was inadequate, the temperature rose due to the failure of the freezing equipment, and thus sand flow (sand bursting) gushed into the cross passage under artesian water. The failure of the cross passage led to the flooding and collapse of the 238 m long tunnel, the overall collapse of the ground, dramatic ground subsidence and the rapid sinking of existing structures. Coupling failure mechanisms developed in these cases, in which the failure of one structure resulted in the failures of adjacent structures caused by rapid sand flow, in partial failure, and in overall collapse initiated from construction disturbances. It is noted that the tunnel failure was of a large scale, and the induced damage was catastrophic.

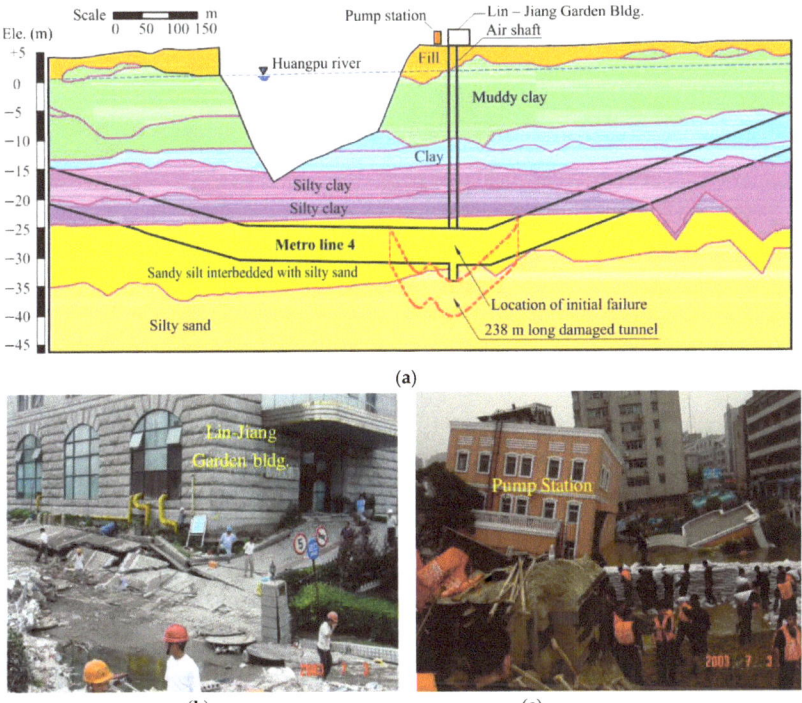

Figure 2. Destructions at Shanghai Metro Line 4: (**a**) Location of initial failure and 238 m long damaged tunnel; (**b**) Ground subsidence before Lin−Jiang Garden building; (**c**) Pump station sinking [1].

Physical modeling has played an important role in studies related to the excavation of tunnels [2–22]. It has been employed by many researchers to address the behavior of tunnel faces [2,23–26], stress transfer [25–28], multi-tunnel construction [29], deformation and the instability of structures [30–39]. However, most studies have focused on the response of a single structure to tunneling. The mechanisms of a single structure and a group of structures differ in that the latter is influenced by the interactions between structures, the arrangement of the structures with respect to the tunnel face, the failure pattern of the face, the gushing water encountered, etc. At present, theoretical and experimental studies on new tunnels underneath existing structures are still in the experience exploratory stage due to complex geological conditions and influencing factors. Research is still underway in this area within the international scientific community. It is essential to understand the coupling failure mechanism of existing underground structures to ensure the safe construction of new tunnels and the safe operation of existing structures.

In this study, four centrifuge model tests were performed at an 80 g level to investigate the coupling failure mechanism of existing underground structures subject to construction disturbances. A simple modeling technique was developed to simulate the instability of a tunnel face during construction. Three major mechanisms of sand flow, partial failure and overall collapse, associated with different soil conditions, were reproduced in the centrifuge. Observations of soil movement and the deformations of existing structures were made. The geometry of the failure zone is depicted for different tunnel face movements. The effects of soil properties, underground water and the presence of existing structures on deformations and failure mechanisms are discussed.

2. Centrifuge Model Testing
2.1. Model Setup

Figure 3 depicts the layout of the centrifuge model in a container. The container had internal dimensions of 0.6 m long × 0.2 m wide × 0.53 m high, accommodating existing underground structures underlaid by a new tunnel with a tunnel face at the center line of the container. A transparent front window enabled visual monitoring during the test. The model structures included a building basement of 0.12 m long × 0.04 m wide × 0.04 m high, a tunnel of 0.56 m × 0.05 m × 0.05 m and two storehouses (denoted as Store L of 0.1 m × 0.05 m × 0.05 m and Store R of 0.15 m × 0.05 m × 0.05 m) on either side of a sewer line (denoted as Sewer of 0.196 m × 0.05 m × 0.05 m).

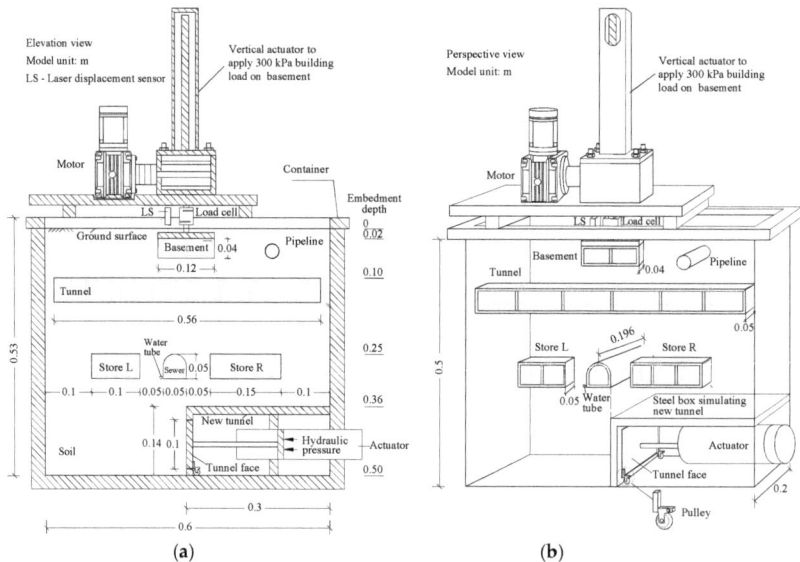

Figure 3. Centrifuge model setup: (**a**) Elevation view; (**b**) Perspective view.

The soil depth in the container was 0.5 m. The embedment depths of the basement and the tunnel were 0.02 m and 0.1 m, respectively. The two storehouses and the sewer line were buried at the same depth of 0.25 m. The model structures were made from 5 mm thick transparent acrylic plates and a colored acrylic plate facing the front window, with supporting plates of the same material inside the box, as shown in Figure 4. The stiffness of the model structure was measured to be 327 MPa. The length of the model tunnel (0.56 m) was smaller than the length (0.6 m) of the container, and the length of the model sewer line

(0.196 m) was smaller than the width (0.2 m) of the container so that direct contact between the models and the interior of the container side could be avoided.

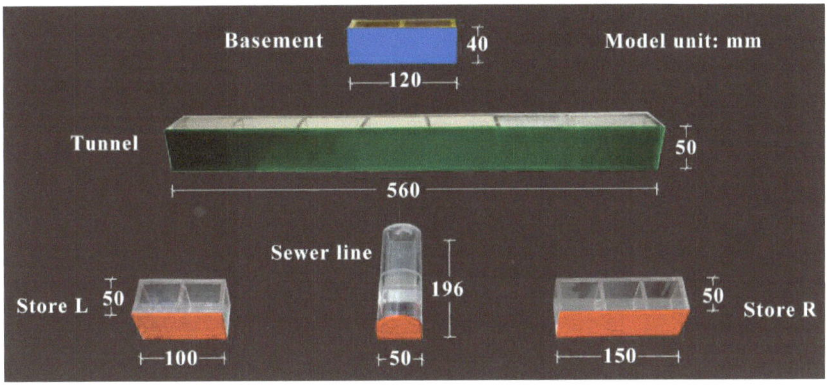

Figure 4. Dimensions of the model structures that were made of transparent acrylic plate.

A new tunnel under construction was modeled with a steel box of 0.3 long × 0.2 wide × 0.14 m high at the bottom with a tunnel face of 0.16 m wide × 0.1 m high. The tunnel face of a steel plate was connected to a horizontal actuator mounted within the steel box. The actuator with hydraulic pressure on the right-hand side supported the face (Figure 3a). It later applied hydraulic pressure on the opposite side to displace the tunnel face away from the soil, simulating the instability of the face. Two small pulleys were attached to the tunnel face, as shown in Figure 3b, supporting the amplified weight of the face under 80 g, and contact was avoided between the face and the surrounding frame so that the frictional resistance at the areas of contact was reduced. This technique allowed the tunnel face to move smoothly under high centrifugal acceleration.

The centrifuge model tests were carried out in the geotechnical centrifuge at Tsinghua University [40]. The soil models were scaled down to satisfy the principles of mechanical similitude between a model and its prototype [41]. Table 1 summarizes the typical scaling factors for centrifuge model testing. For the centrifuge model at 80 g, the dimensions of the model and the displacements measured on the model were multiplied by 80 for the prototype.

Table 1. Scaling law for centrifuge model test [41].

Parameter	Model/Prototype
Macroscopic length (m)	$1/N$
Gravitational acceleration (m/s^2)	N
Microscopic length (m)	1
Stress (kPa)	1
Strain (–)	1
Time for soil consolidation	$1/N^2$

2.2. Test Program

The test program had four models, as listed in Table 2. The sand model consisted of uniform sand with a configuration as shown in Figure 3, aiming to simulate sand flow caused by instability of the tunnel face. The low interlayer model, as shown in Figure 5a, was made to reproduce partial collapse, limited to the front of the tunnel face, which comprised silt containing 0.05 m of thick silty clay beneath the sewer line. To evaluate the impact of overall collapse and compare the effects of soil properties and water, two models were used, i.e., the silt model consisting of uniform silt and the high interlayer model (Figure 5b) containing 0.05 m of thick silty clay above the sewer line, as water is always a key factor involved in the safety of tunneling. A tiny tube was placed above the silty clay to bring water into the soil in the two interlayer models.

Table 2. Four centrifuge models in the test program.

Model Name	Soil Description	Water Effect	Failure Mechanism
Sand model	Uniform sand	Not involved	Sand flow
Low interlayer model	Silt with an interlayer below the sewer line	1.67 kg water	Partial failure
Silt model	Uniform silt	Not involved	Overall collapse
High interlayer model	Silt with an interlayer above the sewer line	0.75 kg water	Overall collapse

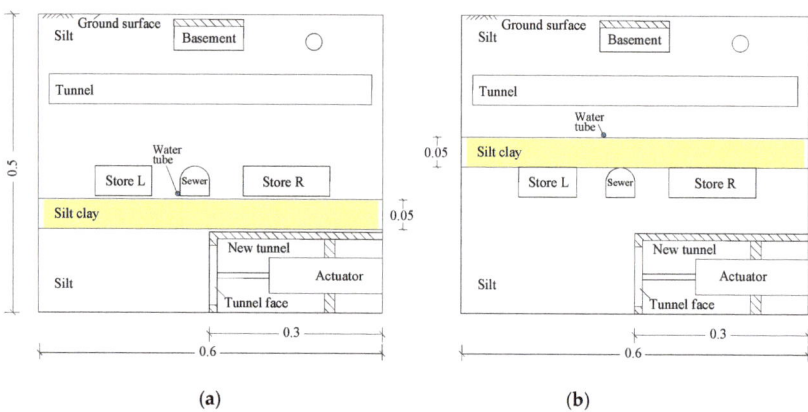

Figure 5. Two models consisting of silt with an interlayer of silty clay: (**a**) Low interlayer model with the silty clay beneath the sewer line; (**b**) High interlayer model with the silty clay above the sewer line (model unit: m).

2.3. Soil Properties and Model Preparation

Table 3 summarizes the properties of the three soils. The sand is a clean medium of sand with a mean grain size (D50) of 0.34 mm. It was compacted into a container with a dry density of 1660 kg/m^3 for the sand model. The sand was dense and firm at this density. The model structures, facing the front window, were placed at the designated locations during the compaction process, as shown in Figure 6a. The front window was removed after the preparation of the centrifuge model to place markers that were used to trace the movement of soil during the test, and it was then assembled back afterwards. A frictional coefficient between the model structures and the front window was estimated to be 0.3–0.4. It may have had a slight effect on the measured displacements of the model. To facilitate the placement of the markers, the sand was sprayed with a low water content of about 4%.

The silt had a plasticity index of 6.5 and was compacted with a water content of 8% and a dry density of 1500 kg/m^3. Saturated and drained triaxial tests were conducted to obtain the effective shear strength parameters of the sand and the silt. The silty clay had a plasticity index of 15.8, exhibiting high plasticity. The maximum dry density was 2287 kg/m^3 at a water content of 15% from a laboratory standard compaction test (ASTM D698). The silty clay was compacted with a water content of 17% and a dry density of 1600 kg/m^3 for the two interlayer models. It had a cohesion of 54 kPa and an internal friction angle of 14o through consolidated undrained triaxial tests at a water content of 17%. Markers of small white pebbles were used for the silt model and the two interlayer models, as shown in Figure 6b. The transparent wall was removed for the placement of the markers and was assembled back afterwards.

Table 3. Properties of three types of soil used in centrifuge tests.

Parameter	Sand	Silt	Silty Clay
Specific gravity	2.64	2.65	2.67
Maximum dry density (kg/m^3)	1680	/	2290
Minimum dry density (kg/m^3)	1330	/	/
Dry density of soil model (kg/m^3)	1660	1500	1600
Liquid limit (%)	/	25	30.0
Plastic limit (%)	/	18.5	14.2
Water content of soil model (%)	4	8	17
Cohesion (kPa)	0	6.1	54
Internal friction angle φ	38°	28.9°	14°

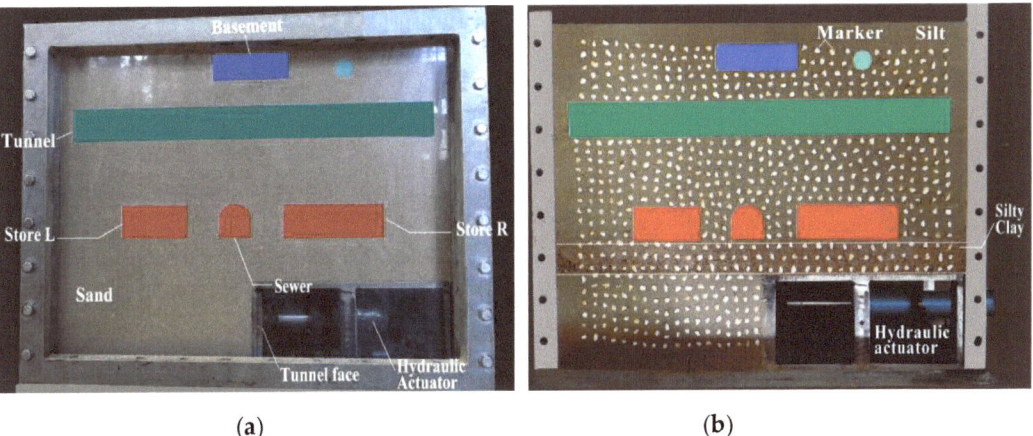

Figure 6. (**a**) Sand model after preparation; (**b**) Low interlayer model with pebble markers (the transparent wall was temporarily removed).

2.4. Instrumentation and Modeling Procedures

Figure 7 shows the instrumentation used in the model. A surcharge loading of 300 kPa, measured by a load cell, was applied to the basement to simulate the weight of the building. A non-contact laser displacement sensor was installed to measure the settlement of the ground surface. Seven tiny pressure cells were used: Nos. #1 and #2 were embedded on the left side of the Sewer, No. #3 was embedded on the right side of Store L, Nos. #4 and #5 were embedded on the base of Store L, and Nos. #6 and #7 were embedded on the base and right side of the Sewer to monitor the earth pressures. Unfortunately, the performance of the pressure cells deteriorated over time due to significant soil displacement. A digital black and white video camera was placed in front of the transparent side wall covering an area of 0.51 m–0.39 m, as indicated by dashed lines in Figure 7a. A photo-imaging technique was used to accurately measure the displacements of the soil and the structures by tracing the markers [39,40].

The centrifuge model was consolidated at 80 g first under self-weight and then under the surcharge load, and it terminated when the readings of the displacement sensor became stable. The deformations during consolidation were measured and deducted in the process under construction disturbance. Following consolidation, the tunnel face moved toward the right at about 10 mm with each step. The induced movement of the soil and the structures were recorded continuously by the video camera at 20 frames/s. Images of key phenomena could be captured during the test. The data logger for the earth pressure cells was set to record data at 0.1 Hz.

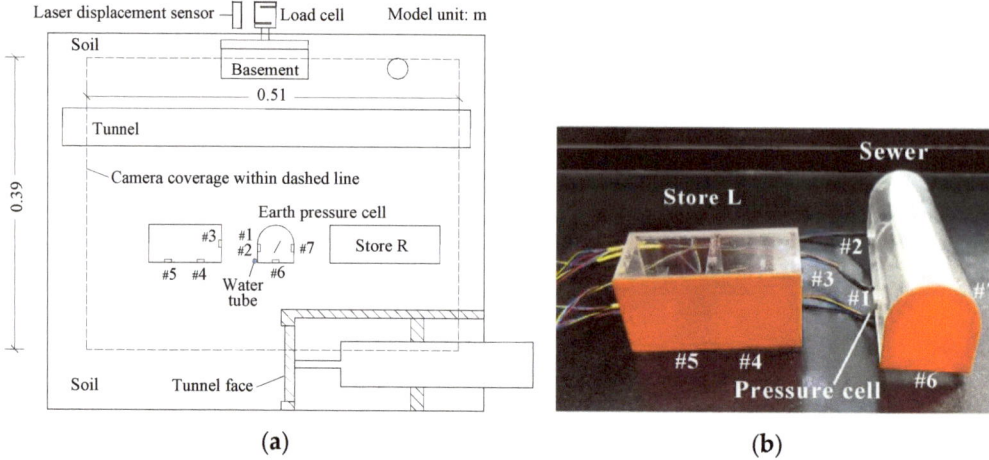

Figure 7. Instrumentation used in the centrifuge model: (**a**) Layout of instrument; (**b**) Placement of earth pressure cells.

3. Results and Discussions

The displacements measured on the model were multiplied by 80 for the prototype with a unit of m, and the underground water in kilograms used the model's scale. A two-dimensional description was adopted so that a major mechanism developed in the model could be captured. The geometries of the gap beneath the structures and the void induced by soil failure are depicted in Figure 8a, in which D = 4 m is the diameter of the tunnel. Settlement S and tilt are indicated in Figure 8b for the basement, the storehouses and the sewer line. Deformation along the longitudinal length of the existing tunnel is highlighted in Figure 8b, in which S_{max} is the maximum deformation.

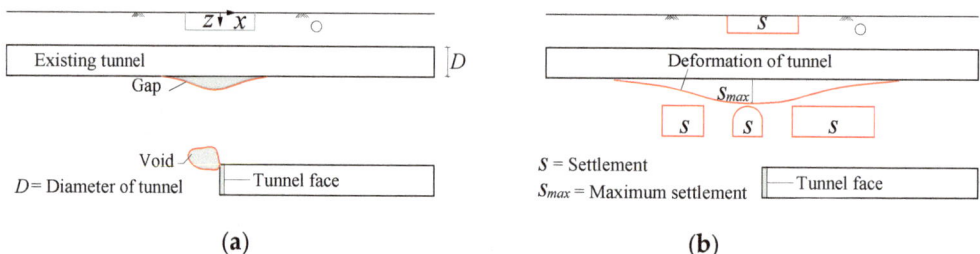

Figure 8. Characterization of deformations and failure: (**a**) Geometries of gap and void in soil; (**b**) Settlement of existing structures.

3.1. Sand Flow

Following the instability of the tunnel face as shown in Figure 9a in the sand model, which moved 0.85 m away from its initial position, sand flow occurred instantly, as reported in case studies [1], with a chimney-like mechanism above the tunnel face [9]. The existing tunnel then promptly deformed and tilted conspicuously. Through tracing the movement of some markers in the flow zone, soil displacements could be estimated to be 0.5 m. The position of the tunnel face remained, but the sand continuously flowed into the new tunnel. Gaps consequently formed beneath the basement, the existing tunnel and the storehouses, as shown in Figure 9b. A 0.13 m settlement was found at the basement, and the sewer line tilted 1 degree. The gaps expanded as shown in Figure 9c when sand flow terminated.

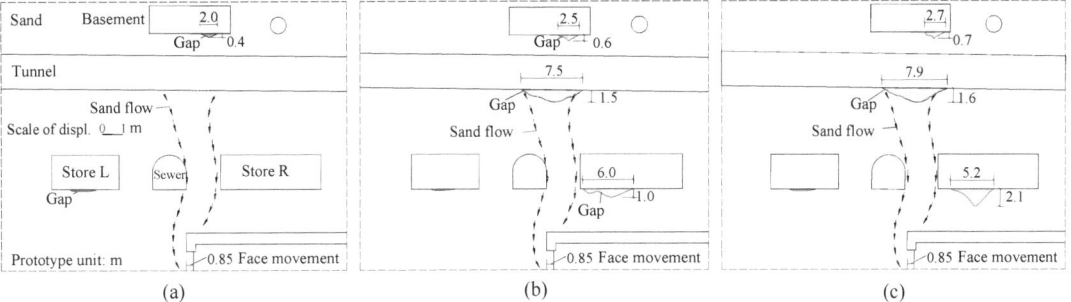

Figure 9. Side view of the model within coverage of the digital camera: (**a**) Sand flow occurring instantly following the instability of the tunnel face; (**b**) Gaps forming beneath structures; (**c**) Existing tunnel bending and gaps expanding.

Failure patterns induced by tunnel face stability have been revealed by greenfield models in sand. Figure 10a shows the recoded failure pattern in a large-scale 1 g model conducted by Sterpi et al. [28]. The failure resulted from air pressure reduction at the tunnel face and extended to the ground surface. Kamata and Masimo [25] showed similar failure patterns through centrifuge tests. The failure appeared in the vicinity of the tunnel face at 25 g and extended to the ground surface at 30 g. The observed failure mechanism in this study is similar to that reported by Sterpi et al. [25] and Kamata and Masimo [22]. However, the presence of the sewer line and the storehouse influenced the shape of the flow zone, and the existing tunnel prevented the flow zone from extending to the ground surface. In fact, the flow zone bypassed the tunnel and the basement and still reached the ground surface.

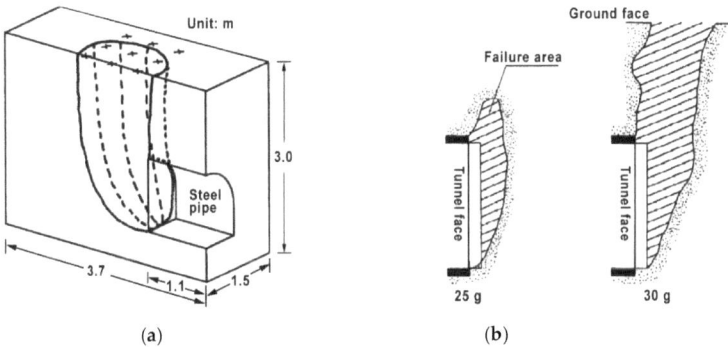

Figure 10. Greenfield failure patterns: (**a**) 1 g model [28]; (**b**) Centrifuge model [25].

Deformations of the existing tunnel were measured through image analysis when the sand flow terminated (Figure 9c), and the induced tensile strains were estimated by considering the tunnel to be equivalent Timoshenko beam [41], as shown in Figure 11, in which x is the distance from the tunnel face. The tunnel generally tilted 1 degree toward the right, which may be attributed to the free contact at the end. As the sand flow was sudden, bending concentrated at the location above the sand flow. Compared with the disturbance induced by tunneling [26,37], the scale of the construction disturbance was very extensive and, as a consequence, the maximum induced tensile strain was 2100 $\mu\varepsilon$, which could cause severe damage to the tunnel.

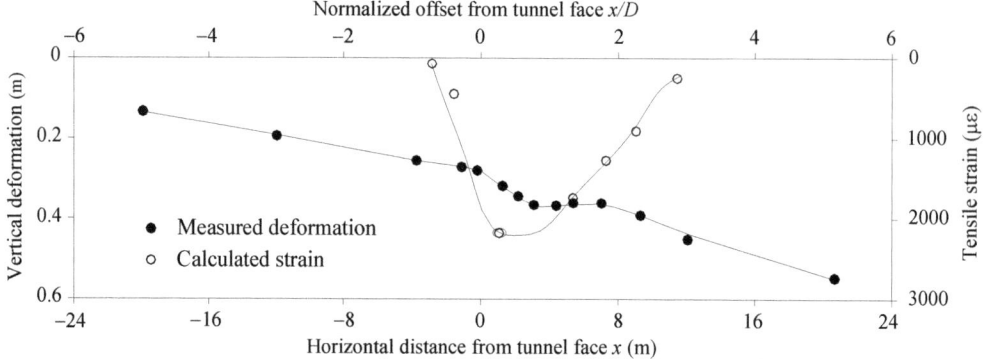

Figure 11. Measured deformations and calculated tensile strains of existing tunnel in sand model.

3.2. Partial Failure

Partial failure refers to a failure zone limited in front of the tunnel face in cohesive soil due to an arching effect. Figure 12 depicts the geometry of the failure zone for different tunnel face movements in the low interlayer model. In the beginning, the soil remained stable even when the tunnel face moved 1.6 m, as shown in Figure 12a. Then, water was brought in at a speed of 1.67 kg per minute and lasted for one minute, and it gushed down under high centrifugal acceleration and caused a void of 3.4 m wide and 8.0 m high (Figure 12b) in front of the face. At the end of water discharge (total water amount of 1.67 kg), the tunnel face moved from 1.6 m to 1.9 m, and a curved arch formed in the silty clay stratum, as shown in Figure 12c. The soil failure continued to propagate and break through the silty clay, resulting in increments of structure settlement and tilt (Figure 12d). A curved arch formed in the silt, as indicated in Figure 12e, which prevented the failure from developing upward. Therefore, later, when the tunnel face moved significantly from 1.9 m to 6.6 m, no further failure happened, as shown in Figures 12f and 13.

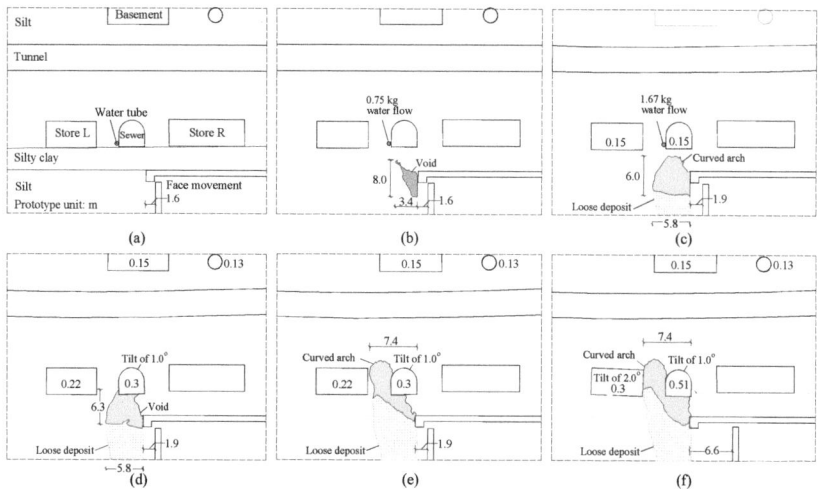

Figure 12. Partial failure in low interlayer model: (**a**) No changes at face movement of 1.6 m; (**b**) Void initiated by 0.75 kg of water flow; (**c**) Curved arch in silty clay at face movement of 1.9 m and 1.67 kg of water flow; (**d**) Breakthrough of silt clay layer and structures settling after water discharge; (**e**) Curved arch formed in silt; (**f**) Collapse zone stabilizing at face movement of 6.6 m.

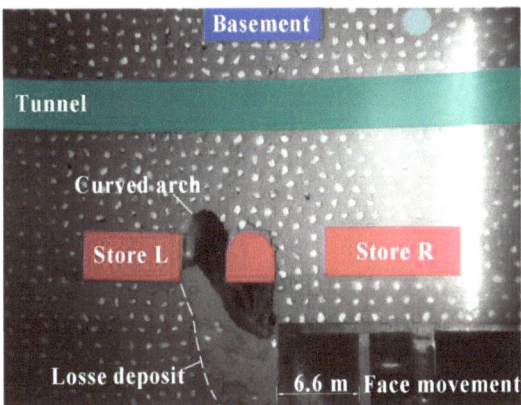

Figure 13. Photo of low interlayer model corresponding to Figure 12f.

Figure 14 illustrates the measured maximum deformations and calculated tensile strains of the existing tunnel at face movements of 6.6 m. Compared to the sand model, the arching had a strong effect on the deformations and induced strains on the existing tunnel. As the failure zone was limited, its impact on existing tunnel was greatly reduced. Consequently, the maximum settlement of the tunnel was 0.15 m, much lower than that in the sand model. The maximum strain in the low interlayer model was 850 με, only 40% of that in the sand model. However, the presence of the flexible interlayer of the silty clay may have increased the bending through width of the tunnel and thus had a greater influence on the performance of adjacent underground structures.

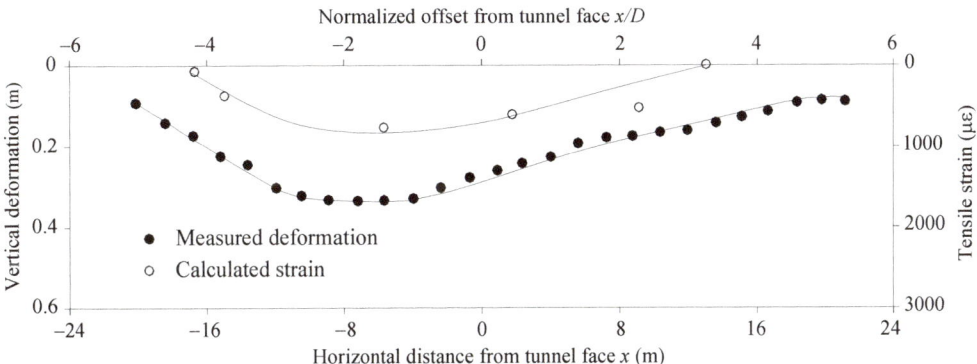

Figure 14. Measured deformations and calculated tensile strains of existing tunnel in low interlayer model.

3.3. Overall Collapse

In the case of cohesive soils, face failure involves a large volume of ground ahead of the working front, presenting an overall collapse, a failure mode of a ground block bounded by two single or multiple shear planes extending from the tunnel face to the surface [42]. To reproduce overall collapse in the centrifuge, two model tests were performed using the silt model and the high interlayer model. Figure 15 presents the failure mechanism in the silt model developed at different face movements. It was noticed that the curved arch formed with a face movement from 0 to 5.0 m, as shown in Figure 15a–d. With a face movement of 5.0 m, a failure developed in the sewer line (Figure 15e). By further increasing the face movement to 6.9 m, as depicted in Figures 15f and 16, a sudden fall-down of 3.9 m for the

Sewer triggered an overall collapse above the face, leaving a 12.8 m long and 1.7 m high gap beneath the tunnel. The overall failure was bounded by two single shear planes. The occurrence of the overall collapse may be attributed to the low cohesion strength of the silt.

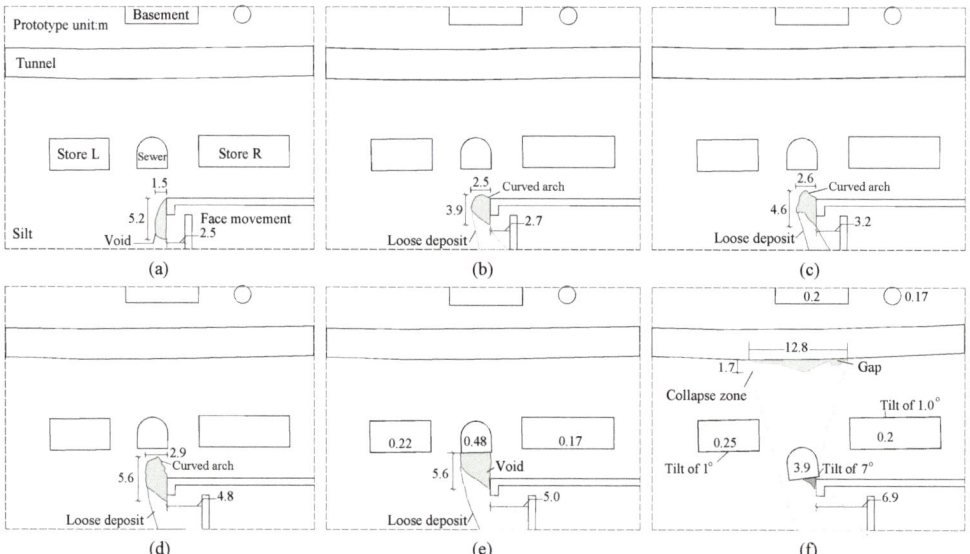

Figure 15. Overall collapse in silt model: (**a**) Void initiating with face movement of 2.5 m; (**b**–**d**) Curved arch with face movement from 2.5 to 4.8 m; (**e**) Void moving up to Sewer with face movement of 5.0 m; (**f**) Overall collapse with face movement of 6.9 m.

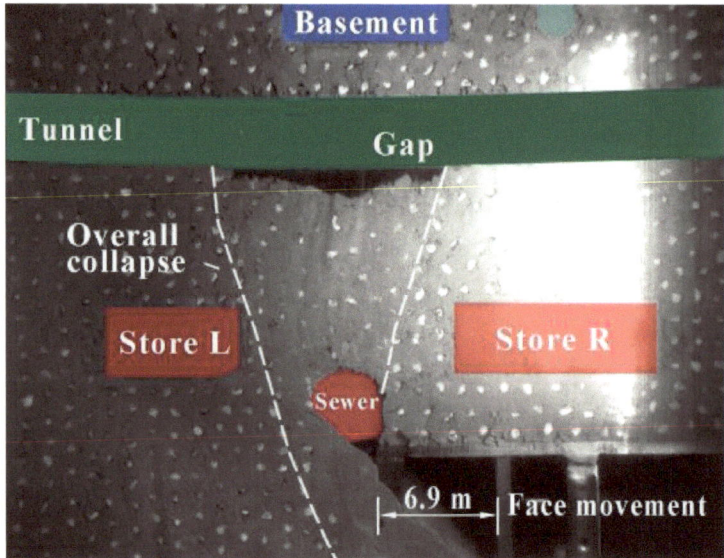

Figure 16. Photo of the silt model after failure.

Figure 17 illustrates the measured deformations of the existing tunnel for different face movements. When failure was confined with a face movement of 2.5–5.0 m, the bending deformation of the existing tunnel developed steadily. After the sudden brittle failure of the ground, the deformation increased sharply, leading to significant bending of the existing tunnel at the location above the gap. The maximum deformation of the existing tunnel was 0.47 m, about 12% of tunnel diameter. It consequently led to 1 degree of tilt and an increment of settlement for Store L and Store R. Shielded by the existing tunnel, 0.2 m of settlement was caused at the basement. Figure 18 depicts the earth pressures of #4, #5 and #6 over the entire process, with sharp changes in the curves that are consistent with the overall collapse.

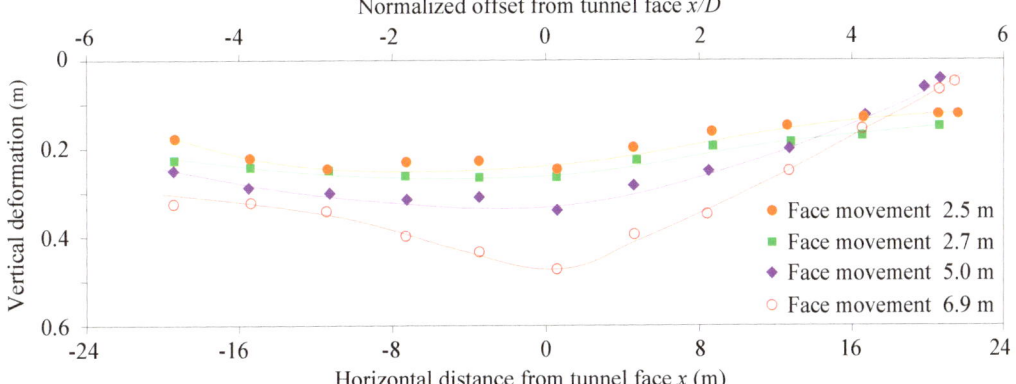

Figure 17. Measured deformations of existing tunnel in the silt model.

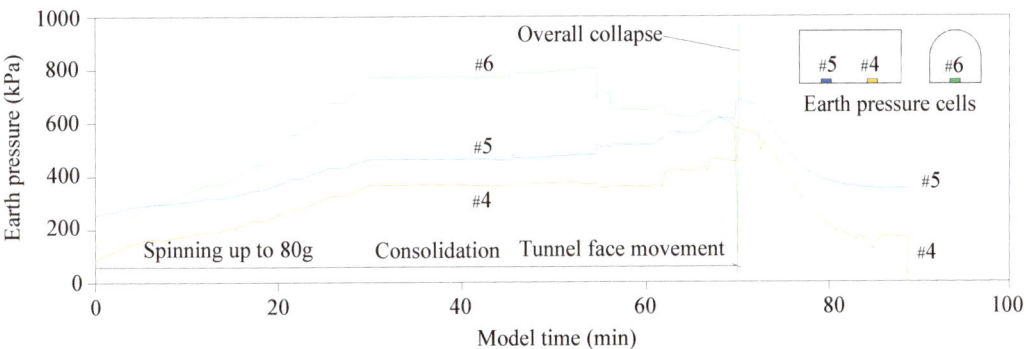

Figure 18. Earth pressure vs. model time in the silt model.

The high interlayer model presented an identical failure mechanism as that in the silt model, as shown in Figure 19. The silt predominated the behavior in the high interlayer model and exhibited brittle failure similar to that in the silt model. In the comparison of the two models in Figure 20, the silty clay layer above the sewer had a slight effect of reducing the induced bending deformation of the existing tunnel due to the flexibility of the interlayer. Table 4 summarizes the maximum deformations of the buried structures in the four centrifuge models. As indicated in Table 4, the bending deformation of the existing tunnel is well correlated with the failure mode, and a limited partial collapse (in the low interlayer model) had the smallest impact on the tunnel. The magnitude of the deformation of the structures depended not only on the failure mode but also on the scope and orientation of the failure.

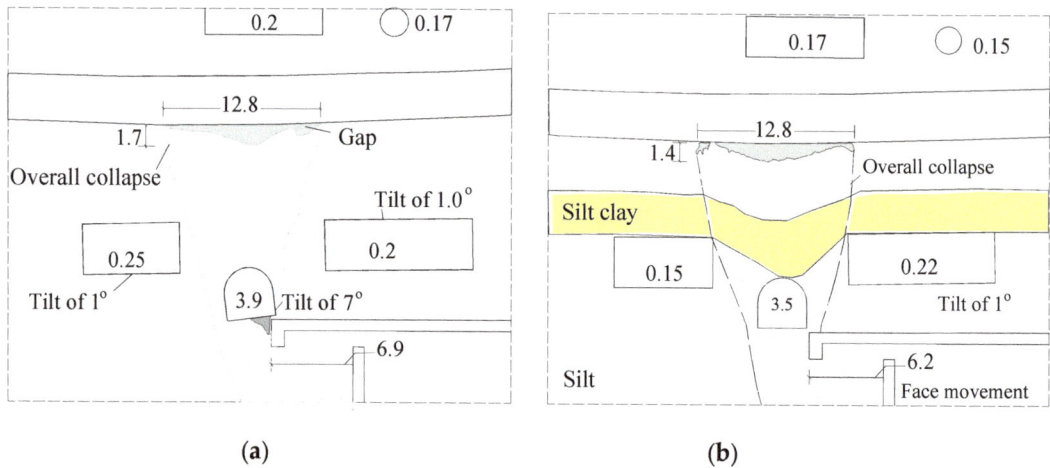

Figure 19. Identical overall collapse mechanism in silt model and high interlayer model: (**a**) silt model; (**b**) High interlayer model.

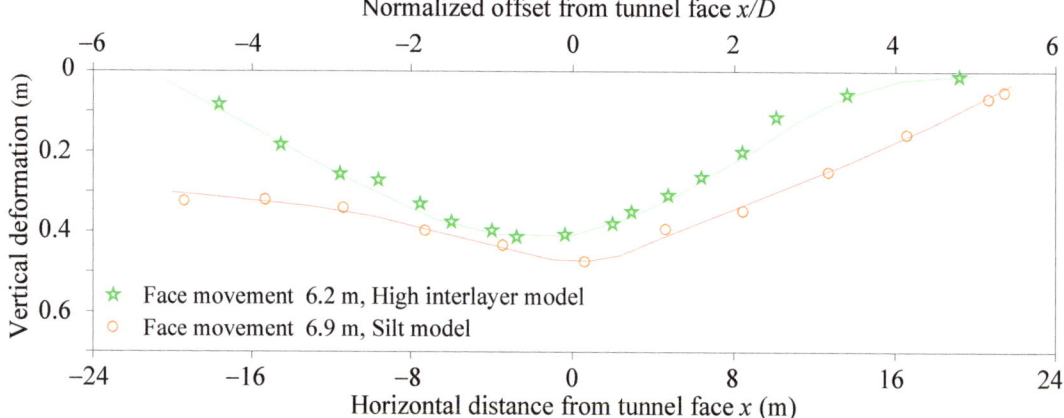

Figure 20. Comparison of bending deformations in silt model and high interlayer model.

Table 4. Maximum deformations of buried structures induced by instability of tunnel face (m).

Model Name	Tunnel	Sewer	Store L	Store R	Basement
Low interlayer model	0.13	0.51	0.3	0.24	0.15
Sand model	0.45	0.09	0	0.05	0.13
Silt model	0.47	3.9	0.09	0.14	0.20
High interlayer model	0.41	3.5	0.15	0.22	0.17

4. Summary and Conclusions

This paper presents the results of four centrifuge model tests for investigating the coupling failure mechanisms of underground structures subjected to instability of the tunnel face. The physical investigation offered some new insights and led to the following conclusions:

(a) Rapid sand flow occurred instantly following a relatively small movement of 0.85 m of the tunnel face. This may be the main cause that induced the catastrophic failure in

Shanghai Metro Line 4 and Guangdong Foshan Metro Line 2. A chimney-like mechanism created gaps underneath the existing structures.

(b) An arching effect in cohesive soil and the influence of adjacent structures led to a partial failure even with a large face movement of 6.6 m, a failure that was limited to the front of the tunnel face, having a lower impact on the existing tunnel.

(c) An overall collapse may occur in conditions of soil with lower cohesion strength or when involving changes in the ground water table, which is a failure mode of a ground block bounded by two single shear planes extending from the tunnel face to the surface.

(d) The maximum bending deformation and the induced tensile strain of the existing tunnel are well correlated with the failure mode. The maximum tensile strain was about 2000 με for cases of sand flow and overall collapse. The partial failure had the smallest impact on the tunnel, and the maximum tensile strain was only 40% of the former two cases. The magnitude of the deformation of the structures depended not only on the failure mode but also on the scope and orientation of the failure.

As indicated by case studies on Shanghai Metro Line 4 and Guangdong Foshan Metro Line 2, rapid occurrence of large-scale tunnel failure can cause serious damage to existing structures. Further studies can investigate the impact of the large-scale failures of tunnels during construction, especially for existing tunnels.

Author Contributions: Methodology, J.Z. and X.C.; investigation, J.Z. and A.W.; writing, J.Z.; editing, L.Z. All authors have read and agreed to the published version of the manuscript.

Funding: This research was funded by the National Natural Science Foundation of China, grant number 52090084 and 52279101.

Institutional Review Board Statement: Not applicable.

Informed Consent Statement: Not applicable.

Data Availability Statement: Not applicable.

Conflicts of Interest: The authors declare no conflict of interest.

References

1. Tan, Y.; Lu, Y.; Wang, D.L. Catastrophic Failure of Shanghai Metro Line 4 in July, 2003: Occurrence, Emergency Response, and Disaster Relief. *J. Perform. Constr. Facil.* **2021**, *35*, 04020125. [CrossRef]
2. Mair, R.J. Centrifugal Modelling of Tunnel Construction in Soft Clay. Ph.D. Thesis, University of Cambridge, Cambridge, UK, 1979.
3. Davis, E.H.; Gunn, M.J.; Mair, R.J.; Seneviratine, H.N. The stability of shallow tunnels and underground openings in cohesive material. *Géotechnique* **1980**, *30*, 397–416. [CrossRef]
4. Burford, D. Heave of tunnels beneath the Shell Centre, London, 1959–1986. *Géotechnique* **1988**, *38*, 135–137. [CrossRef]
5. Anagnostou, G.; Kovari, K. Face stability of slurry-shield-driven tunnels. *Tunn. Undergr. Space Technol.* **1994**, *9*, 165–174. [CrossRef]
6. Chang, C.T.; Sun, C.W.; Duann, S.W.; Hwang, R.N. Response of a Taipei Rapid Transit System (TRTS) tunnel to adjacent excavation. *Tunn. Undergr. Space Technol.* **2001**, *16*, 151–158. [CrossRef]
7. Zhang, J.H.; Pu, J.; Zhang, M.; Qiu, T. Model tests by centrifuge of soil nail reinforcements. *J. Test. Eval.* **2001**, *29*, 315–328.
8. Bezuijen, A.; Brassinga, H.M. Blow-Out Pressures Measured in a Centrifuge Model and in the Field. In *Tunnelling*; Bezuijen, A., Lottum, H.V., Eds.; A Decade of Progress—GeoDelft 1995–2005; Taylor & Francis: London, UK, 2005; pp. 143–148.
9. Leca, E.; New, B. Settlements induced by tunneling in Soft Ground. *Tunn. Undergr. Space Technol.* **2007**, *22*, 119–149. [CrossRef]
10. Meguid, M.A.; Saada, O.; Nunes, M.A.; Mattar, J. Physical modeling of tunnels in soft ground: A review. *Tunn. Undergr. Space Technol.* **2008**, *23*, 185–198. [CrossRef]
11. Zhang, L.M.; Zhang, G.; Zhang, J.M.; Lee, C.F. Centrifuge model tests on a cohesive soil slope under excavation conditions. *Soils Found.* **2011**, *51*, 801–812. [CrossRef]
12. Chen, X.S. A space-time-dependant design method and the stability of ice wall for deep shafts. In *Applied Mechanics and Materials*; Trans tech publications: Stafa-Zurich, Switzerland, 2012; Volume 204–208, pp. 3275–3281. [CrossRef]
13. Nghiem, H.L.; Heib, M.A.L.; Emeriault, F. Physical model for damage prediction in structures due to underground excavations. In Proceedings of the International Conference on Geotechnical Engineering (Geoshanghai 2014), Reston, VA, USA, 26 May 2014; pp. 155–164.
14. Senent, S.; Jimenez, R. A tunnel face failure mechanism for layered ground, considering the possibility of partial collapse. *Tunn. Undergr. Space Technol.* **2015**, *47*, 182–192. [CrossRef]

15. Lu, H.; Shi, J.W.; Ng, C.W.W.; Lv, Y. Three-dimensional centrifuge modeling of the influence of side-by-side twin tunneling on a piled raft. *Tunn. Undergr. Space Technol.* **2020**, *103*, 103486. [CrossRef]
16. Wang, H.Y.; Leung, C.F.; Huang, M.S.; Fu, Y. Axial response of short pile due to tunnelling-induced soil movement in soft clay. *Int. J. Phys. Model. Geotech.* **2020**, *20*, 71–82. [CrossRef]
17. Weng, X.L.; Sun, Y.F.; Yan, B.H.; Niu, H.S.; Lin, R.A.; Zhou, S.Q. Centrifuge testing and numerical modeling of tunnel face stability considering longitudinal slope angle and steady state seepage in soft clay. *Tunn. Undergr. Space Technol.* **2020**, *101*, 103406. [CrossRef]
18. Song, G.Y.; Marshall, A.M. Centrifuge study on the use of protective walls to reduce tunnelling-induced damage of buildings. *Tunn. Undergr. Space Technol.* **2021**, *115*, 104064. [CrossRef]
19. Xu, J.M.; Franza, A.; Marshall, A.M.; Losacco, N.; Boldini, D. Tunnel-framed building interaction: Comparison between raft and separate footing foundations. *Géotechnique* **2021**, *71*, 631–644. [CrossRef]
20. Alkhdour, A.; Tiutkin, O.L.; Marochka, V.V.; Boboshko, S.H. The centrifugal modeling of reinforcement on approaches to railway bridges. *Acta Polytech. Hungarica* **2022**, *19*, 131–142. [CrossRef]
21. Benmebarek, M.A.; Benmebarek, S.; Rad, M.M.; Ray, R. Pile optimization in slope stabilization by 2D and 3D numerical analyses. *Int. J. Geotech. Eng.* **2022**, *16*, 211–224. [CrossRef]
22. Esmaeili, M.; Astaraki, F.; Yaghouti, H.; Rad, M.M. Laboratory Investigation on the Effect of Microsilica Additive on the mechanical behavior of deep soil mixing columns in saline dry sand. *Period. Polytech. Civ. Eng.* **2021**, *65*, 1080–1091. [CrossRef]
23. Corte, J.F. Presentation of the LCPC centrifuge. In *International Symposium in Geotechnical Centrifuge Model Testing*; Tokyo Institute of Technology: Tokyo, Japan, 1984; pp. 120–126.
24. Chambon, P.C.; Corte, J.F. Shallow tunnels in cohesionless soil: Stability of tunnel face. *J. Geotech. Eng.* **1994**, *120*, 1148–1165. [CrossRef]
25. Kamata, H.; Masimo, H. Centrifuge model test of tunnel face reinforcement by bolting. *Tunn. Undergr. Space Technol.* **2003**, *18*, 205–212. [CrossRef]
26. Ng, C.W.W.; Wong, K.S. Investigation of passive failure and deformation mechanisms due to tunnelling in clay. *Can. Geotech. J.* **2013**, *50*, 359–372. [CrossRef]
27. Konig, D.; Grittier, U.; Jessberger, H.L. Stress redistributions during tunnel and shaft constructions. In *International Conference Centrifuge 1991*; Balkema: Rotterdam, The Netherlands, 1991; pp. 129–138.
28. Sterpi, D.; Cividini, A.; Sakurai, S.; Nishitake, S. Laboratory model tests and numerical analysis of shallow tunnels. In Proceedings of the International Symposium on Eurock 96—ISRM, Turin, Italy, 2–5 September 1996; Barla, G., Ed.; OnePetro: Richardson, TX, USA, 1996; Volume 1, pp. 689–696.
29. Champan, D.N.; Ahn, S.K.; Hunt, D.V.L.; Chan, H.C. The use of model tests to investigate the ground displacement associated with multiple tunnel construction in soil. *Tunn. Tunn.* **2006**, *21*, 413.
30. Hagiwara, T.; Grant, R.J.; Calvello, M.; Taylor, R.N. The effect of overlying strata on the distribution of ground movements induced by tunneling in clay. *Soils Found.* **1999**, *39*, 63–73. [CrossRef] [PubMed]
31. Sharma, J.S.; Hefny, A.M.; Zhao, J.; Chan, C.W. Effect of large excavation on deformation of adjacent MRT tunnels. *Tunn. Undergr. Space Technol.* **2001**, *16*, 93–98. [CrossRef]
32. Zhang, J.H.; Chen, Z.Y.; Wang, X.G. Centrifuge modelling of rock slopes susceptible to block toppling. *Rock Mech. Rock Eng.* **2007**, *40*, 363–382. [CrossRef]
33. Farrell, R.P.; Mair, R.J. Centrifuge modelling of the response of buildings to tunnelling. In Proceedings of the 7th International Conference on Physical Modelling in Geotechnics, Zurich, Switzerland, 28 June–1 July 2010; Volume 1, pp. 549–554.
34. Zheng, G.; Wei, S.W.; Peng, S.Y.; Diao, Y.; Ng, C.W.W. Centrifuge modeling of the influence of basement excavation on existing tunnel. In Proceedings of the International Conference on Physical Modelling in Geotechnics; Taylor & Francis Group: London, UK, 2010; pp. 523–527.
35. Giardina, G.; DeJong, M.J.; Mair, R.J. Interaction between surface structures and tunnelling in sand: Centrifuge and computational modelling. *Tunn. Undergr. Space Technol.* **2015**, *50*, 465–478. [CrossRef]
36. Yokota, Y.; Date, K.; Yamamoto, T. Verification of reinforcing effects of a tunnel face reinforcement method by centrifuge model tests and numerical analysis. In Proceedings of the 12th ISRM International Congress on Rock Mechanics, Harmonising Rock Engineering and The Environment, Beijing, China, 17–21 October 2011; Qian, Q., Zhou, Y., Eds.; OnePetro: Richardson, TX, USA, 2011; pp. 2173–2176.
37. Franza, A.; Marshall, A.M.; Zhou, B. Greenfield tunnelling in sands: The effects of soil density and relative depth. *Geotechnique* **2019**, *69*, 297–307. [CrossRef]
38. Ritter, S.; Giardina, G.; Franza, A.; DeJong, M.J. Building deformation caused by tunneling: Centrifuge modeling. *J. Geotech. Geoenviron. Eng.* **2020**, *146*, 04020017. [CrossRef]
39. Meng, F.Y.; Chen, R.P.; Xu, Y.; Wu, H.N.; Li, Z.C. Centrifuge modeling of effectiveness of protective measures on existing tunnel subjected to nearby excavation. *Tunn. Undergr. Space Technol.* **2021**, *112*, 103880. [CrossRef]
40. Zhang, J.H.; Lin, H.L.; Wang, K.Z. Centrifuge modeling and analysis of submarine landslides triggered by elevated pore pressure. *Ocean. Eng.* **2015**, *109*, 419–429. [CrossRef]

41. Taylor, R.N. *Geotechnical Centrifuge Technology*; Blackie Academic and Professional: London, UK, 1995.
42. White, D.J.; Take, W.A.; Bolton, M.D. Soil deformation measurement using particle image velocimetry (PIV) and photogrammetry. *Géotechnique* **2003**, *53*, 619–631. [CrossRef]

Disclaimer/Publisher's Note: The statements, opinions and data contained in all publications are solely those of the individual author(s) and contributor(s) and not of MDPI and/or the editor(s). MDPI and/or the editor(s) disclaim responsibility for any injury to people or property resulting from any ideas, methods, instructions or products referred to in the content.

Article

An Iterative PSD-Based Procedure for the Gaussian Stochastic Earthquake Model with Combined Intensity and Frequency Nonstationarities: Its Application into Precast Concrete Structures

Xu-Yang Cao

College of Civil and Transportation Engineering, Hohai University, Nanjing 210024, China; caoxy@hhu.edu.cn

Abstract: Earthquakes cause severe damage to human beings and financial development, and they are commonly associated with a lot of uncertainties and stochastic factors regarding their frequency, intensity and duration. Thus, how to accurately select an earthquake record and determine an earthquake's influence on structures are important questions that deserve further investigation. In this paper, the author developed an iterative power spectral density (PSD)-based procedure for the Gaussian stochastic earthquake model with combined intensity and frequency nonstationarities. In addition, they applied this procedure to five precast concrete structures for dynamic analysis and verification. The research proved the effectiveness of the iterative procedure for matching the target response spectra and for generating the required seismic records. The application examples verified the accuracy of the seismic design for the precast concrete structures and indicated the reliable dynamic demands of the precast concrete structures under the stochastic excitation of nonstationary earthquakes. In general, the research provided a meaningful reference for further stochastic earthquake selections, and it could play an effective role in further assessments of precast structures.

Keywords: stochastic earthquake model; nonstationarity; Gaussian; PSD; precast concrete structure; performance assessment

MSC: 65-04

1. Introduction

An earthquake is a sudden and rapid shaking of the ground caused by crustal movement and plate compression. Earthquakes can cause fires, tsunamis, landslides or avalanches and they can lead to severe damage to human societies. During the past few decades, the influence of earthquakes has been gradually recognized by researchers, and lots of solutions (e.g., retrofitting, upgrading or strengthening strategies) have been proposed by researchers all over the world [1–7].

Commonly, an earthquake is associated with a lot of uncertainties in terms of its source, attenuation and site amplification, and an earthquake occurance generally includes a series of stochastic factors in terms of its frequency, intensity and duration [8–12]. Taking the intensity as an example, the peak ground acceleration of an unknown earthquake is commonly stochastic in a probabilistic way, which means that it may exceed the fortification earthquake level and may lead to severe postdisaster damage [13–17]. Thus, how to accurately select an earthquake record and determine an earthquake's influence on structures are important questions that deserve further investigation [18–22]. At this stage, a commonly adopted method is to select earthquake records from the existing database and match them with the target response spectra in the corresponding seismic regulations. It has been noted that this approach can be effective in choosing the required records to a certain extent, but, commonly, the generated average response spectra are different to the target response spectra with respect to their statistical details [23–27]. Meanwhile, as earthquake theory develops, researchers hope to focus more on the stochastic parameters of earthquakes, but the traditional selection strategy from the database shows limitations and cannot reflect so many parameters. Thus, the stochastic earthquake model was developed by researchers to characterize these stochastic parameters and to capture specific information for structural dynamic analysis [28–32].

Shinozuka and Deodatis [33] gave a state-of-the-art review of the stochastic process models for earthquake simulations, and the research proved the effectiveness and importance of the stochastic earthquake model, which laid a critical foundation for further research. Loh and Yeh [34] carried out spatial variation research and performed the stochastic modelling of seismic differential ground motions. It was observed that the corner frequency and phase velocity were the controlling parameters in estimating multiple differential grep deformations. Chen and Ahmadi [35] analyzed the seismic response of secondary substructures in base-isolated systems via the stochastic earthquake model, and the data for the Mexico City earthquake indicated the sensitivity of the base-isolated structures in terms of long periods of excitation. Grigoriu [36] proposed two models (i.e., $X_n(t)$ and $Y_n(t)$) to generate the stochastic band-limited samples of Gaussian stationary processes in light of the spectral representation, as well as the harmonic superposition, which gave an important basis for further stochastic earthquake simulation. Rietbrock et al. [37] proposed a stochastic earthquake model for the UK based on peak ground acceleration, peak ground velocity and pseudospectral acceleration, and the model indicated an ideal accuracy and predicting effect. Yamamoto and Baker [38] adopted wavelet packets to simulate the stochastic earthquake model, and the proposed stochastic earthquake model showed great consistency with existing established models for earthquake prediction in terms of the variabilities and means. Huang [39] proposed the orthogonal decomposition algorithm in the simulation of the multivariate nonstationary stochastic process, and the fast Fourier transform operation was introduced during the process, which distinctively enhanced the generating efficiency of the stochastic process. Bhattacharyya et al. [40] proposed a novel time-frequency representation approach based on the enhanced wavelet transform, and Fourier-to-Bessel expansions were further adopted to generate stochastic nonstationary signals, which provided some references for the efficient modelling of stochastic earthquakes. Cao et al. [41] performed the probabilistic seismic fragility comparison of different approaches under the stochastic nonstationary earthquake, and the research proved the importance of the stochastic earthquake model in the probabilistic performance assessment and fragility method selection. Feng et al. [42] proposed a nonparametric probabilistic density evolution method (PDEM)-based approach for seismic fragility evaluation of frame structures under the stochastic earthquake model, and the results showed that the stochastic earthquake model was directly related to the accuracy of the fragility calculation.

On the other hand, precast concrete structures are a type of construction method that involves the use of prefabricated concrete components, such as beams, columns, slabs, walls and foundations, that are manufactured off-site in a workshop setting and then transported to the construction site for assembly [43–46]. Utilizing precast concrete offers many advantages over traditional construction methods in terms of speed, efficiency, cost and quality. The prefabricated components are manufactured off-site in a controlled environment, meaning they are produced in a much shorter timeframe than traditional construction methods. This also eliminates the need for weather delays and other issues that can slow down the construction process [47–50]. The cost of the materials is often much lower than traditional construction methods, and there is a wide range of prefabricated components available for use. Additionally, as the components are produced off-site and can be delivered to the project site, the labor costs associated with traditional construction methods are eliminated. The quality of precast concrete structures is also higher than that of traditional construction methods [51–54]. The components are manufactured in a controlled environment, meaning they can be designed to exact specifications and with high-quality materials, resulting in a structure that is much stronger and more durable than one constructed using traditional methods. The environmental impact of precast concrete structures is also less than that of traditional construction methods. The materials used in precast concrete components are generally easier to recycle than traditional construction materials, and, as the components are manufactured off-site, there is less waste produced on-site. Overall, precast concrete structures offer many advantages over traditional construction methods in terms of speed, cost, quality and environmental impact. By utilizing prefabricated components, the construction process can be completed much faster, at a lower cost and environmental impact and, most importantly, with a higher construction quality [55–60].

Elliott [61] summarized the superiorities of earthquake-resistant precast concrete structures in terms of the precast concept, materials in the precast structures, precast frame systems, precast floor systems, precast beam systems, precast column systems, precast shear wall systems, precast joint systems, etc., which provided an overall literature review of precast concrete structures for further research. Kurama et al. [62] gave a state-of-the-art review of earthquake-resistant precast concrete structures and divided the structural forms into moment frames, structural walls, floor diaphragms and bridges, which contributed greatly to the literature review and laid an important foundation for further analysis. Polat [63] conclusively defined the parameters that affected the application of precast concrete structures in the United States and gave the development tendency of the precast-concrete industry through the past few decades, which provided some important references for future explorations of precast concrete structures. Koskisto and Ellingwood [64] gave an optimization strategy for precast concrete structures in view of reliability theory, and they formulated the design limitations of flexural failure probability, shear failure probability, cracking probability and excessive deflection probability. Ozden et al. [65] analyzed the seismic performance of precast concrete structures affected by the Van earthquakes in Turkey, and reported the importance of proper design, as well as seismic details of precast concrete joints, in the construction stages for structures in high-seismicity areas. Belleri et al. [66] assessed the seismic damage of a three-story precast concrete structure through large-scale experiments and structural identifications, which indicated the effectiveness of the structural form in seismic repairing regions. Kataoka et al. [67] performed nonlinear numerical analysis of a precast concrete slab–beam–column joint for its seismic behaviors, and they gave suggestions for the influence of critical parameters in the seismic design. Lacerda et al. [68] experimentally investigated the influence of vertical groutings in precast concrete structures, and the result implied an increase in the rotational flexural stiffness, as well as the flexural strength capacity, of the precast concrete structures via the vertical filling. Cao et al. [69] proposed innovative external precast concrete structural forms for seismic retrofitting without any inner disturbance, and their experiments validated the effectiveness of the novel precast structures in practical application. Lago et al. [70] investigated the effectiveness of diaphragms in precast concrete structures with cladding panels, and they proposed a novel fastening system to increase the total energy dissipation capacity of the structural system. Feng et al. [71] performed a comparative study of numerical approaches for precast concrete structures based on damage mechanics, and three practical strategies were proposed for efficient performance prediction in static cyclic modelling. Ye et al. [72] proposed a novel hybrid beam–column joint for precast concrete structures and carried out experimental and numerical studies of its seismic performance, which proved the effectiveness of the precast form. Xu et al. [73] used spectrum-compatible stochastic earthquakes with near-field nonstationarities to conduct a comparative study of precast steel-reinforced concrete substructures for seismic retrofitting, and the precast substructures potentially indicated a superior upgrading capacity and effectively alleviated the premature damage of existing buildings.

From the above literature review, it can be found that the stochastic earthquake model is developing rapidly and needs a better record-selection strategy and a more realistic uncertainty-quantification method in terms of seismic excitation. In the meantime, precast concrete structures have indicated a lot of superiorities, and they are promising for practical engineering in high-seismicity regions [74–79]. At this stage, the research of the nonstationary stochastic dynamic performance of precast concrete structures is scarce and deserves further exploration. It is meaningful research work and possesses value in terms of practical applications, which require the consideration of more stochastic input factors and reflect more realistic seismic capacities in the life cycle period. Thus, in this paper, the author has developed an iterative power spectral density (PSD)-based procedure for the Gaussian stochastic earthquake model with combined intensity and frequency nonstationarities, and they have applied this model to five precast concrete structures for dynamic analysis and verification. During the analysis, four iterative calculations were performed for the stochastically generated nonstationary earthquakes, and it was observed that the deviations with the target spectrum distinctively dropped along with the iterative procedure. Meanwhile, two system-level indexes were adopted for the assessment of the precast structures (i.e., the maximum and residual interstory drift ratio) to obtain a more comprehensive evaluation. In general, the research proved the effectiveness of the iterative procedure for matching the target response spectra and for generating the required seismic records. The application examples verified the accuracy of the seismic design for the precast concrete structures and indicated the reliable dynamic demands of the precast concrete structures under the stochastic excitation of nonstationary earthquakes. The detailed principles and applications of the iterative PSD-based procedure for the Gaussian stochastic earthquake model with combined intensity and frequency nonstationarities are illustrated in the following sections.

2. The Principles of the Iterative PSD-Based Procedure for the Gaussian Stochastic Earthquake Model

Generally, structures have many stochastic variables, including geometry variables ($\Theta_s = (\Theta_1, \Theta_2, \ldots, \Theta_x)^T$) and force variables ($\Theta_f = (\Theta_{x+1}, \Theta_{x+2}, \ldots, \Theta_n)^T$). The variable Θ is then adopted to reflect the structural uncertainty (i.e., $\Theta = (\Theta_s, \Theta_f)$). The variable Θ has n groups of matrices, and the dynamic equation for balance is denoted in Equation (1), where M, D and K are the mass matrix, damping matrix and stiffness matrix of the structure, respectively. The values $\ddot{G}(\Theta, t)$, $\dot{G}(\Theta, t)$ and $G(\Theta, t)$ denote the acceleration matrix, velocity matrix and displacement matrix of the structure, respectively. For any concerned stochastic response of a structure, $G(\Theta, t)$ can be assigned for analysis, which depends on the structural stochastic variable Θ. The value $\ddot{g}_{inp}(\Theta, t)$ denotes the stochastic earthquake model with combined intensity and frequency nonstationarities [16].

$$M \cdot \ddot{G}(\Theta, t) + D \cdot \dot{G}(\Theta, t) + K \cdot G(\Theta, t) = -M \cdot \ddot{g}_{inp}(\Theta, t) \qquad (1)$$

There are quite a few approaches to characterizing the stochastic earthquake model. In this paper, the spectral representation theory is utilized for the stochastic earthquake model, and the function of the bilateral evolutionary power spectral density (PSD) is introduced, as shown in Equation (2). The equation $\beta_k = k \cdot \beta_{if}$ holds, and β_{if} denotes the interval frequency. The set $\{\Theta 1_k, \Theta 2_k\}$ ($k = 1, 2, \ldots, N_{tr}$) denotes the orthogonal stochastic variable in standard form, and it is obtained from a stochastic mapping from $\{\Psi 1_n, \Psi 2_n\}$ ($n = 1, 2, \ldots, N_{tr}$).

$$\ddot{g}_{inp}(\Theta, t) = \sum_{k=1}^{N_{tr}} \sqrt{2 S_{\ddot{g}_{inp}}(t, \beta_k) \cdot \beta_{if}} \cdot \left[\cos(\beta_k t) \cdot \Theta 1_k + \sin(\beta_k t) \cdot \Theta 2_k \right] \qquad (2)$$

As for the Gaussian-based stochastic earthquake model, the Gaussian-based orthogonal forms of $\{\Psi 1_n, \Psi 2_n\}$ are incorporated. Equations (3) and (4) show the principles, where one or two phase angles are introduced as stochastic variables (i.e., PA_1 and PA_2). By this mapping strategy, the parameter dimensions are obviously lowered from $2N_{tr}$ to 2, and the systematic efficiency in the calculation is, consequently, increased [80]. In this approach, both PA_1 and PA_2 are uniformly distributed.

$$\Theta 1_k = \Psi 1_n = \Phi^{-1}\left[\frac{1}{\pi}arcsin(\frac{sin(n \cdot PA_1) + cos(n \cdot PA_1)}{\sqrt{2}}) + \frac{1}{2}\right], k \text{ or } n = 1,2,\ldots,N_{tr} \quad (3)$$

$$\Theta 2_k = \Psi 2_n = \Phi^{-1}\left[\frac{1}{\pi}arcsin(\frac{sin(n \cdot PA_2) + cos(n \cdot PA_2)}{\sqrt{2}}) + \frac{1}{2}\right], k \text{ or } n = 1,2,\ldots,N_{tr} \quad (4)$$

To incorporate and consider both the intensity and frequency nonstationarities, the classic Clough–Penzien model is introduced, and Equation (5) shows the Clough–Penzien model for the evolutionary power spectral density (i.e., $S_{\ddot{g}_{inp}}(t,\beta)$), which incorporates both the nonstationary intensity parameter and the nonstationary frequency parameter, as explained in Equations (6) and (7). In Equation (6), $\xi_g(t)$, $\xi_f(t)$, $\beta_g(t)$ and $\beta_f(t)$ reflect the stochastic characteristics of the earthquake model for the frequency nonstationarities, and in Equation (7), $A_{amp}(t)$ and $S_{amp}(t)$ reflect the stochastic characteristics of the earthquake model for intensity nonstationarities. Table 1 gives the symbols and definitions of the stochastic earthquake model with frequency and intensity nonstationaries. Based on the different soil sites, the detailed values can be found in [81].

$$S_{\ddot{g}_{inp}}(t,\beta) = A^2_{amp}(t) \cdot S_{amp}(t) \cdot \frac{\beta_g^4(t) + 4\xi_g^2(t)\beta_g^2(t)\beta^2}{\left[\beta^2 - \beta_g^2(t)\right]^2 + 4\xi_g^2(t)\beta_g^2(t)\beta^2} \cdot \frac{\beta^4}{\left[\beta^2 - \beta_f^2(t)\right]^2 + 4\xi_f^2(t)\beta_f^2(t)\beta^2} \quad (5)$$

$$\xi_g(t) = \xi_0 + \mu_2\frac{t}{T_{inp}}, \quad \xi_f(t) = \xi_g(t), \quad \beta_g(t) = \beta_0 - \mu_1\frac{t}{T_{inp}}, \quad \beta_f(t) = 0.1\beta_g(t) \quad (6)$$

$$A_{amp}(t) = \left[\frac{t}{\mu_3} \cdot exp(1 - \frac{t}{\mu_3})\right]^{\mu_4}, \quad S_{amp}(t) = \frac{\bar{a}^2_{max}}{\gamma_e^2 \pi \beta_g(t) \cdot \left[2\xi_g(t) + 1/(2\xi_g(t))\right]} \quad (7)$$

Table 1. The symbols and definitions of the stochastic earthquake model with frequency and intensity nonstationaries.

Number	Symbol	Definition
1	ξ_0	Soil damping.
2	β_0	Primary angular frequency.
3	μ_1	Field classification.
4	μ_2	Seismic group.
5	μ_3	Peak acceleration arrival time.
6	μ_4	Shape factor.
7	γ_e	Equivalent peak parameter.
8	T_{inp}	Total duration.
9	$\bar{a}_{max}$	Average peak acceleration.

In order to improve the accuracy of the stochastic nonstationary earthquake model with combined intensity and frequency nonstationarities, and to fit it with the target spectral acceleration, an iterative procedure was further introduced to adjust the evolutionary power spectral density. The corresponding iterative procedure is listed in Equation (8), and it includes the following four steps: (1) first, spectral representation theory is utilized to generate the initial stochastic earthquakes and to obtain the initial spectral acceleration, on average; (2) second, the gaps between the target spectral acceleration and the average spectral acceleration are analyzed, as indicated in Equation (8); (3) third, a new group of stochastic earthquakes with intensity and frequency nonstationarities is generated by the aforementioned equations; (4) fourth, the above PSD-based steps are repeated 4–5 times, and the target-spectrum-compatible stochastic earthquakes with required nonstationarities and less deviations are obtained. Figure 1 displays the flow diagram of the PSD-based iterative procedure of the stochastically generated nonstationary earthquakes in the practical application.

$$S_{\ddot{g}_{inp}}(t,\beta)|_{i+1} = \begin{cases} S_{\ddot{g}_{inp}}(t,\beta), & 0 < \beta \le \beta_c \\ S_{\ddot{g}_{inp}}(t,\beta)|_i \cdot \frac{Q^T(\beta,D)^2}{Q^S(\beta,D)^2|_i}, & \beta > \beta_c \end{cases} \quad (8)$$

where $\beta = 2\pi/T_0$, β represents the structural frequency and T_0 represents the basic period. The values $S_{\ddot{g}_{inp}}(t,\beta)|_{i+1}$ and $S_{\ddot{g}_{inp}}(t,\beta)|_i$ represent the $(i+1)$th and ith iterative procedure of the evolutionary power spectral density, respectively. The value $Q^T(\beta,D)$ represents the target response spectra in the code requirement with a damping ratio of D, and $Q^S(\beta,D)|_i$ represents the average response spectra of the generated stochastic nonstationary earthquakes with a damping ratio of D after the ith iteration. The value β_c represents the truncated frequency and it reflects the adjusting range of the evolutionary power spectral density in the PSD-based iterative procedure.

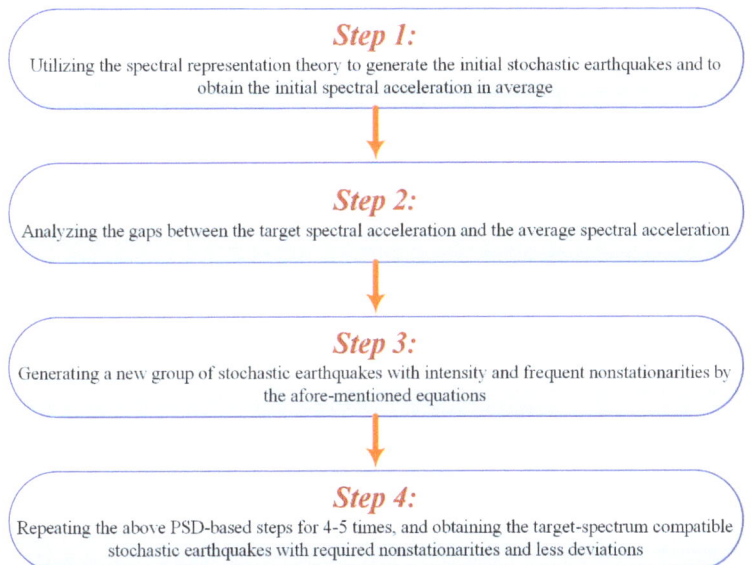

Step 1: Utilizing the spectral representation theory to generate the initial stochastic earthquakes and to obtain the initial spectral acceleration in average

Step 2: Analyzing the gaps between the target spectral acceleration and the average spectral acceleration

Step 3: Generating a new group of stochastic earthquakes with intensity and frequent nonstationarities by the afore-mentioned equations

Step 4: Repeating the above PSD-based steps for 4-5 times, and obtaining the target-spectrum compatible stochastic earthquakes with required nonstationarities and less deviations

Figure 1. The flow diagram of the PSD-based iterative procedure of the stochastically generated nonstationary earthquakes.

3. Application of the Iterative PSD-Based Procedure for the Gaussian Stochastic Earthquake Model

In this section, an application of the iterative PSD-based procedure for the Gaussian stochastic earthquake model with combined intensity and frequency nonstationarities is described, based on the precast concrete structures. In total, five precast concrete frames (PCFs) were well designed according to the principle of 'equivalence to monolithic behavior'. That is, the reinforcements and dimensions were the same as the conventional cast in the place of the concrete structures, but the constructional details corresponded to the precast assembly operations. The five PCFs were 5 spans wide and 10 stories high; 5 spans wide and 8 stories high; 4 spans wide and 8 stories high; 4 spans wide and 6 stories high; and 3 spans wide and 6 stories high, respectively, and the dimensional details are displayed in Figure 2. To perform a dynamic assessment, an appropriate software is commonly required, and, in this analysis, the OpenSees software was utilized [82,83], which is a well-known and efficient platform in the earthquake community. The simulation approach of a PCF is given in Figure 3, in which the precast beams and precast columns are modelled via the nonlinear beam–column elements. To reflect the precast characteristics in the PCF, the Joint2D element was introduced, which can reflect the joint flexural moment–rotation relationship via the central spring and reflect the interfacial moment–rotation relationship via the four interfacial springs. For the central spring, Pinching4 material was used to reflect the pinching effects and joint shear deformation. For the interfacial spring, hysteresis material was used to reflect the degradation effects and interfacial bond–slip phenomenon. Figure 3 gives a verification example with experimental data in terms of the cyclic hysteresis curves [84], which, in a sense, indicate the accuracy and effectiveness of the numerical strategy. More details of the modelling details of the PCF can be found in Cao et al. [85–87].

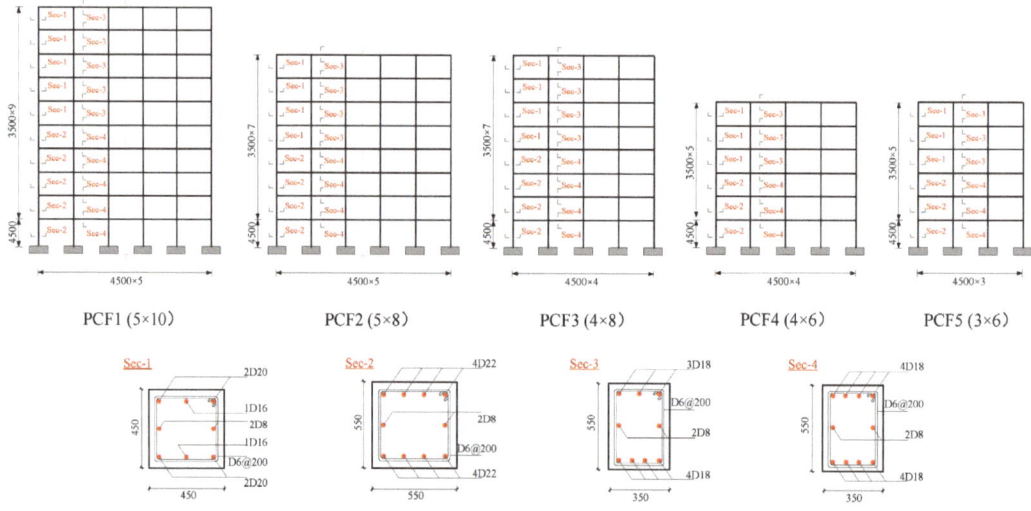

Figure 2. The dimensional details of the five PCFs in the application example.

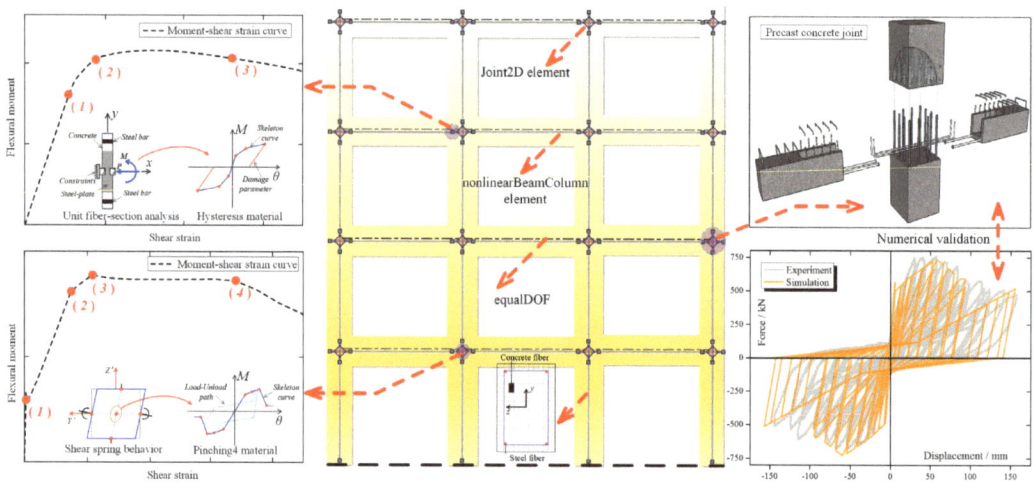

Figure 3. The simulation approach and experimental verification of a PCF in the application example.

According to the principle of the iterative PSD-based procedure for the Gaussian stochastic earthquake model with combined intensity and frequency nonstationarities, in total, four iterative scenarios were performed in this example. Meanwhile, 10 sets of values for PA_1 and PA_2 in Equations (3) and (4) were sampled (ranging from 0 to 2π, as indicated in Table 2), and 10 stochastic nonstationary earthquakes were generated in this example for the evaluation of their seismic behavior. Additionally, the PCF in this example was located on a fortification site of 8 degrees, which means the corresponding peak ground acceleration (PGA) for the design was 0.2 g, followed by a probability of 10% in fifty years. Figure 4 displays the individual stochastic spectral acceleration (gray lines), the average spectral acceleration (blue lines) and the target spectral acceleration (red lines) of all four iterative scenarios, and the corresponding deviations are also given in Figure 4 and Table 3. It was found that with an increase in iteration times, the matching degree between the average spectral acceleration and the target spectral acceleration was enhanced. In the meantime, the deviations obviously dropped between Iteration 0 and Iteration 4. In this analysis, two deviation parameters were adopted, and the expressions are given in Equations (9) and (10), where Tar_i and Ave_i present the target spectral acceleration and the average spectral acceleration at the ith period, respectively, and n represents the total number of structural periods in the matching range of the spectral acceleration.

$$\text{Deviation 1} = \sum_{i}^{n} (Tar_i - Ave_i)^2 \qquad (9)$$

$$\text{Deviation 2} = \sqrt{\sum_{i}^{n} (Tar_i - Ave_i)^2 / (n-1)} \qquad (10)$$

Table 2. The information of stochastic variables for the Gaussian stochastic earthquake model.

Number	Random Variables	Symbol	Distribution	Mean (Unit)	COV
1	Earthquake phase angle 1.	PA_1	Uniform.	3.142 (1)	0.577
2	Earthquake phase angle 2.	PA_2	Uniform.	3.142 (1)	0.577

For Deviation 1, the result before the iteration was 0.2231, and the result after the fourth iteration was 0.0114, with a dropping ratio of 94.89%. For Deviation 2, the result before iteration was 0.0236, and the result after the fourth iteration was 0.0053, with a dropping ratio of 77.54%. The dropping ratios proved the accuracy and effectiveness of the iterative PSD-based procedure for the Gaussian stochastic earthquake model with combined intensity and frequency nonstationarities, and, meanwhile, they provided a critical basis for the subsequent dynamic assessment of the PCF. Figure 5 presents the relationship between the evolutional PSD, the earthquake's frequency and the earthquake's duration in the iterative PSD-based stochastic model. Figure 5a–c presents the results of Iteration 0, and Figure 5d–f presents the results of Iteration 4. It was shown that after the fourth iteration, the peak values and general densities of the evolutional PSD were elevated. Meanwhile, Figure 6 presents the means and standard deviations of the iterative PSD-based stochastic model. Figure 6a,b presents the means and standard deviations of Iteration 0, and Figure 6c,d presents the means and standard deviations of Iteration 4. The blue lines represent the target values, and the gray lines represent the average values. In general, the results of the 10 stochastic nonstationary earthquakes satisfied the target values and showed the same varying trends. Figure 7 presents a typical stochastic earthquake and iteration comparison, in which the gray lines represent the earthquakes before an iteration and the red lines represent the earthquakes after an iteration. Figure 7a,b shows the comparison of two typical earthquakes after the first iteration, Figure 7c,d shows the comparison of two typical earthquakes after the second iteration, Figure 7e,f shows the comparison of two typical earthquakes after the third iteration and Figure 7g,h shows the comparison of two typical earthquakes after the fourth iteration.

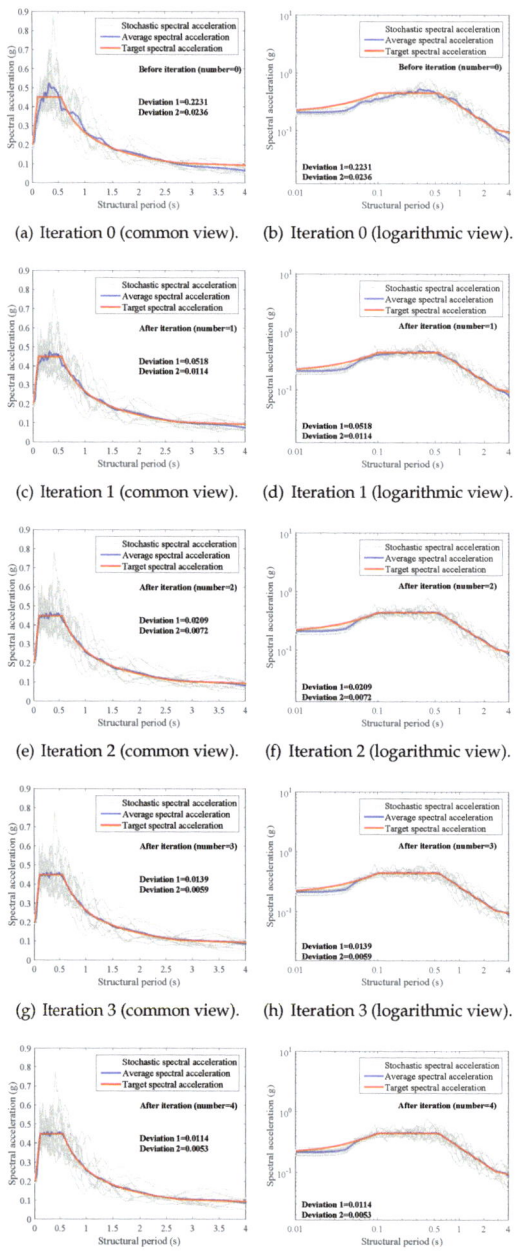

Figure 4. The individual, average and target spectral acceleration of all four iterative scenarios.

Table 3. The deviations between the target and average spectral acceleration for all four iterative scenarios.

Iterative Scenario	Iteration 0	Iteration 1	Iteration 2	Iteration 3	Iteration 4
Deviation 1.	0.2231	0.0518	0.0209	0.0139	0.0114
Deviation 2.	0.0236	0.0114	0.0072	0.0059	0.0053

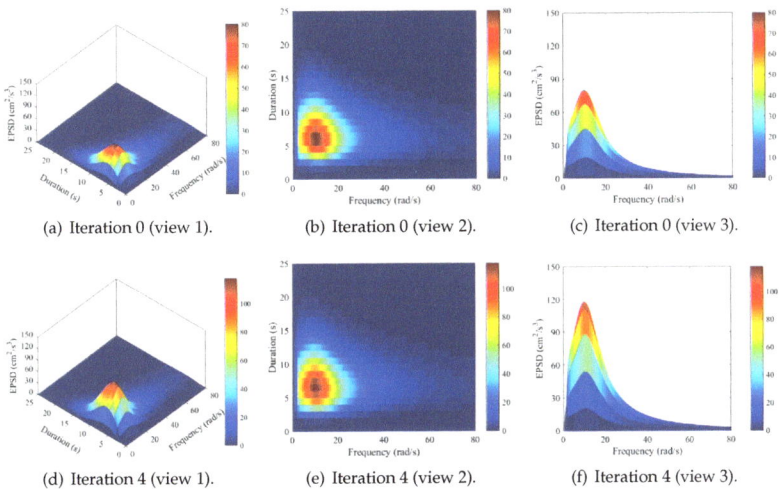

Figure 5. The relationship between the evolutional PSD, the earthquake frequency and the earthquake duration in the iterative PSD-based stochastic model.

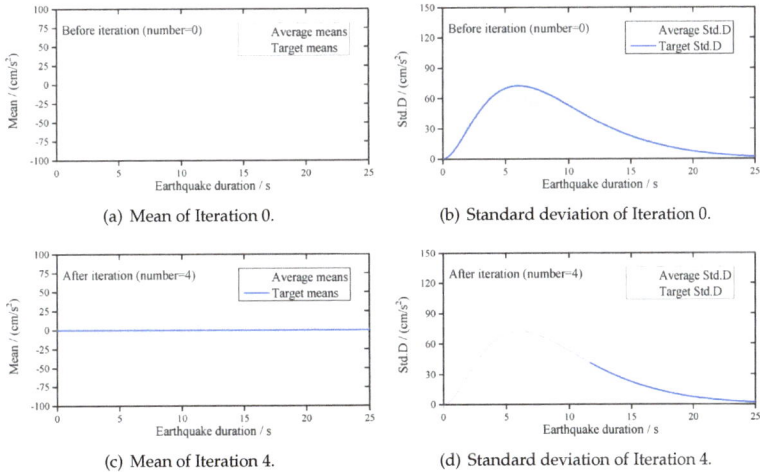

Figure 6. The means and standard deviations of the iterative PSD-based stochastic earthquake model.

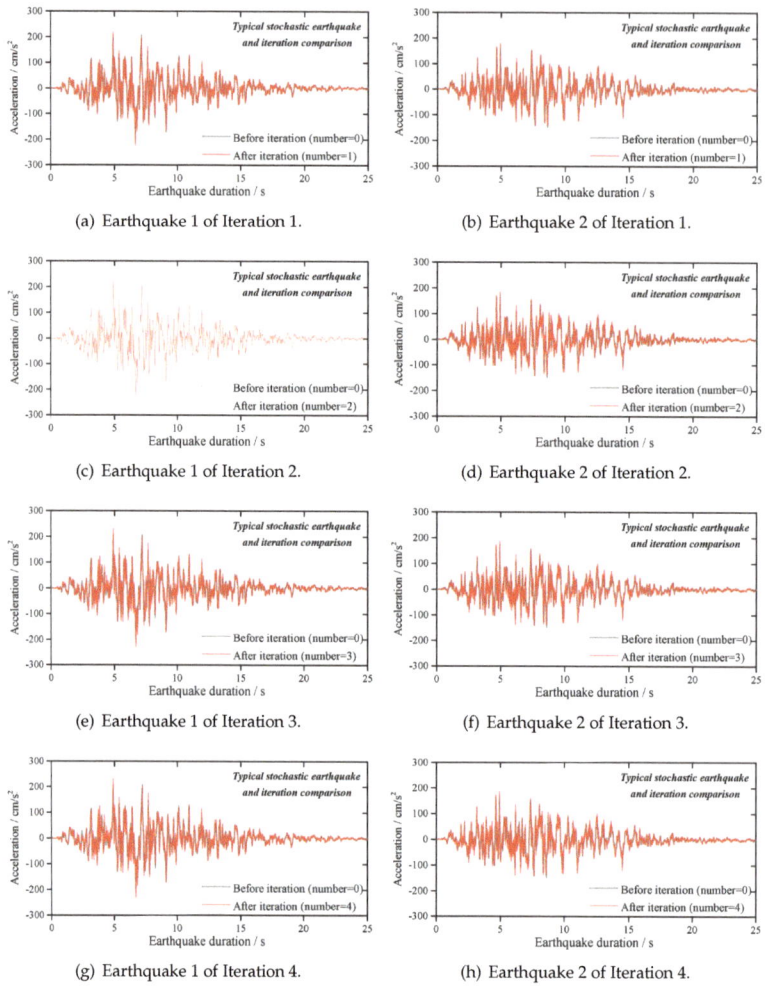

Figure 7. The typical stochastic earthquake and iteration comparison via the iterative PSD-based model.

For the performance assessment of the PCF in this example, two engineering demand parameters were utilized, which were the maximum interstory drift ratio (MIDR) and residual interstory drift ratio (RIDR), respectively. These two indexes are broadly accepted in the fields of building engineering and dynamic assessment [69,88,89]. Two intensity levels were defined, which were the frequent earthquake level (FEL) with a probability exceeding 63% in 50 years and the rare earthquake level (REL) with a probability exceeding 2% in 50 years. According to GB50011 [90] and FEMA-356 [91], the thresholds for the MIDR and RIDR were adopted as 0.0018 and 0.00036 for the FEL, respectively, and the corresponding thresholds for the MIDR and RIDR were adopted as 0.02 and 0.004 for the REL, respectively. It is worth mentioning that the generated 10 stochastic nonstationary earthquakes in Figure 4 were for the fortification earthquake level (with a probability exceeding 10% in 50 years), and the corresponding accelerations were adjusted to the FEL and REL linearly in this analysis according to the generating principle of the stochastic earthquake model. Figure 8 presents the average roof accelerations of the five PCFs under three typical stochastic nonstationary earthquakes. Figure 9 presents the MIDR development along the structural height under the stochastic nonstationary earthquakes for both the FEL and REL, and Figure 10 presents the RIDR development along the structural height under the stochastic nonstationary earthquakes for both the FEL and REL. For the MIDR, the average results for all the conditions were calculated using the blue lines, and for the RIDR, the average results for all the conditions were calculated using the pink lines. The thresholds for both the MIDR and RIDR are shown by the red lines. Generally, the seismic performances of the five PCFs were satisfied within the thresholds in terms of the MIDR and RIDR. Especially for the average lines, they were all obviously lower than the red threshold lines for all the dynamic scenarios, which verified the accuracy of the seismic design for the precast concrete structures and indicated the reliable dynamic demands of the precast concrete structures under the stochastic excitation of nonstationary earthquakes. In general, the research provided a meaningful reference for further stochastic earthquake selections and could play an effective role in further precast structure assessments.

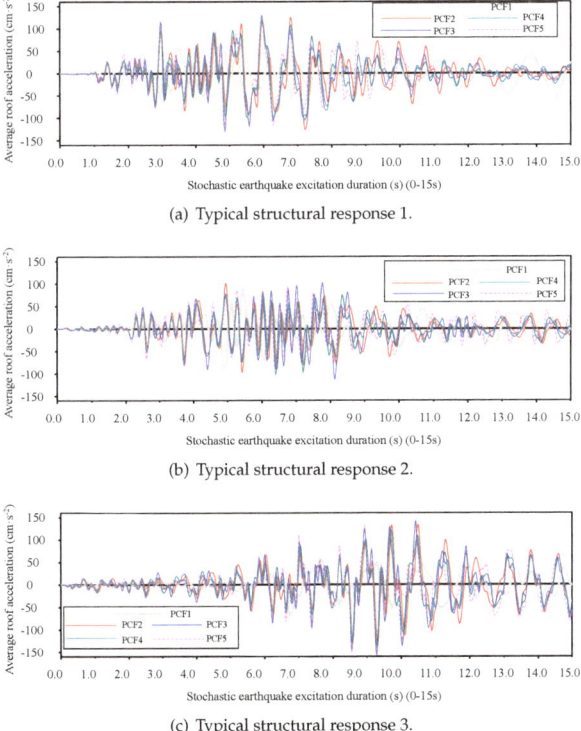

Figure 8. Average roof accelerations of the five PCFs under three typical stochastic nonstationary earthquakes.

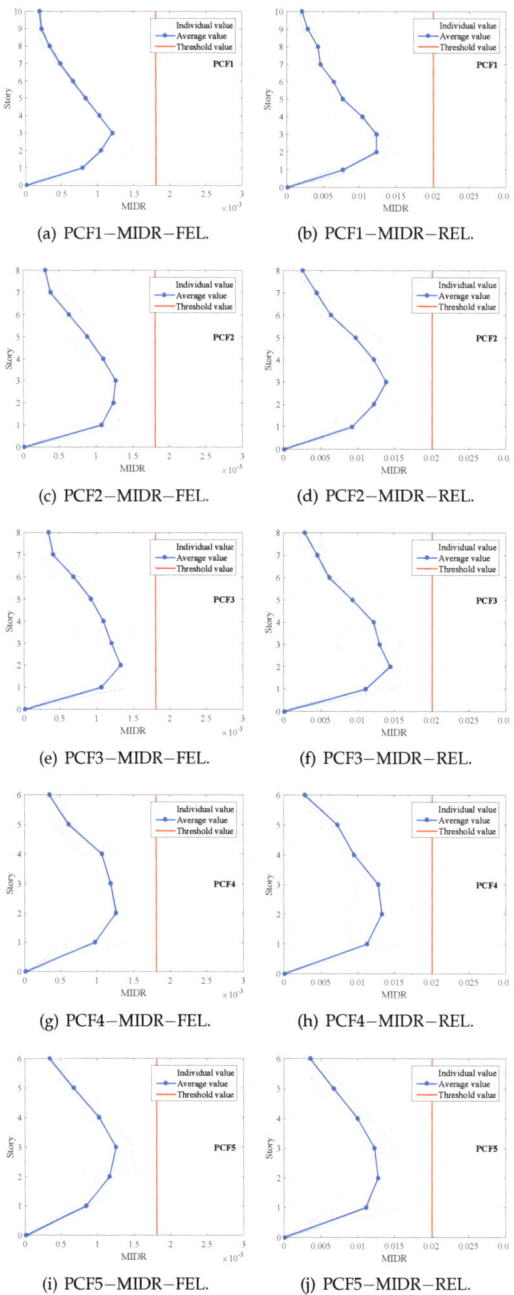

Figure 9. MIDR development along the structural height under the stochastic nonstationary earthquakes for both the FEL and the REL.

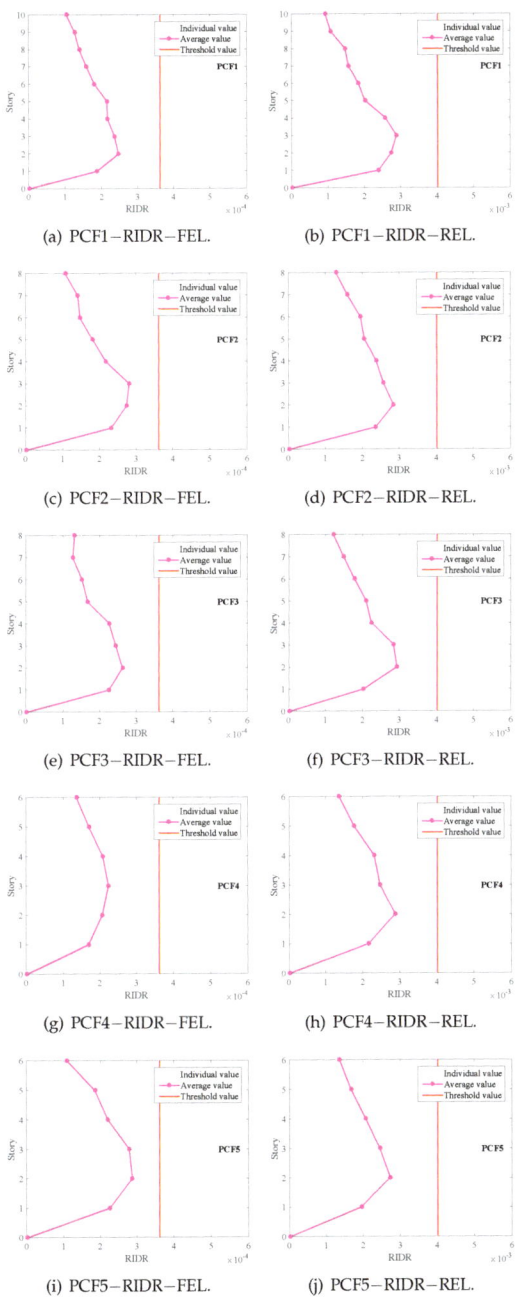

Figure 10. RIDR development along the structural height under the stochastic nonstationary earthquakes for both the FEL and the REL.

4. Conclusions

In this paper, an iterative PSD-based procedure for the Gaussian stochastic earthquake model was developed with combined intensity and frequency nonstationarities, and it was applied to five precast concrete structures for dynamic analysis and validation, from which the following findings can be drawn:

(1) An earthquake contains a lot of uncertainties and stochastic factors in terms of its frequency, intensity and duration, and accurately defining an earthquake's influence on structures is an important task that deserves further exploration. In order to improve the accuracy of the stochastic nonstationary earthquake model and to fit it with target spectral acceleration, an iterative procedure was developed to adjust the evolutionary power spectral density. The iterative procedure included four steps, and a series of stochastic parameters associated with the earthquake can be considered during the procedure. An example of four iterative scenarios was performed to verify the procedure. It was found that, with an increase in iteration times, the matching degree between the average spectral acceleration and the target spectral acceleration was enhanced. The deviations obviously dropped between Iteration 0 and Iteration 4. For Deviation 1, the result before iteration was 0.2231, and the result after the fourth iteration was 0.0114, with a dropping ratio of 94.89%. For Deviation 2, the result before iteration was 0.0236, and the result after the fourth iteration was 0.0053, with a dropping ratio of 77.54%. The dropping ratios proved the accuracy and effectiveness of the iterative PSD-based procedure for the Gaussian stochastic earthquake model with combined intensity and frequency nonstationarities, and they provided an important basis for the dynamic assessment of engineering structures in the future.

(2) An application of the iterative PSD-based procedure for the Gaussian stochastic earthquake model was performed, based on five PCFs designed according to the principle of 'equivalence to monolithic behavior'. Two engineering demand parameters were utilized, which were the MIDR and RIDR, and two intensity levels were defined, which were the FEL with a probability exceeding 63% in 50 years, and the REL with a probability exceeding 2% in 50 years. The thresholds for the MIDR and RIDR were adopted as 0.0018 and 0.00036 for the FEL, respectively, and the corresponding thresholds for the MIDR and RIDR were adopted as 0.02 and 0.004 for the REL, respectively. It is worth noting that the accelerations were linearly adjusted to the FEL and REL from the fortification level in this analysis, according to the generating principle of the stochastic earthquake model. Generally, the seismic performances of the five PCFs were within the thresholds, in terms of the MIDR and the RIDR. Especially for the average lines, they were all obviously lower than the red threshold lines for all the dynamic scenarios, which verified the accuracy of the seismic design for the precast concrete structures and indicated the reliable dynamic demands of the precast concrete structures under the stochastic excitation of nonstationary earthquakes. In general, the research provided some meaningful references for further stochastic earthquake selections and precast-structure assessments.

Funding: This research was funded by the National Natural Science Foundation of China (Grant No. 52208164), the Natural Science Foundation of Jiangsu Province (Grant No. BK20220984), the China Postdoctoral Science Foundation (Grant No. 2022M711028) and the Jiangsu Funding Program for Excellent Postdoctoral Talent (Grant No. 2022ZB187).

Data Availability Statement: The raw data required to reproduce these findings are available on request. The processed data required to reproduce these findings are available on request.

Acknowledgments: The author greatly appreciates the National Natural Science Foundation of China (Grant Nos. 52208164), the Natural Science Foundation of Jiangsu Province (Grant No. BK20220984), the China Postdoctoral Science Foundation (Grant No. 2022M711028) and the Jiangsu Funding Program for Excellent Postdoctoral Talent (Grant No. 2022ZB187).

Conflicts of Interest: The author declares that they have no financial and personal relationships with other people or organizations that could have inappropriately influenced this work.

References

1. Cao, X.Y.; Shen, D.; Feng, D.C.; Wang, C.L.; Qu, Z.; Wu, G. Seismic retrofitting of existing frame buildings through externally attached sub-structures: State of the art review and future perspectives. *J. Build. Eng.* **2022**, *57*, 104904. [CrossRef]
2. Hu, L.; Feng, P. Theoretical Analysis and Design of Prestressed CFRP-Reinforced Steel Columns. *J. Compos. Constr.* **2022**, *26*, 04022029. [CrossRef]
3. Wang, Z.; Feng, D.C.; Cao, X.; Wu, G. Seismic performance assessment of code-conforming precast reinforced concrete frames in China. *Earthq. Struct.* **2021**, *21*, 277–289.
4. Shi, J.; Wang, X.; Wu, Z.; Wei, X.; Ma, X. Long-term mechanical behaviors of uncracked concrete beams prestressed with external basalt fiber-reinforced polymer tendons. *Eng. Struct.* **2022**, *262*, 114309. [CrossRef]
5. Peng, Z.; Wang, X.; Ding, L.; Wu, Z. Integrative tensile prediction and parametric analysis of unidirectional carbon/basalt hybrid fiber reinforced polymer composites by bundle-based modeling. *Mater. Des.* **2022**, *218*, 110697. [CrossRef]
6. Li, M.; Shen, D.; Yang, Q.; Cao, X.; Liu, C.; Kang, J. Rehabilitation of Seismic-damaged Reinforced Concrete Beam-column Joints with Different Corrosion Rates Using Basalt Fiber-reinforced Polymer Sheets. *Compos. Struct.* **2022**, *289*, 115397. [CrossRef]
7. Zhang, B.; Zhu, H.; Dong, Z.; Yang, Z. Mechanical properties and durability of FRP-reinforced coral aggregate concrete structures: A critical review. *Mater. Today Commun.* **2023**, *35*, 105656. [CrossRef]
8. Huang, Z.K.; Pitilakis, K.; Argyroudis, S.; Tsinidis, G.; Zhang, D.M. Selection of optimal intensity measures for fragility assessment of circular tunnels in soft soil deposits. *Soil Dyn. Earthq. Eng.* **2021**, *145*, 106724.
9. Li, H.; Li, L.; Zhou, G.; Xu, L. Time-dependent seismic fragility assessment for aging highway bridges subject to non-uniform chloride-induced corrosion. *J. Earthq. Eng.* **2022**, *26*, 3523–3553. [CrossRef]
10. Zhang, Q.; Zheng, N.H.; Gu, X.L.; Wei, Z.Y.; Zhang, Z. Study of the confinement performance and stress-strain response of RC columns with corroded stirrups. *Eng. Struct.* **2022**, *266*, 114476. [CrossRef]
11. Huang, L.; Zhou, Z.; Wei, Y.; Xie, Q.; Sun, X. Seismic performance and resilience assessment of friction damped self-centering prestressed concrete frames. *Eng. Struct.* **2022**, *263*, 114346. [CrossRef]
12. Cao, X.Y.; Feng, D.C.; Beer, M. Consistent seismic hazard and fragility analysis considering combined capacity-demand uncertainties via probability density evolution method. *Struct. Saf.* **2023**. [CrossRef]
13. Conte, J.; Peng, B. Fully nonstationary analytical earthquake ground-motion model. *J. Eng. Mech.* **1997**, *123*, 15–24. [CrossRef]
14. Iyama, J.; Kuwamura, H. Application of wavelets to analysis and simulation of earthquake motions. *Earthq. Eng. Struct. Dyn.* **1999**, *28*, 255–272. [CrossRef]
15. Chrysanidis, T.; Tegos, I. Axial and transverse strengthening of R/C circular columns: Conventional and new type of steel and hybrid jackets using high-strength mortar. *J. Build. Eng.* **2020**, *30*, 101236. [CrossRef]
16. Feng, D.C.; Cao, X.Y.; Beer, M. An enhanced PDEM-based framework for reliability analysis of structures considering multiple failure modes and limit states. *Probab. Eng. Mech.* **2022**, *70*, 103367. [CrossRef]
17. Hu, S.; Qiu, C.; Zhu, S. Floor acceleration control of self-centering braced frames using viscous dampers. *J. Build. Eng.* **2023**, 105944, in press. [CrossRef]
18. Lu, Y.; Liu, Y.; Ge, Q.; Lv, Q.; Wang, Z. Experimental and numerical studies on hysteretic behavior of friction-strip coupled damper. *Eng. Struct.* **2022**, *265*, 114519. [CrossRef]
19. Zhang, Q.; Jia, W.; Lee, D.S.H.; Cai, J.; Feng, J. Inverse design of planar morphing scissor structures with end constraints. *Struct. Multidiscip. Optim.* **2022**, *65*, 1–14. [CrossRef]
20. Hu, S.; Zhu, S.; Wang, W. Machine learning-driven probabilistic residual displacement-based design method for improving post-earthquake repairability of steel moment-resisting frames using self-centering braces. *J. Build. Eng.* **2022**, *61*, 105225. [CrossRef]
21. Pang, R.; Zhou, Y.; Chen, G.; Jing, M.; Yang, D. Stochastic Mainshock–Aftershock Simulation and Its Applications in Dynamic Reliability of Structural Systems via DPIM. *J. Eng. Mech.* **2023**, *149*, 04022096. [CrossRef]
22. Ke, K.; Chen, Y.; Zhou, X.; Yam, M.C.; Hu, S. Experimental and numerical study of a brace-type hybrid damper with steel slit plates enhanced by friction mechanism. *Thin-Walled Struct.* **2023**, *182*, 110249. [CrossRef]
23. Al Atik, L.; Abrahamson, N. An improved method for nonstationary spectral matching. *Earthq. Spectra* **2010**, *26*, 601–617. [CrossRef]
24. Jayaram, N.; Lin, T.; Baker, J.W. A computationally efficient ground-motion selection algorithm for matching a target response spectrum mean and variance. *Earthq. Spectra* **2011**, *27*, 797–815. [CrossRef]
25. Li, H.; Li, L.; Wu, W.; Xu, L. Seismic fragility assessment framework for highway bridges based on an improved uniform design-response surface model methodology. *Bull. Earthq. Eng.* **2020**, *18*, 2329–2353. [CrossRef]
26. Chrysanidis, T.; Mousama, D.; Tzatzo, E.; Alamanis, N.; Zachos, D. Study of the effect of a seismic zone to the construction cost of a five-story reinforced concrete building. *Sustainability* **2022**, *14*, 10076. [CrossRef]
27. Zheng, X.W.; Li, H.N.; Gardoni, P. Hybrid Bayesian-Copula-based risk assessment for tall buildings subject to wind loads considering various uncertainties. *Reliab. Eng. Syst. Saf.* **2023**, *233*, 109100. [CrossRef]
28. Pang, R.; Xu, B.; Kong, X.; Zhou, Y.; Zou, D. Seismic performance evaluation of high CFRD slopes subjected to near-fault ground motions based on generalized probability density evolution method. *Eng. Geol.* **2018**, *246*, 391–401. [CrossRef]
29. Xu, B.; Pang, R.; Zhou, Y. Verification of stochastic seismic analysis method and seismic performance evaluation based on multi-indices for high CFRDs. *Eng. Geol.* **2020**, *264*, 105412. [CrossRef]

30. Shang, Q.; Wang, T.; Li, J. Seismic resilience assessment of emergency departments based on the state tree method. *Struct. Saf.* **2020**, *85*, 101944. [CrossRef]
31. Huang, Z.; Zhang, D.; Pitilakis, K.; Tsinidis, G.; Huang, H.; Zhang, D.; Argyroudis, S. Resilience assessment of tunnels: Framework and application for tunnels in alluvial deposits exposed to seismic hazard. *Soil Dyn. Earthq. Eng.* **2022**, *162*, 107456. [CrossRef]
32. Jia, X.; Sedehi, O.; Papadimitriou, C.; Katafygiotis, L.S.; Moaveni, B. Hierarchical Bayesian modeling framework for model updating and robust predictions in structural dynamics using modal features. *Mech. Syst. Signal Process.* **2022**, *170*, 108784. [CrossRef]
33. Shinozuka, M.; Deodatis, G. Stochastic process models for earthquake ground motion. *Probab. Eng. Mech.* **1988**, *3*, 114–123. [CrossRef]
34. Loh, C.H.; Yeh, Y.T. Spatial variation and stochastic modelling of seismic differential ground movement. *Earthq. Eng. Struct. Dyn.* **1988**, *16*, 583–596. [CrossRef]
35. Chen, Y.; Ahmadi, G. Stochastic earthquake response of secondary systems in base-isolated structures. *Earthq. Eng. Struct. Dyn.* **1992**, *21*, 1039–1057. [CrossRef]
36. Grigoriu, M. On the spectral representation method in simulation. *Probab. Eng. Mech.* **1993**, *8*, 75–90. [CrossRef]
37. Rietbrock, A.; Strasser, F.; Edwards, B. A stochastic earthquake ground-motion prediction model for the United Kingdom. *Bull. Seismol. Soc. Am.* **2013**, *103*, 57–77. [CrossRef]
38. Yamamoto, Y.; Baker, J.W. Stochastic model for earthquake ground motion using wavelet packets. *Bull. Seismol. Soc. Am.* **2013**, *103*, 3044–3056. [CrossRef]
39. Huang, G. Application of proper orthogonal decomposition in fast fourier transform—Assisted multivariate nonstationary process simulation. *J. Eng. Mech.* **2015**, *141*, 04015015. [CrossRef]
40. Bhattacharyya, A.; Singh, L.; Pachori, R.B. Fourier–Bessel series expansion based empirical wavelet transform for analysis of non-stationary signals. *Digit. Signal Process.* **2018**, *78*, 185–196. [CrossRef]
41. Cao, X.Y.; Feng, D.C.; Li, Y. Assessment of various seismic fragility analysis approaches for structures excited by non-stationary stochastic ground motions. *Mech. Syst. Signal Process.* **2023**, *186*, 109838. [CrossRef]
42. Feng, D.C.; Cao, X.Y.; Wang, D.; Wu, G. A PDEM-based non-parametric seismic fragility assessment method for RC structures under non-stationary ground motions. *J. Build. Eng.* **2023**, *63*, 105465. [CrossRef]
43. Chen, Z.P.; Zhu, S.; Yu, H.; Wang, B. Development of novel SMA-based D-type self-centering eccentrically braced frames. *Eng. Struct.* **2022**, *260*, 114228. [CrossRef]
44. Cao, X.Y.; Feng, D.C.; Wu, G.; Wang, Z. Experimental and theoretical investigations of the existing reinforced concrete frames retrofitted with the novel external SC-PBSPC BRBF sub-structures. *Eng. Struct.* **2022**, *256*, 113982. [CrossRef]
45. Huang, X.; Liu, Y.; Sun, X. Concept and analysis of resilient frictional shear connector for coupled system. *J. Build. Eng.* **2022**, *50*, 104172. [CrossRef]
46. Xu, J.G.; Cao, X.Y.; Wu, G. Seismic collapse and reparability performance of reinforced concrete frames retrofitted with external PBSPC BRBF sub-frame in near-fault regions. *J. Build. Eng.* **2023**, *64*, 105716. [CrossRef]
47. Chen, Z.P.; Zhu, S. Development of a novel shape memory alloy-based self-centering precast segmental concrete column. *Struct. Control Health Monit.* **2022**, *29*, e3099. [CrossRef]
48. Zhang, Q.; Wei, Z.Y.; Gu, X.L.; Yang, Q.C.; Li, S.Y.; Zhao, Y.S. Confinement behavior and stress–strain response of square concrete columns strengthened with carbon textile reinforced concrete (CTRC) composites. *Eng. Struct.* **2022**, *266*, 114592. [CrossRef]
49. Ouyang, X.; Zhang, Y.; Ou, X.; Shi, Y.; Liu, S.; Fan, J. Seismic fragility analysis of buckling-restrained brace-strengthened reinforced concrete frames using a performance-based plastic design method. *Structures* **2022**, *43*, 338–350. [CrossRef]
50. Huang, L.; Zeng, B.; Zhou, Z.; Zhang, W.; Wei, Y.; Li, C. Seismic behavior and reliability of variable friction damped self-centering prestressed concrete frames considering bolt bearing. *Soil Dyn. Earthq. Eng.* **2023**, *164*, 107643. [CrossRef]
51. Zhang, Y.; Ouyang, X.; Sun, B.; Shi, Y.; Wang, Z. A comparative study on seismic fragility analysis of RC frame structures with consideration of modeling uncertainty under far-field and near-field ground motion excitation. *Bull. Earthq. Eng.* **2022**, *20*, 1455–1487. [CrossRef]
52. Chen, Z.P.; Feng, D.C.; Cao, X.Y.; Ma, K.J.; Zhu, S.; Wu, G. Probabilistic seismic demand and fragility analysis of a novel mid-rise large-span cassette structure. *Bull. Earthq. Eng.* **2022**, *20*, 383–413. [CrossRef]
53. Huang, Z.; Argyroudis, S.; Zhang, D.; Pitilakis, K.; Huang, H.; Zhang, D. Time-dependent fragility functions for circular tunnels in soft soils. *Asce-Asme J. Risk Uncertain. Eng. Syst. Part Civ. Eng.* **2022**, *8*, 04022030. [CrossRef]
54. Li, Y.; Geng, F.; Ding, Y. Design procedure and seismic response of low-damage self-centering precast concrete frames. *Soil Dyn. Earthq. Eng.* **2023**, *166*, 107780. [CrossRef]
55. Cao, X.Y.; Wu, G.; Feng, D.C.; Zu, X.J. Experimental and Numerical Study of Outside Strengthening with Precast Bolt-Connected Steel Plate Reinforced Concrete Frame-Brace. *J. Perform. Constr. Facil.* **2019**, *33*, 04019077. [CrossRef]
56. Pang, R.; Xu, B.; Zhou, Y.; Song, L. Seismic time-history response and system reliability analysis of slopes considering uncertainty of multi-parameters and earthquake excitations. *Comput. Geotech.* **2021**, *136*, 104245. [CrossRef]
57. Shang, Q.; Guo, X.; Li, J.; Wang, T. Post-earthquake health care service accessibility assessment framework and its application in a medium-sized city. *Reliab. Eng. Syst. Saf.* **2022**, *228*, 108782. [CrossRef]
58. Cao, X.Y.; Wu, G.; Feng, D.C.; Wang, Z.; Cui, H.R. Research on the seismic retrofitting performance of RC frames using SC-PBSPC BRBF substructures. *Earthq. Eng. Struct. Dyn.* **2020**, *49*, 794–816. [CrossRef]

59. Shi, J.; Wang, X.; Zhang, L.; Wu, Z.; Zhu, Z. Composite-Wedge Anchorage for Fiber-Reinforced Polymer Tendons. *J. Compos. Constr.* **2022**, *26*, 04022005. [CrossRef]
60. Cao, X.Y.; Feng, D.C.; Wu, G.; Zeng, Y.H. Reusing & replacing performances of the AB-BRB with thin-walled concrete-infilled steel shells. *Thin-Walled Struct.* **2020**, *157*, 107069.
61. Elliott, K.S. *Precast Concrete Structures*; CRC Press: Boca Raton, FL, USA, 2019.
62. Kurama, Y.C.; Sritharan, S.; Fleischman, R.B.; Restrepo, J.I.; Henry, R.S.; Cleland, N.M.; Ghosh, S.; Bonelli, P. Seismic-resistant precast concrete structures: State of the art. *J. Struct. Eng.* **2018**, *144*, 03118001. [CrossRef]
63. Polat, G. Factors affecting the use of precast concrete systems in the United States. *J. Constr. Eng. Manag.* **2008**, *134*, 169–178. [CrossRef]
64. Koskisto, O.J.; Ellingwood, B.R. Reliability-based optimization of plant precast concrete structures. *J. Struct. Eng.* **1997**, *123*, 298–304. [CrossRef]
65. Ozden, S.; Akpinar, E.; Erdogan, H.; Atalay, H.M. Performance of precast concrete structures in October 2011 Van earthquake, Turkey. *Mag. Concr. Res.* **2014**, *66*, 543–552. [CrossRef]
66. Belleri, A.; Moaveni, B.; Restrepo, J.I. Damage assessment through structural identification of a three-story large-scale precast concrete structure. *Earthq. Eng. Struct. Dyn.* **2014**, *43*, 61–76. [CrossRef]
67. Kataoka, M.N.; Ferreira, M.A.; de Cresce El, A.L.H. Nonlinear FE analysis of slab-beam-column connection in precast concrete structures. *Eng. Struct.* **2017**, *143*, 306–315. [CrossRef]
68. Lacerda, M.M.S.; da Silva, T.J.; Alva, G.M.S.; de Lima, M.C.V. Influence of the vertical grouting in the interface between corbel and beam in beam-to-column connections of precast concrete structures–An experimental analysis. *Eng. Struct.* **2018**, *172*, 201–213. [CrossRef]
69. Cao, X.Y.; Feng, D.C.; Wu, G. Seismic performance upgrade of RC frame buildings using precast bolt-connected steel-plate reinforced concrete frame-braces. *Eng. Struct.* **2019**, *195*, 382–399. [CrossRef]
70. Dal Lago, B.; Bianchi, S.; Biondini, F. Diaphragm effectiveness of precast concrete structures with cladding panels under seismic action. *Bull. Earthq. Eng.* **2019**, *17*, 473–495. [CrossRef]
71. Feng, D.C.; Wang, Z.; Cao, X.Y.; Wu, G. Damage mechanics-based modeling approaches for cyclic analysis of precast concrete structures: A comparative study. *Int. J. Damage Mech.* **2020**, *29*, 965–987. [CrossRef]
72. Ye, M.; Jiang, J.; Chen, H.; Zhou, H.; Song, D. Seismic behavior of an innovative hybrid beam-column connection for precast concrete structures. *Eng. Struct.* **2021**, *227*, 111436. [CrossRef]
73. Xu, J.G.; Cao, X.Y.; Shi, J.; Wang, Z. A comparative study of the novel externally-attached precast SRC braced-frames for seismic retrofitting under near-field spectrum-compatible non-stationary stochastic earthquake. *Structures* **2023**, *50*, 200–214. [CrossRef]
74. Cao, X.Y. Probabilistic Seismic Performance Evaluation of Existing Buildings through Non-stationary Stochastic Ground Motions and Incremental Dynamic Analysis. In Proceedings of the 2021 7th International Conference on Hydraulic and Civil Engineering & Smart Water Conservancy and Intelligent Disaster Reduction Forum (ICHCE & SWIDR), Nanjing, China, 6–8 November 2021, pp. 1167–1170.
75. Xu, J.G.; Feng, D.C.; Mangalathu, S.; Jeon, J.S. Data-driven rapid damage evaluation for life-cycle seismic assessment of regional reinforced concrete bridges. *Earthq. Eng. Struct. Dyn.* **2022**, *51*, 2730–2751. [CrossRef]
76. Hu, S.; Zhu, S.; Alam, M.S.; Wang, W. Machine learning-aided peak and residual displacement-based design method for enhancing seismic performance of steel moment-resisting frames by installing self-centering braces. *Eng. Struct.* **2022**, *271*, 114935. [CrossRef]
77. Shang, Q.; Qiu, L.; Wang, T.; Li, J. Experimental and analytical study on performance of seismic sway braces for suspended piping systems. *J. Build. Eng.* **2022**, *57*, 104826. [CrossRef]
78. Shi, J.; Sun, S.; Cao, X.; Wang, H. Pullout behaviors of basalt fiber-reinforced polymer bars with mechanical anchorages for concrete structures exposed to seawater. *Constr. Build. Mater.* **2023**, *373*, 130866. [CrossRef]
79. Cao, X.Y.; Feng, D.C.; Wu, G. Pushover-based probabilistic seismic capacity assessment of RCFs retrofitted with PBSPC BRBF sub-structures. *Eng. Struct.* **2021**, *234*, 111919. [CrossRef]
80. Liu, Z.; Liu, W.; Peng, Y. Random function based spectral representation of stationary and non-stationary stochastic processes. *Probab. Eng. Mech.* **2016**, *45*, 115–126. [CrossRef]
81. Liu, Z.; Zeng, B.; Wu, L. Simulation of non-stationary ground motion by spectral representation and random functions (in Chinese). *J. Vib. Eng.* **2015**, *28*, 411–417.
82. Mazzoni, S.; McKenna, F.; Scott, M.H.; Fenves, G.L. *OpenSees Command Language Manual*; Pacific Earthquake Engineering Research (PEER) Center: Berkeley, CA, USA, 2006.
83. Cao, X.Y.; Feng, D.C.; Wu, G.; Xu, J.G. Probabilistic Seismic Performance Assessment of RC Frames Retrofitted with External SC-PBSPC BRBF Sub-structures. *J. Earthq. Eng.* **2021**, *26*, 1–24. [CrossRef]
84. Im, H.J.; Park, H.G.; Eom, T.S. Cyclic Loading Test for Reinforced-Concrete-Emulated Beam-Column Connection of Precast Concrete Moment Frame. *ACI Struct. J.* **2013**, *110*, 115–125.
85. Cao, X.Y.; Wu, G.; Ju, J.W.W. Seismic performance improvement of existing RCFs using external PT-PBSPC frame sub-structures: Experimental verification and numerical investigation. *J. Build. Eng.* **2022**, *46*, 103649. [CrossRef]
86. Cao, X.Y.; Feng, D.C.; Wang, Z.; Wu, G. Parametric investigation of the assembled bolt-connected buckling-restrained brace and performance evaluation of its application into structural retrofit. *J. Build. Eng.* **2022**, *48*, 103988. [CrossRef]

87. Cao, X.Y.; Xiong, C.Z.; Feng, D.C.; Wu, G. Dynamic and probabilistic seismic performance assessment of precast prestressed reinforced concrete frames incorporating slab influence through three-dimensional spatial model. *Bull. Earthq. Eng.* **2022**, *20*, 6705–6739. [CrossRef]
88. Zhang, Y.; Shi, Y.; Sun, B.; Wang, Z. Estimation of aleatory randomness by Sa (T1)-based intensity measures in fragility analysis of reinforced concrete frame structures. *CMES-Comput. Model. Eng. Sci.* **2022**, *130*, 73–96. [CrossRef]
89. Cao, X.; Xu, J.; Chen, S. A Comparison Between PDEM-Based Approach and Linear-Regression-Based Approach in Seismic Fragility Assessment: Application into Low-Rise Frame Buildings. In *Proceedings of the 2022 International Conference on Green Building, Civil Engineering and Smart City, Guilin, China, 8–10 April 2022*; Springer: Berlin/Heidelberg, Germany, 2022; pp. 869–875.
90. *GB50011*; Code for Seismic Design of Buildings. MHURD-PRC (Ministry of Housing and Urban-Rural Development of the People's Republic of China): Bejing, China, 2010. (In Chinese)
91. *FEMA-356*; Commentary for the Seismic Rehabilitation of Buildings. Federal Emergency Management Agency: Washington, DC, USA, 2000.

Disclaimer/Publisher's Note: The statements, opinions and data contained in all publications are solely those of the individual author(s) and contributor(s) and not of MDPI and/or the editor(s). MDPI and/or the editor(s) disclaim responsibility for any injury to people or property resulting from any ideas, methods, instructions or products referred to in the content.

Article

Intelligent Analysis of Construction Costs of Shield Tunneling in Complex Geological Conditions by Machine Learning Method

Xiaomu Ye [1], Pengfei Ding [2], Dawei Jin [3], Chuanyue Zhou [1,3], Yi Li [3] and Jin Zhang [3,*]

1. PowerChina Huadong Engineering Corporation Limited, Hangzhou 311122, China
2. Hangzhou City Infrastructure Management Center, Hangzhou 310026, China
3. Key Laboratory of Ministry of Education for Geomechanics and Embankment Engineering, Hohai University, Nanjing 210024, China
* Correspondence: zhangjin90@hhu.edu.cn

Abstract: The estimation of construction costs for shield tunneling projects is typically based on a standard quota, which fails to consider the variation of geological parameters and often results in significant differences in unit cost. To address this issue, we propose a novel model based on a random forest machine learning procedure for analyzing the construction cost of shield tunnelling in complex geological conditions. We focus specifically on the unit consumption of grease, grouting, labor, water, and electricity. Using a dataset of geotechnical parameters and consumption quantities from a shield tunneling project, we employ KNN and correlation analysis to reduce the input dataset dimension from 17 to 6 for improved model accuracy and efficiency. Our proposed approach is applied to a shield tunneling project, with results showing that the compressive strength of geomaterial is the most influential parameter for grease, labor, water, and electricity, while it is the second most influential for grouting quantity. Based on these findings, we calculate the unit consumption and cost of the tunnelling project, which we classify into three geological categories: soil, soft rock, and hard rock. Comparing our results to the standard quota value, it is found that the unit cost of shield tunneling in soil is slightly lower (6%), while that in soft rock is very close to the standard value. However, the cost in the hard rock region is significantly greater (38%), which cannot be ignored in project budgeting. Ultimately, our results support the use of compressive strength as a classification index for shield tunneling in complex geological conditions, representing a valuable contribution to the field of tunneling cost prediction.

Keywords: random forest; shield tunneling; budget; complex geological conditions; construction cost

MSC: 68T09

1. Introduction

Project budgets during the bidding stage and project final accounts after completion are the two important steps of construction project management [1,2] of shield tunneling projects. The core of construction project management is the investment estimation of the construction cost for shield tunneling engineering [3,4]. The investment estimation of the construction cost governs project profitability. Since it is a crucial component of the economic analysis of a subway line or underground tunnel, the cost of a shield tunneling project has a substantial impact on the overall economic benefit. The accurate cost prediction of tunneling projects is critical, as it can provide a powerful source of help for reducing the project costs and optimizing construction management. Therefore, it is essential to thoroughly examine the cost prediction in order to increase its speed and accuracy and make correct investment decisions [5].

In practice, the shield tunneling project cost is normally estimated by the use of an official budget standard, which defines the quota of main construction consumption containing the unit quantities of grease, grouting, labor, and so forth. Theoretically, the total construction cost can be calculated as the standard consumption multiplied by the unit price. However, concerning the tunneling, quantities of consumption exhibit an obvious relationship with the geological condition of the construction site [6,7]. Consequently, the usual computation procedure of shield tunneling without considering different geological conditions will lead to great errors in the construction cost. Especially in underground tunneling projects, the excavation site usually has composite geological layers. This implies proposing a new computation method with the consideration of influences of geotechnical parameters on the total cost [8–10].

Numerous studies have been devoted to the factors that affect tunneling costs by researchers in recent years. Aiming at avoiding unexpected variations of time and cost during the construction process, different studies have been published concerning the influences of composite geological conditions [11–13]. By the use of mathematical models [14,15], the random process and time it takes for the excavation process have been fully discussed by considering the geological conditions around the tunnel route. Besides, in order to gather information on the geological conditions in the complex tunneling region, in situ equipment was applied by Carrière et al. [16] for pilot-drilling, subsurface-boring, and advanced geophysical prospecting. Daraei et al. [17] proposed the application of value engineering principles to decrease construction costs and increase safety in tunnel construction projects in Iraqi Kurdistan, demonstrated through the optimization of the Heybat Sultan twin tunnels project. Particularly, Mahmoodzadeh et al. [18] has proposed a novel model to estimate the construction time and cost in tunneling projects. The influences of uncertain geological conditions in tunneling construction on the time and cost were analyzed by applying the Markov chain and considering opinions of experts.

In addition, with the development of artificial intelligence [19,20], various machine learning algorithms have been successfully applied to the prediction of construction cost. Ye [21] established an intelligent algorithm for the construction cost estimation, which was developed from the Particle Swarm Optimization (PSO) Guided BP Neural Network. Combined with the Support Vector Machine (SVM) method, the construction cost of substations has been successfully predicted by a PSO-based procedure in the Ref. [22]. Considering the gray fuzzy theory, a gray fuzzy predictive model was proposed by Liu et al. [23] to calculate the cost of an unfinished construction. The Decision Aids for Tunneling (DAT) [24] is a computer-based tool which has also been widely used for computing the distributions of tunnelling cost and time, considering uncertainties of the geological conditions. On the other hand, aiming at using the official quota for the consumption quantities in complex geological conditions, the degrees of impact of the geotechnical parameters [25,26] are essential for the classification, indicating the application of random forest method [27]. Concerning the application of machine learning algorithms for engineering practice, development of a user-friendly software tool has been considered by researchers [28–30]. The software is easily used by engineers and practitioners without the need for extensive knowledge of the underlying machine learning algorithms.

As an ensemble learning technique for classification, regression, and other problems, random forests build a large number of decision trees during the training process [31–33]. The result of the random forest for classification (RFC) tasks is the class that the majority of the trees choose [34,35]. For regression tasks (RFR), the mean or average forecast of each individual tree is returned [36,37]. Random choice forests correct the tendency of decision trees to overfit their training set. The potential of forecasting the fatty acids and tocopherols content has been explored by Rajković et al. [38], by combining two machine learning methods, namely the artificial neural network (ANN) and random forest regression (RFR) algorithms. In particular, the random forest method can be used to compute the feature importance score of input datasets due to the bootstrap structure [39–41]. Gu et al. [42] carried out a random forest-based computation and found that the annual average daily traffic on a minor road from the roadway traffic characteristics group makes the highest contribution to rear-end crashes. Similarly, the feature importance of different variables has also been evaluated by the random forest procedure for fatal fall-from-heights accidents [43], vegetation mapping in savannah regions [44] and contributions from LiDAR and orthoimagery data to map urban objects [45].

Considering the difficulty of the classification of budget quotas in complex geological conditions, the present study is devoted to analyzing the influences of geotechnical parameters on the main unit consumption in shield tunneling. The excavation consumption and geotechnical data were collected from a shield tunneling project in China, in which different soil and rock geological layers are involved. In order to obtain the most impactful geotechnical parameter in complex conditions, the random forest machine learning technique is employed with the consumption factor as the target in this study. Referring to the opinions of experts, four consumption factors for shield tunneling, quantity of grease, grouting, labor and water and electricity are studied for different geological conditions. The main purpose of our study was to find out the most impactful geological parameter and propose a new budget quota for classification. Thus, the random forest classification algorithm is applied and the collected data will be classified in different categories. In comparison with the DAT method, the proposed random forest-based model is data-driven, which allows us to take into account the full range of geotechnical parameters and their interactions in a more comprehensive manner. It does not require specific knowledge and can be easily implemented in engineering practice. The most influential geotechnical parameter on the consumption of shield tunneling is obtained from the comprehensive result of four factors by the random forest procedure. Consequently, the shield tunneling consumption in different geological conditions is computed with the classification of the parameter, which will provide the basis for novel quotas in this situation.

The present paper is organized in the following way. In Section 2, the background of the shield tunneling project is briefly introduced, and the collection and ordering of geotechnical and consumption data are also described. In order to improve the computation accuracy and efficiency, the dimension of the datasets is reduced before model training. Section 3 is devoted to recalling the principle formulation of the random forest algorithm, as well as the general flowchart of this machine learning method in analysis of the construction cost of shield tunneling in complex geological conditions. In Section 4, the constructed random forest model is applied to calculate the importance score of considered geotechnical parameters for four consumption factors. The accuracy of the proposed method is accessed by comparison with the unit consumption and cost in the soil, soft rock and hard rock conditions with those of the standard one. In the last section, some concluding points are provided.

2. Problem Description and Data Pre-Processing

2.1. Background of the Project

The present study is based on data and reports from the Zhijiang Road Tunneling (ZRT) project in Hangzhou, China, as shown in Figure 1. The tunnel was excavated using a combination of shield tunneling (mud–water balancing shield machine with inner diameter 14.5 m and outer diameter 15.03 m) and open-cut methods. The shield tunneling portion, marked by the red point in Figure 1, spans a distance of 3.6 km and is divided into east and west sections.

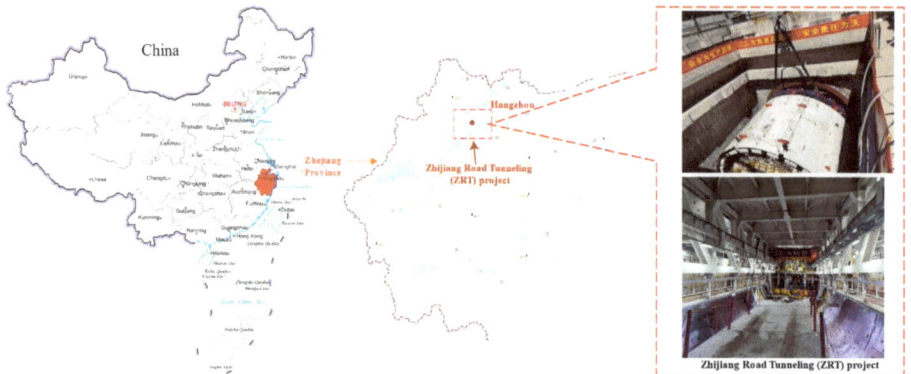

Figure 1. The background and location of the Zhijiang Road Tunneling (ZRT) project in Hangzhou, China.

Based on the geological engineering investigation report, the tunnel geology of the entire west section is primarily composed of extremely soft and soft rock, where moderately weathered argillaceous siltstone accounts for approximately 53% and moderately weathered tuffaceous sandstone accounts for about 19%. In the east tunneling excavation section, hard rock predominates, including moderately weathered siltstone accounting for 60% and moderately weathered quartz sandstone accounting for 10% (Figure 2).

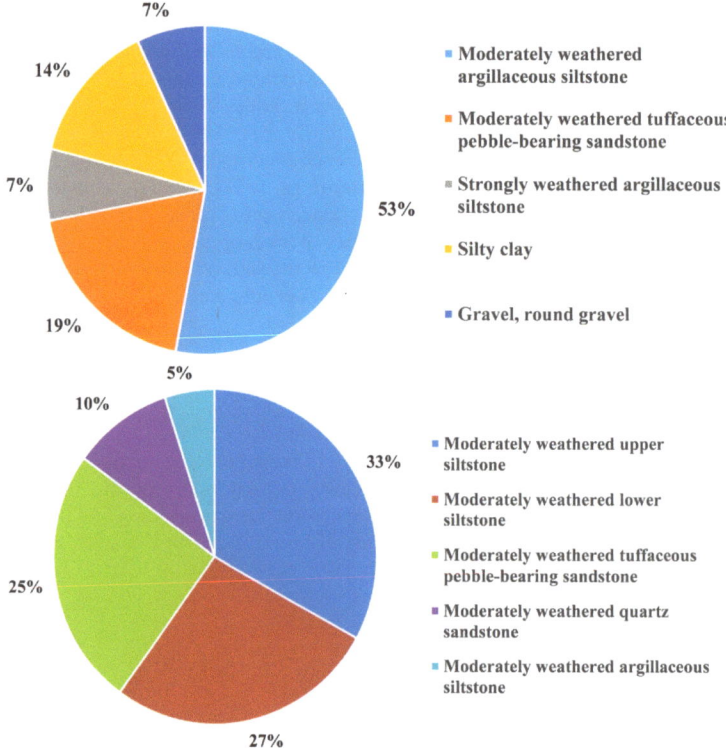

Figure 2. Main geological compositions of west (above) and east (below) sections of shield tunneling excavation in ZRT project.

2.2. Collection of Geological Data and Tunneling Consumption

The distribution of main geological conditions along the east tunneling part of ZRT project is displayed in Figure 3. We take it as an example to explain the collection and preparation of geological data on site of the project and of the shield operational consumption. Noticing that the width of standard shield segments is 2 m, the datasets of tunneling consumption are consequently collected per 2 m. As shown in Figure 4, the arrangement of geological data and material consumption are in the same order of shield segments, which is crucial for training the random forest model developed in our study.

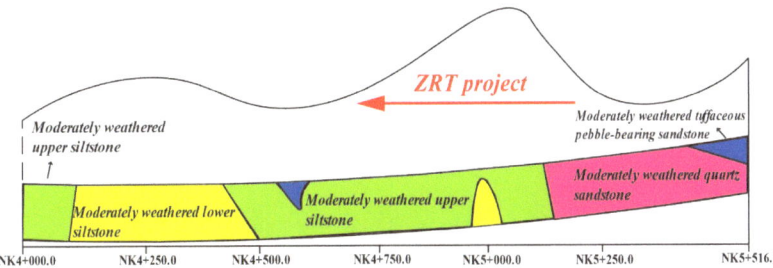

Figure 3. Profile of main geological conditions along the east tunnel.

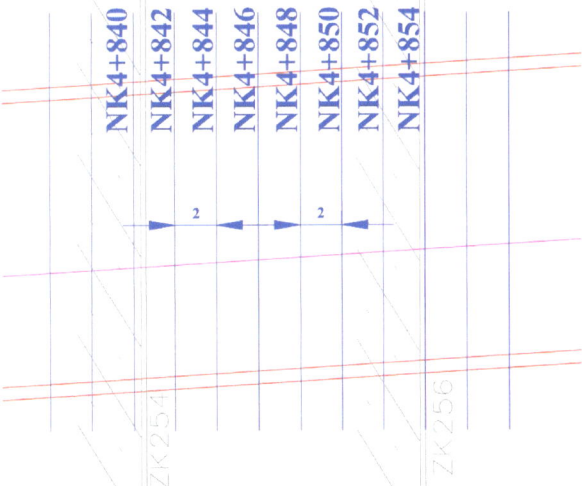

Figure 4. Shield segments index.

In order to improve the the generalization ability of the constructed model in the present study, 17 geological parameters in the geological report are all taken into account. The statistical information of geological parameters which will be analyzed in the following machine learning model is provided in Table 1 for different geological layers. For the sake of simplicity, the abbreviations of each geotechnical parameter are also provided in this table, and will be used in the following part of this study. Besides, it can be found that some specific values of the geotechnical parameters are missing, so additional pre-processing for the missing values is needed. The objective of this paper concerns the influence of complex geological conditions on economic factors in shield tunneling, so the feature importance of different geological parameters should be considered. Thus, it would be better to find out the main influence geological factors, providing a basis for the cost classification of budgets.

Table 1. Statistical information of 17 geological parameters of different layers.

Geotechnical Parameters and Abbreviations	Soil 1	Soil 2	Soil 3	Soil 4	...	Rock 9
Moisture content (W_0 %)	28.98	45.24	41.87	41.59	...	-
Natural density (γ kN/m^3)	19.10	17.40	17.40	17.80	...	26.00
Specific gravity (G_s)	2.70	2.73	2.73	2.73	...	-
Void ratio (e)	0.80	1.30	1.15	1.23	...	0.032
Saturability (S_r)	95.66	95.25	96.12	92.47	...	-
Liquid limit (WL)	-	40.51	38.64	39.75	...	-
Plastic limit (WP)	-	24.34	23.94	23.97	...	-
liquidity index (IL)	-	16.17	14.70	15.77	...	-
plasticity index (IP)	-	1.32	1.20	0.97	...	-
Bearing capacity (fak kPa)	130	65	65	100	...	3500
Modulus of compressibility (E_s MPa)	7.0	2.3	2.4	4.0	...	-
Lateral pressure coefficient (k_0 MPa^{-1})	0.40	0.58	0.58	0.54	...	0.25
Horizontal permeability coefficient (KH cm/s)	1.0×10^3	4.0×10^6	2.0×10^6	2.0×10^6	...	3.0×10^6
Vertical permeability coefficient (KV cm/s)	9.0×10^4	3.0×10^6	1.5×10^6	1.5×10^6	...	2.5×10^6
Cohesion (c kPa)	3.0	13.0	13.0	24.0	...	450
Friction angle (ϕ °)	25	9.5	10	12	...	43
Compressive strength (σ MPa)	5000	4×10	9.4021	0.9954	...	60.40

Similarly, the main consumption factors in the tunneling process are also recorded per segment (2 m). In the present paper, four main consumption indicators, the amount of grease, grouting, labor and water and electricity, are studied for the purpose of economic classification in complex geological conditions. From this perspective, the main components of each indicator are given in Table 2 based on the official Quota Booklet of shield tunneling (Version 2018). The unit prices of each consumption component are also provided for the computation of construction cost in the following part. The key influencing economic consumptions are arranged in the order of shield segment, as those of geological data. Moreover, the objective consumption indicators are ordered by the Y_i index in order to be implemented in the random forest program.

Table 2. Statistical information of 4 concerned consumption indicators.

Consumption Indicator	Components	Unit Price [1]	Index
Grease	Tail grease	17.5	Y_1
	EP2 grease	25.0	Y_2
	Seal grease	55.0	Y_3
Grouting	Grouting	1.3–1.8	Y_4
Labor	Labor	135.0	Y_5
Water & electricity	Water	4.27	Y_6
	Electricity	0.78	Y_7

[1] The currency for the unit price is CNY.

2.3. Pre-Processing of the Datasets

For the purpose of determination of shield tunneling consumption in complex geological conditions, especially for the four indicators in Table 2, the collected data will be used in a random forest-based procedure to train the model. The accuracy of the prediction model is significantly influenced by the quality of the input data. Before the implementation, data pre-processing is needed for the missing and abnormal values.

As shown in Figure 5, the values of geotechnical parameters are displayed in the arranged order of shield segment. The abbreviations for the concerned geotechnical parameters are given in Table 1. It can be seen that there are too much missing data for 8 parameters (W_0, G_s, S_r, WL, WP, IP, IL and E_s), which will be neglected for the following analysis. Besides, some recorded values for tunneling consumption data could be abnormal due to incorrect recording or other reasons. Those abnormal values (too large or too small) will be removed, and the missing data of σ and e will be replaced by that calculated by the KNN algorithm (k-Nearest Neighbor) [46]. The distribution of original data (red dash line) and that treated by the KNN algorithm (blue solid line) are plotted in Figure 6, respectively. It is obviously seen that the distribution of compressive strength (σ) and void ratio (e) are not changed, and they can be accepted for the following analysis by the random forest procedure.

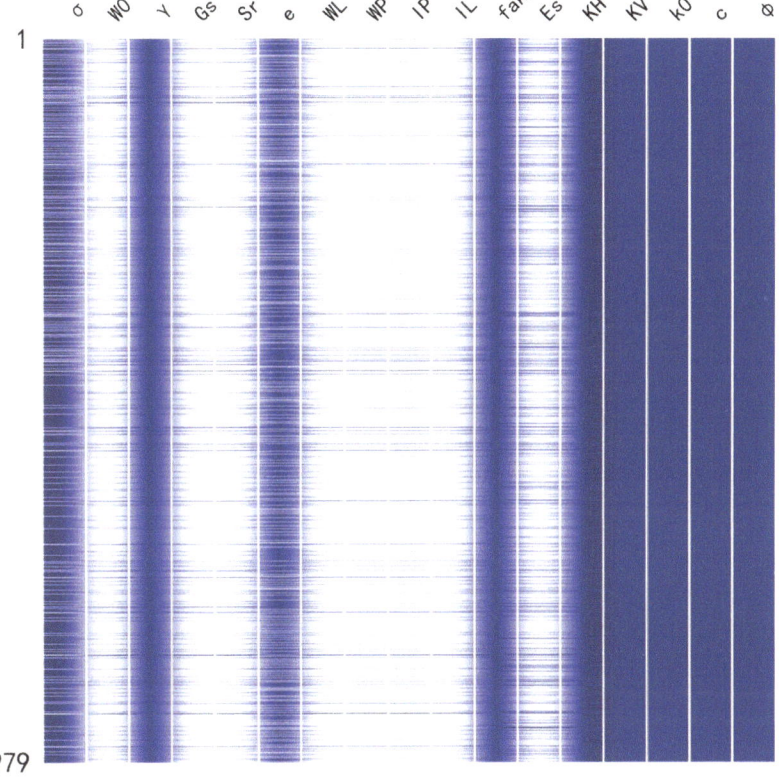

Figure 5. Missing values of all 17 geotechnical parameters arranged in the order of shield segment.

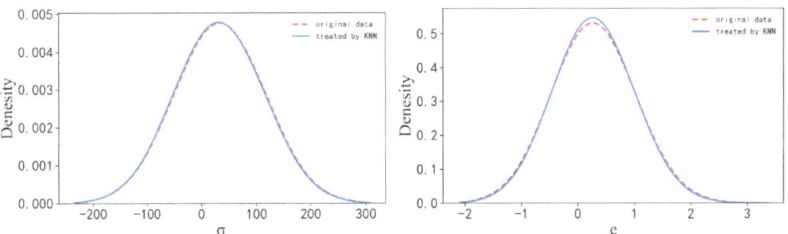

Figure 6. Distribution of original data and that treated by the KNN algorithm of compressive strength (σ) (**left** subfigure) and void ratio (e) (**right** subfigure).

Moreover, in the random forest program, the performance of the random forest model will get worse if the degree of correlation between involved geotechnical parameters is greater. In order to improve the accuracy of the random forest procedure, the collected geological data also need to be analyzed for the correlation coefficient. Consequently, the correlation matrix is used to display the correlation coefficients among all the geological parameters, before being implemented in the program. The heat map (Figure 7), also known as the correlation coefficient map, can visually judge the magnitude of the correlation between variables based on the color of different squares on the heat map. The correlation coefficient can be calculated directly by the following formulation:

$$\rho = \frac{Cov(X_1, X_2)}{\sqrt{DX_1, DX_2}} = \frac{E(X_1X_2) - E(X_1) \cdot E(X_2)}{\sqrt{DX_1, DX_2}} \quad (1)$$

where Cov denotes the covariance and E is the mathematical expectation. By the use of the heat map, the involved geotechnical features with high correlation can be screened out to prevent overfitting in the random forest model. As shown in Figure 7, the correlation coefficients of nine different geotechnical variables (after the remove of missing data) are displayed in the form of a heat map by different colors. Notice that the abbreviations for the parameters have already been provided in Table 1.

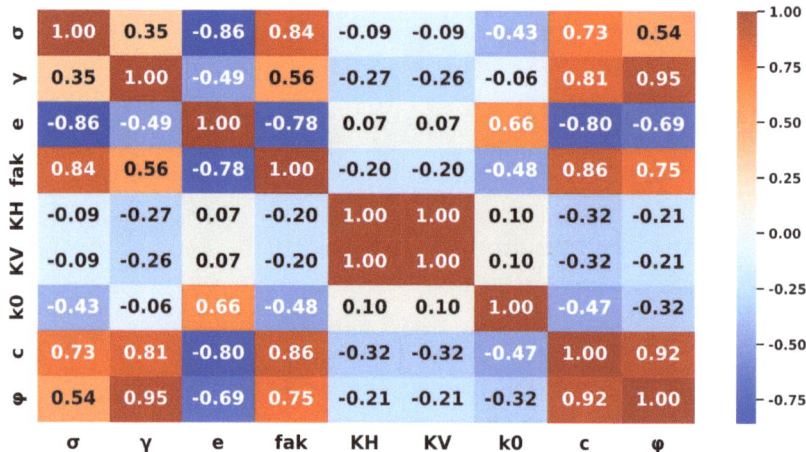

Figure 7. Correlation matrix heat map of nine geological parameters.

It is clear from Figure 7 that any of the nine features recovered exhibit a high degree of association. The nine datasets will again be shrunk in dimension to avoid features with strong correlations that would have a significant impact on the obtained prediction. It is demonstrated that there is a strong correlation between the cohesion and bearing capacity (0.86), natural density and friction angle (0.95), and horizontal and vertical permeability coefficients (1.00). Consequently, we only need to reserve one of the mentioned pair of geotechnical parameters. In practice, the natural density and bearing capacity are important geological parameters according to experts and need to be reserved. By reserving the vertical permeability coefficient, nine parameters are reduced to six for the variable importance analysis by random forest. Figure 8 displays the final data preparation after reductions from 17 to 6 geotechnical input parameters for the model training. Each of the input data contains 1979 sets.

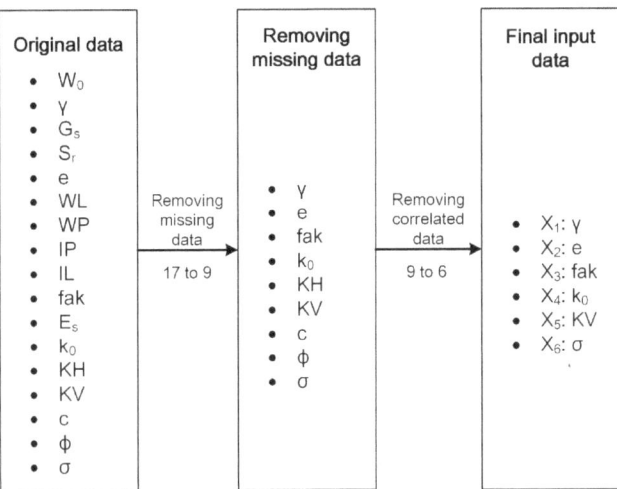

Figure 8. Final six geotechnical features in random forest model by dimension reduction.

3. Methodology

Random forests is an ensemble learning method for classification, regression and other tasks that operates by constructing a multitude of decision trees at the training time. The class that the majority of the trees chose is the output of the random forest for classification tasks. The mean or average prediction of each individual tree is returned for regression tasks. The tendency of decision trees to overfit their training set is corrected by random decision forests. By randomly sampling the sample data, multiple different decision trees are formed, and then the results are combined to obtain the prediction results of the random forest. The variable importance in the objective tunneling consumption indicators will be calculated by the constructed model in this paper. Thus, this section is devoted to the basic principle of the random forest model and the algorithm applied to this study.

3.1. Principle Technique of Random Forest

Decision Trees is a non-parametric supervised learning method. The goal is to create a model that predicts the value of a target variable by learning simple decision rules inferred from the data features. A tree can be seen as a piecewise constant approximation. Given a training set $X = \{X_1, X_2, \ldots, X_n\}$ with responses $Y = \{Y_1, Y_2, \ldots, Y_n\}$, a decision tree recursively partitions the feature space such that the samples with the same labels or similar target values are grouped together.

Let the data at node m be represented by Q_m with n_m samples. For each candidate split $\theta = (j, t_m)$ consisting of a feature j and threshold t_m, partition the data into $Q_m^l(\theta)$ and $Q_m^r(\theta)$ subsets:

$$Q_m^l(\theta) = \{(x,y) \mid x_j \leq t_m\}$$
$$Q_m^r(\theta) = Q_m \backslash Q_m^l(\theta) \qquad (2)$$

The quality of a candidate split of node m is then computed using an impurity function or loss function H, the choice of which depends on the task being solved

$$G(Q_m, \theta) = \frac{n_m^l}{n_m} H(Q_m^l(\theta)) + \frac{n_m^r}{n_m} H(Q_m^r(\theta)) \qquad (3)$$

Select the parameters that minimises the impurity

$$\theta^* = \mathrm{argmin}_\theta G(Q_m, \theta) \tag{4}$$

Recurse for subsets $Q_m^l(\theta^*)$ and $Q_m^r(\theta^*)$ until the maximum allowable depth is reached $n_m < \min_{samples}$ or $n_m = 1$.

If a target is a classification outcome taking on values $0, 1, \ldots, K-1$, for node m, let

$$p_{mk} = \frac{1}{n_m} \sum_{y \in Q_m} I(y = k) \tag{5}$$

be the proportion of class k observations in node m. Two common measures of impurity are the Gini index:

$$H(Q_m) = \sum_k p_{mk}(1 - p_{mk}) \tag{6}$$

and log loss or Entropy:

$$H(Q_m) = -\sum_k p_{mk} \log(p_{mk}) \tag{7}$$

The Random Forest algorithm [33] is a classification algorithm composed of multiple decision trees, with each tree producing a category that contributes to the final output category. It is built using the bagging method and categorical regression trees and has been successfully used in various disciplines (see Figure 9). Random forests consist of different decision trees that are independent of each other. When a sample is inputted, each tree in the forest will make a decision and vote to determine the best category. Typically, $\sqrt{p}$ features are used in each split for classification problems with p features. However, each problem requires tuning to identify the best values for these parameters.

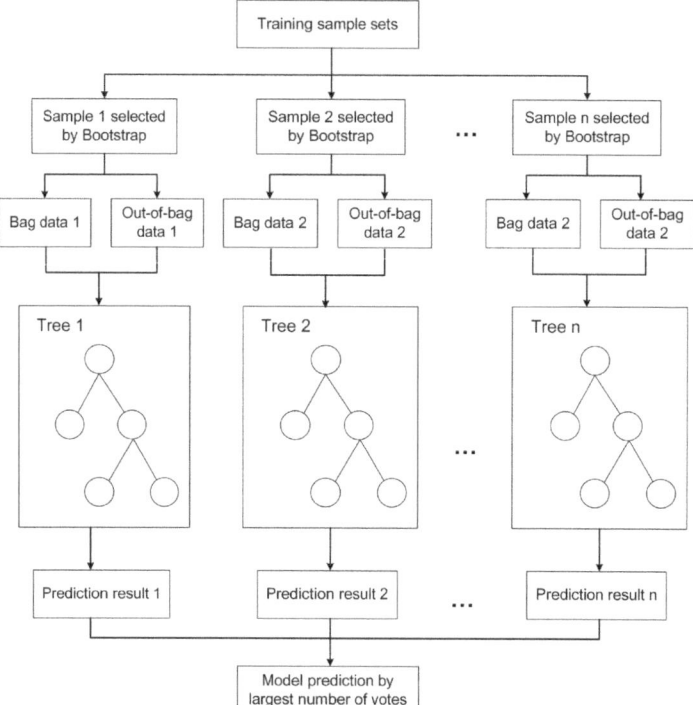

Figure 9. Expansion of Random Forest structure.

Each dataset is used to construct the largest decision tree possible without any additional processing. Then, the information gain is determined using the entropy or Gini index in the randomly selected feature factors. After computing each accuracy information, the candidate feature factor with the highest information gain (entropy or Gini) among them is divided. These stages are iteratively repeated until the entropy or Gini becomes smaller than the predetermined value, resulting in the development of a random forest algorithm with n decision trees. The training data for feature identification is then classified using the established random forest model, and the decision trees in the forest vote to determine the best classification prediction.

The random forest approach can be utilized to order the relevance of variables in a classification or regression task in a natural way. During training, the error is tracked and averaged over the forest. The contribution (Gini) can be computed using the Gini index. After training, the jth feature values are permuted among the training data, and the error is computed once again on this perturbed dataset to determine the jth feature's relevance. By averaging the difference between before and after the permutation over all trees, the importance score for the jth feature is calculated. The score is standardized using the standard deviation of these differences.

We take the Gini index as a measure to show the calculation of variable importance. Considering n categories, the weight of the k-th category can be computed from Equation (6). For feature j, the change value of feature j at node m (VI_{jm}) is obtained as:

$$\text{VI}_{jm} = \text{GI}_m - \text{GI}_l - \text{GI}_r \tag{8}$$

where GI_m is the Gini index before branch; GI_l and GI_r is the new Gini index after the node m. The normalized value of the contribution of feature j is the importance score of feature j, which is calculated as follows:

$$\text{VI}'_j = \frac{\text{VIM}_j}{\sum_{i=1}^{c} \text{VIM}_i} \tag{9}$$

The detailed derivation of variable importance can be found in the Ref. [42].

Actually, the random forest model is used to rank the importance of variables (geotechnical parameters) (Equation (9)) by a classification problem in the present paper meaning, that the most impactful geotechnical parameter can be selected for the quota of budget of shield tunneling in complex geological conditions.

3.2. Application of the Random Forest-Based Method in Analysis of Tunneling Consumption in Complex Geological Conditions

The considered economic factors (consumption of grease, grouting, labor and water and electricity) in shield tunneling project will be analyzed by the random forest-based model. The contributions of geological parameters (feature importance) are expected to be calculated, so that the proof for classification in complex geological conditions will be provided based on the random forest result.

In order to avoid repetition, only the calculation and analysis of grease will be detailed provided here for example. As mentioned in the previous section, the original collected data of consumption of grease is firstly pre-processed to replace the abnormal and empty values, and transformed into the form that random forest model can recognize. Besides, concerning the geotechnical parameters in the tunneling area, 17 features from the geological report are reduced to 6 for dimension reduction (see Figure 8). The grease consumption is set as the target of random forest model (Y^k), in which k denotes the index of input datasets corresponding to the label of shield segment. There are 1979 sets of input data for the concerned geotechnical parameters.

Next, considering the complex geological conditions, 6 geotechnical parameters are selected for the features to be implemented in the random forest model as natural density X_1^k, void ratio X_2^k, bearing capacity X_3^k, lateral pressure coefficient X_4^k, vertical permeability coefficient X_5^k and compressive strength X_6^k. Consequently, the variable importance of grease will be computed by implementing the random forest model with the prepared input datasets. Besides, the model parameters, such as number of classifiers, random state and minimum numbers of samples leaf and split, also need to be provided for training. Then the trained tree for each classifier and the prediction for unseen sample will be put out after training process, which is predicted by taking the majority vote for classification. Thus, the variable importance for consumption of grease can also be obtained from this procedure.

In practice, we can modify the structure of random forest model by taking different values of model parameters (criterion, number of classifiers, minimum number pf samples leaf and minimum number of samples split), so as to obtain the best prediction accuracy. Due to the complexity of geological conditions, this sensitivity comparison is necessary. Besides, the error between the predicted value and the target value need to be evaluated by an accuracy index function. In this study, the Gini (6) and Entropy index (7) are chosen to estimate the accuracy.

The above procedure will repeated for other tunneling consumption factors by replacing the target set Y, in order to obtain the variable importance for all the concerned geotechnical features. Generally considering the obtained results by random forest model, we will try to find out the most influential geotechnical parameters on all the consumption factors. For the sake of simplicity in engineering, normally one geotechnical parameter is adopted for classification in the quota of construction budget in complex geological conditions. Then, referred to the Geotechnical Engineering Survey Code (China), all the tunneling consumption will be calculated for the chosen parameter based on the classification rules. The unit shield tunneling cost can be consequently computed by multiplied by the corresponding unit price. By comparison with the existing cost quota, the accuracy of obtained results by the proposed random forest-based procedure will be accessed, and the influence of geotechnical parameters on the shield tunneling cost will also be discussed in the following section. The full flowchart of intelligent analysis on shield tunneling cost in complex geological conditions is illustrated in Figure 10.

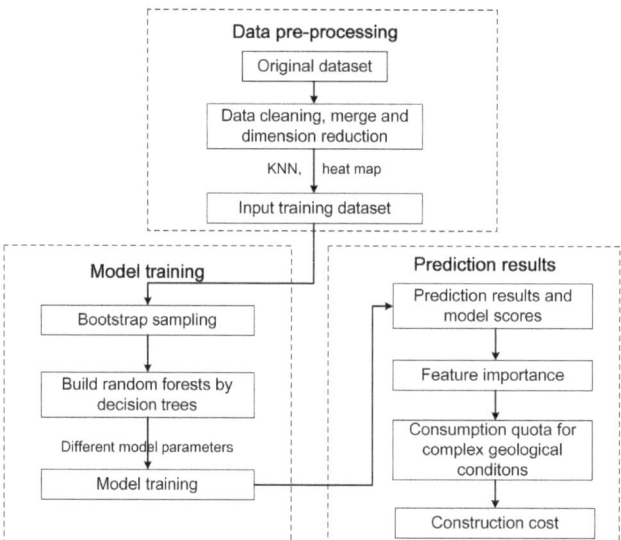

Figure 10. Flowchart of analysis on main consumption factors of shield tunneling in complex geological conditions by random forest algorithm.

4. Predictions of Construction Cost of Shield Tunneling in Complex Geological Conditions

In this section, the constructed Random Forest procedure will be applied to predict the construction cost of shield tunneling in complex geological conditions, in which the dataset for training the random forest model is collected from the ZRT project. In Section 4.1, the feature importance of geotechnical parameters are firstly calculated by the proposed model for each of the considered consumption factors. Then, the unit cost for shield tunneling is predicted by multiplying the price, and compared with the standard cost defined by the official quota to access the obtained result in Section 4.2. In order to validate the accuracy, no additional parameter is introduced for model training.

4.1. Feature Importance of Geotechnical Parameters for Consumption Factors

The training dataset for random forest method is crucial to its prediction accuracy. Consequently, the pre-processing described in the previous section is necessary for the dataset before analysis. 6 parameters of different geological layers are taken into account in variable importance analysis for main consumption factors (greases, grouting, labor, electricity and water) in this subsection.

The strategy of the data preparation are arranged as follows. The reduced input dataset contains 6 geotechnical parameters: natural density, void ratio, bearing capacity, lateral pressure coefficient, vertical permeability coefficient and compressive strength. The objective parameter is set as the concerned factors, and they will be analyzed one by one in the established random forest model. Arranged in the order of the shield segment index, 1979 sets containing above 6 parameters in different geological conditions are derived as the dataset of the model. Among them, 1485 (75%) sets are used as the training set of random forest model, and 494 (25%) sets will be predicted by the trained model (test set) and compared to the true values, aiming at validating the prediction accuracy.

The direct use of original data may result in accuracy issues caused by the dominance of large dimension values, as the input and output data of the model have different units and can fluctuate substantially in value. As the model training process uses gradient descent optimization, the difference in dimensions can slow down the rate at which model parameters are updated in each iteration. To prevent these issues, we normalize the input and output data during the preprocessing step and scale them linearly to the interval of [0, 1] using Equation (10). This normalization and scaling procedure ensures that the model is not affected by differences in data dimensions.

$$x^* = \frac{x - x_{\min}}{x_{\max} - x_{\min}} \tag{10}$$

where x denotes the original input and output data values, x_{min} and x_{max} are the minimum and maximum values, and x^* is the objective normalized value that can be employed in the proposed model.

The suggested random forest model has been trained using the aforementioned stages, taking various model parameters into consideration (criterion, number of estimators, minimum samples leaf and split). The ideal answer can be found by comparing the forecast accuracy with various structures. Different numbers of estimators (50, 100, 400, 700, 1000) with 1, 5, 10, 15, 20 minimum samples leaves and 2, 4, 10, 12, 16 minimum samples splits have been attempted.

Inspired by Santos et al. [47], we have plotted the six geological parameters and the quantity of material consumption in the same order of shield segment in Figures 11 and 12. To avoid repetition, we will only discuss tail grease (red curve in Figure 11) and grouting (purple curve in Figure 12). The values of the geological parameters have been normalized using Equation (10). It is observed that the different geological conditions in the excavation area can be reflected by the variation of geological parameters, and there is a correlation with material consumption. However, the most important geological feature and exact relation cannot be directly seen and need to be analyzed using the constructed random forest model.

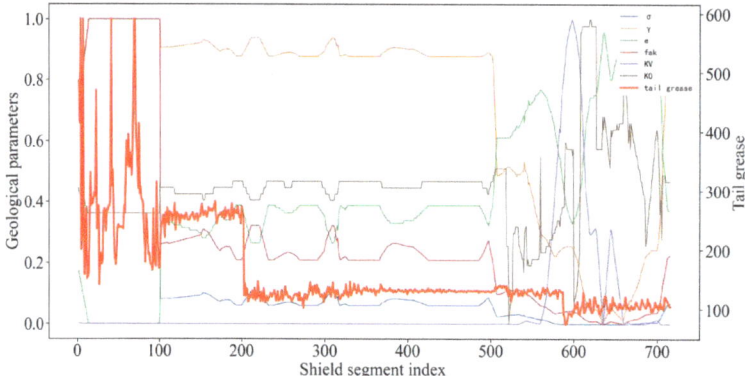

Figure 11. Collected geological parameters and tail grease in the order of shield segment.

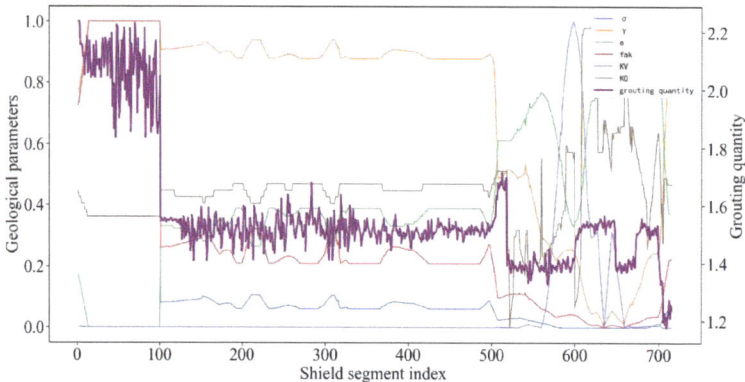

Figure 12. Collected geological parameters and grouting in the order of shield segment.

For the sake of clarity, the final value of the best score at the end of the training process and calculation efficiency of different random forest structures are illustrated in Figure 13 (the criterion Gini is always chosen by the program instead of Entropy). It can be concluded in Figure 13a that except for 400 and 700, the final value of the best score does not have remarkable changes with the variation of the number of estimators, where it takes the maximum value with 50. Besides, as shown in Figure 13b,c, the values of accuracy levels are all acceptable for different numbers of the minimum samples leaf and samples split. Consequently, considering the best performance, the random forest model with 50 estimators with one minimum samples leaves and two samples splits was adopted for the training and prediction steps. The final accuracy level (best score) of the test data is 0.9403.

With the above set of model parameters, the importance of each geotechnical feature is firstly calculated in the random forest model for the consumption factor grease (tail grease, EP2 grease and seal grease). The obtained results are shown in Figure 14, with the vertical axis being the geotechnical features and the horizontal axis being the magnitude of corresponding importance. It can be seen from the three subfigures that the compressive strength (σ) of material has the most important impact on the prediction of all the three types of greases. More precisely, the strength parameter exhibits obviously the greatest importance than other geotechnical parameters for consumption of tail grease (first subfigure of Figure 14), where the correlation is more than 48%. While for seal grease (third subfigures), the most significant geotechnical parameter is also the strength, the difference with the second parameter is not that much greater than that in the first one (the following important feature is a void ratio). Notice for the EP2 grease, for the strength in the second impactful geotechnical feature, the difference with the first one (fak) is not great. Consequently, the strength can be concluded as the most impactful geotechnical parameter on the consumption of greases in general. The accuracy levels for Figure 14 are 0.9413, 0.9357 and 0.9608, respectively.

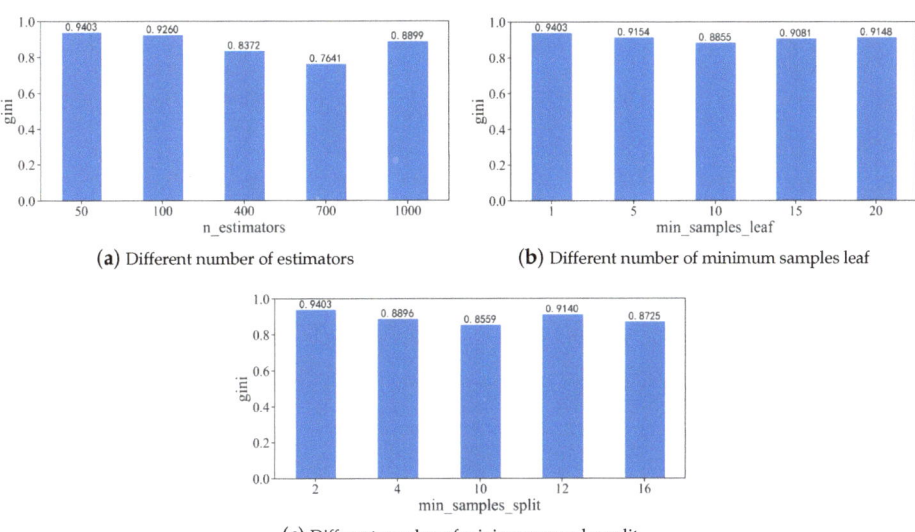

Figure 13. Comparison of the best score with different random forest structures.

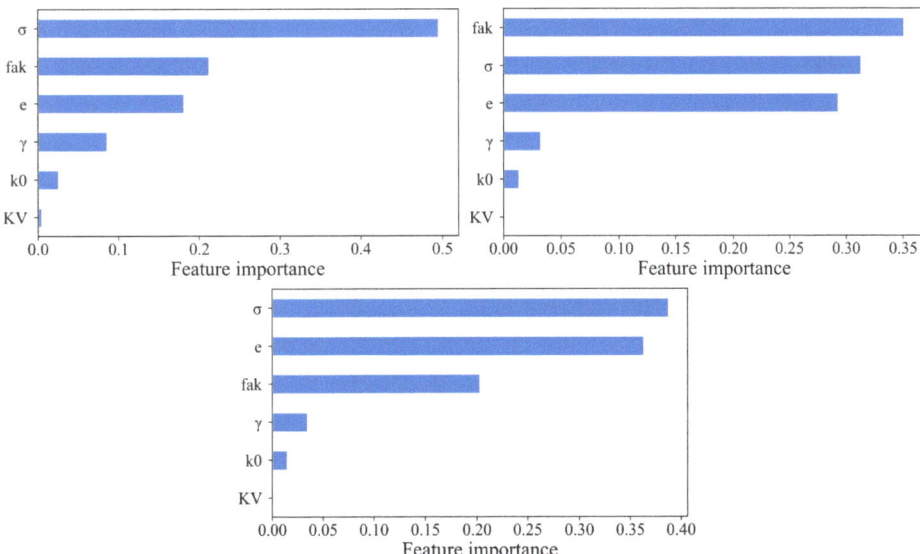

Figure 14. Variable importance for tail grease, EP2 grease and seal grease by random forest model in shield tunneling.

Figures 15–18 display the geotechnical feature importance for the consumption of grouting, labor and electricity and water in shield tunneling, respectively. Similar to the variable importance analysis of grease, the most impactful geotechnical parameter for the consumption of grouting and labor is also the strength of material, obviously (see Figures 16 and 18). The accuracy levels are 0.893, 0.7333, 0.9317 and 0.9252, respectively.

On the contrary, concerning the consumption of grouting, the most important geotechnical parameter is obtained as the void ratio (e) of the material, instead of the strength (Figure 15), which is in second place. The corresponding importance is 0.27. It is reasonable that the grouting quantity is related to the void ratio of the material from the point of view of geomechanics, because large porosity will lead to more backfill grouting in shield tunneling. As a result, the strength of soil or rock is not the most important feature for all the considered consumption factors. In order to find a single geotechnical parameter for the classification of the quota of budget in complex geological conditions, more computation of the total cost is needed to verify the selected feature, verifying if it can be used as the classification index in general. This will be provided in the next subsection.

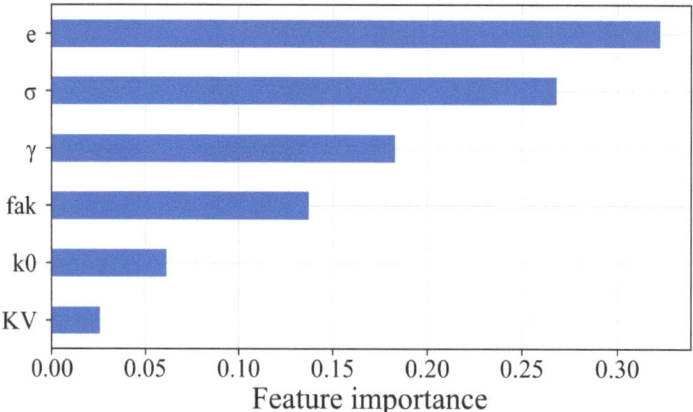

Figure 15. Variable importance for grouting quantity by random forest model in shield tunneling.

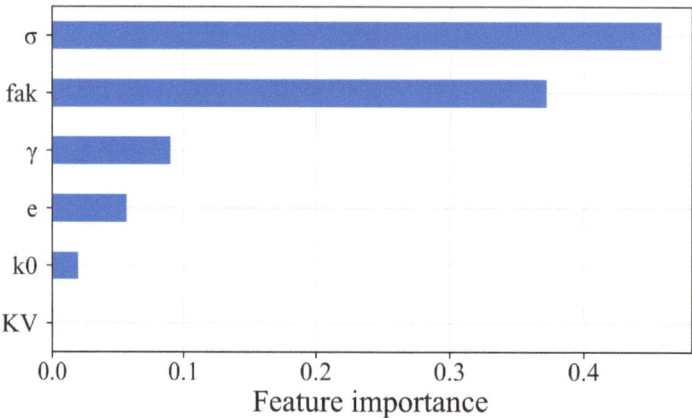

Figure 16. Variable importance for labor by random forest model in shield tunneling.

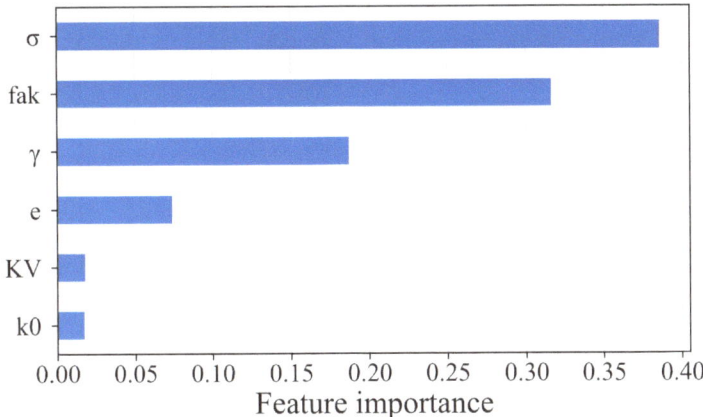

Figure 17. Variable importance for water consumption by random forest model in shield tunneling.

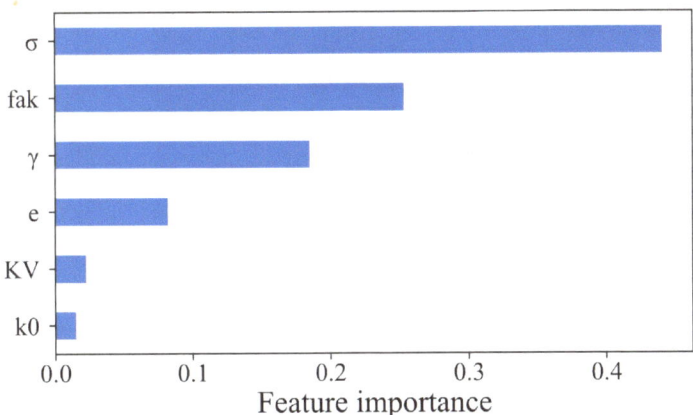

Figure 18. Variable importance for electricity consumption by random forest model in shield tunneling.

In addition, for the purposes of evaluation of the prediction by random forest model, the confusion matrix for each target consumption factor was also carried out. The confusion matrix displays predictions that are both correct and incorrect, and the results are evaluated in light of the actual values. The confusion matrix can show how the random forest classification model gets confused while making predictions. The four values in the matrix are True Positive (TP), False Positive (FP), False Negative (FN), and True Negative (TN), respectively. Thus, the accuracy levels for each target can be calculated as:

$$AC = \frac{TP + TN}{TP + FP + FN + TN}. \tag{11}$$

In Figure 19, the number of correct predictions and the number of incorrect predictions for tail grease are displayed in two subfigures (left: training set; right: test set), respectively. Consequently, the accuracy levels for calculating the variable importance can also be obtained by Equation (11). It is seen that the obtained results by the proposed model are reliable. In order to avoid repetition, the confusion matrix for other factors is not illustrated here.

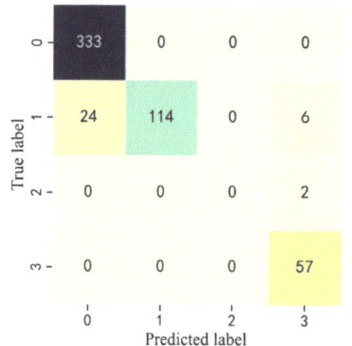 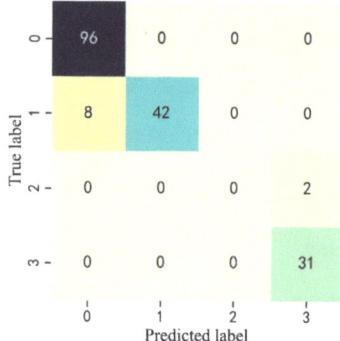

Figure 19. Confusion matrix for the consumption of tail grease (**left**: training set; **right**: test set).

4.2. Quota of Budget for Shield Tunneling in Complex Geological Conditions Based on the Random Forest Results

In this part, we aim at establishing a quota budget for shield tunneling in complex geological conditions based on the random forest results obtained in the previous subsection. From the above computation, the compressive strength (σ) is the most important feature for the consumption of grease, labor and electricity and water, while it is the second influencing geotechnical parameter for grouting (the most impactful parameter is the void ratio). For the sake of simplicity in engineering, it is supposed to consider only one geotechnical parameter to produce the classification in the quota of budgets in complex conditions. As a result, we assume that all the considered economic factors can be classified by the compressive strength index. We will also verify the prediction accuracy by comparing the total cost computed by the constructed model with that defined by the available quota.

Inspired by the classification standard for the engineering rock mass and code for geotechnical engineering investigation of China, let us introduce the following classification based on the compressive strength of geomaterials, as shown in Table 3. Consequently, we propose a classification with three categories (hard rock, soft rock and soil) by identifying the compressive strength, and continue the analysis.

Table 3. Classification of engineering geomaterials by compressive strength.

Type	Compressive Strength (MPa)
Soil	≤ 1
Soft rock	≤ 30
Hard rock	≥ 30

The collected data of the concerned consumption in shield tunneling have been reclassified by the compressive strength as in Table 3, so all the consumption data for grease, grouting, labor and electricity and water are recounted in the above three categories. The obtained average values for each category with respect to tunneling consumption are displayed in Table 4. The standard value defined by the available official quota is also provided in the same table for comparison (per meter). In general, the considered consumption quantities exhibit an obvious positive correlation with the compressive strength of geomaterial. It can be seen that the consumption per meter in shield tunneling is increasing from soil to hard rock, also for the grouting quantity.

Table 4. Comparison of main consumption and cost in different geological conditions with the standard values.

Factor	Quota	Soil		Soft Rock		Hard Rock	
Tail grease		70.50		84.99		145.88	
EP2 grease	81.90	14.18	118%	14.16	136%	70.79	399%
Seal grease		12.72		12.58		110.46	
Grouting	1.3–1.8	1.49		1.60		2.12	
Labor	51.73	51.34	99%	61.90	120%	106.24	205%
Water	78.93	176.74	223%	227.92	289%	334.65	424%
Electricity	10,800	7449.25	69%	9565	89%	25,885	239%
Total cost	72,153	68,039	94%	72,996	101%	99,719	138%

Only the concerned consumption (part of the main materials and labor) have been listed in this Table, other materials and machine-teams which remain the same have not been listed, but included in the total cost.

To elaborate, for soft rock and soil, the differences of main consumption are not as great as that between soft rock and hard rock. Consequently, the construction cost of shield tunneling is much more expensive, which is consistent with the actual situation. This proves the rationality of the classification for the quota from the side. Comparing with the standard values, the obtained results in soil are slightly smaller, while those in soft rock are close to the standard quantities. Concerning the consumption of hard rock, all the tunneling consumption is obviously greater than the standard value, even greater than two times. Consequently, for the tunneling project in complex geological conditions, the total budget cannot be calculated accurately by the present standard quota. It must be pointed out that only the concerned varying consumption has been listed in Table 4, other materials and machine-teams which remain the same have been not listed, but included in the total cost.

The total cost of the tunneling project per meter is provided in Figure 20. The cost for each factor can be calculated by the use of the values in Table 4, and the total cost can be obtained by accumulating the components. It is seen that the total cost in tunneling also has an evident positive correlation with the compressive strength, increasing from soil to hard rock. Although the most impactful geotechnical feature for grouting is not the strength (because the most impactful geotechnical parameter is a void ratio), the strength can still be used for defining the new quota of budgets in complex geological conditions. The total cost for soft rock is close to the original budget of the shield tunneling project, while that for soil is 6% lower than the standard cost. What is more, the total cost for hard rock is 38% higher than the standard cost, which cannot be ignored in complex conditions. This is the most important remark of this study, that the compressive strength can be chosen as the classification index, and the proposed categories in Table 3 are an effective reference scheme.

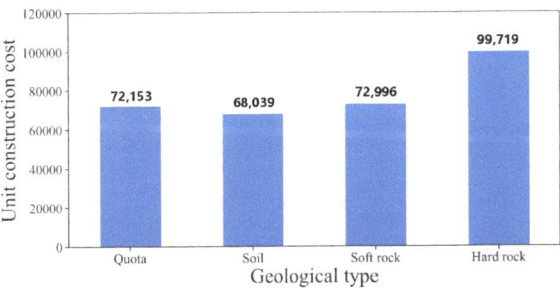

Figure 20. Comparison of unit cost of standard quota and by random forest algorithm for different geological conditions (Currency: CNY).

It must be pointed out by recent research that the random forest model can have limited extrapolation ability, and it may not perform well when applied to data that fall outside the range of the training set [48,49]. However, the main objective of our study was to determine the most influential geological parameter for material consumption in shield tunneling. In this context, the random forest algorithm is suitable for determining feature importance. Besides, increasing the size of datasets can help random forest models capture more patterns in the data, which we have done in our study by collecting geological parameters from soft soil to hard rock. Additionally, we have carefully selected the hyperparameters of the random forest model to optimize its performance and improve its ability, as explained in the previous section. These efforts have helped us to mitigate the limitation of extrapolation in the random forest model to a certain extent. Moreover, due to the limitation of data sources, the constructed model was trained with the data collected from a single project, which may lead to inaccuracy if applied to other projects with varying geometric parameters. This needs to be improved in further research by collecting more data from different projects.

On the other hand, according to recent studies on Bayesian neural networks [50,51], the strong spatial variability of soil properties can affect the accuracy of deterministic data-driven models. Thus, deterministic data-driven models may incur large errors and its prediction results cannot be evaluated. Advanced developments need to be taken into account in incorporating uncertainty to enhance the robustness of the proposed model, such as exploring the possibility of incorporating probabilistic models or stochastic techniques to account for the inherent variability and uncertainty of soil properties. This could potentially improve the reliability and accuracy of our model in predicting the material consumption in shield tunneling under various geological conditions.

5. Conclusions

In this study, we have proposed a random forest-based machine learning procedure to analyze the construction cost of shield tunneling in complex geological conditions. We identified the unit consumption of grease, grouting, labor, and water and electricity as the main factors affecting construction cost, based on engineering practice and expert opinions. To improve the accuracy of the model, we replenished empty and abnormal values in the input datasets and reduced its dimensionality from 17 to 6 using KNN and correlation analysis.

The proposed machine learning model was applied to the ZRT shield tunneling project and found that the compressive strength of geomaterial was the most influential geotechnical parameter for grease, labor, water, and electricity consumption. The consumption of grouting was mostly impacted by the void ratio, with compressive strength in second place. Based on these findings, we calculated and classified the unit consumption and cost of the ZRT tunneling project for three geological categories: soil, soft rock, and hard rock. Comparison with the standard value given by the official quota revealed that the unit cost of shield tunneling in soil was slightly lower (6%) than the standard cost, while that in soft rock was very close to the standard value. However, the cost in hard rock regions was significantly greater (38%) and cannot be ignored in budgeting. Thus, we recommend using the compressive strength as the classification index for shield tunneling in complex geological conditions.

In the outlook, collecting more data from different projects with varying tunnel diameters is an essential task in the future to improve the generalizability of the proposed model. Another interesting topic is to take into account advanced developments in incorporating uncertainty to enhance the robustness of the proposed model.

Author Contributions: Conceptualization, P.D.; Methodology, X.Y.; Software, C.Z.; Investigation, Y.L.; Data curation, P.D. and D.J.; Writing—original draft, X.Y.; Writing—review & editing, D.J., Y.L. and J.Z.; Supervision, J.Z.; Project administration, X.Y. All authors have read and agreed to the published version of the manuscript.

Funding: This study is supported by the project "Study on influencing economic factors in large diameter shield tunneling under complex geological conditions".

Data Availability Statement: The experimental data used to support the findings of this study are available from the corresponding author upon request.

Conflicts of Interest: The authors declare that they do not have any financial or nonfinancial conflict of interests.

References

1. Demirkesen, S.; Ozorhon, B. Impact of integration management on construction project management performance. *Int. J. Proj. Manag.* **2017**, *35*, 1639–1654. [CrossRef]
2. Kim, S.; Chang, S.; Castro-Lacouture, D. Dynamic modeling for analyzing impacts of skilled labor shortage on construction project management. *J. Manag. Eng.* **2020**, *36*, 04019035. [CrossRef]
3. Kim, Y.; Bruland, A. A study on the establishment of Tunnel Contour Quality Index considering construction cost. *Tunn. Undergr. Space Technol.* **2015**, *50*, 218–225. [CrossRef]
4. Huang, Z.; Zhang, D.; Pitilakis, K.; Tsinidis, G.; Huang, H.; Zhang, D.; Argyroudis, S. Resilience assessment of tunnels: Framework and application for tunnels in alluvial deposits exposed to seismic hazard. *Soil Dyn. Earthq. Eng.* **2022**, *162*, 107456. [CrossRef]
5. Mesároš, P.; Mandičák, T. Exploitation and benefits of BIM in construction project management. *IOP Conf. Ser. Mater. Sci. Eng.* **2017**, *245*, 062056. [CrossRef]
6. Chmelina, K.; Rabensteiner, K.; Krusche, G. A tunnel information system for the management and utilization of geo-engineering data in urban tunnel projects. *Geotech. Geol. Eng.* **2013**, *31*, 845–859. [CrossRef]
7. Li, J.; Jing, L.; Zheng, X.; Li, P.; Yang, C. Application and outlook of information and intelligence technology for safe and efficient TBM construction. *Tunn. Undergr. Space Technol.* **2019**, *93*, 103097. [CrossRef]
8. Vargas, J.P.; Koppe, J.C.; Pérez, S.; Hurtado, J.P. Planning tunnel construction using Markov chain Monte Carlo (MCMC). *Math. Probl. Eng.* **2015**, 797953. [CrossRef]
9. Park, J.; Lee, K.H.; Park, J.; Choi, H.; Lee, I.M. Predicting anomalous zone ahead of tunnel face utilizing electrical resistivity: I. Algorithm and measuring system development. *Tunn. Undergr. Space Technol.* **2016**, *60*, 141–150. [CrossRef]
10. Park, J.; Lee, K.H.; Kim, B.K.; Choi, H.; Lee, I.M. Predicting anomalous zone ahead of tunnel face utilizing electrical resistivity: II. Field tests. *Tunn. Undergr. Space Technol.* **2017**, *68*, 1–10. [CrossRef]
11. Leu, S.S.; Joko, T.; Sutanto, A. Applied real-time Bayesian analysis in forecasting tunnel geological conditions. In Proceedings of the 2010 IEEE International Conference on Industrial Engineering and Engineering Management, Macao, China, 7–10 December 2010; pp. 1505–1508.
12. Mahmoodzadeh, A.; Zare, S. Probabilistic prediction of expected ground condition and construction time and costs in road tunnels. *J. Rock Mech. Geotech. Eng.* **2016**, *8*, 734–745. [CrossRef]
13. Lee, J.; Sagong, M.; Cho, G.C.; Choo, S. Experimental estimation of the fallout size and reinforcement design of a tunnel under excavation. *Tunn. Undergr. Space Technol.* **2010**, *25*, 518–525. [CrossRef]
14. Guan, Z.; Deng, T.; Jiang, Y.; Zhao, C.; Huang, H. Probabilistic estimation of ground condition and construction cost for mountain tunnels. *Tunn. Undergr. Space Technol.* **2014**, *42*, 175–183. [CrossRef]
15. Zhang, Q.; Liu, Z.; Tan, J. Prediction of geological conditions for a tunnel boring machine using big operational data. *Autom. Constr.* **2019**, *100*, 73–83. [CrossRef]
16. Carrière, S.D.; Chalikakis, K.; Sénéchal, G.; Danquigny, C.; Emblanch, C. Combining electrical resistivity tomography and ground penetrating radar to study geological structuring of karst unsaturated zone. *J. Appl. Geophys.* **2013**, *94*, 31–41. [CrossRef]
17. Daraei, A.; H Sherwani, A.F.; Faraj, R.H.; Kalhor, Q.; Zare, S.; Mahmoodzadeh, A. Optimization of the outlet portal of Heybat Sultan twin tunnels based on the value engineering methodology. *SN Appl. Sci.* **2019**, *1*, 1–10. [CrossRef]
18. Mahmoodzadeh, A.; Mohammadi, M.; Abdulhamid, S.N.; Nejati, H.R.; Noori, K.M.G.; Ibrahim, H.H.; Ali, H.F.H. Predicting construction time and cost of tunnels using Markov chain model considering opinions of experts. *Tunn. Undergr. Space Technol.* **2021**, *116*, 104109. [CrossRef]
19. Shi, L.; Zhang, J.; Zhu, Q.; Sun, H. Prediction of mechanical behavior of rocks with strong strain-softening effects by a deep-learning approach. *Comput. Geotech.* **2022**, *152*, 105040. [CrossRef]
20. Mahmoodzadeh, A.; Mohammadi, M.; Daraei, A.; Farid Hama Ali, H.; Ismail Abdullah, A.; Kameran Al-Salihi, N. Forecasting tunnel geology, construction time and costs using machine learning methods. *Neural Comput. Appl.* **2021**, *33*, 321–348. [CrossRef]
21. Ye, D. An Algorithm for Construction Project Cost Forecast Based on Particle Swarm Optimization-Guided BP Neural Network. *Sci. Program.* **2021**, *2021*, 4309495. [CrossRef]
22. Lin, T.; Yi, T.; Zhang, C.; Liu, J. Intelligent prediction of the construction cost of substation projects using support vector machine optimized by particle swarm optimization. *Math. Probl. Eng.* **2019**, 7631362. [CrossRef]
23. Liu, J.B.; Ren, H.; Li, Z.M. Model on dynamic control of project costs based on GM (1, 1) for construction enterprises. In *Fuzzy Information and Engineering Volume 2*; Springer: Berlin/Heidelberg, Germany, 2009; pp. 1611–1620.
24. Min, S.; Einstein, H.; Lee, J.; Kim, T. Application of decision aids for tunneling (DAT) to a drill & blast tunnel. *KSCE J. Civ. Eng.* **2003**, *7*, 619–628.

25. Maruvanchery, V.; Zhe, S.; Robert, T.L.K. Early construction cost and time risk assessment and evaluation of large-scale underground cavern construction projects in Singapore. *Undergr. Space* **2020**, *5*, 53–70. [CrossRef]
26. Shi, S.S.; Li, S.C.; Li, L.P.; Zhou, Z.Q.; Wang, J. Advance optimized classification and application of surrounding rock based on fuzzy analytic hierarchy process and Tunnel Seismic Prediction. *Autom. Constr.* **2014**, *37*, 217–222. [CrossRef]
27. Belgiu, M.; Drăguţ, L. Random forest in remote sensing: A review of applications and future directions. *ISPRS J. Photogramm. Remote Sens.* **2016**, *114*, 24–31. [CrossRef]
28. Feng, X.; Jimenez, R. Predicting tunnel squeezing with incomplete data using Bayesian networks. *Eng. Geol.* **2015**, *195*, 214–224. [CrossRef]
29. Zhang, P.; Yin, Z.Y.; Jin, Y.F. Machine learning-based modelling of soil properties for geotechnical design: Review, tool development and comparison. *Arch. Comput. Methods Eng.* **2022**, *29*, 1229–1245. [CrossRef]
30. Lu, L.; Meng, X.; Mao, Z.; Karniadakis, G.E. DeepXDE: A deep learning library for solving differential equations. *SIAM Rev.* **2021**, *63*, 208–228. [CrossRef]
31. Ho, T.K. Random decision forests. In Proceedings of the 3rd International Conference on Document Analysis and Recognition, Montreal, QC, Canada, 14–16 August 1995; Volume 1, pp. 278–282.
32. Ho, T.K. The random subspace method for constructing decision forests. *IEEE Trans. Pattern Anal. Mach. Intell.* **1998**, *20*, 832–844.
33. Breiman, L. Random forests. *Mach. Learn.* **2001**, *45*, 5–32. [CrossRef]
34. Strobl, C.; Boulesteix, A.L.; Augustin, T. Unbiased split selection for classification trees based on the Gini index. *Comput. Stat. Data Anal.* **2007**, *52*, 483–501. [CrossRef]
35. Palomino, A.F.; Espino, P.S.; Reyes, C.B.; Rojas, J.A.J.; y Silva, F.R. Estimation of moisture in live fuels in the mediterranean: Linear regressions and random forests. *J. Environ. Manag.* **2022**, *322*, 116069. [CrossRef] [PubMed]
36. Smith, P.F.; Ganesh, S.; Liu, P. A comparison of random forest regression and multiple linear regression for prediction in neuroscience. *J. Neurosci. Methods* **2013**, *220*, 85–91. [CrossRef] [PubMed]
37. Piryonesi, S.M. The Application of Data Analytics to Asset Management: Deterioration and Climate Change Adaptation in Ontario Roads. Ph.D. Thesis, University of Toronto, Toronto, ON, Canada, 2019.
38. Rajković, D.; Jeromela, A.M.; Pezo, L.; Lončar, B.; Grahovac, N.; Špika, A.K. Artificial neural network and random forest regression models for modelling fatty acid and tocopherol content in oil of winter rapeseed. *J. Food Compos. Anal.* **2023**, *115*, 105020. [CrossRef]
39. Kang, K.; Ryu, H. Predicting types of occupational accidents at construction sites in Korea using random forest model. *Saf. Sci.* **2019**, *120*, 226–236. [CrossRef]
40. Tixier, A.J.P.; Hallowell, M.R.; Rajagopalan, B.; Bowman, D. Application of machine learning to construction injury prediction. *Autom. Constr.* **2016**, *69*, 102–114. [CrossRef]
41. Wang, L.; Mao, Z.; Xuan, H.; Ma, T.; Hu, C.; Chen, J.; You, X. Status diagnosis and feature tracing of the natural gas pipeline weld based on improved random forest model. *Int. J. Press. Vessel. Pip.* **2022**, *200*, 104821. [CrossRef]
42. Gu, Y.; Liu, D.; Arvin, R.; Khattak, A.J.; Han, L.D. Predicting intersection crash frequency using connected vehicle data: A framework for geographical random forest. *Accid. Anal. Prev.* **2023**, *179*, 106880. [CrossRef]
43. Zermane, A.; Tohir, M.Z.M.; Zermane, H.; Baharudin, M.R.; Yusoff, H.M. Predicting fatal fall from heights accidents using random forest classification machine learning model. *Saf. Sci.* **2023**, *159*, 106023. [CrossRef]
44. Mishra, N.B.; Crews, K.A. Mapping vegetation morphology types in a dry savanna ecosystem: Integrating hierarchical object-based image analysis with Random Forest. *Int. J. Remote Sens.* **2014**, *35*, 1175–1198. [CrossRef]
45. Guan, H.; Li, J.; Chapman, M.; Deng, F.; Ji, Z.; Yang, X. Integration of orthoimagery and lidar data for object-based urban thematic mapping using random forests. *Int. J. Remote Sens.* **2013**, *34*, 5166–5186. [CrossRef]
46. Peterson, L.E. K-nearest neighbor. *Scholarpedia* **2009**, *4*, 1883. [CrossRef]
47. Santos, O.J., Jr.; Celestino, T.B. Artificial neural networks analysis of Sao Paulo subway tunnel settlement data. *Tunn. Undergr. Space Technol.* **2008**, *23*, 481–491. [CrossRef]
48. Takoutsing, B.; Heuvelink, G.B. Comparing the prediction performance, uncertainty quantification and extrapolation potential of regression kriging and random forest while accounting for soil measurement errors. *Geoderma* **2022**, *428*, 116192. [CrossRef]
49. Carrasco, L.; Toquenaga, Y.; Mashiko, M. Extrapolation of random forest models shows scale adaptation in egret colony site selection against landscape complexity. *Ecol. Complex.* **2015**, *24*, 29–36. [CrossRef]
50. Yang, L.; Meng, X.; Karniadakis, G.E. B-PINNs: Bayesian physics-informed neural networks for forward and inverse PDE problems with noisy data. *J. Comput. Phys.* **2021**, *425*, 109913. [CrossRef]
51. Zhang, P.; Yin, Z.Y.; Jin, Y.F. Bayesian neural network-based uncertainty modelling: Application to soil compressibility and undrained shear strength prediction. *Can. Geotech. J.* **2022**, *59*, 546–557. [CrossRef]

Disclaimer/Publisher's Note: The statements, opinions and data contained in all publications are solely those of the individual author(s) and contributor(s) and not of MDPI and/or the editor(s). MDPI and/or the editor(s) disclaim responsibility for any injury to people or property resulting from any ideas, methods, instructions or products referred to in the content.

Article

Analytical Predictions on the Ground Responses Induced by Shallow Tunneling Adjacent to a Pile Group

Caixia Guo [1], Yingying Tao [1], Fanchao Kong [1,*], Leilei Shi [1,2], Dechun Lu [1] and Xiuli Du [1]

[1] Key Laboratory of Urban Security and Disaster Engineering of Ministry of Education, Beijing University of Technology, Beijing 100124, China
[2] Beijing Municipal Construction Group Co., Ltd., Beijing 100089, China
* Correspondence: kongfc@bjut.edu.cn

Abstract: Prevalent buildings are supported by pile foundations in urban areas, and the importance of nearby excavation prediction is indisputable due to various engineering accidents caused by the density of urban buildings and the complexity of the underground environment. Recently, a case of tunneling adjacent to a pile group has received a lot of attention from the research community and engineers. In this study, a mechanical model of a shallow tunnel adjacent to a pile group is established. The proposed stress-release function is taken as the stress boundary condition of the tunnel periphery. Considering the pile group, the elastic stresses are calculated by complex variable theory, combined with the Mindlin's solution. Then, the new analytical solutions to stress are obtained to predict the stratum responses induced by tunneling adjacent to the existing pile group loads inside the stratum in a gravity field. Ultimately, this study provides parameters to analyze their influence on ground stress and potential plastic zone, such as the stress release coefficient, pile group locations, and soil parameters. This research provides a theoretical basis for stratum stresses' prediction in shallow tunneling engineering fields when tunneling adjacent to a pile group, and it can be applied to the construction of resilient cities.

Keywords: adjacent crossing; complex variable theory; pile group; shallow tunnel; plastic zone

MSC: 74A10

1. Introduction

Owing to the continuous expansion of cities and decreases in available land, the demand for urban tunnels has sharply increased in recent years [1–5]. Unavoidably, tunnel construction is disturbed by the foundations of nearby existing structures, particularly in densely constructed areas located adjacent to tunnel construction sites. More and more buildings are supported by pile foundations. Under the coupling effect of pile foundation loadings and tunnel excavation, the soil around the tunnel and pile foundations may experience stress redistribution or yield prior to support installation, which can adversely affect and even destabilize the surrounding ground. To ensure the safety of tunneling operations and nearby existing structures, a new analytical solution is required, by means of which the ground responses around shallow tunnels adjacent to pre-existing pile group loads can be reasonably predicted.

Traditional methods, namely empirical methods, analytical methods, numerical methods and model test methods have made great accomplishments in the study of ground displacement and stress by tunneling. The empirical methods [6–10] are routinely used to investigate ground responses using the Peck theory, Celestino theory. Additionally, these methods are fitted intuitively from measured data and lack rigorous theory. With the development of computer technology, a more accurate prediction, considering complex excavation process and geological conditions such as the soil elastoplastic or elasto-viscoplastic property, can be obtained via numerical analysis [11–13]. Numerical simulation can consider various tunnel cross-section shapes, nonlinear effects of stratum mechanics, complex construction procedures, and the coupling interaction between surrounding rock and tunnel structures. It is a commonly used method for studying the response of strata and tunnel structures induced by tunneling. The model test methods [14] can more realistically reflect the ground deformation laws due to the reliability of soil parameters.

Compared with other three methods, the analytical methods based on a rigorous mathematical derivation can consider the quantitative effects of geomechanical and geometric parameters [15–17]. At present, there are four main theoretical analysis methods for predicting the ground stresses caused by tunneling, namely the Airy stress function method [18], the virtual image method [19,20], the bipolar coordinate method [21,22] and complex variable theory [23–25]. The stress function method can obtain the elastic solution of a deep circular tunnel, but it cannot obtain the analytical solution of a deep tunnel of other shapes, nor can it obtain the analytical solution of a shallow tunnel. The bipolar coordinate method can obtain the analytical solution of stress field, but cannot obtain the accurate displacement solution. The complex variable theory can solve the shortcomings of the above methods well, and has been widely used to solve the elastic solution of tunnel excavation in recent years.

Markedly, considering the existence of surface and gravity field, the problem of shallow tunnels is more complicated than that of deep tunnels, and the complex variable theory using the Laurent series and conformal mapping is appropriate for shallow tunnels. This method uses conformal mapping on the ring so that the depth of the tunnel only affects the thickness of the ring wall and does not affect the function analysis in the complex variable solution procedure. The characteristics of this solution are that the complex variable method can guarantee the continuity of the boundary in the theoretical analysis, and reasonable boundary conditions are a key factor to obtain the solution of shallow tunnels [26,27]. For instance, Lu et al. [28] provided the analytical solution of a shallow tunnel that had excavation stress on the tunnel periphery and was stress-free on the ground surface, considering the linear variations of the initial stresses with depth and lateral stress coefficients. Lu et al. [29] discussed the case of a shallow circular hydraulic tunnel filled with water in an elastic rock mass with gravity. Furthermore, Kong et al. [30] proposed a unified stress function as the stress boundary condition of a tunnel periphery to describe the vertical and horizontal stress distributions of an underwater shallow tunnel. Using complex variable theory and the integration of Flamant's solutions, Wang et al. [31] obtained an elastic analytical solution with surcharge loadings on ground surface. Yang et al. [32] solved the problem of a shallow tunnel with a nearby cavern; they used a complex variable method and the Schwarz alternating method to study the interaction between the tunnel and the cavern. However, these provided analytical solutions cannot determine the ground stress field under the influence of an adjacent pile group.

With regard to the analytical study of a combination of tunnel and pile foundations, Marshall et al. [33] used a spherical cavity expansion analysis method to evaluate the end-bearing capacity of the pile and estimate the effect that constructing a new tunnel will have on an existing pile. Cao et al. [6] investigated the mechanical mechanism of the effects of the isolation piles on the ground vertical displacements using a modified Loganathan–Poulos formula and the Melan solution of the vertical displacement in a general form. Xiang et al. [34] mainly studied the potential plastic zone caused by tunneling in the vicinity of single pile foundation; however, the gravity field was not considered. Generally, these solutions cannot clearly estimate the stratum stress field induced by shallow tunneling adjacent to vertical pile group loads.

For abovementioned studies, nevertheless, existing studies have generally focused on the ground responses of tunneling in greenfield; with caverns and with surcharge loadings on the ground surface, the case of existing pile group loads in the interior of the stratum has not been highlighted. Accordingly, to fill a gap in the area of theoretical analytic solutions, this study paves the way for predicting ground stresses induced by tunneling in non-greenfield.

This study reports a combinatory strategy, including Mindlin's solution and complex variable theory, to further improve the influence mechanism of shallow tunnel excavation under the influence of a pile group in a gravity field. In this paper, based on the plane strain condition and the elastic constitutive relation, the analytical solutions of stress induced by shallow tunneling adjacent to pile group loads are obtained using analytical methods; due to the limitations of the conformal mapping function, the current shallow buried semi-infinite domain mechanical model can only obtain analytical solutions for circular tunnels. Therefore, the proposed method may only be used to solve the analytical solutions of strata induced by circular tunnels. Notably, the proposed stress release function is introduced as the boundary condition into the complex variable solving process, which is detailed in Section 3.3.1. The remainder of the paper is organized as follows: Section 2 introduces the mechanical model and method framework of theoretical prediction; Section 3 presents the derivation process of new analytical solution and its feasibility; and Section 4 illustrates the application of the solution and analyzes the influence of the stress release coefficient, pile group parameters and soil parameters on the stratum stress field and potential plastic zone. Eventually, the authors believe that it will be useful to decide a reasonable location for tunnel construction in preliminary designs.

2. Mechanical Model and Method Framework

In urban tunnel engineering, it is common for shallow tunnels to pass through an adjacent superstructure. The smaller the depth of shallow tunnel, the more significant the impacts on adjacent buildings, such as building cracking, distortion, uneven settlement, and collapse [35–38]. This factor should be seriously emphasized. Furthermore, the loads of superstructures are transferred to the stratum through pile group foundations. If the loads are simplified as vertical loads in the ground, this case can be modelled as a tunnel being excavated after the application of vertical loads in the ground. Based on these assumptions, a mechanical model that demonstrates excavation of a shallow tunnel with existing pile group loads in the ground is proposed.

2.1. Establishment of Mechanical Model

Referring to the three-dimensional mechanical model shown in Figure 1, the plane $y = y_t$ vertical to the tunnel axis is considered. Notably, the pile group and shallow tunnel are in the same plane when $y_t = y_p$; the pile group is not in the same plane as the tunnel when $y_t \neq y_p$, which is a three-dimensional problem.

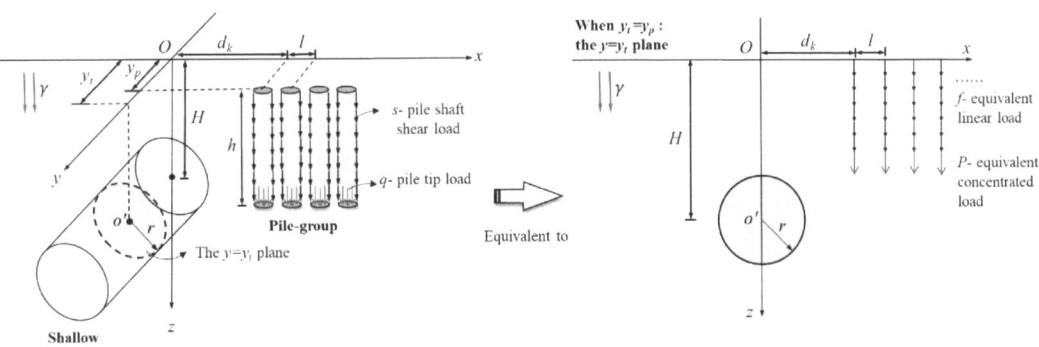

Figure 1. Mechanical analysis model of shallow tunnel adjacent to pile group.

In Figure 1, y_t, y_p are y coordinates of the tunnel section and pile group, respectively. The pile loads in the ground consist of two parts: the pile tip load q and the pile shaft shear load s. For the convenience of calculations, the pile loads are simplified to an equivalent concentrated load P and equivalent linear load f along the longitudinal axis. The horizontal coordinate of the first pile load d_k is adopted to represent the location of the pile group, and l is the pile spacing.

As shown in Figure 1, this is a semi-infinite domain model which considers the surface boundary to realize the stratum stress analysis of shallow tunnel with existing pile group loads. The shallow tunnel is affected by the surface boundary and the gravity is the main external load, so the load change of gradient should be considered. Assuming that the ground is a homogeneous, isotropic and ideal elastic-plastic material, the changes in stratum stress caused by pile group loads and tunneling can be considered a linear elastic response.

2.2. Method Framework

According to the mechanical model in Figure 1, the final ground stress solution can be divided into two parts: (1) the stress induced by pile group loads, (2) the stress induced by tunneling in greenfield (where there are no existing foundations in the ground). The former uses the Mindlin's solution [39] in the classical elastic theory, which gives the solution of the displacement and stress of the stratum caused by the vertical force acting on a point in the semi-infinite space. Complex variable theory is used as the latter's method to predict tunneling-induced stress. The prediction process of the stress solution and potential plastic zone of ground are yielded as follows:

(I) The elastic theory Mindlin's solution and its integral along the pile length, respectively, to equivalent concentrated load P and equivalent linear load f are used to calculate the ground stress solution.

(II) The analytical solution of the ground stress caused by shallow tunneling in the gravity field is obtained by complex variable theory using the stress boundary condition considering the stress release coefficient, and the ground stress is calculated by substituting the parameter values and coordinate values.

(III) The ground stress induced by tunneling and pile group loads is superimposed.

(IV) The Mohr–Coulomb criterion is substituted and the mathematical software Matlab is used to calculate the total ground stress and predict the shape and extent of the potential plastic zone.

The theoretical calculation steps are shown in Figure 2.

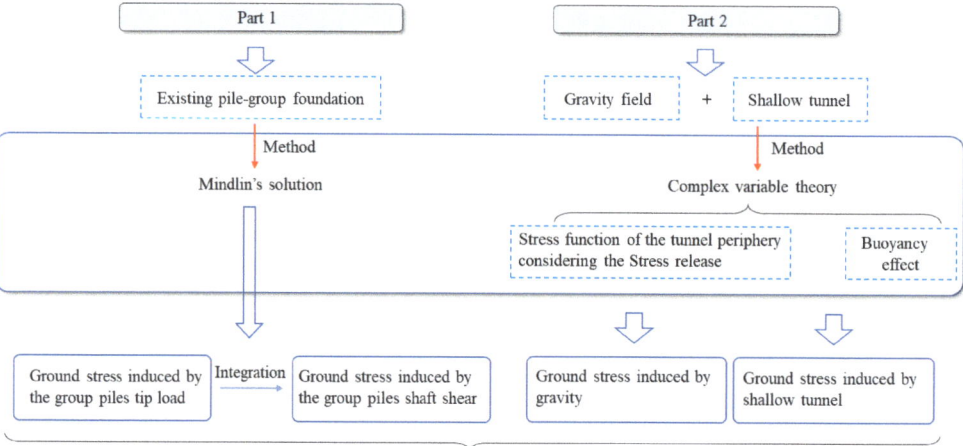

Figure 2. Flowchart of the calculation.

3. Analytical Solutions of Stress for Tunneling Adjacent to Pile Group

The elastic analytical stresses induced by a pile group for the vertical force acting at a point in the ground have been provided by Mindlin [39]. Thus, the solutions of stress for tunneling adjacent to a pile group proposed in this study use Mindlin's solution and its integral combined with a complex variable method. In order to reflect the factual situation, the gravity is applied in the vertical direction, and the arbitrary stress in the horizontal direction before the excavation. Besides, the buoyancy effect and the stress release are considered in the tunnel periphery after the excavation.

3.1. Stress Boundary Conditions

The general boundary conditions corresponding to the mechanical model in Figure 1 are shown in Figure 3. The boundary equations are given in Equation (1):

$$\begin{cases} \sigma_{z=0} = 0 \\ \sigma_{x \to \infty} = k_0 \gamma z + \sigma_{x1} \\ \sigma_{z \to \infty} = \gamma z + \sigma_{z1} \\ \sigma_s = p_x + i p_z \end{cases} \quad (1)$$

where γ is uniform volumetric weight. k_0 is the lateral stress coefficient and is equal to $v/(1-v)$. v is the Poisson's ratio. σ_{x1} and σ_{z1} are the ground stresses induced by the pile group, σ_s is the stress boundary condition of the tunnel periphery, and p_x, p_z are the stress boundary functions of tunnel paralleled to the x and z axes, respectively.

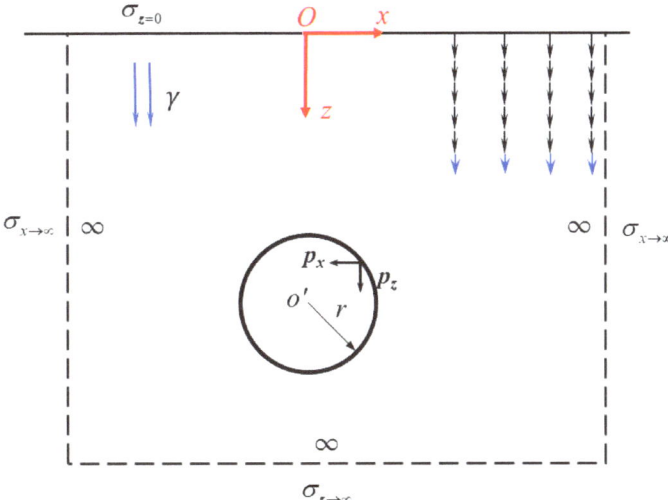

Figure 3. General boundary conditions of mechanical model.

The general boundary conditions can be broken into three parts, as shown in Figure 4, i.e., Part 1, Part 2a and Part 2b. Part 1 indicates that only pile group loads are applied in the ground, and there is no excavation of the tunnel, i.e., the tunnel section is in the initial stress state (Section 3.2). Part 2 is broken down into two parts: Part 2a in the unexcavated state of the tunnel and Part 2b in the excavated state of the tunnel (Section 3.3).

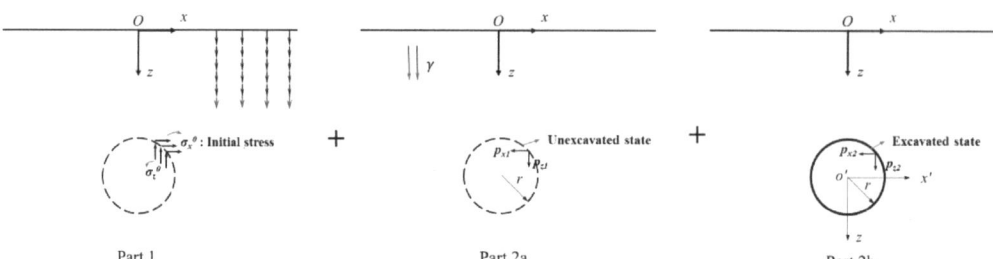

Figure 4. Disassembly of boundary conditions.

3.2. Analytical Solution of Pile Group Loads

The ground stresses due to simplified pile group loads in the x–z plane can be obtained using the Mindlin's solution, which consists of two sections: the equivalent concentrated load P and the equivalent linear load f.

3.2.1. Ground Stress Induced by Pile Group Tip Loads

The pile group tip loads can be simplified to equivalent concentrated load P at the pile tip. Then, by the principle of Mindlin's solution and summation, the stresses generated at any point (x, y, z) in the ground when multiple loads are applied in a three-dimensional semi-infinite elastomer are as follows:

$$\sigma_{x1}^p = \sum_{k=1}^{m} \frac{-P_k}{8\pi(1-v)} f_x(x,z;h)$$

$$= \sum_{k=1}^{m} \frac{-P_k}{8\pi(1-v)} \left\{ \begin{array}{l} \frac{(1-2v)(z-h)}{R_1^3} - \frac{3(x-d_k)^2(z-h)}{R_1^5} + \frac{(1-2v)[3(z-h)-4v(z+h)]}{R_2^3} \\ - \frac{3(3-4v)(x-d_k)^2(z-h)-6h(z+h)[(1-2v)z-2vh]}{R_2^5} - \frac{30hz(x-d_k)^2(z+h)}{R_2^7} \\ - \frac{4(1-v)(1-2v)}{R_2(R_2+z+h)} \left(1 - \frac{(x-d_k)^2}{R_2(R_2+z+h)} - \frac{(x-d_k)^2}{R_2^2}\right) \end{array} \right\} \quad (2)$$

$$\sigma_{z1}^p = \sum_{k=1}^{m} \frac{-P_k}{8\pi(1-v)} f_z(x,z;h)$$

$$= \sum_{k=1}^{m} \frac{-P_k}{8\pi(1-v)} \left\{ \begin{array}{l} -\frac{(1-2v)(z-h)}{R_1^3} - \frac{3(z-h)^3}{R_1^5} + \frac{(1-2v)(z-h)}{R_2^3} - \frac{3(3-4v)z(z+h)^2 - 3h(z+h)(5z-h)}{R_2^5} \\ - \frac{30hz(z+h)^3}{R_2^7} \end{array} \right\} \quad (3)$$

$$\sigma_{xz1}^p = \sum_{k=1}^{m} \frac{-P_k(x-d_k)}{8\pi(1-v)} f_{xz}(x,z;h)$$

$$= \sum_{k=1}^{m} \frac{-P_k(x-d_k)}{8\pi(1-v)} \left\{ -\frac{1-2v}{R_1^3} - \frac{3(z-h)^2}{R_1^5} + \frac{1-2v}{R_2^3} - \frac{3(3-4v)z(z+h) - 3h(3z+h)}{R_2^5} - \frac{30hz(z+h)^2}{R_2^7} \right\} \quad (4)$$

where m represents the number of piles, σ_{x1}^p, σ_{z1}^p and σ_{xz1}^p denote the horizontal stress, vertical stress and shear stress in the $y = y_t$ plane, respectively, induced by equivalent concentrated load P_k at the pile tip.

$$R_1 = \sqrt{(x-d_k)^2 + (y_t-y_p)^2 + (z-h)^2}, \quad R_2 = \sqrt{(x-d_k)^2 + (y_t-y_p)^2 + (z+h)^2}, \quad k = 1,2,3,4,\ldots$$

3.2.2. Ground Stress Induced by Pile Group Shaft Shear Loads

For the shaft shear loads simplified to equivalent linear load f along the longitudinal axis, the analytical solutions of the ground stress obtained by integrating Equations (5)–(7) are as follows:

$$\sigma_{x1}^f = \sum_{k=1}^{m} \int_0^h \frac{-f_k}{8\pi(1-v)} f_x(x,z;b) db \quad (5)$$

$$\sigma_{z1}^f = \sum_{k=1}^{m} \int_0^h \frac{-f_k}{8\pi(1-v)} f_z(x,z;b)db \tag{6}$$

$$\sigma_{xz1}^f = \sum_{k=1}^{m} \int_0^h \frac{-f_k(x-d_k)}{8\pi(1-v)} f_{xz}(x,z;b)db \tag{7}$$

where h is the pile length and b is the integration variable along the pile length, and σ_{x1}^f, σ_{z1}^f and σ_{xz1}^f denote the horizontal stress, vertical stress and shear stress in the $y = y_t$ plane, respectively, induced by equivalent linear load f_k along the pile length.

$$R_1' = \sqrt{(x-d_k)^2 + (y_t - y_p)^2 + (z-l)^2}, \; R_2' = \sqrt{(x-d_k)^2 + (y_t - y_p)^2 + (z+l)^2}, \; k = 1,2,3,4,\ldots$$

3.2.3. Stress Superposition

Considering the joint effect of the tip loads and the shaft shear loads of pile group, the stress solution of Part 1 can be obtained using Equation (8):

$$\begin{cases} \sigma_{x1} = \sigma_{x1}^p + \sigma_{x1}^f \\ \sigma_{z1} = \sigma_{z1}^p + \sigma_{z1}^f \\ \sigma_{xz1} = \sigma_{xz1}^p + \sigma_{xz1}^f \end{cases} \tag{8}$$

3.3. Analytical Solution of Shallow Tunnel in Greenfield

The shallow tunnel excavated in an elastic soil can be considered an elastic half-plane problem (Part 2). Firstly, under the influence of gravity field, the ground stress is as shown in Equation (12) before excavation (Part 2a). Then, using the complex variable theory for the shallow tunnel, the ground stress after excavation in free strata can be obtained (Part 2b).

3.3.1. Stress-Release Function

In the unexcavated state, the stress at the tunnel periphery stays in the initial stress state. As the excavation process advances, stress redistribution occurs in the strata around the tunnel, and stress release will inevitably occur in the tunnel. In the tunnel simulation, the longitudinal direction of the tunnel is taken as 1 m for calculation, which is a plane strain calculation; it is therefore necessary to consider the stress release problem after excavation. The stress release of the tunnel periphery proposed here corresponds to the FEM; accordingly, a more reasonable excavation surface stress was applied to the tunnel boundary.

The stress for any point Q of the tunnel periphery is shown in Figure 5. The points o' and r_o are the center and radius of the circular tunnel, respectively. The angle of point Q is expressed as

$$\angle Q = \theta + 2k\pi, k = 0,1,2,3,4\ldots \tag{9}$$

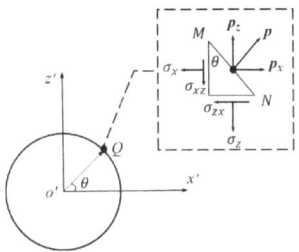

Figure 5. Stress at a point Q on the circular tunnel periphery.

The stress function of tunnel perimeter is considered as Equation (10). s_r denotes the stress release coefficient. The ground displacement caused by the pile group loads has been completed before the tunnel excavation, so this part of the displacement is no longer of concern during the tunnel excavation and is cleared to 0. Then, the release loads are applied in the opposite direction to the initial stresses (Figure 4, Part 1), and the value of release loads are the initial stresses multiplied by the stress release coefficient.

When $s_r = 0$, the tunnel periphery is in the initial stress state before excavation, or in a no-stress release state while the lining is applied immediately after the excavation, the stress solution equals Equation (12). When $s_r = 1$, σ in Equation (10) is equal to 0, which means that the tunnel has no lining during excavation and the stress is in a completely released state. When $0 \leq s_r \leq 1$, Equation (10) reflects the different degrees of stress release.

$$\begin{cases} \sigma_x(\theta) = k_0\gamma(1-s_r)(H-r\sin\theta) \\ \sigma_z(\theta) = \gamma(1-s_r)(H-r\sin\theta) \\ \sigma_{xz}(\theta) = 0 \end{cases} \quad (10)$$

In Figure 5, the plane MN is infinitely close to point Q, and p_x and p_z represent the principal stress of point Q and are the projection of the normal stress on the x' and z' axes on the plane MN. Then, the process of transforming the normal stress into the principal stress can be expressed by Equation (11). The stress function of the tunnel perimeter is

$$\begin{bmatrix} p_x \\ p_z \end{bmatrix} = \begin{bmatrix} \sigma_x & \sigma_{xz} \\ \sigma_{zx} & \sigma_z \end{bmatrix} \begin{bmatrix} l' \\ m' \end{bmatrix} = \begin{bmatrix} k_0\gamma(1-s_r)(H-r\sin\theta)\cos\theta \\ \gamma(1-s_r)(H-r\sin\theta)\sin\theta \end{bmatrix} \quad (11)$$

where $l' = \cos\theta$, $m' = \sin\theta$, H is the depth of the tunnel, and h is the pile length.

3.3.2. Part 2a Solution

In the Part 2a, the tunnel periphery with a dashed line represents that the stress is also in the initial stress state at this time; the ground stress boundary equation is

$$\begin{cases} \sigma_{x2}^a = k_0\gamma z \\ \sigma_{z2}^a = \gamma z \\ \sigma_{xz2}^a = 0 \end{cases} \quad (12)$$

Combining the stress tensor equation and Equation (13) indicates that the stress boundary function of virtual tunnel periphery in Part 2a, θ, is positive counter-clockwise, and $z = H - r\sin\theta$.

$$\begin{cases} p_{x1} = k_0\gamma z\cos\theta \\ p_{z1} = \gamma z\sin\theta \end{cases} \quad (13)$$

Then, the stress boundary function of tunnel periphery in Part 2b is as follows:

$$\begin{cases} p_{x2} = p_x - p_{x1} \\ p_{z2} = p_z - p_{z1} \end{cases} \quad (14)$$

3.3.3. Part 2b Solution

Analytical solutions of the total stress for the shallow tunnel in Part 2b are obtained by the complex variable method. It is assumed that the z-plane can be mapped conformally onto a ring in the ζ-plane using the suitable conformal transformation function Equation (16), see Figure 6. In the complex variable method, the solutions are expressed by two complex potential functions $\phi(z)$ and $\varphi(z)$, which must be analytic in the z-plane occupied by the elastic material. Then, the stresses are shown in Equation (15):

$$\begin{cases} \sigma_{x2}^b + \sigma_{z2}^b = 2[\phi'(z) + \overline{\varphi'(z)}] \\ \sigma_{z2}^b - \sigma_{x2}^b + 2i\sigma_{xz2}^b = 2[\bar{z}\phi''(z) + \varphi'(z)] \end{cases} \quad (15)$$

$$z = \omega(\zeta) = -ia\frac{1+\zeta}{1-\zeta} \qquad (16)$$

where $a = H\frac{1-\alpha^2}{1+\alpha^2}$, $\alpha = \frac{H}{r}(1 - \sqrt{(1-\frac{r^2}{H^2})})$.

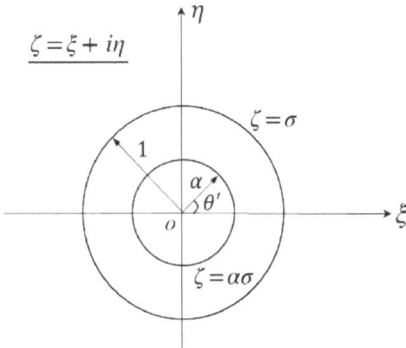

Figure 6. ζ-plane of conformal mapping.

During tunnel excavation, the removal of soil will be synchronized by the generation of concentrated forces F_x and F_z around the tunnel periphery, both of which are equal to the weight of excavated soil minus the weight of the tunnel lining. The "buoyancy effect" will occur when the weight of excavated soil is greater than the lining [15,40], and is incorporated into the method in this study by using the complex potential functions of Equations (17) and (18).

$$\phi(z) = -\frac{F_x + iF_z}{2\pi(1+\kappa)}[\kappa \log(z-\overline{z_c}) + \log(z-z_c)] + \phi_0(z) \qquad (17)$$

$$\varphi(z) = \frac{F_x - iF_z}{2\pi(1+\kappa)}[\log(z-\overline{z_c}) + \kappa \log(z-z_c)] + \varphi_0(z) \qquad (18)$$

where $\kappa = 3 - 4v$ for plane strain:

$$z_c = -ia\frac{1+\zeta_c}{1-\zeta_c} = -ia \qquad (19)$$

The stress is taken as the boundary condition of both the ground surface and tunnel periphery, where C is an integral constant.

I. Ground surface:

$$\zeta = \sigma : \phi(z) + z\overline{\phi'(z)} + \overline{\varphi(z)} = 0 \qquad (20)$$

II. Tunnel periphery:

$$\zeta = \alpha\sigma : \phi(z) + z\overline{\phi'(z)} + \overline{\varphi(z)} = i\int (p_{x2} + ip_{z2})ds + C \qquad (21)$$

Combining Equations (16)–(19), Equation (21) can be converted to Equation (22), where p_{x2} and p_{z2} are stress boundary functions and F_x and F_z are the concentrated forces generated by the buoyancy effect. The right side of the equation can be written as the series expansion

$$(1-\alpha\sigma)i\int (p_{x2} + ip_{z2})ds + (1-\alpha\sigma)F(F_{x2}, F_{z2}) = \sum_{k=-\infty}^{\infty} A_k \sigma^k \qquad (22)$$

where

$$F(F_{x2}, F_{z2}) = \left\{ \begin{array}{c} \frac{F_{x2}+iF_{z2}}{2\pi}\ln(\frac{\sigma-\alpha}{\alpha\sigma-1}) + \frac{F_{x2}+iF_{z2}}{2\pi(1+\kappa)}\ln\alpha \\ -\frac{F_{x2}-iF_{z2}}{4\pi(1+\kappa)}(\frac{\kappa}{\sigma}+\alpha^{-1})\frac{(\sigma-\alpha+\alpha\sigma^2-\alpha^2\sigma)}{1-\alpha\sigma} \end{array} \right\} \quad (23)$$

The coefficient of the complex potential function can be determined by selecting the fixed point of displacement, and the value of a_1 is obtained through series convergence. Then, $\phi(z)$ and $\varphi(z)$ are obtained by Equations (17) and (18). Eventually, the stress solution of Part 2b can be obtained by substituting them into Equation (15).

3.4. Stress Solution

Considering the gravity field and tunneling, the stress solution of Part 2 can be obtained using Equation (24):

$$\left\{ \begin{array}{l} \sigma_{x2} = \sigma_{x2}^a + \sigma_{x2}^b \\ \sigma_{z2} = \sigma_{z2}^a + \sigma_{z2}^b \\ \sigma_{xz2} = \sigma_{xz2}^a + \sigma_{xz2}^b \end{array} \right. \quad (24)$$

Assuming that the soil is linear elastic, accordingly, a superposition principle is introduced to obtain the analytical solution of the model in Figure 1 by superimposing the solutions of the pile group and tunneling. Therefore, the total stress of the mechanical model of the shallow tunnel adjacent to the pile group loads in the gravity field shown in Figure 1 is the sum of Part 1 and Part 2:

$$\left\{ \begin{array}{l} \sigma_x = \sigma_{x_1} + \sigma_{x2} \\ \sigma_z = \sigma_{z1} + \sigma_{z2} \\ \sigma_{xz} = \sigma_{xz1} + \sigma_{xz2} \end{array} \right. \quad (25)$$

4. Parametric Analysis

In this section, a parametric analysis with regard to the influences of different parameters on the stress and potential plastic zone of the ground is deliberated; these parameters are the soil parameters, pile parameters and the stress release degree of the tunnel periphery. We established some basic parameters: (1) the geometrical parameters of the tunnel are radius $r = 3$ m, depth $H = 12$ m; (2) the soil parameters are a Young's modulus of $E = 20$ MPa and a Poisson's ratio of $\nu = 0.3$; (3) the pile parameters are considered as the number of piles $m = 4$.

4.1. Stress Analysis

With regard to the influences of the stress release function in Equation (10) on the ground stress, the contour diagrams of major principal stress under different s_r values are presented in Figure 7, wherein the pile group loads are 4 m to the right side of the tunnel.

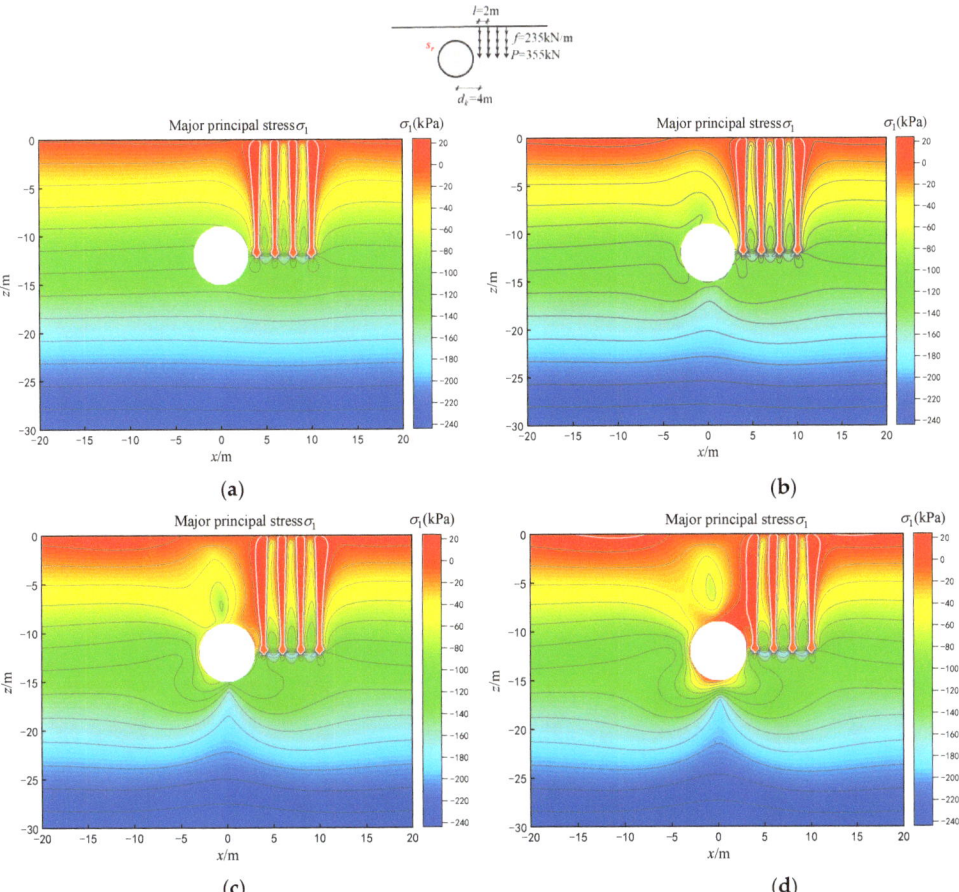

Figure 7. Contour diagrams of major principal stresses with various s_r: (**a**) $s_r = 0$; (**b**) $s_r = 0.3$; (**c**) $s_r = 0.7$; (**d**) $s_r = 1$.

Considering the plane strain condition, the major and minor principal stresses are

$$\sigma_1 = \frac{\sigma_x + \sigma_z}{2} + \sqrt{\left(\frac{\sigma_x - \sigma_z}{2}\right)^2 + \sigma_{xz}^2} \qquad (26)$$

$$\sigma_3 = \frac{\sigma_x + \sigma_z}{2} - \sqrt{\left(\frac{\sigma_x - \sigma_z}{2}\right)^2 + \sigma_{xz}^2} \qquad (27)$$

The stress around the tunnel is in the initial stress state when the stress release coefficient equals 0; moreover, the stress field around the pile group is symmetrical about the vertical centerline of the pile group due to the existence of the loads, as shown in Figure 7a. The tensile stress zone is mainly concentrated on the ground surface and pile group when s_r is small, as shown in Figure 7b. With the increase in the value of s_r, the tensile stress zone on the ground surface gradually develops downward as well as beginning to appear on the upper right side of the tunnel, due to the influence of the pile group load (see Figure 7d). The greater the value of s_r, the greater the disturbance of the stratum stress field.

Figure 8 shows the stresses field with various pile group tip loads P and shaft shear loads f. Clearly, the compressive stress zone of σ_3 mainly appears at the arch waist on both sides of the tunnel, and owing to the influence of the pile group loads, the compressive stress zone on the right side is larger. It can be noted from Figure 8a,b that the stratum stress field is less disturbed when the pile group load is small. The greater the pile group tip loads and shaft shear loads, the greater the degree of stratum disturbance.

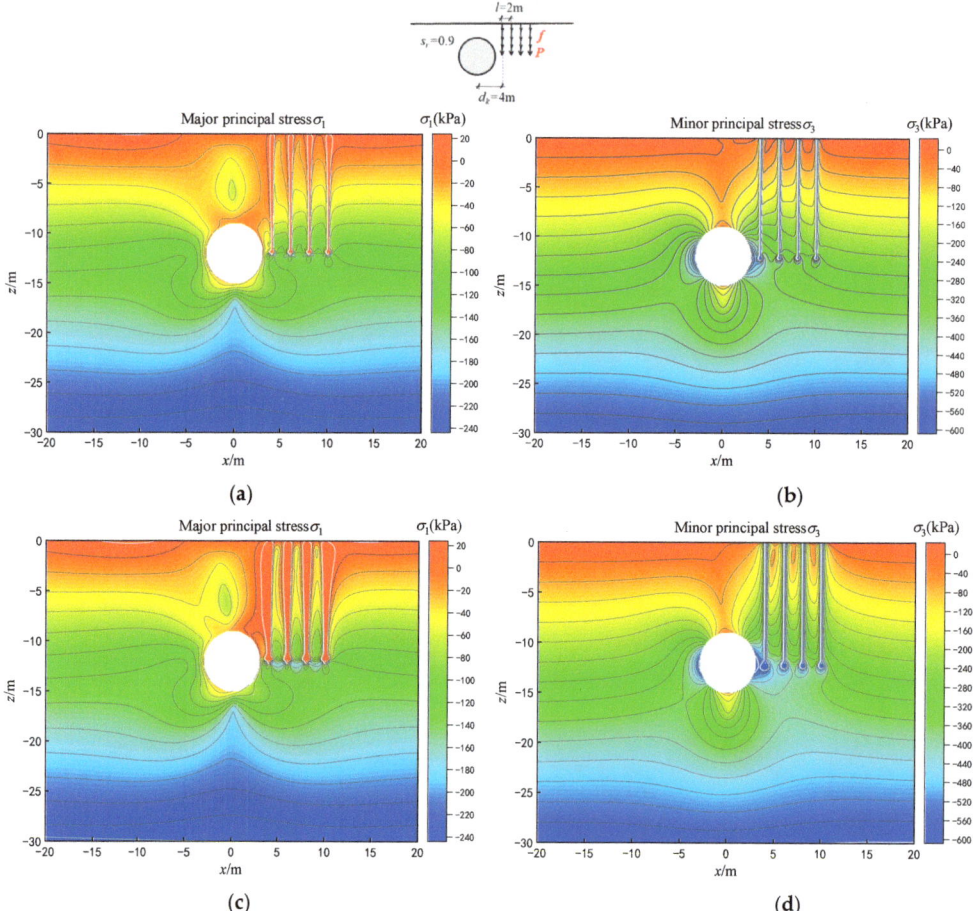

Figure 8. Contour diagrams of major and minor principal stresses with various pile group tip loads P and shaft shear loads f when $s_r = 0.9$: (**a**,**b**) $P = 150$ kN, $f = 70$ kN/m; (**c**,**d**) $P = 355$ kN, $f = 235$ kN/m.

Figure 9 provides the stress distribution of major principal stresses with various pile lengths and relative positions of the pile group and tunnel. As shown in Figure 9a, the pile group is located 1 m above the tunnel crown, and the stratum stress is disturbed in the horizontal range of approximately -5 m~5 m ($h = 8$ m, $l = 2$ m). Compared with bottom of pile group, the compressive stress on both sides of the tunnel above the pile group tip is smaller than that in Figure 9b. Moreover, it may also be noted from Figure 9c,d that the disturbed range of stratum stress increases with the increase in pile length. Meanwhile, the tensile stress zone appears at the upper right of the tunnel.

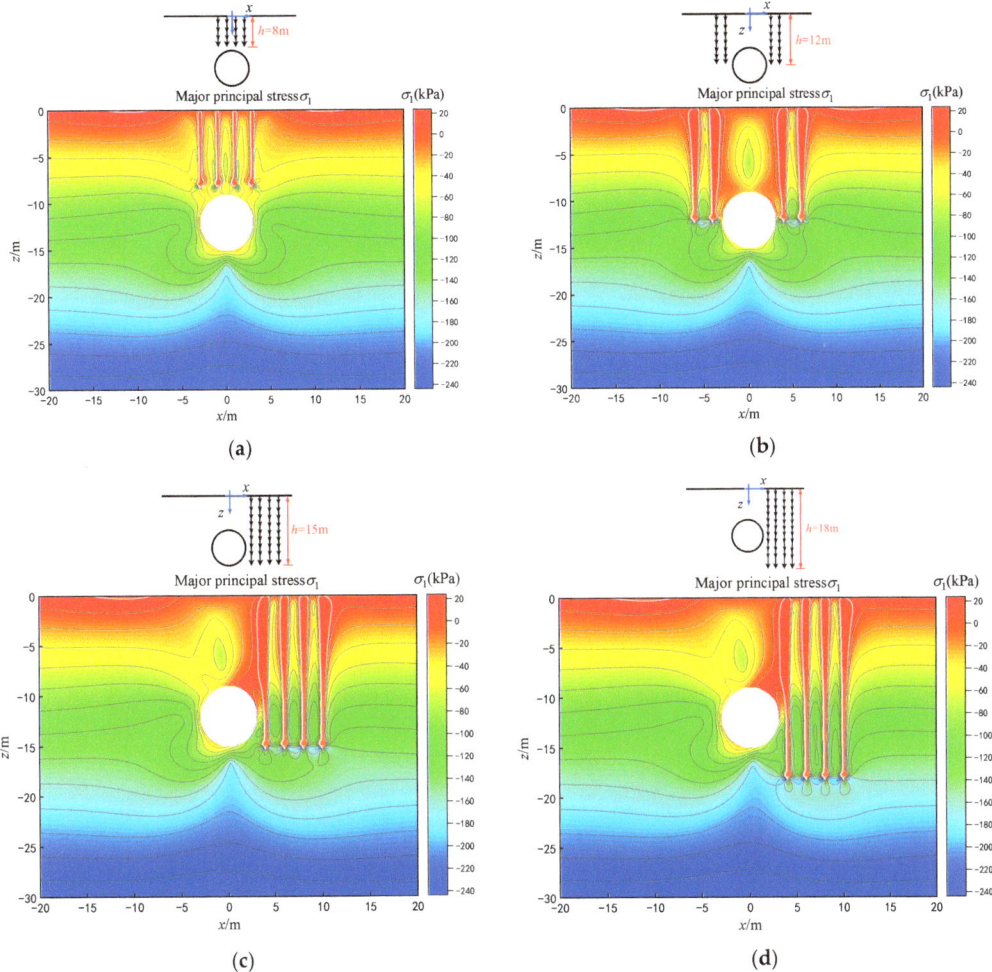

Figure 9. Contour diagrams of major principal stresses with various pile lengths and relative positions of the pile group and tunnel when $s_r = 0.9$: (**a**) the pile group right on top of the tunnel; (**b**) the pile group distributed on both sides of the tunnel; (**c**) the depth of the pile group tip close to the tunnel spring line; (**d**) the depth of the pile group tip deeper than the tunnel spring line.

4.2. Analysis of Potential Plastic Zone

Consequently, the method proposed in this paper can also introduce prediction of a potential plastic zone. In this way, we can solve not only the ground stress distribution but also the potential plastic zone, which provides a more intuitive way to ensure the safety of tunnel construction and existing structures.

Based on the Mohr–Coulomb yield criterion, combining Equation (26) as well as Equation (27), the judgment equation of potential plastic zone induced by tunneling with adjacent pile group loads in a gravity field can be obtained as Equation (28). The stress in the potential plastic zone meets $\tau_0 \geq \tau_f$.

$$\tau_0 \geq \tau_f = c - \sigma \tan \varphi \tag{28}$$

where c and φ are the soil's cohesion and internal friction angle, respectively,

$$\tau_0 = \frac{(\sigma_1 - \sigma_3)}{2} \cos \varphi, \ \sigma = \frac{\sigma_1 + \sigma_3}{2} + \frac{(\sigma_1 - \sigma_3)}{2} \sin \varphi.$$

4.2.1. Influence of the Pile Group

In this section, the control parameters are assumed to be $r = 3$ m, $H = 12$ m, $s_r = 0.9$, $h = 12$ m, $P = 355$ kN, $f = 235$ kN/m, $\gamma = 20$ kN/m^3, $c = 40$ kPa, $\varphi = 20°$. Figure 10 plots the potential plastic zones for different offsets d_k, and the potential plastic zones are merged in Figure 10a. It can be noted from Figure 10b that the potential plastic zone of the tunnel begins separated from the potential plastic zone of the pile group when $d_k = 7$ m. Furthermore, the degree of separation increases gradually with the increase in the value of d_k, as shown in Figure 10c,d; In Figure 10e, the potential plastic zone of the tunnel and pile group are completely separated when $d_k = 10$ m; however, there is some influence between them; In Figure 10d, the potential plastic zone of the tunnel is almost not affected by the pile group, and the potential plastic zone of the tunnel is approximately symmetrical when $d_k = 12$ m.

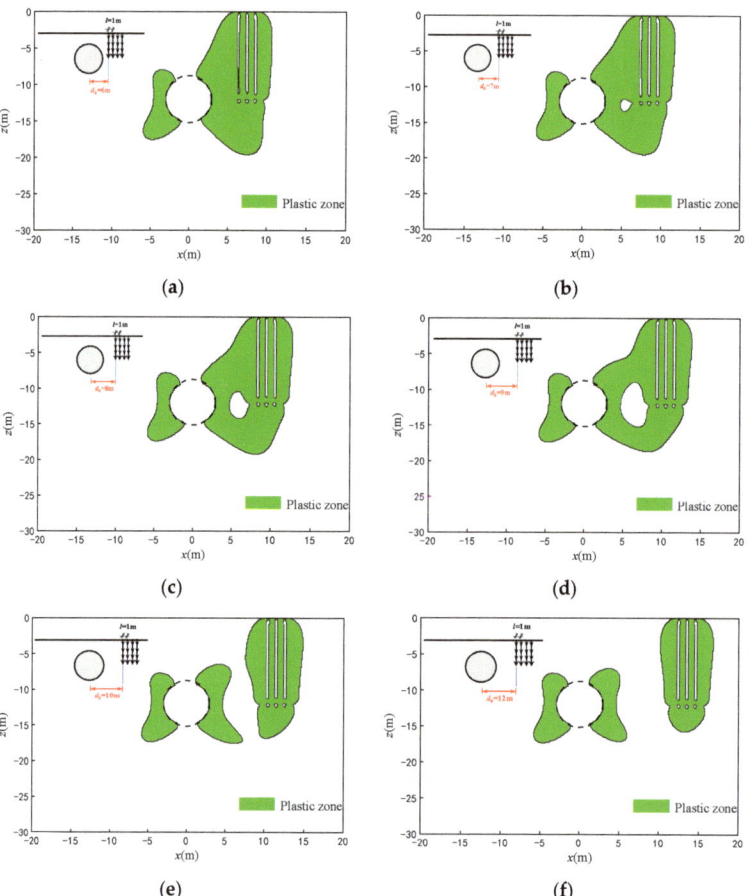

Figure 10. Potential plastic zones for different offsets d_k of the pile group from the tunnel: (**a**) $d_k = 6$ m; (**b**) $d_k = 7$ m; (**c**) $d_k = 8$ m; (**d**) $d_k = 9$ m (**e**) $d_k = 10$ m; (**f**) $d_k = 12$ m.

Moreover, the aforementioned analysis suggests that the potential plastic zone induced by tunneling is butterfly shaped when the gravity field is involved; however, the shape of the potential plastic zone is circular when the gravity field is not involved [34].

4.2.2. Influence of Soil Parameters

Figure 11 shows the influence of different soil parameters on the ranges of the potential plastic zones. The influence of four different magnitudes of volumetric weight of soil on the ranges of the potential plastic zones is shown in Figure 11a. The results indicate that the potential plastic zones of the pile group and tunnel coalesce, and the range of the potential plastic zone increases as the volumetric weight increases. The influence of different soil cohesion (c = 35 kPa, 45 kPa, 55 kPa and 65 kPa) on the range of the potential plastic zone is plotted in Figure 11b. Figure 11c particularly presents the influence of different magnitudes of the angle of internal friction (φ = 20°, 25°, 30°, and 40°) on the range of the potential plastic zone. It is worth noting that the influence rules of c and φ are similar to each other, based on Figure 11b,c. Moreover, it can be observed that the butterfly shape of the potential plastic zone is obvious at a relatively low cohesion value or a low angle of internal friction of the soil.

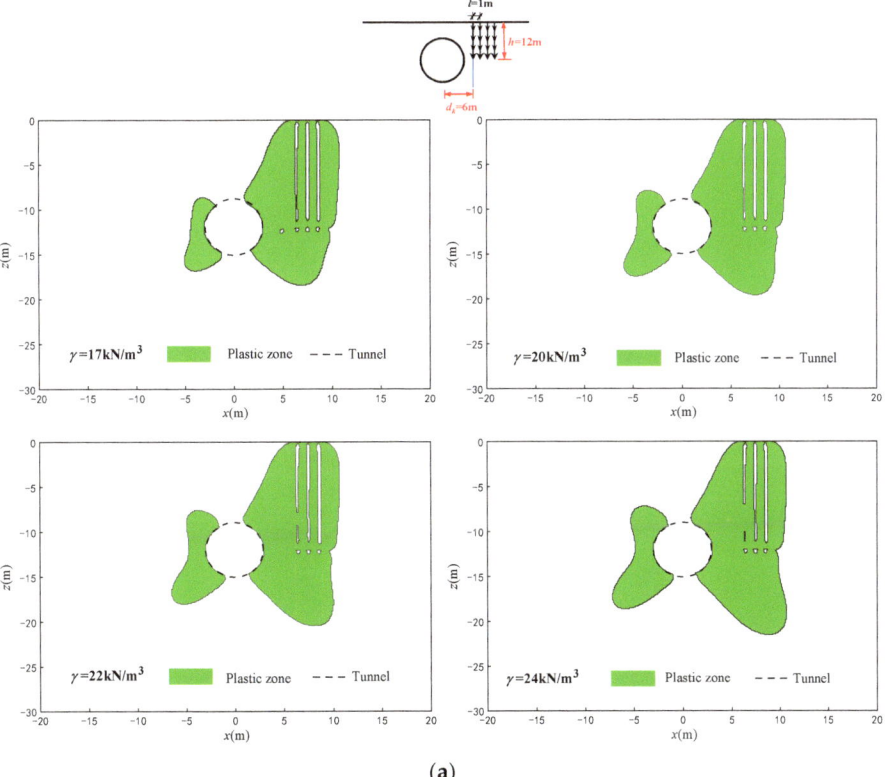

(a)

Figure 11. *Cont.*

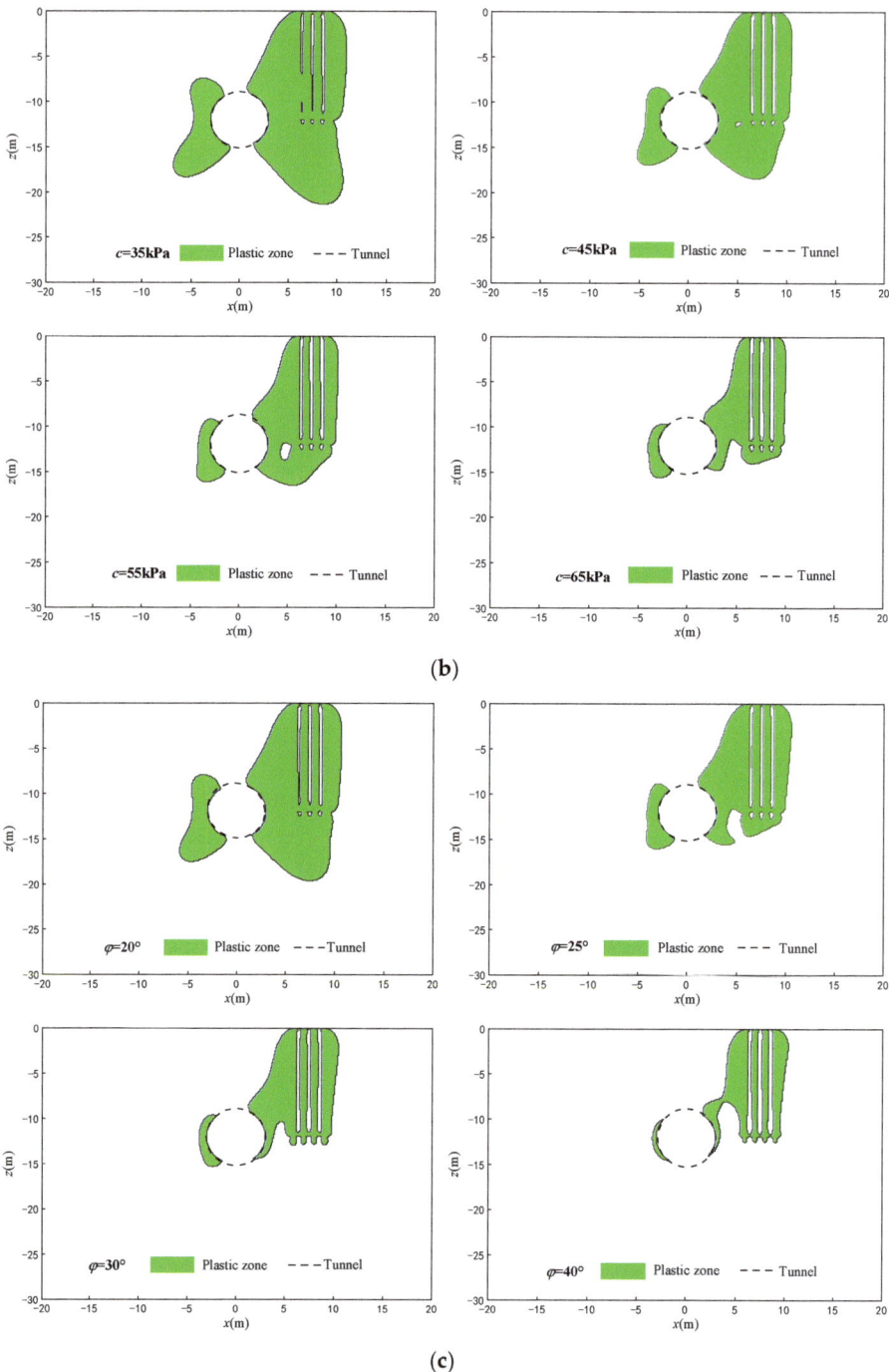

Figure 11. Potential plastic zones for different soil parameters when $d_1 = 6$ m, $d_2 = 7$ m, $d_3 = 8$ m, $d_4 = 9$ m (x coordinate of each pile) and $h = 12$ m. (**a**) Different magnitudes of volumetric weight; (**b**) Different magnitudes of cohesion; (**c**) Different magnitudes of the angle of internal friction.

In this paper, a theoretical calculation procedure is developed for prediction of the secondary stress field and the related potential plastic zone caused by tunneling adjacent to crossing existing building/structures foundations. The working conditions set in this paper are very common in practical projects, and rely on the background project of a section of the Beijing subway adjacent to the bridge pile foundations, which is a typical working condition. To address this problem, most scholars currently use numerical methods and model test methods to predict the influence of tunneling in the vicinity of pile foundations in soils. In the light of this, this study provides a theoretical analysis method for this type of engineering, which is important for understanding the generation mechanisms of stress and deformation, and is able to study the basic relationship between different variables and parameters involved in this type of problem. Moreover, this study more comprehensively considers the influence of stress release s_r, the relative distance d_k between pile group and tunnel, the pile length h, the pile loads P and f, and soil parameters (γ, c, φ). The working conditions match the real working conditions, so based on the established procedures, incorporating engineering parameters will allow us to qualitatively predict the secondary stress field and potential plastic zone. In future related research, a coupling analysis with analytical solutions and the additional effects of adjacent structures will be proposed to consider more complex underground space structures. The reasonable boundary condition is a key factor.

5. Conclusions

Herein, new analytical solutions have been proposed to predict ground responses caused by tunneling alongside existing pile group loads in the interior of the stratum in a gravity field. The stress-release function is proposed to reflect the stress release behavior of the tunnel periphery during excavation, which makes it a good tool to more accurately describe ground responses under different degrees of stress release. The following conclusions of this work have been drawn.

(1) The stress around the tunnel is greatly affected by a change in the stress release coefficient. When the s_r is large enough, the tensile stress zone appears in the tunnel crown; notably, the tensile stress zone appears at the right of the tunnel crown due to the influence of pile group loads. The greater the pile group tip loads and shaft shear loads, the greater the degree of stratum disturbance.

(2) The stratum stress is disturbed in the horizontal range of approximately −5 m~5 m (h = 8 m, l = 2 m), when the pile group is located 1 m above the tunnel crown; the disturbed range of stratum stress increases with the increase in pile length.

(3) Considering the gravity field, the potential plastic zone of the tunnel is butterfly shaped, and the range of lower part is larger than the upper. The potential plastic zones are merged when the horizontal distance between the pile group and the tunnel $d_k \leq 3r$; the potential plastic zone is completely separated when $d_k > 3r$; the potential plastic zone of the tunnel is almost unaffected by the pile group when $d_k \geq 4r$, and the law of the influence of the relative position of the pile group and tunnel on the plastic zone is consistent with the law presented in Xiang et al. (2013).

(4) Shear strength parameters have similar influence rules on the potential plastic zone, and the ranges of the potential plastic zone decrease as the c and φ increase; on the contrary, the ranges of the potential plastic zone increase as the volumetric weight increases.

Because this study does not consider the lining effect, the result of such an analysis is biased towards safety. The solutions provide a simple and effective approach to quickly estimate the stability of shallow tunnels and minimize the risk of damage as a result of tunnel construction under the conditions of existing pile group loads in the planning stage.

Author Contributions: Conceptualization, C.G. and F.K.; Methodology, C.G., F.K. and D.L.; Software, Y.T.; Validation, Y.T.; Formal analysis, Y.T. and L.S.; Investigation, Y.T. and L.S.; Writing—original draft, C.G.; Writing—review & editing, F.K. and D.L.; Visualization, L.S.; Supervision, X.D.; Project administration, X.D.; Funding acquisition, C.G. All authors have read and agreed to the published version of the manuscript.

Funding: This research was funded by the National Key R&D Program of China (Grant No. 2022YFC3800901), the National Natural Science Foundation of China (Grant No. 52278385), and the Beijing Municipal Education Commission (Grant No. KM202210005019).

Data Availability Statement: Data sharing not applicable.

Conflicts of Interest: The authors declare no conflict of interest.

References

1. Guo, C.; Fan, L.; Han, K.; Li, P.; Zhang, M. Progressive failure analysis of shallow circular tunnel based on the functional catastrophe theory considering strain softening of surrounding rock mass. *Tunn. Undergr. Space Technol.* **2023**, *131*, 104799. [CrossRef]
2. Huang, Z.K.; Zhang, D.M.; Pitilakis, K.; Tsinidis, G.; Argyroudis, S. Resilience assessment of tunnels: Framework and application for tunnels in alluvial deposits exposed to seismic hazard. *Soil Dyn. Earthq. Eng.* **2022**, *162*, 107456. [CrossRef]
3. Kong, F.C.; Lu, D.C.; Ma, Y.D.; Tian, T.; Yu, H.T.; Du, X.L. Novel hybrid method to predict the ground-displacement field caused by shallow tunnel excavation. *Sci. China Technol. Sci.* **2023**, *66*, 101–114. [CrossRef]
4. Zhang, J.Z.; Phoon, K.K.; Zhang, D.M.; Huang, H.W.; Tang, C. Novel approach to estimate vertical scale of fluctuation based on CPT data using convolutional neural networks. *Eng. Geol.* **2021**, *294*, 106342. [CrossRef]
5. Zhao, Y.; Chen, X.; Hu, B.; Wang, P.; Li, W. Evolution of tunnel uplift induced by adjacent long and collinear excavation and an effective protective measure. *Tunn. Undergr. Space Technol.* **2023**, *131*, 104846. [CrossRef]
6. Cao, L.Q.; Chen, X.S.; Zhang, D.L.; Su, D. Theoretical investigation of restraint effect of isolation piles on vertical ground displacements due to tunneling under the plane state. *Chin. J. Geotech. Eng.* **2022**, *44*, 916–925. (In Chinese)
7. Chapman, D.N.; Rogers, C.D.F.; Hunt, D.V.L. Predicting the settlements above twin tunnels constructed in soft ground. *Tunn. Undergr. Space Technol.* **2004**, *19*, 378.
8. Fang, Q.; Zhang, D.L.; Li, Q.Q.; Wong, L.N.Y. Effects of twin tunnels construction beneath existing shield-driven twin tunnels. *Tunn. Undergr. Space Technol.* **2015**, *45*, 128–137. [CrossRef]
9. Lu, D.C.; Lin, Q.T.; Tian, Y. Formula for predicting ground settlement induced by tunnelling based on Gaussian function. *Tunn. Undergr. Space Technol.* **2020**, *103*, 103443. [CrossRef]
10. Peck, R.B. Deep excavations and tunnelling in soft ground. In Proceedings of the International Conference on Soil Mechanics and Foundation Engineering, State-of-the-Art, Mexico City, Mexico, 25–29 August 1969; pp. 225–290.
11. Huang, M.S.; Li, Z.; Yang, C. Analysis of the shielding effect of a pile group adjacent to tunneling. *China Civil. Eng. J.* **2007**, *40*, 69–74. (In Chinese)
12. Lee, C.J.; Bolton, M.D.; Tabbaa, A.A. Numerical modeling of group effects on the distribution of dragloads in pile foundations. *Géotechnique* **2002**, *52*, 325–335. [CrossRef]
13. Zhu, F.B.; Yang, P.; Ong, C.W. Numerical analysis on influence of shield tunnel excavation to neighboring piles. *Chin. J. Geotech. Eng.* **2008**, *30*, 298–302. (In Chinese)
14. Lee, Y.J.; Banssett, R.H. Influence zones for 2D pile-soil-tunneling interaction based on model test and numerical analysis. *Tunn. Undergr. Space Technol.* **2007**, *22*, 325–342. [CrossRef]
15. Lu, D.C.; Kong, F.C.; Du, X.L.; Shen, C.P.; Gong, Q.M.; Li, P.F. A unified displacement function to analytically predict ground deformation of shallow tunnel. *Tunn. Undergr. Space Technol.* **2019**, *88*, 129–143. [CrossRef]
16. Verruijt, A. A complex variable solution for a deforming circular tunnel in an elastic half-plane. *Int. J. Numer. Anal. Methods GeoMech.* **1997**, *21*, 77–89. [CrossRef]
17. Zhang, Z.; Wo, W.; Mu, L.; Chen, J.; Zhu, Z.; Pan, Y. Mathematical modelling for shield tunneling induced displacement effects on in-service tunnel: Theoretical solution including shearing deformation of segment and stiffness reduction of circumferential joints. *Appl. Math. Model.* **2023**, *118*, 322–345. [CrossRef]
18. Bobet, A. Analytical solutions for shallow tunnels in saturated ground. *J. Eng. Mech.* **2001**, *127*, 1258–1266. [CrossRef]
19. Li, P.F.; Gou, B.L.; Zhu, M.; Gao, X.J.; Guo, C.X. Calculation method of time-dependent behavior for tunneling-induced ground movements based on virtual image technique. *Rock Soil Mech.* **2022**, *43*, 799–807. (In Chinese)
20. Sagaseta, C. Analysis of undrained soil deformation due to ground loss. *Geotechnique* **1987**, *37*, 301–320. [CrossRef]
21. Howland, R.C.J.; Knight, R.C. Stress functions for a plate containing groups of circular holes. *Philos. Trans. R. Soc. Lond. Ser. A Math. Phys. Sci.* **1939**, *238*, 357–392.
22. Radi, E. Path-independent integrals around two circular holes in an infinite plate under biaxial loading conditions. *Int. J. Eng. Sci.* **2011**, *49*, 893–914. [CrossRef]
23. Verruijt, A. Deformations of an elastic half plane with a circular cavity. *Int. J. Solid Struct.* **1998**, *35*, 2795–2804. [CrossRef]

24. Verruijt, A.; Strack, O.E. Buoyancy of tunnels in soft soils. *Géotechnique* **2008**, *58*, 513–515. [CrossRef]
25. Zhang, Z.; Huang, M.; Pan, Y.; Li, Z.; Ma, S.; Zhang, Y. Time-dependent analyses for ground movement and stress field induced by tunnelling considering rainfall infiltration mechanics. *Tunn. Undergr. Space Technol.* **2022**, *122*, 104378. [CrossRef]
26. Kong, F.C.; Lu, D.C.; Ma, C.; Shen, C.P.; Yang, X.D.; Du, X.L. Fractional viscoelastic solution of stratum displacement of a shallow tunnel under the surface slope condition. *Undergr. Space* **2023**, *10*, 233–247. [CrossRef]
27. Zhang, Z.; Huang, M.; Xi, X.; Yang, X. Complex variable solutions for soil and liner deformation due to tunneling in clays. *Int. J. Geomech.* **2018**, *18*, 04018074. [CrossRef]
28. Lu, A.Z.; Zeng, X.T.; Xu, Z. Solution for a circular cavity in an elastic half plane under gravity and arbitrary lateral stress. *Int. J. Rock Mech. Min. Sci.* **2016**, *89*, 34–42. [CrossRef]
29. Lu, A.; Cai, H.; Wang, S. A new analytical approach for a shallow circular hydraulic tunnel. *Meccanica* **2019**, *54*, 223–238. [CrossRef]
30. Kong, F.C.; Lu, D.C.; Du, X.L.; Li, X.Q.; Su, C.C. Analytical solution of stress and displacement for a circular underwater shallow tunnel based on a unified stress function. *Ocean Eng.* **2021**, *219*, 108352. [CrossRef]
31. Wang, H.N.; Chen, X.P.; Jiang, M.J.; Song, F.; Wu, L. The analytical predictions on displacement and stress around shallow tunnels subjected to surcharge loadings. *Tunn. Undergr. Space Technol.* **2018**, *71*, 403–427. [CrossRef]
32. Yang, G.; Zhang, C.; Min, B.; Chen, W. Complex variable solution for tunneling-induced ground deformation considering the gravity effect and a cavern in the strata. *Comput. Geotech.* **2021**, *135*, 104154. [CrossRef]
33. Marshall, A.M.; Haji, T. An analytical study of tunnel-pile interaction. *Tunn. Undergr. Space Technol.* **2015**, *45*, 43–51. [CrossRef]
34. Xiang, Y.; Feng, S. Theoretical prediction of the potential plastic zone of shallow tunneling adjacent to pile foundation in soils. *Tunn. Undergr. Space Technol.* **2013**, *38*, 115–121. [CrossRef]
35. Guo, C.; Qi, J.; Shi, L.; Fang, Q. Reasonable overburden thickness for underwater shield tunnel. *Tunn. Undergr. Space Technol.* **2018**, *81*, 35–40. [CrossRef]
36. Shang, H.S.; Zhang, H.; Liang, F.Y. Lateral bearing capacity of pile foundation due to shallow tunneling. *Chin. J. Geotech. Eng.* **2013**, *35*, 740–743. (In Chinese)
37. Zhang, J.Z.; Huang, H.W.; Zhang, D.M.; Phoon, K.K.; Liu, Z.Q.; Tang, C. Quantitative evaluation of geological uncertainty and its influence on tunnel structural performance using improved coupled Markov chain. *Acta Geotech.* **2021**, *16*, 3709–3724. [CrossRef]
38. Zhao, Y.; Chen, X.; Hu, B.; Huang, L.; Li, W.; Fan, J. Evolution of tunnel uplift and deformation induced by an upper and collinear excavation: A case study from Shenzhen metro. *Transp. Geotech.* **2023**, *39*, 100953. [CrossRef]
39. Mindlin, R.D. Force at a point in the interior of a semi-infinite solid. *Physics* **1936**, *7*, 195–202. [CrossRef]
40. Strack, O.E.; Verruijt, A. A complex variable solution for a deforming buoyant tunnel in a heavy elastic half-plane. *Int. J. Numer. Anal. Methods GeoMech.* **2002**, *26*, 1235–1252. [CrossRef]

Disclaimer/Publisher's Note: The statements, opinions and data contained in all publications are solely those of the individual author(s) and contributor(s) and not of MDPI and/or the editor(s). MDPI and/or the editor(s) disclaim responsibility for any injury to people or property resulting from any ideas, methods, instructions or products referred to in the content.

Article

Experimental Research on the Settlement Feature of Two Ground Deformation Modes Induced by Tunnelling

Qingtao Lin [1,2], Caixia Guo [2], Xu Meng [2], Hongyu Dong [2] and Fanchao Kong [2,*]

[1] Department of Civil Engineering, School of Civil Engineering, Tsinghua University, Beijing 100084, China; linqingtao@tsinghua.edu.cn

[2] Institute of Geotechnical and Underground Engineering, Beijing University of Technology, Beijing 100124, China; guocaixia@bjut.edu.cn (C.G.); mengxu@emails.bjut.edu.cn (X.M.); donghy@emails.bjut.edu.cn (H.D.)

* Correspondence: kongfc@bjut.edu.cn

Abstract: Two ground deformation modes, i.e., the arching mode and collapsing mode, may be caused by tunnel excavation. However, the development of the ground deformation corresponding to the two modes is unclear. A piece of a model test facility is designed to study the ground settlement induced by tunnel excavation. Tunnel excavation is realized by decreasing the area of the model tunnel. Two model tests with different soil cohesion are conducted, and the two ground deformation modes form in the two tests, respectively. The former mode is observed at higher soil cohesion while the latter is found to develop at lower soil cohesion. Whether the failure surface develops to the ground surface or not is the most significant difference between the two ground deformation modes. In the two modes, the failure surface occurs at the position where the ground settlement contours distribute densely, and the shape of the failure surface can be described by the semi-oval for both modes. Meanwhile, for both the arching mode and the collapsing mode, Gaussian curves can reasonably describe the ground settlement troughs before the ground surface settlement becomes stable or increases sharply, and distribution of the trough width parameter is similar.

Keywords: tunnel excavation; model test; arching mode; collapsing mode; ground settlement

MSC: 74S25

1. Introduction

Soil above the tunnel crown may collapse during tunnel excavation. A failure surface can occur between the collapsed soil body and surrounding intact soil. If the failure surface extends to the ground surface, the soil between the tunnel crown and the ground surface collapse completely. This failure condition is called the "collapsing mode". However, when the failure surface does not extend to the ground surface, the soil between the failure surface and the ground surface does not collapse even if the tunnel is unlined. This condition is defined as the "arching mode". The geometry of the tunnel and mechanical properties of the soil determine the formation of the ground deformation mode together. In general, the arching mode is observed when the cover-to-diameter ratio Z_0/D is large and/or the shear strength of the soil is high (high cohesion c and/or high internal friction angle φ) [1–3].

Trapdoor tests [3–6] have been frequently used to study the ground deformation modes, where attention is mainly placed on the evolution of earth pressure. The ground settlement is not monitored. However, the ground settlement induced by tunnelling has significant impact on both surface buildings and underground structures [7–9]. Proper consideration of the ground settlement caused by tunnelling is of more importance when the collapsing mode occurs, as catastrophic damages to the neighboring structures and foundations can be caused.

Nakai et al. (1997) [10] and Marshall et al. (2012) [11] studied the contours of the ground settlement at a specific moment based on the model test results. However, these tests cannot reveal the development process of the two failure modes because the contours of the ground settlement corresponding to different ground volume loss is not known. In addition, development of the ground settlement trough is directly related to the ground deformation mode. Both field observations [12–18] and model tests [11,19–21] have been used to investigate the ground settlement trough induced by tunnelling. Peck (1969) [22] analyzed the field observation data and indicated that Gaussian curves can well fit the surface settlement trough. Mair et al. (1993) [23] made further development in Peck's method and pointed out that Gaussian curves can also provide a good fit for the subsurface settlement trough. Similar conclusions have been obtained from model tests [19,21,24–26]. However, several studies [27–29] indicated that the ground settlement trough approximates the plug-shape or triangular-shape at the collapsed position. Gaussian curves may not provide an adequate fit for the ground settlement trough at the collapsed position [27–29]. In sum, the development of the ground deformation, including the maximum settlement, the contours of the ground settlement, and surface and subsurface settlement troughs corresponding to the arching mode and collapsing mode are unclear.

This paper presents a new study on the formation of arching and collapsing mode. A new test facility is designed for the model tests. Sand with different water content is used in the tests, which simulates soil with different cohesion. At the initial state, the tunnel to be excavated is filled by a pressurized water bag. Water is then released during the tests to simulate the excavation process. The surface and the subsurface settlement at different soil volume loss states are monitored to obtain the ground settlement contours and the ground settlement troughs. The feature of the failure surface and the ground settlements are analyzed for the two ground deformation modes.

2. Physical Model Test of Tunnel Excavation

2.1. Test Equipment

The test equipment consists of a model strongbox, a model tunnel, and a ground deformation monitoring system.

2.1.1. Model Strongbox

Though the deformation of the ground near the tunnel heading shows 3D features, the final ground deformation is similar for different transverse cross-sections. Therefore, the effect of tunnelling on the ground can be studied using a simplified plain strain model [3,11,23]. In this work, a model strongbox for plain strain tests is designed. The model strongbox is rectangular with a Perspex window on its front face (Figure 1). The main body of the model strongbox is made using several 10-mm-thick steel plates. A 20-mm-thick acrylic plate Perspex window is fitted in the front face, enabling observation of the subsurface ground deformation. Stiffness of the strongbox is large enough to ensure that the deformation of the strongbox is small in the tests. Internal dimensions of the strongbox are 1500 mm long, 400 mm wide, and 1500 mm high. The Perspex window is 900 mm high and 1000 mm wide. The tunnel to be excavated is in the horizontal center of the strongbox. To reduce the boundary effect, the diameter D of the model tunnel is designed to be 200 mm. The distance between the tunnel crown and the top of the strongbox is 600 mm. The maximum cover-to-diameter ratio z_0/D of the model tunnel can reach 3.0. Boundary conditions for the strongbox are shown in Figure 2.

Figure 1. Front view of the model.

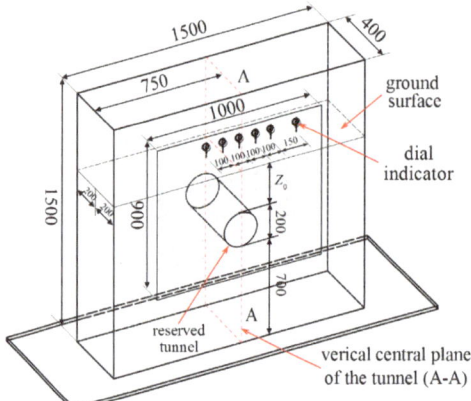

Figure 2. Dimensions of the model strongbox.

2.1.2. Model Tunnel and Excavation Simulation

Reduction of the area of the tunnel transverse section to schematically realize a ground volume loss V_s is an approach adopted by many researchers to simulate the tunnelling process in model tests [8,11]. A model tunnel that can realize different V_s by releasing water was designed (Figure 3a,b), consisting of a water bag and a needle valve, as illustrated in Figure 3c. The diameter of the water bag is 200 mm, and the length is 500 mm. The water bag is filled with water through a high-pressure water pump before it is buried in the model. The needle valve is closed to seal the water bag when the diameter of the tunnel reaches 200 mm. Reduction of the tunnel diameter is simulated by releasing the water from the water bag, as shown in Figure 3a,b. The volume of the discharged water is defined as the tunnel volume loss V_t. The advantage of this system is that V_t can be controlled precisely, and V_t can reach a considerable value so that stable ground deformation can be formed. The ground volume loss V_s is indirectly realized by controlling the tunnel volume loss V_t. Tunnel volume loss can be calculated by Equation (1) [25]:

$$V_t = \frac{V_{wd}}{V_w} = \frac{4V_{wd}}{\pi D^2 L} \tag{1}$$

where V_w is the volume of the model tunnel, V_{wd} is the volume of the discharged water, D (=200 mm) is the diameter of the model tunnel, and L (=500 mm) is the length of the model tunnel.

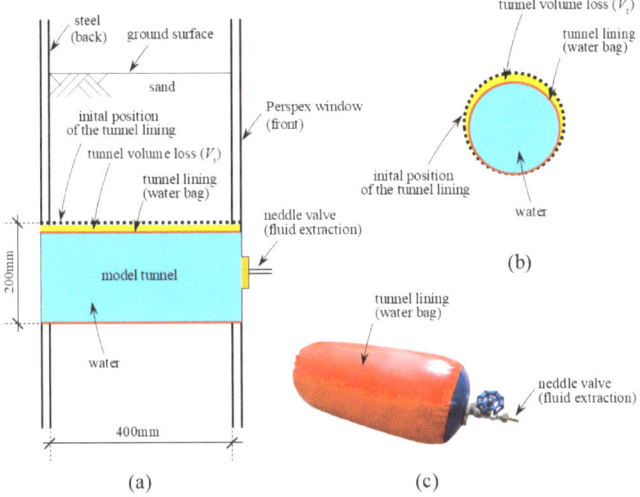

Figure 3. Model tunnel. (**a**) The vertical central plane A-A; (**b**) Cross-section of model tunnel; (**c**) Image of the model tunnel.

2.1.3. Monitoring System

The surface and the subsurface settlements are monitored in the test. As shown in Figure 4, the DSCM monitoring system [30] was chosen to measure the subsurface settlement. The basic principle of DSCM is to match the geometric positions of the digital speckle images and then track the movement of each point. The camera of the DSCM monitoring system is placed in front of the model. The acrylic plate not only ensures the rigidity of the strongbox but also enables the ground deformation to be monitored by the DSCM monitoring system. Data collection points, which are symmetrical about the vertical central plane A-A, are set at each silica sand layer. DSCM computational software is used to conduct the correlation operation so that the displacement of each silica sand layer can be collected. Currently, the DSCM can achieve a precision of 0.01 pixels.

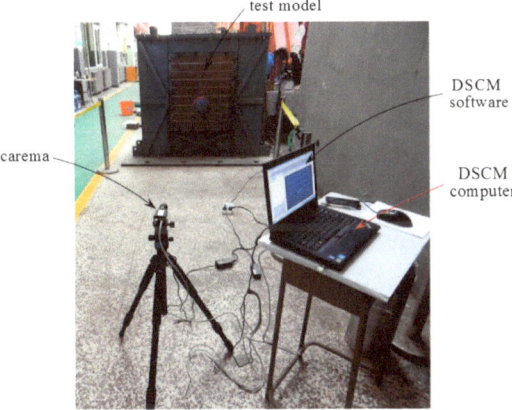

Figure 4. DSCM monitoring system.

Dial indicators are used to monitor the surface settlement (Figure 5). The measurement range of the dial indicator is 30 mm, and the maximum precision is 10 μm. In the tests of this study, the surface and the subsurface settlement troughs are symmetrical about the vertical central plane A-A. Therefore, the dial indicators are arranged only on the right side of A-A. In addition, there is still one dial indicator that is installed on the left side of A-A to check the surface settlement monitored by other dial indicators. The layout of the dial indicators is shown in Figure 2, and the interval between adjacent dial indicators is 100 mm or 150 mm. Dial indicators are fixed on the designed position through supporting frames. The measuring rod of the dial indicator is perpendicular to the ground surface, and a glass pad is placed between the measuring rod and the ground surface (Figure 5). The surface settlement can be monitored reasonably when these measures are implemented.

Figure 5. Monitoring of the surface settlement. (**a**) Arrangement of the dial indicator; (**b**) installation details of the dial indicator.

2.2. Soil for the Tests

Sand was used in the model tests. The grading curve of the sand is shown in Figure 6. When the water content w is less than approximately 10%, cohesion c of the sand increases as w increases [31–33]. The water content w is 5% in Group T1 and 2% in Group T2. Meanwhile, previous studies have shown that the internal friction angle φ of the sand changes very little when w increases from 2% to 5% [34–36].

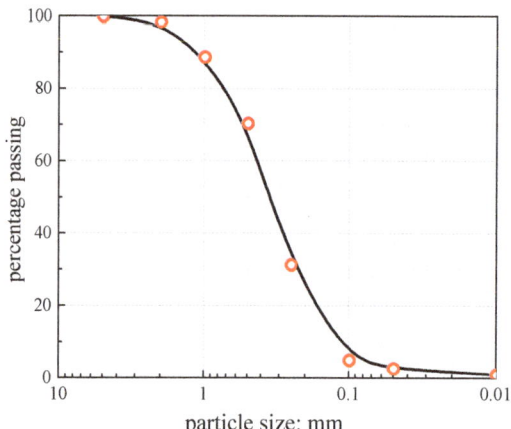

Figure 6. Grading curve of sandy soil.

For the sand in Group T1 and Group T2, the direct shear test is carried out to determine the shear strength of the sand under different vertical pressure. In each group of direct shear tests, the vertical pressure is taken for 100 kPa, 200 kPa, 300 kPa, and 400 kPa, respectively. As shown in Figure 7, values of c and φ of the sand in Group T1 and Group T2 are determined by fitting the measured results of shear strength of the sand with the linear regression method using Equation (2), which is an expression for the Mohr–Coulomb failure criterion [37,38].

$$\tau_f = \sigma \cdot \tan \varphi + c \qquad (2)$$

where τ_f is the shear strength of the sand and σ is the vertical pressure. For the sand used in the test, c and φ are, respectively, equal to 1.60 kPa and 33.0° when w = 2%. The values of c and φ, respectively, equal 7.34 kPa and 30.1° when w increases to 5%, as shown in Figure 7. To evaluate the quality of values of c and φ in Groups T1 and T2, coefficients of determination (R^2) between the fitting line and the measured data are calculated using Equation (3).

$$R^2 = 1 - \frac{\sum_{i=1}^{N}\left(y_i^P - y_i\right)^2}{\sum_{i=1}^{N}\left(\overline{y} - y_i\right)^2} \qquad (3)$$

where y_i and y_i^P are the true value and the predicted value of the ith target variable; $\overline{y}$ is the mean value of y_i; N is the number of data samples. Values of R^2 is 0.95 and 0.99 for Groups T1 and T2, respectively, as also shown in Figure 7.

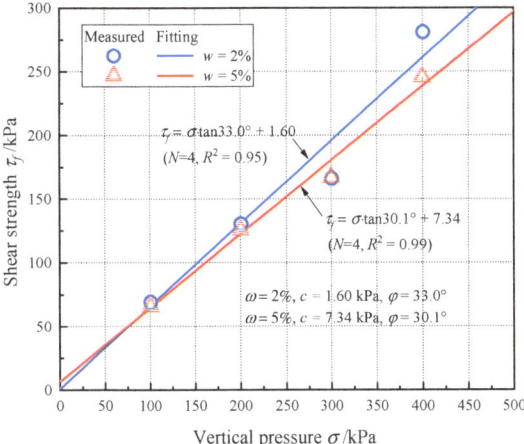

Figure 7. Relationship between the shear strength and the vertical pressure.

2.3. Test Procedure and Conditions

2.3.1. Test Procedure

Sand is preheated and then mixed with a certain amount of water before filling (i.e., w = 5% in Group T1; w = 2% in Group T2). The sand is immediately filled into the strongbox after mixing with water. Lightweight plastic films are placed on the soil to prevent water from evaporating. A total of 103.2 kg (for Group T1) or 100 kg (for Group T2) sand is poured into the strongbox one at a time, and then the sand is compact into a layer 10 cm thick to control the dry density of the sand at 1634 kg/m³. A thin layer of white quartz sand is sprinkled inside the Perspex window for collecting the ground settlement information (Figure 1). The same procedure is repeated until the model reaches the designed height. In particular, the model tunnel is placed at the pre-set location when the sand beneath the tunnel is completed. The sand is in close contact with the lining. After the model is completed, the ground surface is made smooth and the monitoring system is installed.

The data collection points for the DSCM monitoring system are set in the white quartz sand layer.

The test procedure is as follows: (1) fill the test model and install the monitoring system; (2) start the DSCM monitoring system; (3) control the volume of the discharged water and close the needle valve when the volume of the discharged water reaches 100 mL (i.e., V_t = 0.66%); (4) monitor the ground deformation for 10 min to ensure that the ground deformation becomes stable; and (5) repeat steps (3) and (4) until the surface settlement does not change or the surface settlement increases abruptly. In addition, after the model test is completed, the four soil samples at different depths are obtained to measure water content. The test results indicate that the water content remains almost constant.

2.3.2. Test Conditions

Two groups of tests are designed to realize the two ground deformation modes, as shown in Table 1. In Group T1, the water content of the sand is 5% while the buried depth of the tunnel crown is 30 cm, 40 cm, or 50 cm, with the corresponding test numbers being T101, T102, and T103, respectively. In Group T2, the water content of the sand is 2% while the buried depth of the tunnel crown is 25 cm or 50 cm, with the corresponding test numbers being T201 and T202, respectively.

Table 1. Test conditions.

Groups	T1			T2	
Test Number	T101	T102	T03	T201	T202
Tunnel crown depth (cm)	30	40	50	25	50
Water content		5%			2%

3. Two Ground Deformation Modes

The arching mode and collapsing mode are observed in Group T1 and Group T2, respectively. The maximum surface settlements, development of the failure surface, and the ground settlement contours are presented to analyze the features of the ground settlement in the two ground deformation modes. Then, the formation mechanism of the two ground deformation modes is analyzed.

3.1. The Maximum Surface Settlement

In T1 and T2 groups of tests, the development of maximum surface settlement $S_{\max}(0)$ is different. For the T1 groups of tests, $S_{\max}(0)$ tends to converge with the increase in V_t, as shown in Figure 8a. The V_t when $S_{\max}(0)$ begins to converge is defined as $V_{t,c}$. When the buried depths are 30 cm, 40 cm, and 50 cm, the corresponding $V_{t,c}$ are 2.63%, 1.97%, and 1.32%, respectively. The value of $V_{t,c}$ decreases with the increase in Z_0. For the T2 groups of tests, $S_{\max}(0)$ increases sharply when V_t reaches a specific value as shown in Figure 8b. The specific value of V_t is defined as $V_{t,s}$. When the buried depths are 25 cm and 50 cm, the corresponding $V_{t,s}$ are 3.29%, and 5.26%, respectively. $V_{t,s}$ is larger in the deep tunnel. The failure surface does not extend to the ground surface when $S_{\max}(0)$ tends to converge with the increase of V_t, so the arching mode will be formed. Conversely, the failure surface extends to the ground surface after $S_{\max}(0)$ sharply increases with the increase of V_t, which represents that the collapsing mode will be formed.

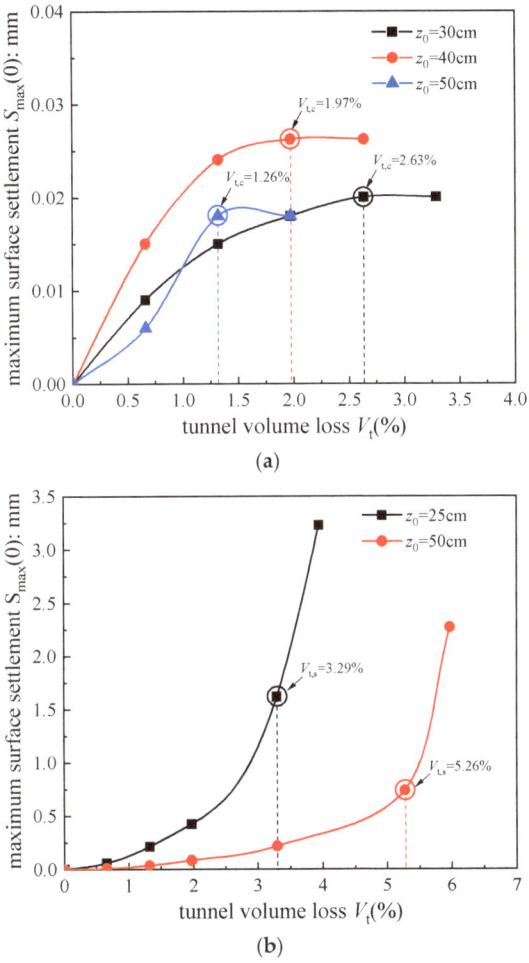

Figure 8. Maximum surface settlement with the tunnel volume loss V_t. (**a**) The arching mode; (**b**) the collapsing mode.

3.2. Development Process of the Failure Surface

The water content of the sand is 5% in Group T1, and the cohesion c is 7.34 kPa. The development process of failure surface is similar in T101, T102, and T103, and therefore, T103 is taken as an example to describe the development process of the failure surface. Figure 9a illustrates that the failure surface cannot be observed when V_t is relatively small. When V_t reaches 2.63%, the failure surface S_1 occurs near the tunnel crown, and the sand between the tunnel crown and S_1 collapses, as shown in Figure 9b. When V_t increases to 4.62%, the failure surface S_2 occurs above S_1, and the sand between S_1 and S_2 collapses as shown in Figure 9c. When V_t reaches 30.66%, the failure surface S_3 occurs, as shown in Figure 9d. After that, additional V_t does not cause new soil failure. When the failure surface does not extend to the ground surface, this condition is defined as the arching mode. As shown in Figure 9, the failure surface is approximately a semi-oval shape. As V_t increases, the lengths of the horizontal axis and the vertical axis gradually increase.

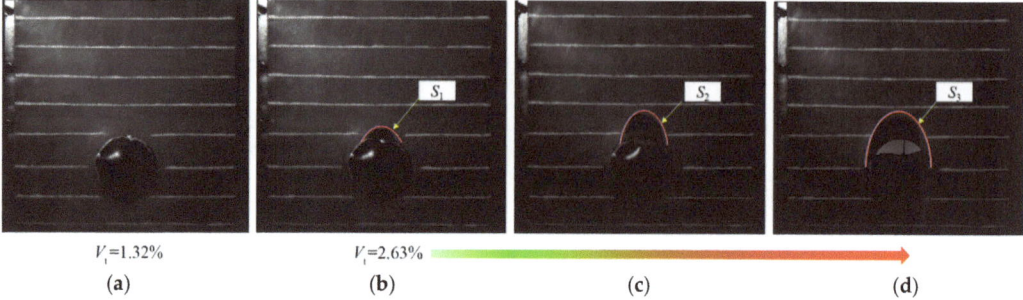

$V_t=1.32\%$
(**a**)

$V_t=2.63\%$
(**b**)

(**c**)

(**d**)

Figure 9. Development of failure surface for the arching mode (T103). (**a**) The failure surface does not occur; (**b**) the failure surface S_1 occurs; (**c**) the failure surface S_2 occurs; (**d**) the failure surface S_3 occurs.

Group T2 includes two test conditions (T201 and T202). The water content of the sand is 2%, and the cohesion c is 1.60 kPa. The development process of the ground deformation is similar in T201 and T202. Thus, T202 is taken as an example to describe the development process of the ground deformation. Obvious ground settlement can be observed even if V_t is relatively small, but the failure surface does not appear. When V_t reaches 5.26%, the failure surface begins to appear near the shoulder of the tunnel, and then the failure surface gradually extends to the ground surface, as shown in Figure 10a. Meanwhile, a sliding block forms between the tunnel crown and the ground surface, and the sliding block moves downward with the increase in V_t, as shown in Figure 10b–d. When the sand between the tunnel crown and the ground surface collapses completely, this condition is defined as the collapsing mode. Figure 10a shows that the failure surface is also approximately a semi-oval-shape, and the similar failure surface was observed by Zheng (2016). As V_t increases, the failure surface gradually evolves into two vertical lines, as shown in Figure 10b–d.

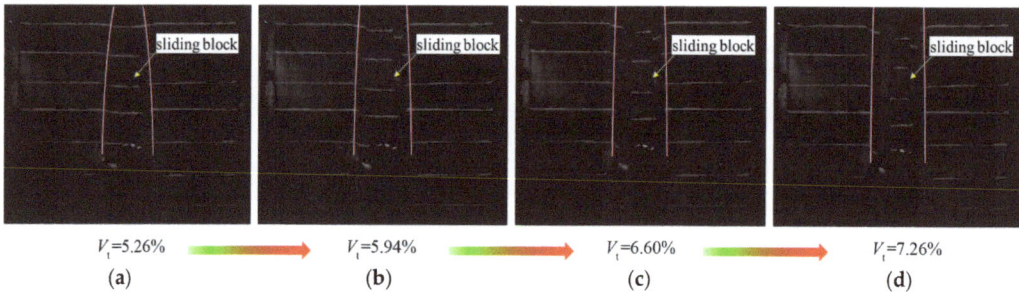

$V_t=5.26\%$
(**a**)

$V_t=5.94\%$
(**b**)

$V_t=6.60\%$
(**c**)

$V_t=7.26\%$
(**d**)

Figure 10. Development of failure surface for the collapsing mode (T202). (**a**) The failure surface extends to the ground surface; (**b**) a sliding block forms; (**c**) the sliding block moves downward when $V_t = 6.60\%$; (**d**) the sliding block moves downward when $V_t = 7.26\%$.

3.3. Ground Settlement Contours

The changing gradient of the ground settlement is larger in the zone that the ground settlement contours distribute densely, which means that the failure surface may occur at the dense zone of the contours. Therefore, distribution of the contours can be used to predict the formation position of the failure surface for the two ground deformation modes. In this study, the contours are obtained by interpolating the measured settlement information, as illustrated in Figure 11 (T103) and Figure 12 (T202). The colors of the contours represent the value of the ground settlement. The settlement differences between two adjacent contours are the same in one figure. Abscissa x represents the horizontal distance from a certain point to the center of the tunnel. Ordinate y represents the vertical distance from a certain point to the center of the tunnel.

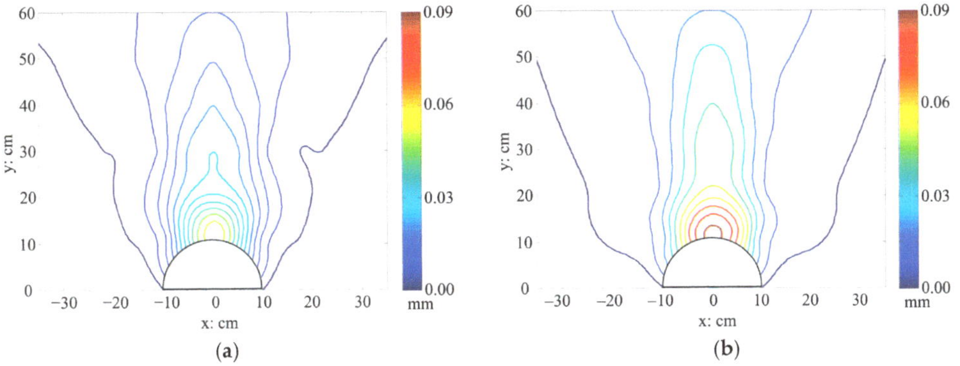

Figure 11. Ground settlement contours before the ground surface settlement becomes stable in the arching mode (T103) (**a**) $V_t = 0.66\%$ (**b**) $V_t = 1.32\%$.

For the arching mode: the surface settlement does not increase when V_t reaches 2.63%, 1.97%, and 1.32% in T101, T102, and T103, respectively. The sand near the tunnel crown does not collapse when the surface settlement begins to become stable. However, contours of the ground settlement, before the ground surface settlement converges, can reflect the position that the failure surface will be formed. In this work, contours of the ground settlement in T103 are presented in Figure 11. To fully present the distribution of displacement in the figure, the range of the legend is from 0 to 0.09 mm because the maximum settlement at the tunnel crown is 0.09 mm when the surface settlement become convergent, i.e., $V_t = 1.32\%$. As shown in Figure 11a, when V_t reaches 0.66%, the contours distribute densely in a zone near the tunnel crown. With the increase in V_t, the range of the dense distribution zone hardly changes, as shown in Figure 11b, indicating that the settlement in the dense distribution zone increases significantly with the increase in V_t, but the settlement outside the dense distribution zone increases minimally. Therefore, the failure surface occurs near the upper boundary of the dense distribution zone. The conclusion can be demonstrated by the comparison of Figures 9d and 11. The position of the failure surface can be determined when the V_t is relatively small for the arching mode.

For the collapsing mode: the maximum surface settlement increases abruptly when V_t reaches 3.29% and 5.26% in T201 and T202, respectively. The failure surface has extended to the ground surface at this moment. For T201 and T202, evolution of the contours of the ground settlement is similar before the ground surface settlement sharply increases. Figure 12 shows the contours of the ground settlement in T202 to analyze the position that the failure surface is formed in the collapsing mode, and the range of the legend is from 0 to 2.80 mm because the maximum settlement at the tunnel crown is 2.80 mm when the collapse extends to the surface, i.e., $V_t = 5.26\%$. The distribution of the contours has significant differences for different values of V_t. As shown in Figure 12a,b, when V_t reaches 0.66% and 1.32%, the contours distribute uniformly in the zone between the tunnel crown and the ground surface. As V_t increases, the contours above the tunnel crown become sparser, as shown in Figure 12c–g. When V_t reaches 5.26%, two vertical bands of the contours occur between the tunnel crown to the ground surface, as shown in Figure 12h. The settlement of the sand inside the two vertical bands is much larger than outside so that the failure surface is formed at the two vertical bands, which can be demonstrated by the comparison between Figures 10a and 12h.

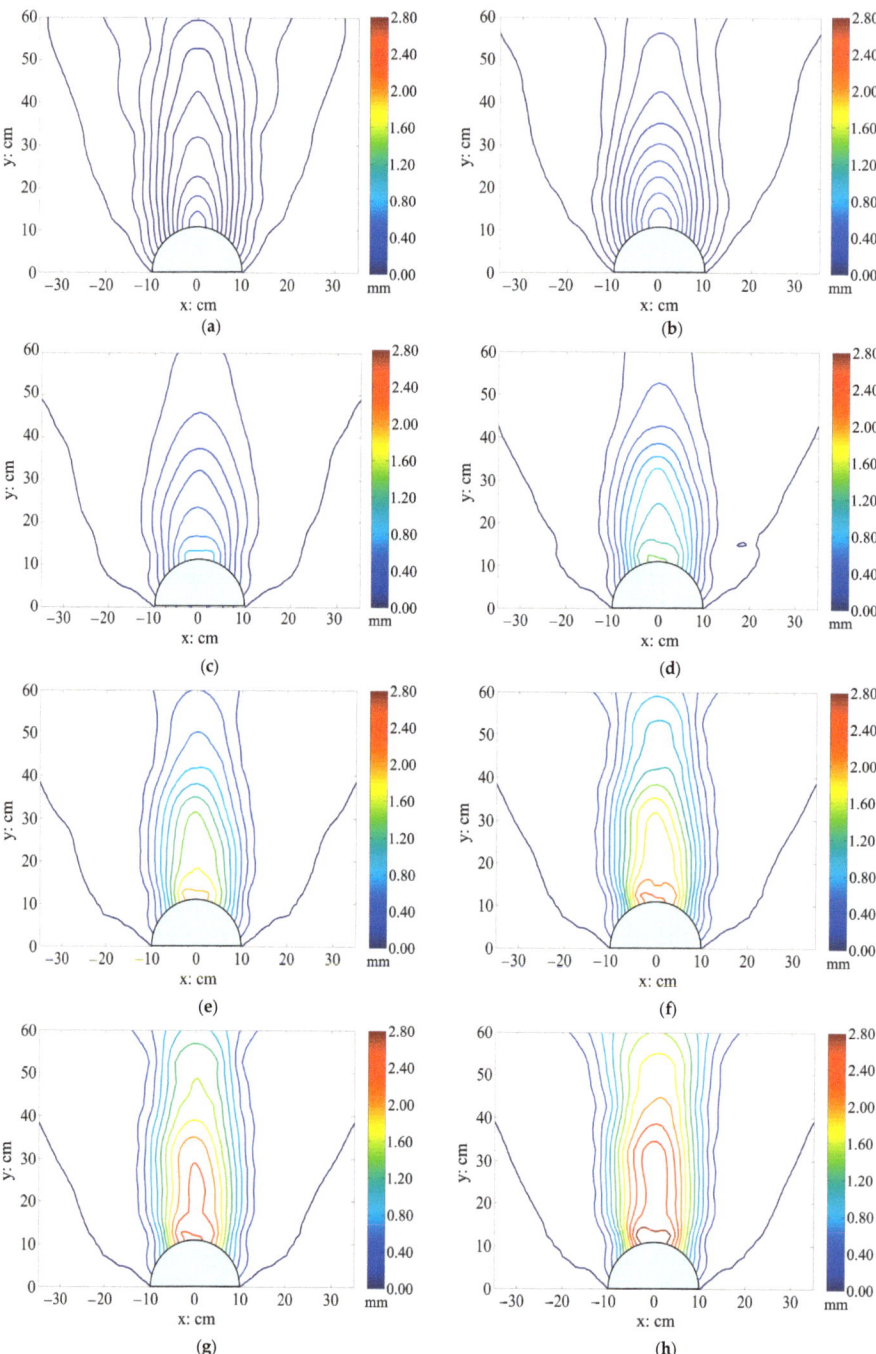

Figure 12. Ground settlement contours before the ground surface settlement increases sharply in collapsing mode (T202); (**a**) $V_t = 0.66\%$; (**b**) $V_t = 1.32\%$; (**c**) $V_t = 1.97\%$ (**d**) $V_t = 2.63\%$ (**e**) $V_t = 3.29\%$ (**f**) $V_t = 3.95\%$ (**g**) $V_t = 4.61\%$ (**h**) $V_t = 5.26\%$.

3.4. Formation Mechanism of the Ground Deformation Mode

Whether the soil above the tunnel crown collapses or not is related to the stress state. As shown in Figure 13a, curve S_1 represents a failure surface before a stable ground deformation mode was formed; soil elements A and B lie on S_1. The length and width of the soil element is dx and dz, respectively. Force balance conditions of soil elements A and B are shown in Figure 13b. The weight of the soil element is larger than the upper resultant of other forces because soil elements A and B tend to collapse, as shown in the equation below:

$$\begin{cases} G_A > c \cdot (dx + 2dz) + 2F_{A1} \cdot \tan \varphi \\ G_B > c \cdot (\sin \alpha_B dx + 2 \cos \alpha_B dz) + 2F_{B1} \cdot (\cos \alpha_B + \sin \alpha_B \tan \varphi) + 2F_{B2} \cdot (\sin \alpha_B + \cos \alpha_B \tan \varphi) \end{cases} \quad (4)$$

where G_A and G_B, respectively, represent the weight of soil elements A and B; F and f, respectively, represent the normal and tangential force acting on the soil element; α is the inclination angle of the soil element. The new failure surface S_2 will be formed above S_1. Soil elements C and D lie on S_2. If the forced state of the soil elements C and D reaches balance as shown in the Equation (5), the soil element above S_2 will not collapse, which means that the arching mode is formed. In contrast, the failure surface will extend upwards. If the failure surface (S_3) is tangent to the ground surface and the force state of the soil elements E and F does not reach balance, as shown in the Equation (6), the soil will collapse completely, which means the collapsing mode is formed.

$$\begin{cases} G_C = c \cdot (dx + 2dz) + 2F_{C1} \cdot \tan \varphi \\ G_D = c \cdot (\sin \alpha_D dx + 2 \cos \alpha_D dz) + 2F_{D1} \cdot (\cos \alpha_D + \sin \alpha_D \tan \varphi) + 2F_{D2} \cdot (\sin \alpha_D + \cos \alpha_D \tan \varphi) \end{cases} \quad (5)$$

$$\begin{cases} G_E > c \cdot (dx + 2dz) + 2F_{E1} \cdot \tan \varphi \\ G_F > c \cdot (\sin \alpha_F dx + 2 \cos \alpha_F dz) + 2F_{F1} \cdot (\cos \alpha_F + \sin \alpha_F \tan \varphi) + 2F_{F2} \cdot (\sin \alpha_F + \cos \alpha_F \tan \varphi) \end{cases} \quad (6)$$

where G_C, G_D, G_E, G_F represent the weight of soil elements A~F.

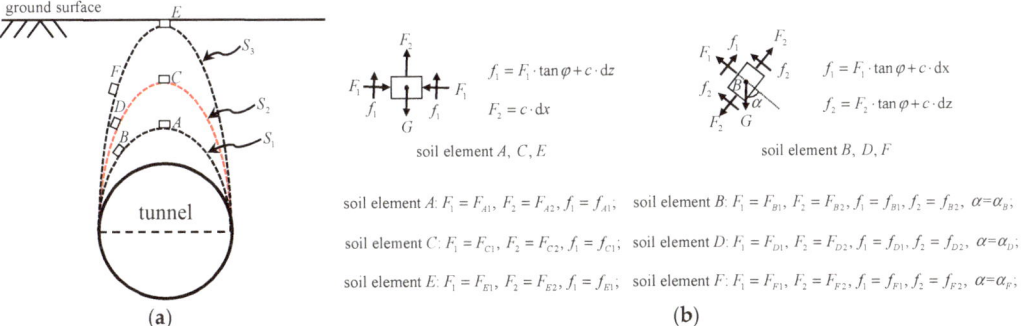

Figure 13. Formation mechanism schematic of the ground deformation mode. (**a**) Schematic diagram for collapse mechanism of the soil; (**b**) Schematic diagram for the force acting on the soil element.

As shown in Equations (4)–(6), both cohesion and internal friction angle affect the formation of the ground deformation mode. Cohesion can resist the tensile stress caused by the weight of the soil above the tunnel crown. The large internal friction angle and cohesion contribute to the formation of the arching mode. The water contents of the sand are 5% and 2% in Group T1 and Group T2, respectively. According to the analysis in Section 2.2, cohesion of the sand in Group T1 is larger than Group T2, and the internal friction angle of Group T1 and Group T2 is almost the same. Therefore, higher cohesion is the main reason that caused the arching mode in Group T1.

4. Surface and Subsurface Settlements

The surface and subsurface settlement troughs are always the focus of research in tunnelling engineering [11,20–23]. The measured surface and subsurface settlements, before the surface settlement no longer increases for the arching mode and the surface settlement sharply increases for the collapsing mode, are shown in Figures 14 and 15, respectively, to analyze the feature of ground settlement during the formation process of the two deformation modes.

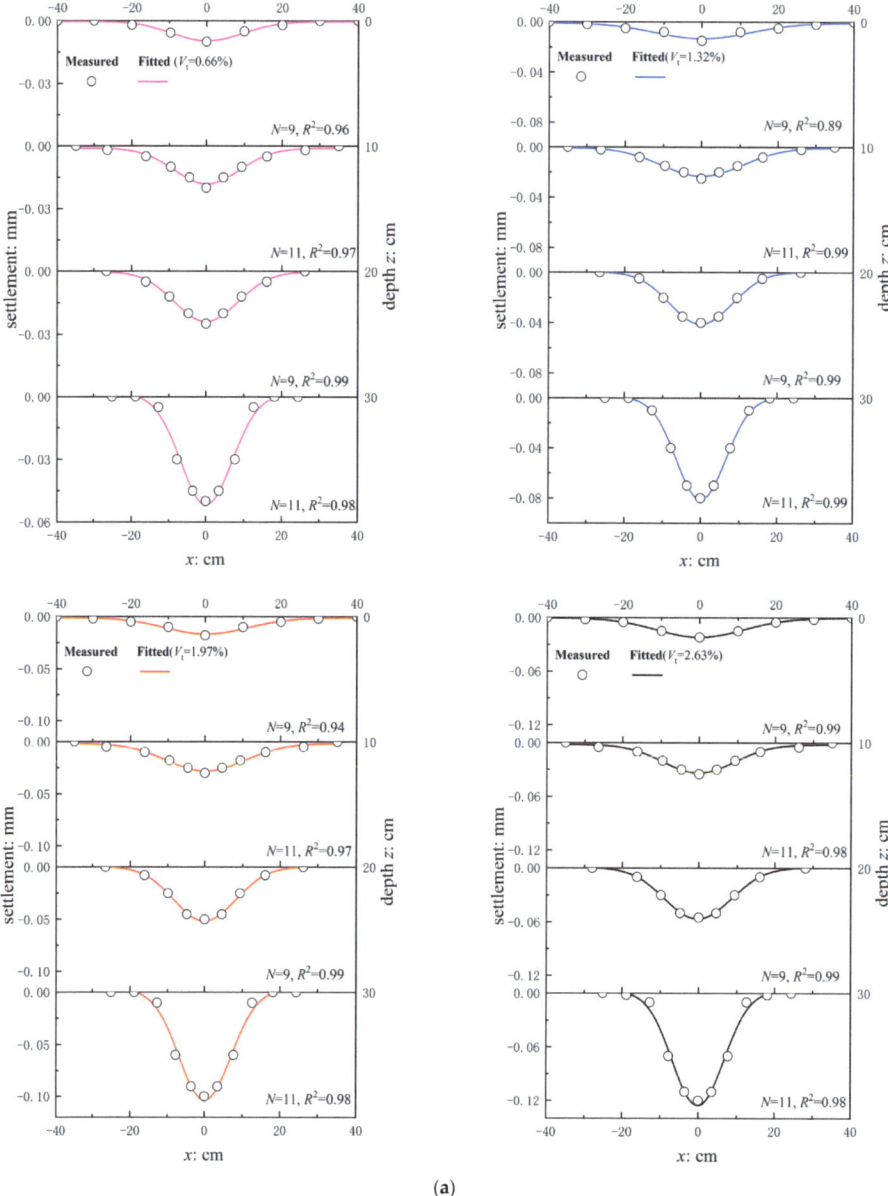

(a)

Figure 14. *Cont.*

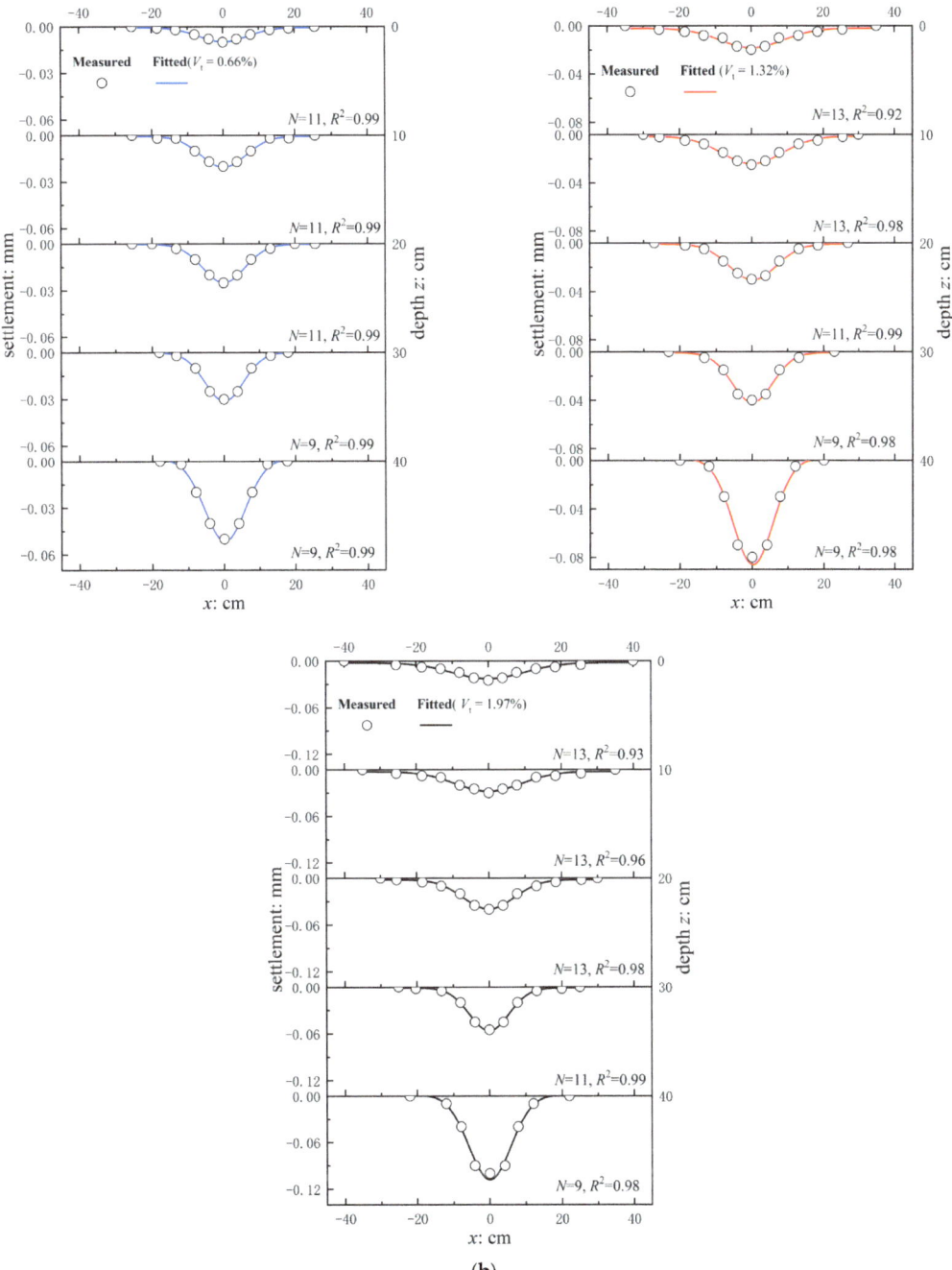

Figure 14. *Cont.*

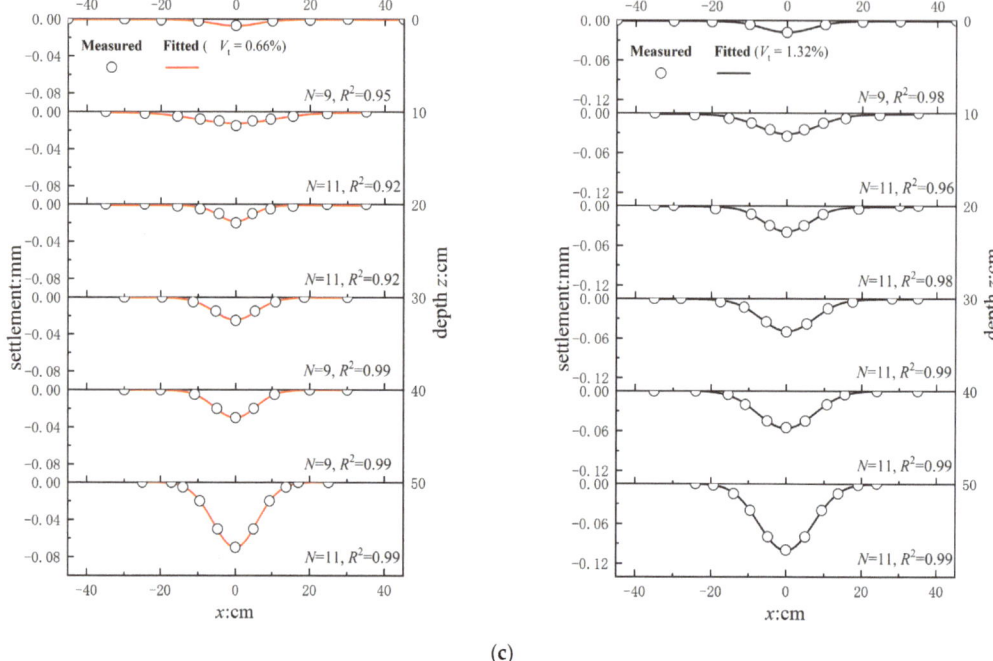

Figure 14. Surface and subsurface settlement troughs in Group T1; (**a**) T101 (**b**) T102 (**c**) T103.

For the arching mode: as shown in Figure 14, the ground settlement of T101, T102, and T103 is similar. Taking T101 as an example, all the ground settlement troughs are approximately the Gaussian curves. For a given V_t, the width of the settlement trough decreases with the increase in the depth, and the settlement increases with the increase of the depth in the same vertical line. When the depth is same, both the width of the settlement trough and the settlement of a point increase with the increase in V_t. The maximum settlement appears in the tunnel crown. In addition, the maximum settlement gradually decreases as the depth of the tunnel increases. For the collapsing mode: as shown in Figure 15, the ground settlement of T201 and T202 is similar. Taking T201 as an example, the ground settlement troughs are also approximately the Gaussian curves when V_t is less than 1.97%, but the ground settlement troughs at different depths become plug-type when V_t reaches 3.29%. In addition, the width of the settlement trough hardly changes with the depth when V_t is fixed.

Existing studies indicate that, in a transverse tunnel section, the surface and subsurface settlement trough can be formulated by the Gaussian function as follows [25]:

$$S(x,z) = S_{\max}(z) \exp\left[-\frac{x^2}{2i(z)^2}\right] \tag{7}$$

where x is the horizontal distance from the vertical tunnel centerline; $S_{\max}(z)$ is the maximum settlement at depth z; and $i(z)$ is the distance from the vertical tunnel centerline to the inflection point of the Gaussian curve at depth z. To analyze the ability of Gaussian function to describe the settlement trough under two deformation modes, Equation (7) is used to fit the data points, as illustrated in Figures 14 and 15. Coefficients of determination (R^2) between the measured settlement troughs and the fitting Gaussian curves are presented in Figure 16. There is only one value of R^2 less than 0.9 in two groups of tests, and most of the data are greater than 0.94. It is indicated that Gaussian curves can well describe the surface and subsurface settlement troughs even before the two deformation modes are formed.

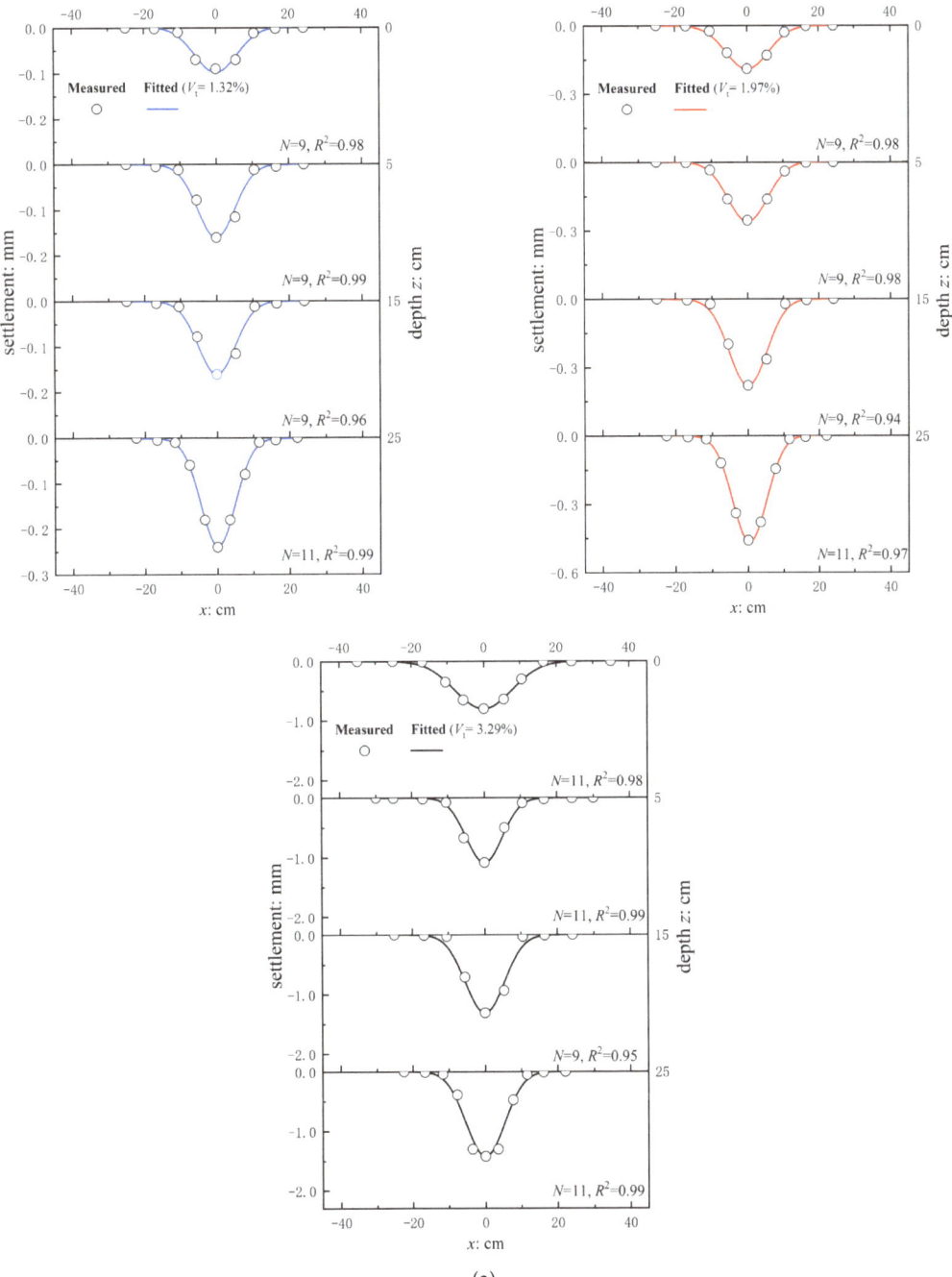

Figure 15. *Cont.*

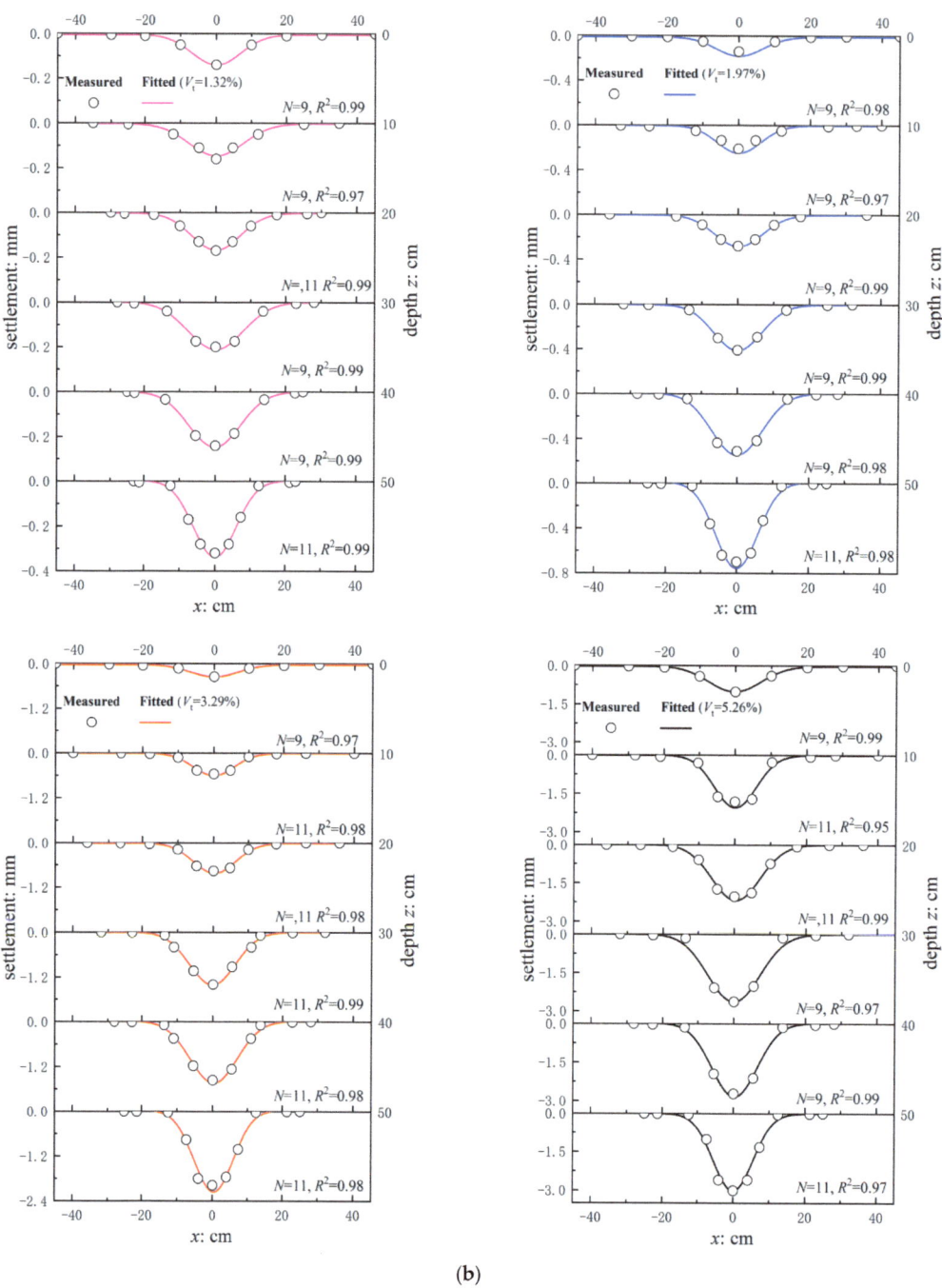

Figure 15. Surface and subsurface settlement troughs in Group T2; (**a**) T201 (**b**) T202.

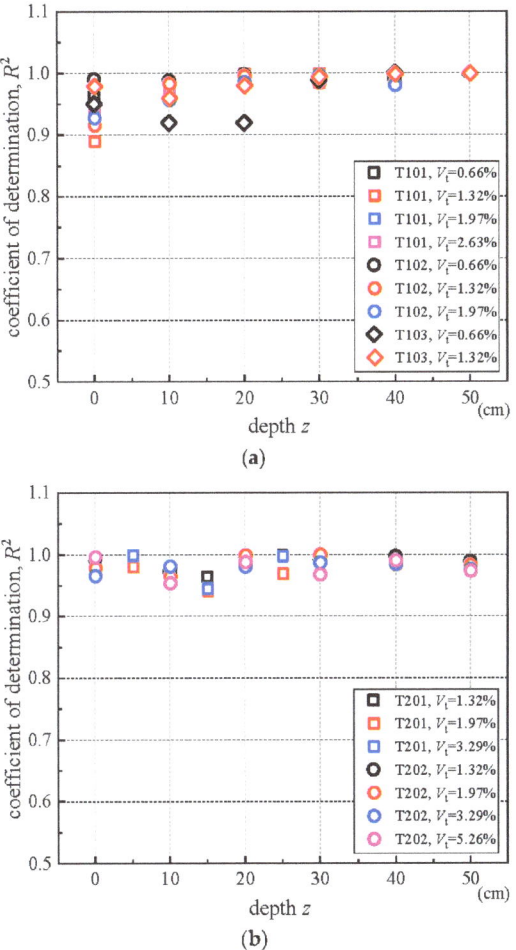

Figure 16. Coefficients of determination between the fitting Gaussian curve and measured results. (**a**) The arching mode; (**b**) the collapsing mode.

4.1. Settlement trough Width Coefficient i(z)

The settlement trough width coefficient $i(z)$ is determined based on the Gaussian curves in Figures 14 and 15. Distribution characteristics of $i(z)$ can be analyzed based on these data. Peck (1969) studied the effect of tunnel crown depth on the surface settlement trough width coefficient, and provided three empirical curves of $2i(0)/D$ against z_0/D that correspond to "rock, hard clays, sands above ground water level", "soft to stiff clays", and "sands below ground level", respectively.

Based on our tests, the settlement trough width coefficient of both surface and subsurface settlement is arranged and compared with Peck's curves, as shown in Figure 17. Note that curves corresponding to different depth form a surface that is parallel to the z/z_0 axis. Figure 17 shows that the test data at the ground surface (i.e., $2i(0)/D$ against z_0/D) is around the curve of "sands above ground water" because this condition agrees with the fact of our test. Meanwhile, the comparison demonstrates that the test data at subsurface is also in accordance with this curve. It can be concluded that z/z_0 does not affect the distribution rule of $2i(z)/D$ against z_0/D.

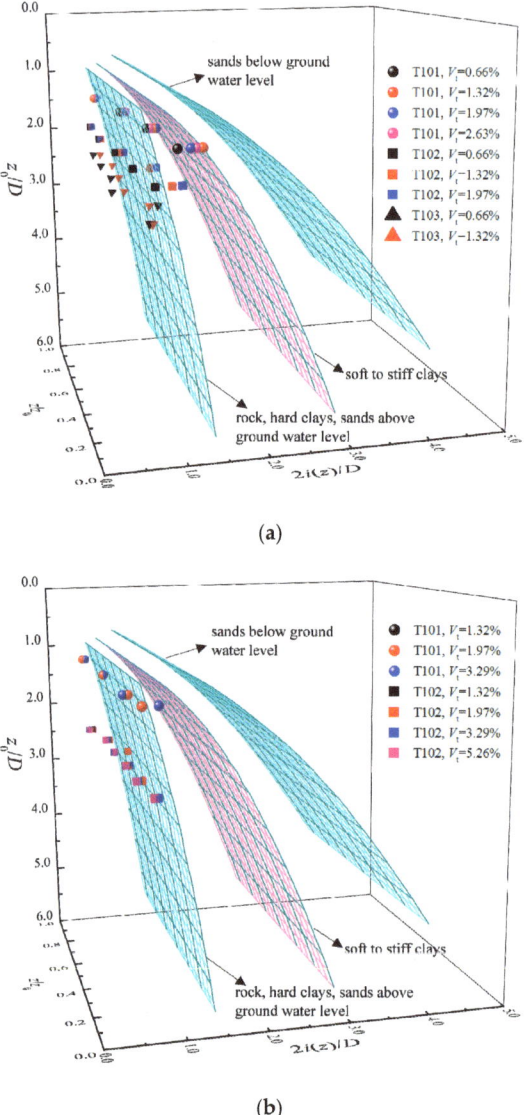

Figure 17. Change rule of *i*(*z*) against tunnel crown depth z_0. (**a**) The arching mode. (**b**) The collapsing mode.

Previous research indicates that *i*(*z*) can be expressed as [23]

$$i(z) = K(z_0 - z) \tag{8}$$

where z_0 is the tunnel crown depth, and *K* is the trough width parameter. The value of *i*(*z*) can be estimated when *K* is determined. Marshall et al. (2012) pointed out that *K* can be described by [11]

$$K = \frac{i(0) + \partial i(z)/\partial z \cdot (z/z_0)}{1 - z/z_0} \tag{9}$$

where $i(0)$ is the value of K at the ground surface, and $\partial i(z)/\partial z$ is the slope of $i(z)$. Mair et al. (1993) [23] found that $\partial i(z)/\partial z = -0.325$ and $i(0) = 0.5$ for clays. The results of K for all measured settlement troughs are plotted in Figure 18, and Equation (9) is used to fit these data to determine to values of $\partial i(z)/\partial z$ and $i(0)$ corresponding to Groups T1 and T2. It can be seen that $\partial i(z)/\partial z = -0.01$ is suitable for both Group T1 and Group T2, but the value of $i(0)$ is 0.24 for Group T1 and 0.27 for Group T2. Meanwhile, coefficients of determination (R^2) between the fitting curve of Equation (9) and measured results, calculated by Equation (3), are 0.96 and 0.97 for Groups T1 and T2, respectively. It can be concluded that Equation (9) can reasonably describe variation of K with depth for both the arching mode and the collapsing mode. In addition, variation of K with depth in clay is presented as the black dash curve in Figure 18, indicating that the value $\partial i(z)/\partial z$ and $i(0)$ in sandy stratum is different from that in the clay stratum. It can be concluded that variation of K with depth is greatly affected by the type of the soil.

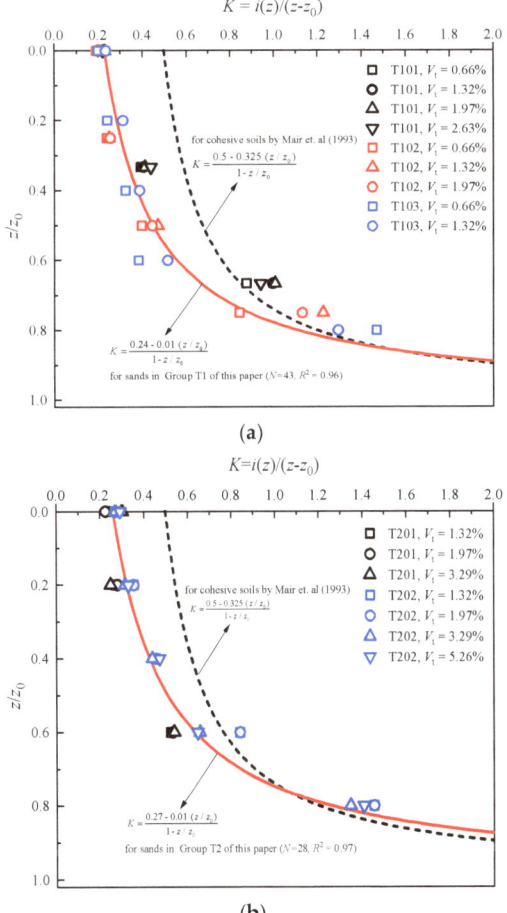

Figure 18. Change rule of K against depth. (**a**) The arching mode; (**b**) the collapsing mode [23].

4.2. Ground Volume Loss $V_s(z)$

$V_s(z)$ is the ground volume loss at depth z and is calculated as the area of the settlement trough. Peck (1969) [22] assumes that $V_s(z)$ is constant during the tunnel excavation process, which means that the area of the settlement trough is independent of depth z.

This assumption is only applicable to clay in the undrained condition. However, some test data show that $V_s(z)$ for sand varies with depth z [11,19], which is consistent with our test results. Figure 19 shows the change of $V_s(z)/Vs(z_0)$ against z/z_0 when the arching mode and the collapsing mode are formed, which illustrates that $V_s(z)$ gradually decreases from tunnel crown to ground surface in two modes. For the arching mode, the change in $V_s(z)$ is similar in T101, T102, and T103. $V_s(z)$ is rapidly reduced from the tunnel crown to the ground surface, especially in the zone between the tunnel crown and the 0.8 z_0. For the collapsing mode, $V_s(z)/V_s(z_0)$ is relatively large, which means the volume loss at different depths approaches that of the tunnel crown, i.e., the sliding block moves downward as a whole. In addition, the value of $V_s(z_0)$ is not equal to V_t, which results from three reasons: the horizontal displacement is also induced by V_t around the model tunnel; dilatation occurs in the sand near the tunnel crown; the soil arching effect appears in the sand above the tunnel crown.

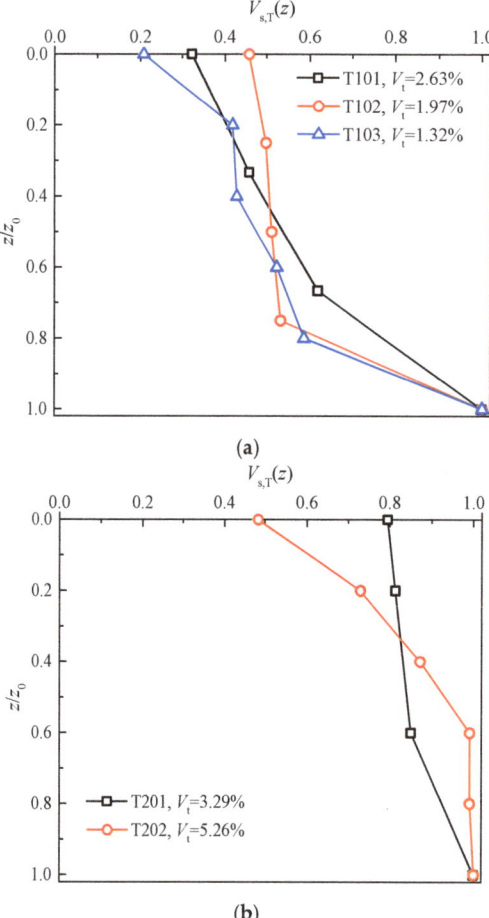

Figure 19. The change rule of $V_{s/T}(z)$ against depth z/z_0. (**a**) The arching mode; (**b**) the collapsing mode.

5. Conclusions

Two groups of tests are conducted through a newly designed test facility. The arching mode is formed in Group T1, in which the cohesion is 7.34 kPa. The collapsing mode is where $i(0)$ is the value of K at the ground surface, and $\partial i(z)/\partial z$ is the slope of $i(z)$. Mair et al. (1993) [23] found that $\partial i(z)/\partial z = -0.325$ and $i(0) = 0.5$ for clays. The results of K for all measured settlement troughs are plotted in Figure 18, and Equation (9) is used to fit these data to determine to values of $\partial i(z)/\partial z$ and $i(0)$ corresponding to Groups T1 and T2. It can be seen that $\partial i(z)/\partial z = -0.01$ is suitable for both Group T1 and Group T2, but the value of $i(0)$ is 0.24 for Group T1 and 0.27 for Group T2. Meanwhile, coefficients of determination (R^2) between the fitting curve of Equation (9) and measured results, calculated by Equation (3), are 0.96 and 0.97 for Groups T1 and T2, respectively. It can be concluded that Equation (9) can reasonably describe variation of K with depth for both the arching mode and the collapsing mode. In addition, variation of K with depth in clay is presented as the black dash curve in Figure 18, indicating that the value $\partial i(z)/\partial z$ and $i(0)$ in sandy stratum is different from that in the clay stratum. It can be concluded that variation of K with depth is greatly affected by the type of the soil.

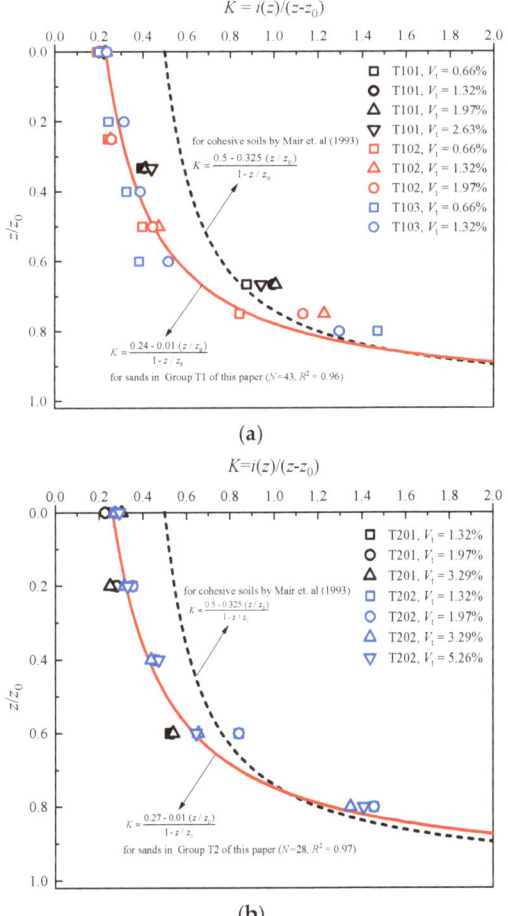

Figure 18. Change rule of K against depth. (**a**) The arching mode; (**b**) the collapsing mode [23].

4.2. Ground Volume Loss $V_s(z)$

$V_s(z)$ is the ground volume loss at depth z and is calculated as the area of the settlement trough. Peck (1969) [22] assumes that $V_s(z)$ is constant during the tunnel excavation process, which means that the area of the settlement trough is independent of depth z.

This assumption is only applicable to clay in the undrained condition. However, some test data show that $V_s(z)$ for sand varies with depth z [11,19], which is consistent with our test results. Figure 19 shows the change of $V_s(z)/Vs(z_0)$ against z/z_0 when the arching mode and the collapsing mode are formed, which illustrates that $V_s(z)$ gradually decreases from tunnel crown to ground surface in two modes. For the arching mode, the change in $V_s(z)$ is similar in T101, T102, and T103. $V_s(z)$ is rapidly reduced from the tunnel crown to the ground surface, especially in the zone between the tunnel crown and the 0.8 z_0. For the collapsing mode, $V_s(z)/V_s(z_0)$ is relatively large, which means the volume loss at different depths approaches that of the tunnel crown, i.e., the sliding block moves downward as a whole. In addition, the value of $V_s(z_0)$ is not equal to V_t, which results from three reasons: the horizontal displacement is also induced by V_t around the model tunnel; dilatation occurs in the sand near the tunnel crown; the soil arching effect appears in the sand above the tunnel crown.

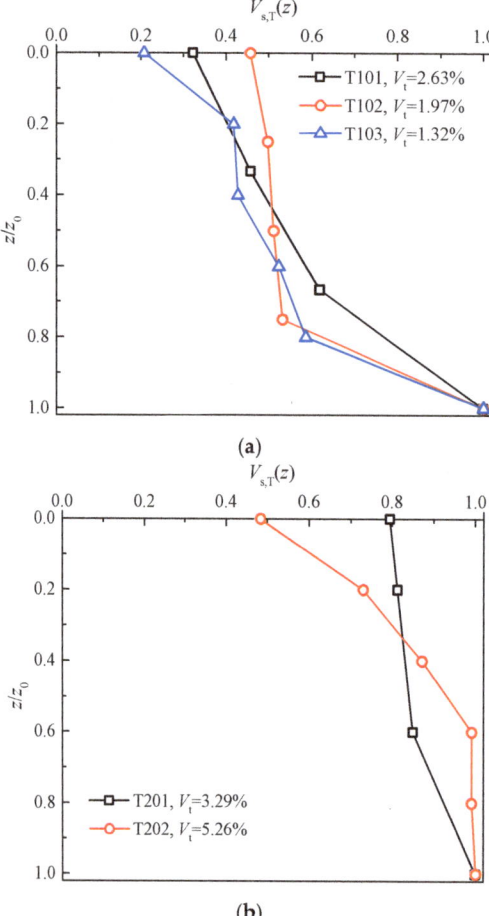

Figure 19. The change rule of $V_{s,T}(z)$ against depth z/z_0. (**a**) The arching mode; (**b**) the collapsing mode.

5. Conclusions

Two groups of tests are conducted through a newly designed test facility. The arching mode is formed in Group T1, in which the cohesion is 7.34 kPa. The collapsing mode is formed in Group T2, in which the cohesion is 1.60 kPa. Characteristics of the two ground deformation modes are studied. The conclusions are as follows:

Before the failure surface occurs, as V_t increases, the maximum surface settlements become convergent in the arching mode and is divergent in the collapsing mode. Development tendency of the maximum surface settlement as V_t increases can be used to predict the two ground deformation modes. Contours of the ground settlement distribute densely in a limited zone above the tunnel crown in the arching mode, but two dense vertical bands of the contours gradually appear between the tunnel crown and the ground surface in the collapsing mode. In the two ground deformation modes, the failure surface occurs at the position where the ground settlement contours distribute densely. For both the arching mode and the collapsing mode, Gaussian curves can reasonably describe the ground settlement troughs before the ground surface settlement becomes stable or increases sharply, and distribution of the trough width parameter is similar. The manuscript only provides the ground deformation under two cohesive forces. More experimental conditions and numerical simulations will be carried out in future works to investigate the influence of cohesion on the ground deformation mode and the corresponding deformation.

Author Contributions: Methodology, Q.L. and F.K.; Validation, X.M. and H.D.; Data curation, C.G. and X.M.; Writing—review & editing, Q.L. and C.G. All authors have read and agreed to the published version of the manuscript.

Funding: This research was funded by National Natural Science Foundation of China (Grant No. 52208396, 52278385), Postdoctoral Science Foundation of China (Grant No. 2021M701934), and Beijing Municipal Education Commission (Grant No. KM202210005019).

Data Availability Statement: Data sharing not applicable.

Conflicts of Interest: The authors declare no conflict of interest.

Abbreviations

c	cohesion strength
D	tunnel diameter and water bag diameter
e_0	initial void ratio
$i(z)$	settlement trough width coefficient
K	trough width parameter
L	water bag length
M_f	peak failure stress ratio
$S_{max}(0)$	maximum settlement of ground surface
$S_{max}(z)$	maximum settlement at a depth of z
V_s	ground volume loss
V_t	tunnel volume loss
$V_{t,c}$	tunnel volume loss when the surface settlement begins to converge
$V_{t,s}$	tunnel volume loss when the surface settlement begins to increase sharply
V_w	volume of water bag
V_{wd}	volume of discharged water
z_0	depth of the buried tunnel crown
z	depth of one point in the model
λ	slope of the isotropic compression curve
κ	slope of the isotropic swelling curve
w	water content
φ	internal friction angle

References

1. Chen, R.P.; Tang, L.J.; Ling, D.S. Face stability analysis of shallow shield tunnels in dry sandy ground using the discrete element method. *Comput. Geotech.* **2011**, *38*, 187–195. [CrossRef]
2. Chen, R.P.; Tang, L.J.; Yin, X.S.; Chen, Y.M.; Bian, X.C. An improved 3D wedge-prism model for the face stability analysis of the shield tunnel in cohesionless soils. *Acta Geotech.* **2015**, *10*, 683–692. [CrossRef]

3. Rui, R.; Tol, F.V.; Xia XLEekelen, S.V.; Hu, G.; Xia, Y.Y. Evolution of soil arching; 2D DEM simulations. *Comput. Geotech.* **2016**, *73*, 199–209. [CrossRef]
4. Dewoolkar, M.M.; Santichaianant, K.; Ko, H.Y. Centrifuge modeling of granular soil response over active circular trapdoors. *Soils Found.* **2007**, *47*, 931–945. [CrossRef]
5. Chevalier, B.; Combe, G.; Villard, P. Experimental and discrete element modeling studies of the trapdoor problem: Influence of the macro-mechanical frictional parameters. *Acta Geotech.* **2012**, *7*, 15–39. [CrossRef]
6. Lu, D.C.; Dong, H.Y.; Lin, Q.T.; Guo, C.X.; Gao, Z.W.; Du, X.L. A method for characterizing the deformation localization in granular materials using the relative particle motion. *Comput. Geotech.* **2023**, *156*, 105262. [CrossRef]
7. Shahin, H.M.; Nakai, T.; Ishii, K.; Iwata, T.; Kuroi, S. Investigation of influence of tunneling on existing building and tunnel: Model tests and numerical simulations. *Acta Geotech.* **2016**, *11*, 679–692. [CrossRef]
8. Ritter, S.; Giardina, G.; DeJong, M.J.; Mair, R.J. Centrifuge modelling of building response to tunnel excavation. *Int. J. Phys. Model. Geotech.* **2018**, *18*, 146–161. [CrossRef]
9. Lin, Q.T.; Lu, D.C.; Lei, C.M.; Tian, Y.; Kong, F.C.; Du, X.L. Mechanical response of existing tunnels for shield under-crossing in cobble strata based on the model test. *Tunn. Undergr. Space Technol.* **2022**, *125*, 104505. [CrossRef]
10. Nakai, T.; Xu, L.; Yamazaki, H. 3D and 2D model tests and numerical analyses of settlements and earth pressures due to tunnel excavation. *Soils Found.* **1997**, *37*, 31–42. [CrossRef]
11. Marshall, A.M.; Farrell, R.; Klar, A.; Mair, R. Tunnels in sands: The effect of size, depth and volume loss on greenfield displacements. *Géotechnique* **2012**, *62*, 385–399. [CrossRef]
12. Lin, Q.T.; Lu, D.C.; Lei, C.M.; Tian, Y.; Gong, Q.M.; Du, X.L. Model test study on the stability of cobble strata during shield under-crossing. *Tunn. Undergr. Space Technol.* **2021**, *110*, 103807. [CrossRef]
13. Miao, J.; Lu, D.; Lin, Q.; Kong, F.; Du, X. Time-dependent surrounding soil pressure and mechanical response of tunnel lining induced by surrounding soil viscosity. *Sci. China Technol. Sci.* **2021**, *64*, 2453–2468. [CrossRef]
14. Zhang, J.Z.; Phoon, K.K.; Zhang, D.M.; Huang, H.W.; Tang, C. Novel approach to estimate vertical scale of fluctuation based on CPT data using convolutional neural networks. *Eng. Geol.* **2021**, *294*, 106342. [CrossRef]
15. Zhang, J.Z.; Huang, H.W.; Zhang, D.M.; Phoon, K.K.; Liu, Z.Q.; Tang, C. Quantitative evaluation of geological uncertainty and its influence on tunnel structural performance using improved coupled Markov chain. *Acta Geotech.* **2021**, *16*, 3709–3724. [CrossRef]
16. Lu, D.C.; Ma, Y.D.; Kong, F.C.; Guo, C.X.; Miao, J.B.; Du, X.L. Support vector regression with heuristic optimization algorithms for predicting the ground surface displacement induced by EPB shield tunnelling. *Gondwana Res.* **2022**. [CrossRef]
17. Kong, F.C.; Lu, D.C.; Ma, Y.D.; Li, J.L.; Tian, T. Analysis and intelligent prediction for displacement of stratum and tunnel lining by shield tunnel excavation in complex geological conditions: A case study. *IEEE Trans. Intell. Transp. Syst.* **2022**, *23*, 22206–22216. [CrossRef]
18. Kong, F.C.; Lu, D.C.; Ma, Y.C.D.; Tian, T.; Yu, H.T.; Du, X.L. Novel hybrid method to predict the ground-displacement field caused by shallow tunnel excavation. *Sci. China-Technol. Sci.* **2023**, *66*, 101–114. [CrossRef]
19. Wang, F.; Miao, L.C.; Yang, X.M.; Du, Y.J.; Liang, F.Y. The Volume of Settlement Trough Change with Depth Caused by Tunneling in Sands. *J. Civ. Eng. KSCE* **2016**, *20*, 2719–2724. [CrossRef]
20. Zheng, G.; Dai, X.; Diao, Y.; Zeng, C.F. Experimental and simplified model study of the development of ground settlement under hazards induced by loss of groundwater and sand. *Nat. Hazards* **2016**, *82*, 1869–1893. [CrossRef]
21. Zhou, M.; Wang, F.; Du, Y.J.; Liu, M.D. Laboratory evaluation of buried high-density polyethylene pipes subjected to localized ground subsidence. *Acta Geotech.* **2019**, *14*, 1081–1099. [CrossRef]
22. Peck, R.B. Deep excavations and tunnelling in soft ground. In Proceedings of the 7th International Conference on Soil Mechanics and Foundation Engineering, State of the Art Volume, Mexico City, Mexico, 1969; pp. 225–290.
23. Mair, R.J.; Taylor, R.N.; Bracegirdle, A. Subsurface settlement profiles above tunnels in clays. *Géotechnique* **1993**, *43*, 315–320. [CrossRef]
24. Lu, D.; Kong, F.; Du, X.; Shen, C.; Gong, Q.; Li, P. A unified displacement function to analytically predict ground deformation of shallow tunnel. *Tunn. Undergr. Space Technol.* **2019**, *88*, 129–143. [CrossRef]
25. Lu, D.C.; Lin, Q.T.; Tian, Y.; Du, X.L.; Gong, Q.M. Formula for predicting ground settlement induced by tunnelling based on Gaussian function. *Tunn. Undergr. Space Technol.* **2020**, *103*, 103443. [CrossRef]
26. Lin, Q.T.; Tian, Y.; Lu, D.C.; Gong, Q.M.; Du, X.L.; Gao, Z.W. A prediction method of ground volume loss variation with depth induced by tunnel excavation. *Acta Geotech.* **2021**, *16*, 3689–3707. [CrossRef]
27. Celestino, T.B.; Gomes, R.A.M.P.; Bortolucci, A.A. Errors in ground distortions due to settlement trough adjustment. *Tunn. Undergr. Space Technol.* **2000**, *15*, 97–100. [CrossRef]
28. Grant, R.J.; Taylor, R.N. Tunnelling-induced ground movements in clay. *ICE Proc. Geotech. Eng.* **2000**, *143*, 43–55. [CrossRef]
29. Huang, Z.K.; Zhang, D.M.; Pitilakis, K.; Tsinidis, G.; Huang, H.W.; Zhang, D.M.; Argyroudis, S. Resilience assessment of tunnels: Framework and application for tunnels in alluvial deposits exposed to seismic hazard. *Soil Dyn. Earthq. Eng.* **2022**, *162*, 107456. [CrossRef]
30. Li, Y.J.; Zhang, D.L.; Fang, Q.; Yu, Q.C.; Xia, L. A physical and numerical investigation of the failure mechanism of weak rocks surrounding tunnels. *Comput. Geotech.* **2014**, *61*, 292–307. [CrossRef]
31. Escario, V.; Juca, F.T. Strength and deformation partly saturated soils. In Proceedings of the 12th International Conference of Soil Mechanics and Foundation Engineering, Rio de Janeiro, Brazil, 13–18 August 1989; pp. 43–46.

32. Lu, N.; Wu, B.; Tan, C.P. Tensile strength characteristics of unsaturated sands. Journal of Geotechnical and Geoenvironmental Engineering. *ASCE* **2007**, *133*, 144–154.
33. Kim, T.H.; Sture, S. Capillary-induced tensile strength in unsaturated sands. *Can. Geotech. J.* **2008**, *45*, 726–737. [CrossRef]
34. Escario, V.; Sàez, J. The shear strength of partly saturated soils. *Géotechnique* **1986**, *3*, 453–456. [CrossRef]
35. Karube, D. New concept of effective stress in unsaturated soil and its proving test. In *Advanced Triaxial Testing of Soil and Rock*; American Society for Testing and Materials: Philadelphia, PA, USA, 1988; pp. 539–552.
36. Drumright, E.E. The Contribution of Matric Suction to the Shear Strength of Unsaturated Soils. Ph.D. Thesis, Colorado State University, Fort Collins, CO, USA, 1989.
37. Lin, Q.T.; Zhu, J.M.; Kang, Y. Active spatial earth pressure behind retaining wall considering arching effects of soil. *Chin. J. Rock Mech. Eng.* **2015**, *34*, 1918–1927.
38. Zhu, J.M.; Lin, Q.T.; Gao, X.J.; Gao, L.S. Research on space earth pressure behind retaining wall adjacent to existing basements exterior wall. *Rock Soil Mech.* **2016**, *37*, 3417–3426.

Disclaimer/Publisher's Note: The statements, opinions and data contained in all publications are solely those of the individual author(s) and contributor(s) and not of MDPI and/or the editor(s). MDPI and/or the editor(s) disclaim responsibility for any injury to people or property resulting from any ideas, methods, instructions or products referred to in the content.

Article

Study on the Reinforcement Mechanism of High-Energy-Level Dynamic Compaction Based on FDM–DEM Coupling

Yiwei Sun [1,2], Kan Huang [1,3,*], Xiangsheng Chen [1,*], Dongmei Zhang [4], Xiaoming Lou [2], Zhongkai Huang [4], Kaihang Han [1] and Qijiang Wu [3]

[1] College of Civil and Transportation Engineering, Shenzhen University, Shenzhen 518060, China; sunyiwei@geoharbour.com (Y.S.); hankaihang@szu.edu.cn (K.H.)
[2] Shanghai Geoharbour Construction Group Co., Ltd., Shanghai 200434, China; louxiaoming@geoharbour.com
[3] School of Civil Engineering, Changsha University of Science & Technology, Changsha 410114, China
[4] Key Laboratory of Geotechnical and Underground Engineering of Ministry of Education, Department of Geotechnical Engineering, Tongji University, Shanghai 200092, China; dmzhang@tongji.edu.cn (D.Z.); 5huangzhongkai@tongji.edu.cn (Z.H.)
* Correspondence: hk_616@csust.edu.cn (K.H.); xschen@szu.edu.cn (X.C.)

Abstract: The high-energy-level dynamic compaction method is widely used in various foundation treatment projects, but its reinforcement mechanism still lags behind the practice. In view of this, a three-dimensional fluid–solid coupling dynamic analysis model was established on the basis of the FDM–DEM coupling method. The variation trends of crater depth, soil void ratio, vertical additional dynamic stress, and pore water pressure during the process of dynamic compaction were analyzed. The results indicate that the curvature of the crater depth fitting curve gradually decreases with the increase in strike times, tending to a stable value. The initial particle structure is altered by the huge dynamic stress induced by dynamic compaction. As strike times increase, the soil void ratio decreases gradually. The vertical additional dynamic stress is the fundamental reason resulting in foundation compaction. Precipitation preloading before dynamic compaction can improve the reinforcement effect of dynamic compaction, making up for the deficiency that the vertical additional dynamic stress attenuates rapidly along the depth direction. The simulated CPT results illustrate that the modulus of foundation soil can be increased by 3–5 times after dynamic compaction. The research results can provide important reference for similar projects.

Keywords: foundation treatment; high-energy dynamic compaction; FDM–DEM coupling; granular soil; vertical dynamic stress; effective reinforcement depth; reinforcement mechanism

MSC: 65P99; 70-10; 74F10

1. Introduction

Dynamic compaction (DC) is an energy-saving and environmentally friendly foundation treatment method. In addition, it has a significant cost-effective advantage over conventional foundation treatment methods [1]. With the rapid development of large infrastructure and coastal land construction projects, the high-energy-level dynamic compaction method emerges to deal with the increasingly complex conditions [2]. In the foundation treatment of marine reclamation land and backfilled granular soil, due to the loose soil quality and large depth of backfill, it takes more than 6 months or even several years to complete the foundation treatment with the preloading method. However, the high-energy dynamic compaction can improve the bearing capacity of foundation in place at one time, shortening the construction period to several months [3].

Dynamic compaction is a design method with double control of deformation and bearing capacity, with an emphasis on deformation control, especially for high-energy dynamic compaction. As a systematic engineering, the following parameters need to be considered in the design of dynamic compaction: the size of the hammer, the energy level of dynamic compaction, the spacing and arrangement of compaction points, the number of strikes, the standard of hammer retraction, the crater depth, the effective reinforcement depth, and the influence range of dynamic compaction. Since dynamic compaction involves complicated transient dynamic response issues, studies on dynamic compaction are mainly conducted by numerical simulations [4–20], model tests [21–23], and field tests [24–32]. Numerical simulation methods adopted by scholars principally include the finite element method (FEM) [4–11], finite difference method (FDM) [12–14], discrete element method (DEM) [15,16], and coupling calculation of various numerical simulation methods [17–20]. Wang et al. [4] established a 2D axisymmetric numerical model in LS-DYNA to investigate the influence of dynamic compaction on the ground surface deformation. On the basis of the results obtained, a forecast model was proposed to assess ground deformation under dynamic compaction. However, the effect of excess pore water pressure generated by DC was not considered in the numerical model. Zhou et al. [5] analyzed the improvement on saturated foundation under dynamic compaction through a dynamic fluid–solid coupled finite element method with soil cap model. The results illustrated that it is crucial to lower the groundwater table before implementing dynamic compaction. Yao et al. [7] performed a parametric study on the densification of sandy soil by conducting three-dimensional finite element analyses. Lastly, a design procedure was proposed to predict the soil relative density associated with dynamic compaction projects. Li et al. [8] investigated the improvement mechanism of DC in saturated soil of a weak layer with high levels of groundwater by performing fluid–solid coupling simulations. The results indicated that, in order to achieve a better compaction effect during DC, the groundwater table should be lowered by dewatering or adding a drainage layer between the ground surface and the groundwater. Chen et al. [12] established a modified constitutive model considering the kinematic hardening effect in FLAC3D under the framework of the Mohr–Coulomb criterion to describe gravelly soils by grain crushing tests and large-scale direct shear tests. However, the dynamic loading was expressed as triangular loading, which could not accurately reflect the actual load effect. Yao et al. [13] chose two sites with different groundwater tables to assess the variation of excess pore pressure during DC and performed a numerical analysis by FLAC3D to examine the liquefaction potential of silty ground. The results demonstrated that a higher water table would lead to higher potential for the ground liquefaction. However, the Finn model adopted in the numerical model could not capture the modulus increase induced by DC. Ma et al. [15] simulated the dynamic compaction process of gravel soil foundation using PFC2D/PFC3D. The findings revealed that the maximum influence depth of the dynamic compaction obtained by the three-dimensional analyses using PFC3D was lower than that by the two-dimensional analyses using PFC2D. However, the accuracy of the results was affected to some extent by using round and spherical hammers. Li et al. [16] studied the micro-dynamic reinforcement mechanism of gravel soil through PFC2D. The results showed that the coordination number of soil particles increased, and the porosity decreased. However, the tamping energy was only 3000 kN·m, and the porosity in the two-dimensional mode was significantly different from that in the three-dimensional mode, which is difficult to promote in a wider application field.

In numerical simulation methods, FEM can only analyze small deformation issues, because, once the displacement gets too large, the mesh of finite elements will be distorted, resulting in inaccuracy of calculation results or nonconvergence of the calculation process. A substantial displacement of soil occurs instantly when a hammer strikes the ground. Therefore, it is difficult to obtain accurate calculation results by using the finite element method to analyze the displacement and additional stress variations induced by high-energy dynamic compaction. The DEM can simulate the large deformation of soil particles, which has unique advantages in reflecting the micromechanical behavior of soil, especially for backfilled granular soil. However, the DEM decomposes the soil mass into a series of particles in space and carries out iterative calculation over time, which requires a huge amount of computation and is far less efficient than continuum methods. As a result, the DEM is limited in model size or can only simplify the three-dimensional problem into a two-dimensional problem analysis. The finite difference method (FDM) provides an approach to solve the large deformation problem in a continuum. However, the necessity for mesh precision is significant when dealing with the dynamic problem of local impact load, and it is still difficult to fully reflect the local punching characteristics around the hammer. With the continuous development of numerical analysis technology, continuum–discrete coupling calculation methods, such as FDM–DEM coupling, provide a new possibility to solve the dynamic problem of local large deformation [33–36].

At present, only a few scholars have simulated the dynamic compaction process using a continuum–discrete coupling method. Jia et al. [17] reproduced the dynamic densification process of granular soils by analyzing the soil displacement field, motion of tracer particles, and evolution of local porosity through PFC/FLAC coupled simulation, but the research was presented for issues with two-dimensional planes. Wang et al. [18] established a 3D continuum–discrete coupling model to simulate the hammer–soil interaction process. The results illustrated that ellipsoidal compaction bands were formed inside the punching surface, and shear bands were formed outside the punching surface. However, the tamping energy was only 2000 kN·m. Meanwhile, the numerical model only considered the effect of one strike, ignoring the characteristics of multiple strikes, as well as the influence of groundwater. Jia et al. [19] introduced a coupled three-dimensional discrete element–finite difference simulation of dynamic compaction. The results indicated that the soil undergoes a transient weakening process induced by dynamic stress propagation. Allocating higher compaction energy to the bearing capacity mechanism could improve the efficiency of dynamic compaction. However, for dynamic analysis, the coupling model did not adopt a suitable boundary to absorb dynamic waves. It is not sufficiently clear how the crater changes during DC. Wang et al. [20] presented a 3D FEM–SPH coupling model in LS-DYNA. It was found that the penetration of the hammer increased with the increase in tamping energy. The coupled simulation method could deal with the DC problem even if the tamping energy was extremely high.

In practice, the design parameters still depend on engineering experience, especially the vertical additional dynamic stress and effective reinforcement depth with a high energy level. Most scholars primarily place emphasis on the influence of one DC on soil displacement, with few studies being performed on the vertical additional dynamic stress propagation law along depth and the effective reinforcement depth during high-energy-level dynamic compaction. Meanwhile, in the aforementioned studies, continuum–discrete two-phase media were rarely adopted to implement a dynamic simulation of high-energy dynamic compaction based on fluid–solid coupling, which is highly consistent with reality. In view of this, it is of great significance to study the reinforcement mechanism of high-energy-level dynamic compaction, which can help us better predict the effect of foundation treatment by high-energy dynamic compaction.

The outline of this paper is as follows: firstly, the soft soil foundation treatment project of Taiping Bay Cooperative Innovation Zone in Wafangdian City, Dalian City is taken as an engineering background. The foundation treatment scheme is determined on the basis of the geological conditions. Secondly, a three-dimensional continuum–discrete fluid–solid coupling dynamic analysis model is established using Particle Flow Code (PFC) and Fast Lagrangian Analysis of Continua (FLAC). The procedure of a hammer's free fall from a given height to strike the ground is performed in clumps. The cumulative crater depth, the variation of soil void ratio, the changing process of vertical additional dynamic stress at different positions along the depth, and the pore water pressure after dynamic compaction were obtained. Lastly, the cone tip resistance before and after dynamic compaction at the center line of the crater was obtained by means of simulated static cone penetration tests (CPTs). Compared with field tests, the reliability of soil particle microparameters and the effectiveness of high-energy dynamic compaction in foundation treatment were verified.

2. FDM–DEM Coupling Numerical Simulation

2.1. Project Overview

Taiping Bay Cooperation Innovation Zone is located in the north of Dalian on the Bohai Sea side of Liaodong Peninsula, 240 km from Shenyang in the north and 106 km from Dalian in the south. The port area is about 13.86 km^2. The port was originally the sea area, and the existing land was composed of new dredger fill. The proposed site is located in the coastal, shoal zone. The location of the foundation treatment project is shown in Figure 1. The site is backfilled with granular soils at present, and the average backfill thickness is 7.5 m. The current situation of the proposed site is shown in Figure 2. In Figure 2, the western side of the proposed site is close to the coastline.

Figure 1. Location of the foundation treatment project.

Figure 2. Current situations of the proposed site: (**a**) western side; (**b**) southern side.

Comprehensive exploration methods combining drilling sampling, standard penetration tests (SPTs), dynamic penetration tests (DPTs), static cone penetration tests (CPTs), and laboratory soil tests were applied to investigate the soil layer on site. The site's groundwater level is primarily affected by seawater, and the groundwater level is basically located at 3 m below the ground surface. The physical and mechanical properties of site soils are shown in Table 1. It should be noted that soil layer 3 contains silty sand interlayer and no mud; hence, this soil layer still has a certain degree of hardness which can be described by SPT.

Table 1. Physical and mechanical properties of site soils.

Soil Layer	Soil Thickness h_s (m)	Density γ (kg/m^3)	Compression Modulus E_s (MPa)	Poisson's Ratio μ	Cohesion c (kPa)	Friction Angle φ (°)	Void Ratio e	Permeability Coefficient k (cm/s)	SPT [1]
1: granular soil	7.5	1800	4.5	0.25	0.5	36	0.790	-	-
2: dredger fill	7.5	1760	3.73	0.3	16.6	11.9	1.377	2.58×10^{-5}	4.9
3: muddy silty clay with silty sand	6	1840	3.58	0.3	15.3	5.8	1.042	1.92×10^{-6}	3.7

[1] Standard penetration test (blow count/30 cm).

2.2. Foundation Treatment Scheme

According to the geological conditions of the site and engineering experience, the available foundation treatment schemes for each soil layer to be treated include the dynamic compaction method, substitution method, vacuum preloading method, and surcharge preloading method. Among them, the substitution method is impracticable due to its substantial material consumption and poor economy. Partial substitution can be carried out in some special areas such as field roads. The project site belongs to the upper hard and lower soft strata, and the soft soil layer is buried deep. In order to reduce the post-construction settlement, the drainage plate needs to be set up at a greater depth, and the preloading period needs to be longer. Meanwhile, higher requirements are put forward for the machine's insertion capacity. Therefore, the construction periods for the vacuum preloading method and the surcharge preloading method are excessively long, and the expenses are considerable.

The dynamic compaction method has higher construction efficiency, has lower project cost, can greatly shorten the construction period, and has a good foundation treatment effect. In addition, the huge shock wave caused by high-energy-level dynamic compaction can change the original structure of granular soil and reduce the soil void ratio. Under the impact of dynamic compaction, the granular soil of the upper hard layer will be squeezed into the lower dredger fill soft soil layer to increase the content of coarse particles in the deep soft soil layer, enhancing the bearing capacity of the entire foundation significantly. According to the previous engineering experience and specification suggestions, in order to make the effective reinforcement depth of dynamic compaction exceed the thickness of hard layer and affect the soft soil filled below, the dynamic compaction energy level of this project was set to 8000 kN·m.

2.3. FDM–DEM Coupling Technique

DEM can realize dynamic large deformation simulation based on Newton's second law, but the size limitation of the numerical model affects the accuracy of the calculation results. FDM can reflect pore pressure changes, dynamic wave propagation, and continuous displacement trends, expand model size, and eliminate dynamic wave reflection through the free field boundary. The coupling calculation makes up for the corresponding shortcomings. In the FDM–DEM coupling calculation, FLAC^{3D} was used to simulate the mechanical behavior of the medium in the continuous domain macroscopically, while PFC^{3D} was used to simulate the mechanical behavior of the medium in the discrete domain microscopically. The flowchart for FDM–DEM coupling calculation is shown in Figure 3.

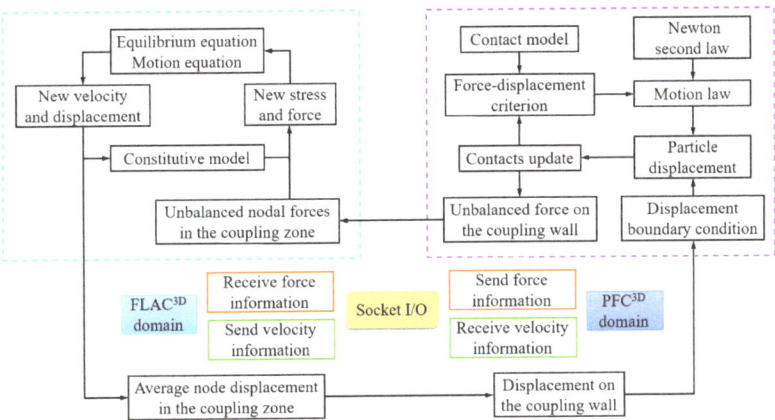

Figure 3. Flowchart for FDM–DEM coupling calculation.

The process of FDM-DEM coupling is to follow the principle of virtual work of continuum element nodes and Newton's second law of discrete element particles in the iterative calculation process. The data such as force and velocity are continuously transmitted through the coupling boundary. The consistency and continuity of the calculated data in the discrete domain and the continuum domain are ensured by timestep control, so as to realize the comprehensive analysis of the mechanical behavior of the medium from the perspective of continuum and discrete macro–micro synergy. At each calculation step, the continuum domain element node transmits the velocity to the discrete domain boundary particles, and then generates displacement and contact force inside the discrete domain material. The generated force is also transmitted to the element nodes of the continuum domain through the particles of the coupling boundary to complete the coupling loop operation.

At each cycle of PFC^{3D}, a force–displacement criterion is applied to each contact, controlling the motion of particles according to Newton's second law, while constantly updating the position of the particles and the wall. The unbalance force on the coupling wall is transmitted to FLAC^{3D} through the embedded Socket I/O interface. After obtaining the new stress and force, the new velocity and displacement are calculated by calling the equilibrium equation (motion equation), and the node displacement on the coupling area is transformed into a new displacement boundary condition through the Socket I/O interface. The displacement of particles in the discrete domain is made, and the cyclic calculation is carried out successively.

2.4. The 3D FDM–DEM Coupling Numerical Model

In the dynamic analysis of geotechnical engineering, the fixed boundary conditions commonly used in static analysis will cause a reflection of dynamic waves on the model boundary, and this phenomenon can be reduced by adopting a wider model range [37,38]. For this reason, a larger model size was used in this numerical simulation, with a length and width of 40 m and height of 21 m. Free field boundaries were set at the four sides and four corners of the model, and a quiet boundary was set at the bottom of the model, which could eliminate the reflection of dynamic waves at the model bottom and achieve an effect similar to an infinite range boundary. The granular soil in the central area with a height of 5 m and a diameter of 5 m was discretized and surrounded by continuum. The size radius of the soil particles was between 0.035 and 0.04 m. In the initial stage, 238,214 balls were generated in the discrete domain. The three-dimensional FDM–DEM coupling numerical model is shown in Figure 4.

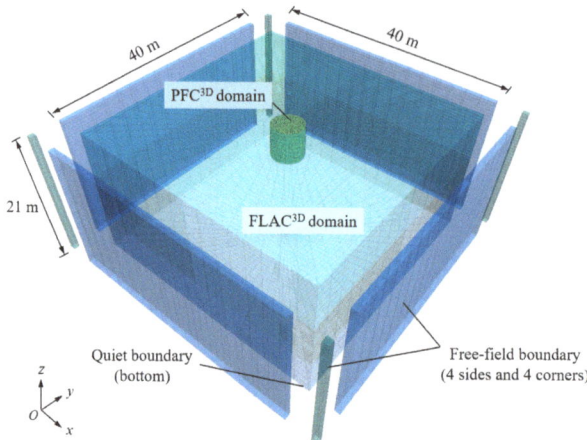

Figure 4. Three-dimensional FDM–DEM coupling numerical model.

In order to simulate the process of dynamic compaction more realistically, the clump composed of pebbles was used to establish the actual size model of the hammer, which could realize the free fall motion of the hammer under the gravity. The hammer weighed 38.288 t, with a diameter of 2.5 m, a height of 1 m, and a density of 7800 kg/m^3. The three-dimensional hammer model is shown in Figure 5.

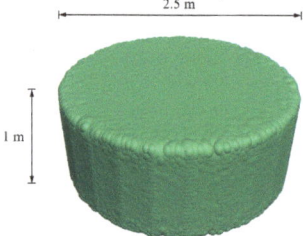

Figure 5. Three-dimensional hammer model.

The linear parallel bond model was a contact constitutive model proposed by Potyondy [39] to represent the bond characteristics between particles, which could reflect the microscopic contact characteristics of rock and soil. The continuum adopted the Mohr–Coulomb constitutive model. The linear parallel bond constitutive model was used for the discrete medium. The microscopic parameters in the coupled numerical model are shown in Table 2. It is significant to note that the ball–wall parallel-bond strengths were set to be larger than normal to ensure that the balls at the boundary remained bonded to neighboring zones. The model parameters in Table 2 were verified by comparing the simulated CPT tests with the field CPT results.

Table 2. Microscopic parameters in FDM–DEM coupled numerical model.

Contact Type	Effective Modulus (MPa)	Normal Bonding (Pa)	Shear Bonding (Pa)	Friction Angle (°)	Friction Coefficient	Normal-to-Shear Stiffness Ratio
Ball–ball	25.0	1.5×10^3	0.5×10^3	36	0.5	1.5
Ball–wall	25.0	1.5×10^4	5×10^3	36	0.3	1.5
Ball–pebble	25.0	-	-	-	0.3	1.0

A flowchart of the methodology is shown in Figure 6.

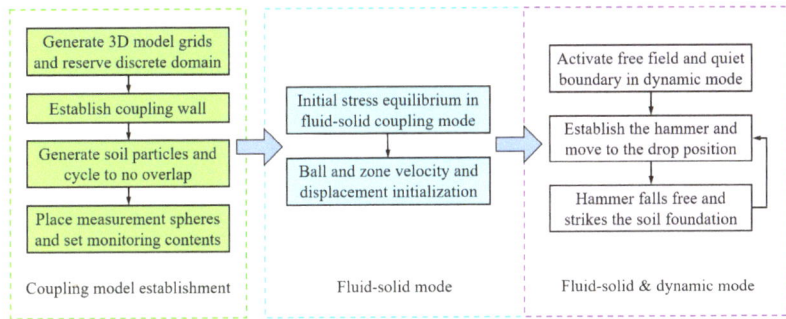

Figure 6. Flowchart of the methodology.

3. Numerical Analysis Results

In order to reduce the impact of groundwater on the reinforcement effect of dynamic compaction, the foundation treatment scheme considered vacuum well point dewatering to drop the groundwater level from 3 m below the ground surface to 9 m below the ground surface. Before dynamic compaction, the groundwater level dropped to 9 m below the ground surface. The dynamic compaction process is shown in Figure 7, where h is the hammer drop height.

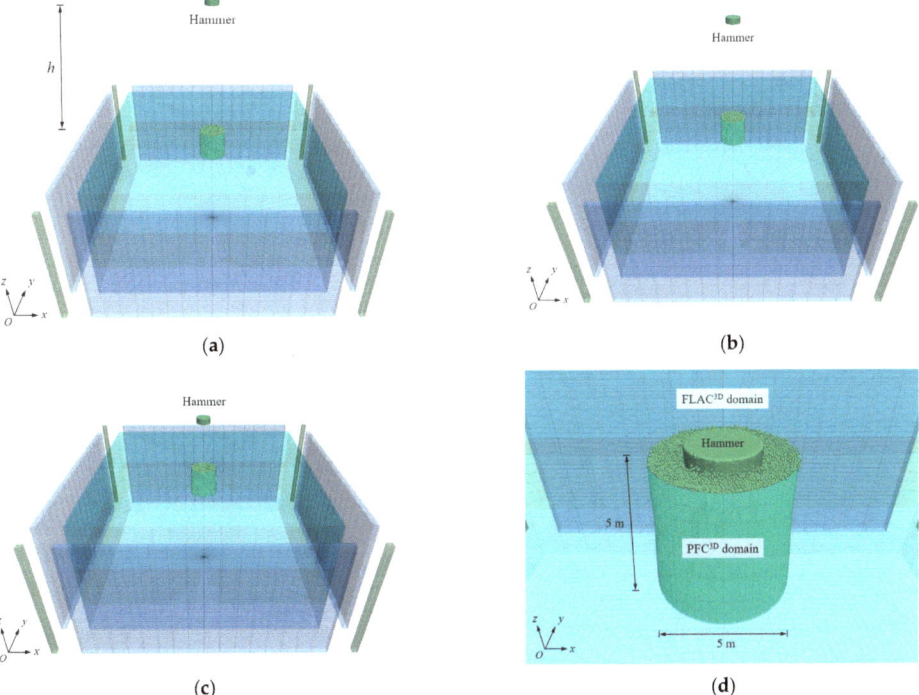

Figure 7. Dynamic compaction process: (**a**) release from rest; (**b**) accelerating due to gravity; (**c**) approaching ground surface; (**d**) hammer–soil impact.

3.1. Crater Depth

According to the site strata and foundation treatment requirements, the 8000 kN·m dynamic compaction energy level was adopted to carry out continuous eight strikes at the same tamping point. The height at which the hammer was released freely from rest was 21.3 m. In the last strike of dynamic compaction, the changing process of hammer drop distance and hammer velocity with time is shown in Figures 8 and 9.

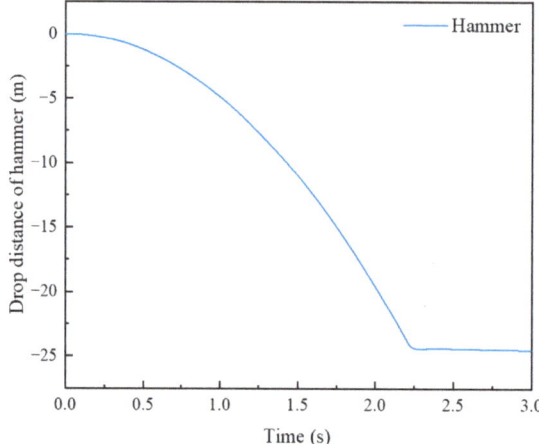

Figure 8. Changing process of hammer drop distance with time.

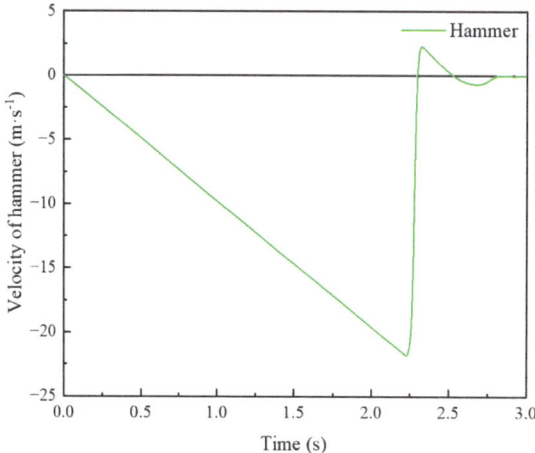

Figure 9. Changing process of hammer velocity with time.

According to the calculation results of Figure 9, the instantaneous hammer–soil contact time was 50 ms at which point the speed of the hammer decreased to zero.

The vertical displacement contours of the crater after each strike are shown in Figure 10. It can be seen from Figure 10 that, with the increase in the number of strikes, the crater depth gradually increased. Due to the huge impact energy caused by DC, the soil around the hammer was squeezed after each strike, with some soil around the hammer exhibiting a certain degree of splash. A little uplift appeared on the ground surface around the crater. After removing the hammer, the surrounding soil progressively slid into the crater.

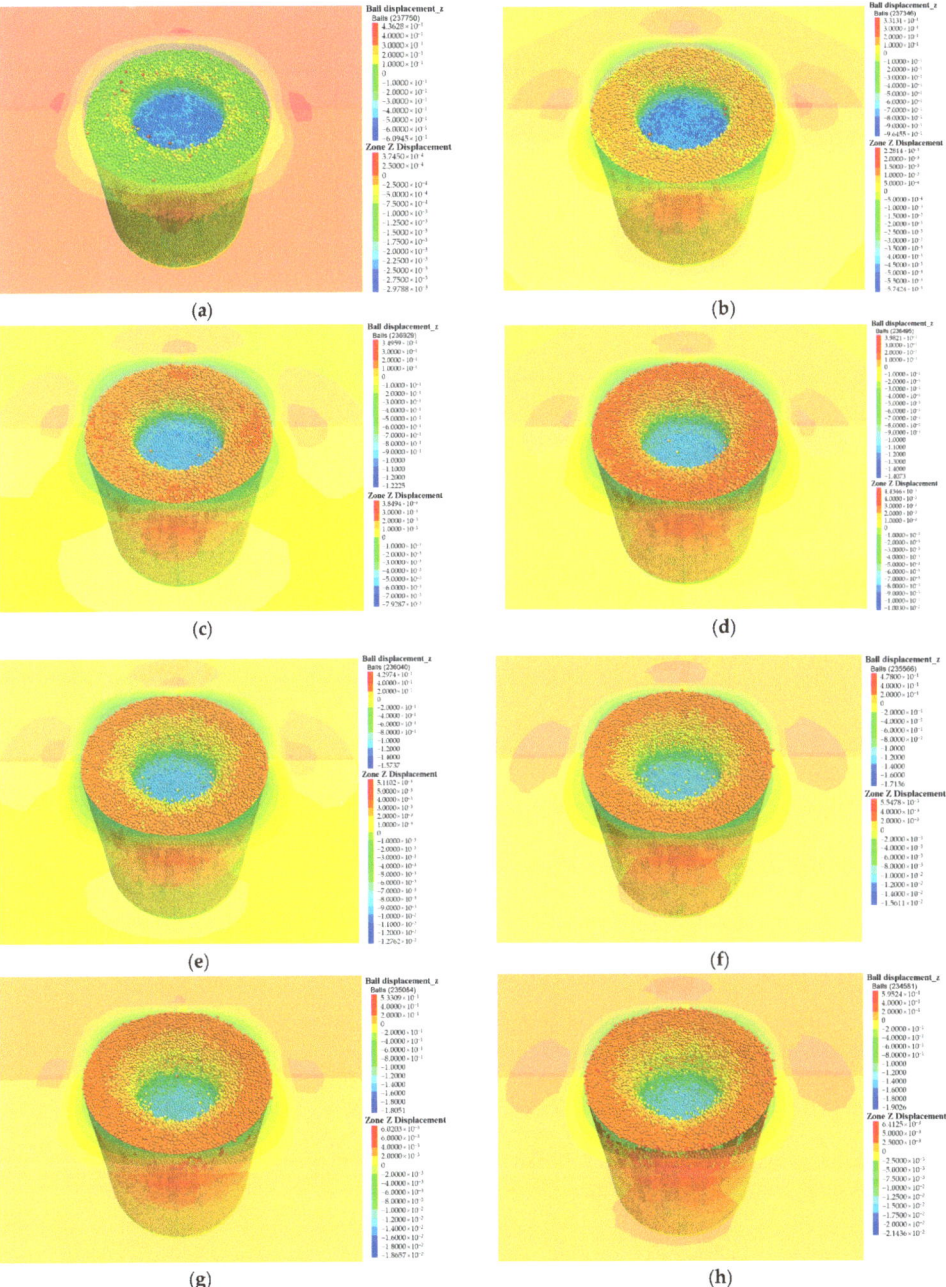

Figure 10. Vertical displacement of crater (m): (**a**) first strike; (**b**) second strike; (**c**) third strike; (**d**) fourth strike; (**e**) fifth strike; (**f**) sixth strike; (**g**) seventh strike; (**h**) eighth strike.

The variations of the cumulative settlement at different depths of the tamping point center with the number of strikes are shown in Figure 11.

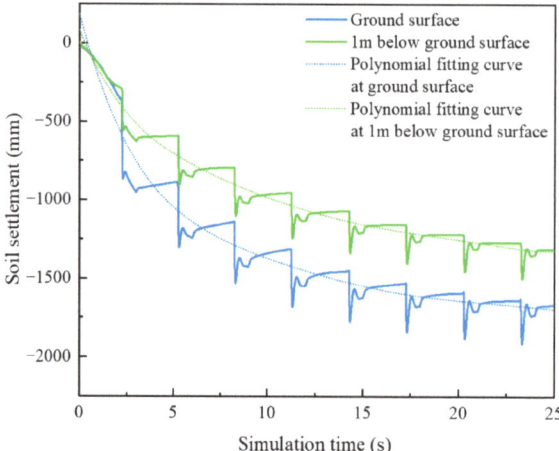

Figure 11. Soil settlement at different depths in crater center.

Figure 11 describes the relationship between crater depth and strike times. Initially, backfilled granular soil would produce a certain amount of settlement under gravity. The soil settlement caused by the first strike was the maximum due to the large soil void ratio before dynamic compaction. The instant rebound at the crater bottom after the first removal of the hammer was small. With the increase in strike times, the instant rebound at the moment when the hammer was removed increased gradually. However, with the increase in strike times, the resilience of soil stabilized after hammer removal first increased and then decreased gradually. The reason is that there were large voids in the soil at first, and the particles were not wedged tightly. The first strike changed the soil from loose to compact. As the soil was gradually compacted, the resilience of he foundation was enhanced. However, the enhancement of resilience indicates that the compaction degree did not reach the requirement of foundation treatment. When the number of strikes reached seven and eight, the soil settlement of a single strike was reduced, and the rebound in the process of soil stabilization after hammer removal was close to zero, demonstrating that the soil foundation reached a satisfying compaction state at this time. In practical engineering, the standard of hammer retraction is determined by the average settlement in the crater of the last two strikes. When the dynamic compaction energy E of each strike is between 8000 kN·m and 12,000 kN·m, the average settlement in the crater of the last two strikes should be less than 200 mm. According to Figure 11, the total crater depth was 1669 mm, the soil settlement at the crater surface in the first strike was 460.7 mm, and the soil settlement at the crater surface in the last strike was 28.8 mm, meeting the standard of hammer retraction. Polynomial fitting of the soil settlement curves revealed that the curvature of the fitting curve gradually decreased, indicating that the foundation's bearing capacity increased progressively with the increase in strikes of dynamic compaction and eventually tended to a stable value.

3.2. Soil Void Ratio

The soil void ratio e variations at different depths were monitored by placing measurement spheres in the discrete domain of the FDM–DEM coupled model. The principle of measurement spheres is to measure the volume of particles in the sphere domain and calculate the porosity. Then, the soil void ratio is obtained by the relationship between porosity and void ratio. The radius of the measurement sphere was 400 mm, and the centers of the sphere were distributed at -2 m, -3 m, and -4 m. The changing process of soil void ratio at different depths during dynamic compaction is shown in Figure 12.

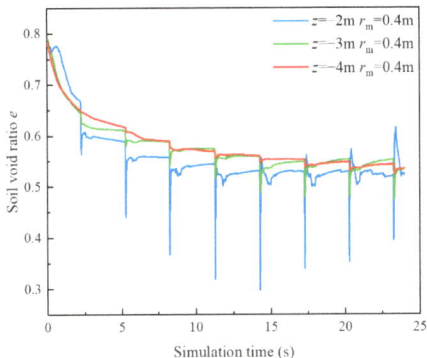

Figure 12. Changing process of soil void ratio at different depths.

It can be seen from Figure 12 that, with the increase in strike times, the soil void ratio decreased gradually, and the soil void ratio reached the minimum value at the moment when the hammer contacted the soil instantaneously. It should be pointed out that the void ratio monitored at $z = -2$ m had an upward trend after the fifth strike. The reason is that the nearest distance between the measurement sphere and the surface was 1.6 m, and the crater depth at this time exceeded 1.6 m, resulting in excess void on the upper part of the measurement sphere. The actual trend was still that the soil void ratio gradually decreased. Through calculation and analysis, it was concluded that, after eight strikes of dynamic compaction, the final void ratio of granular soil could be reduced from 0.790 to 0.523. The soil void ratio could be reduced by 33.8%.

3.3. Vertical Additional Dynamic Stress

The vertical additional dynamic stress is the fundamental reason resulting in foundation compaction. The effective reinforcement depth of dynamic compaction can be deduced from the maximum propagation depth of vertical additional dynamic stress. The vertical additional dynamic stress can be obtained by recording the total vertical stress through measurement spheres and deducting the self-weight stress at the corresponding position. Measurement spheres with a radius of 200 mm were arranged vertically every 1 m in the discrete domain. The variation of the vertical additional dynamic stress at different depths in the discrete domain with strike times of dynamic compaction is shown in Figure 13.

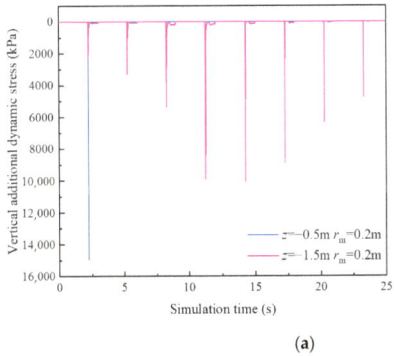

(a)

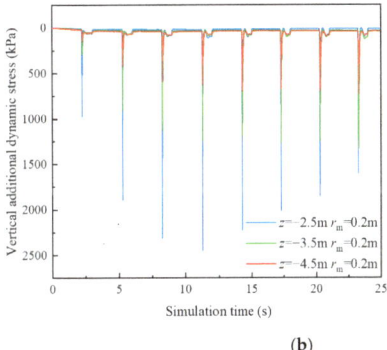

(b)

Figure 13. Variation trends of the vertical additional dynamic stress at different depths: (**a**) range from -2.0 m to 0 m; (**b**) range from -5.0 m to -2.0 m.

It can be seen from Figure 13 that the maximum vertical additional dynamic stress decreased with the increase in depth, among which the maximum vertical additional dynamic stress at 0.5 m below the surface caused by the first strike was 14,953.2 kPa. The maximum vertical additional dynamic stress at 1.5 m below the surface was 2305.5 kPa, which decreased by 84.58% compared with that at $z = -0.5$ m. The maximum vertical additional dynamic stress at 2.5 m below the surface was 972.7 kPa, which decreased by 57.8% compared with that at $z = -1.5$ m. In Figure 10, the maximum vertical additional dynamic stress in part of the measurement spheres gradually decreased in the later period of dynamic compaction, which was caused by the decrease in the number of particles inside the measurement spheres as the crater depth increased. The results indicate that the vertical additional dynamic stress caused by dynamic compaction attenuated rapidly along the depth. When closer to the ground surface, the attenuation of vertical additional dynamic stress was more obvious.

Meanwhile, the fluctuations of the vertical additional dynamic stress of soil in the discrete domain shown in Figure 13 were obvious, indicating that the discrete domain within 5 m below the ground surface was in the effective reinforcement range of dynamic compaction. In order to further study the maximum effective reinforcement depth that the dynamic compaction energy level of 8000 kN·m could achieve onsite, the variation trends of vertical dynamic stress at the distance between -14 m and -9 m from the ground surface in continuum are shown in Figure 14. The vertical dynamic stress in Figure 14 includes the initial self-weight stress.

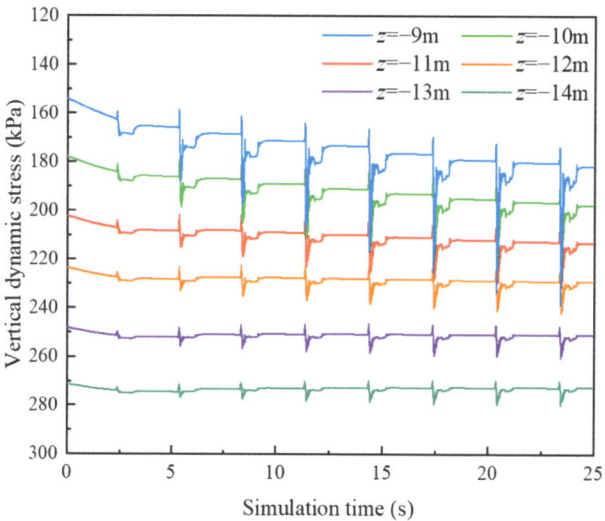

Figure 14. Variation trends of vertical dynamic stress in continuum.

From Figure 14, it can be seen that the maximum vertical dynamic stress at 9 m below the ground surface during the dynamic compaction process could exceed the initial gravity stress at 12 m below the ground surface, indicating that the dynamic compaction continued to have the ability to compact the foundation soil at 9 m below the ground surface. Similarly, the maximum vertical dynamic stress at 11 m below the surface could also approach the initial self-weight stress at 12 m below the surface, while the fluctuations between the maximum vertical dynamic stress and the self-weight stress at -14 m to -12 m were not obvious. It could be determined that the maximum effective reinforcement depth h_d of 8000 kN·m dynamic compaction energy level at this site was -11 m.

The effective reinforcement depth h_d of dynamic compaction can also be estimated using Ménard's empirical formula [1]:

$$h_d = \alpha(Mh)^{1/2}, \tag{1}$$

where M is the mass of the hammer (t), h is the drop height (m), and α is a coefficient depending on the properties of foundation soil. For granular soil, the value of α is 0.5. A higher energy per strike results in a lower value of α [40]. Assuming that the reduction coefficient of α is 0.8, the effective reinforcement depth calculated using Menard's modified formula is 11.42 m, which is in good agreement with the effective reinforcement depth of 11 m calculated by the FDM–DEM coupled numerical model.

3.4. Pore Water Pressure

After eight strikes of dynamic compaction, the pore water pressure at the site is shown in Figure 15.

Figure 15. Pore water pressure at the site after eight strikes of dynamic compaction (mPa).

It can be seen from Figure 15 that the pore water pressure below the crater only increased slightly after dynamic compaction. Therefore, dewatering before dynamic compaction can significantly reduce the instantaneous increase in pore pressure induced by vertical additional dynamic stress. The dewatering depth should be determined according to the initial water level of the site and the dynamic compaction energy level. According to the numerical analysis results, it is generally accepted that the reduction in groundwater level to the effective reinforcement depth of the dynamic compaction can avoid the repeated increase in pore water pressure during the dynamic compaction process and reduce the waiting time for pore water pressure dissipation.

3.5. Total Reinforcement Pressure

Before dynamic compaction, the vacuum well point tubes and tube wells were set for dewatering preloading. As a result, the preloading load could be enhanced by decreasing groundwater, and the increase in pore water pressure could also be decreased during DC. In the dewatering dynamic compaction project, the total reinforcement pressure could be divided into preloading pressure of dewatering in the early stage and vertical additional dynamic stress pressure of dynamic compaction in the later stage. Both of them performed more effectively together to increase the reinforcement pressure and depth of foundation treatment. By superimposing the dewatering pressure and the maximum vertical additional dynamic stress of dynamic compaction, the total reinforcement pressure is shown in Figure 16.

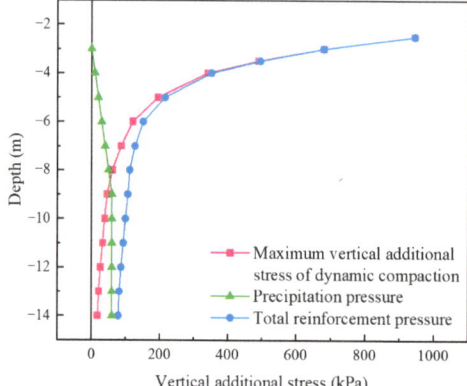

Figure 16. Total reinforcement pressure.

As can be seen from Figure 16, the dewatering preloading induced by groundwater descending from $z = -3$ m to $z = -9$ m was trapezoidal. The vertical additional dynamic stress induced by dynamic compaction decreased rapidly along the depth. The superposition of both could increase the reinforcement effect on deep soil, making up for the limited reinforcement effect of dynamic compaction on deep soil.

3.6. Simulated Static Cone Penetration Tests

In order to verify the reinforcement effect of dynamic compaction on foundation soil, the PFC walls were used to establish a static cone penetration model. The cone tip angle was 60°, the diameter was 43.7 mm, and the penetration velocity was 1.2 m/min. The cone tip resistance q_c along the depth direction was recorded during the penetration process. The simulated static cone penetration tests were carried out in the crater center before and after dynamic compaction. The penetration process of static cone penetration after dynamic compaction is shown in Figure 17. The comparison of simulated static cone penetration tests before and after dynamic compaction is shown in Figure 18.

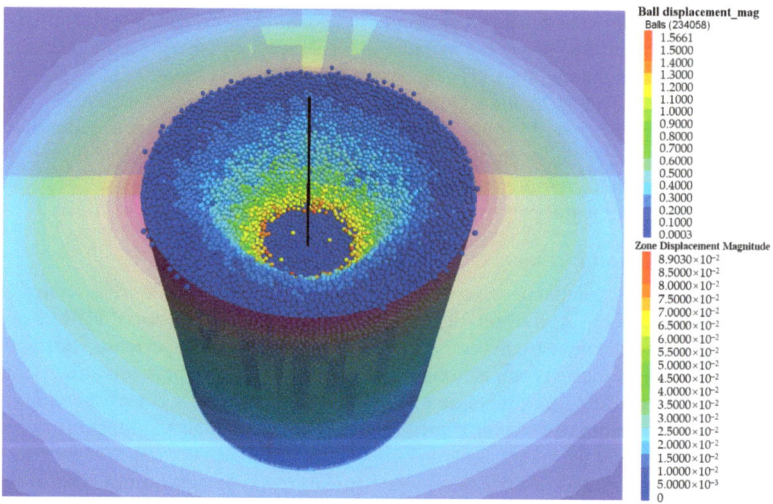

Figure 17. Penetration process of CPT after dynamic compaction (m).

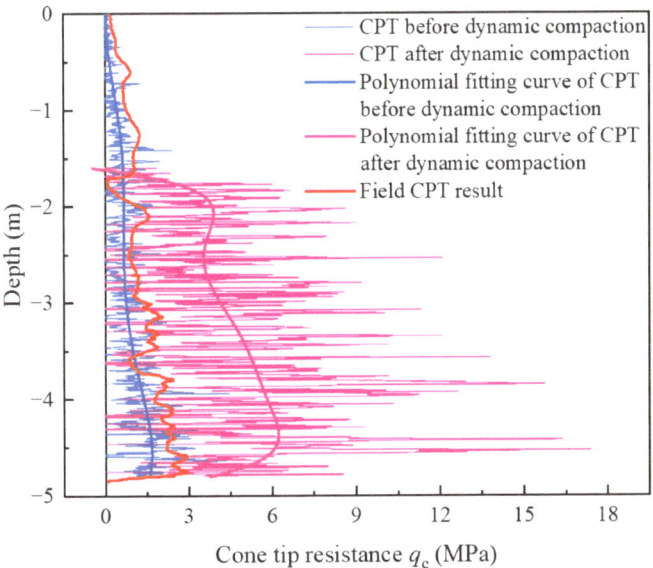

Figure 18. Comparison of simulated CPTs before and after dynamic compaction.

The simulated results of CPT before dynamic compaction had a good agreement with the field CPT results, verifying the reliability of the numerical calculation parameters. It should be pointed out that, due to the computational efficiency of discrete elements, it is difficult for the particle size to be completely consistent with the size of real soil particles; hence, the cone tip resistance would be zero intermittently in the process of simulating CPT. Therefore, the simulated CPT result was slightly lower than the field CPT result. It can be seen from the comparison results that the simulated results of CPT after dynamic compaction were about 3–5 times higher than those before dynamic compaction. The results illustrate that the modulus of foundation soil could be increased by about 3–5 times after eight strikes of 8000 kN·m high-energy-level dynamic compaction.

4. Conclusions

This study established a three-dimensional fluid–solid coupling dynamic analysis numerical model based on the FDM–DEM coupling method. Clumps were adopted to realize the multiple dynamic simulation of a hammer's free-falling compaction on foundation soil from a certain height. The reinforcement mechanism of high-energy-level dynamic compaction was studied. The main conclusions are as follows:

(a) The FDM–DEM coupling method was adopted to realize the three-dimensional refined modeling of continuum–discrete coupling, effectively enlarging the model size, reflecting local large deformation during DC, and improving the efficiency of numerical calculation. The 3D coupled model realized the comprehensive analysis of the mechanical behavior of the medium from the perspective of continuum and discrete macro–micro synergy. Meanwhile, a free field boundary and quiet boundary were applied to eliminate the influence of dynamic wave reflection, obtaining a higher calculation accuracy than that in previous studies.

(b) The crater depth and the instant soil rebound at the crater bottom increased with the number of strikes. After removing the hammer, the soil rebound in the process of soil stabilization increased first and then decreased as the number of strikes increased. The soil settlement at the crater surface in the first strike was 460.7 mm, and the soil settlement at the crater surface in the last strike was 28.8 mm The total crater depth was 1669 mm after eight strikes of 8000 kN·m DC. Through polynomial fitting of the soil settlement curve, it could be found that the curvature gradually decreased, revealing that the foundation bearing capacity eventually tended to a stable value as a result of DC.

(c) In the process of dynamic compaction, the soil void ratio decreased gradually and reached the minimum value at the moment of compaction. The final void ratio of granular soil could be reduced from 0.790 to 0.523. The vertical additional dynamic stress induced by DC was the fundamental reason resulting in foundation compaction, but the vertical additional dynamic stress attenuated rapidly along the depth. The effective reinforcement depth could be determined according to the fluctuation of vertical dynamic stress in different measurement spheres. The effective reinforcement depth of 8000 kN·m DC at this site was 11 m, which is in good agreement with the effective reinforcement depth of 11.42 m calculated using Menard's modified formula.

(d) Dewatering before dynamic compaction could reduce the increase in pore water pressure induced by vertical additional dynamic stress and improve the reinforcement effect. The superposition of dewatering pressure and vertical additional dynamic stress could compensate for the rapid attenuation of vertical additional dynamic stress along the depth direction to a certain extent. By comparing with the field CPT results, the rationality of the microscopic parameters of the model was verified, and the reliability of the CPT simulation was confirmed. The simulated CPT results demonstrate that the dynamic compaction could increase the modulus of soil foundation by about 3–5 times.

Author Contributions: Conceptualization, Y.S.; methodology, Y.S.; software, Y.S., X.C. and D.Z.; validation, Y.S. and X.L.; investigation, Y.S. and Q.W.; resources, Y.S. and X.L.; data curation, X.L. and K.H. (Kaihang Han); writing—original draft preparation, Y.S.; writing—review and editing, Y.S. and X.L.; visualization, Y.S.; supervision, X.L and Z.H.; funding acquisition, K.H. (Kan Huang). All authors have read and agreed to the published version of the manuscript.

Funding: This research was funded by the National Key Research and Development Program of China (No. 2022YFC3800905), the National Natural Science Foundation of China (No. 52078060), and the International Cooperation and Development Project of Double-First-Class Scientific Research at Changsha University of Science and Technology (No. 2018IC19).

Data Availability Statement: The numerical data used to support the findings of this study are available from the corresponding author upon request.

Conflicts of Interest: The authors declare no conflict of interest.

References

1. Ménard, L.; Broise, Y. Theoretical and practical aspect of dynamic consolidation. *Géotechnique* **1975**, *25*, 3–18. [CrossRef]
2. Feng, S.J.; Tan, K.; Shui, W.H.; Zhang, Y. Densification of desert sands by high energy dynamic compaction. *Eng. Geol.* **2013**, *157*, 48–54. [CrossRef]
3. Zhang, R.Y.; Sun, Y.J.; Song, E.X. Simulation of dynamic compaction and analysis of its efficiency with the material point method. *Comput. Geotech.* **2019**, *116*, 103218. [CrossRef]
4. Wang, W.; Chen, J.J.; Wang, J.H. Estimation method for ground deformation of granular soils caused by dynamic compaction. *Soil Dyn. Earthq. Eng.* **2017**, *92*, 266–278. [CrossRef]
5. Zhou, C.; Jiang, H.G.; Yao, Z.Y.; Li, H.; Yang, C.J.; Chen, L.C.; Geng, X.Y. Evaluation of dynamic compaction to improve saturated foundation based on the fluid-solid coupled method with soil cap model. *Comput. Geotech.* **2020**, *125*, 103686. [CrossRef]
6. Zhou, C.; Yang, C.J.; Qi, H.; Yao, K.; Yao, Z.Y.; Wang, K.; Ji, P.; Li, H. Evaluation on improvement zone of foundation after dynamic compaction. *Appl. Sci.* **2021**, *11*, 2156. [CrossRef]
7. Yao, Z.Y.; Zhou, C.; Lin, Q.Q.; Yao, K.; Satchithananthan, U.; Lee, F.H.; Tang, A.M.; Jiang, H.G.; Pan, Y.T.; Wang, S.T. Effect of dynamic compaction by multi-point tamping on the densification of sandy soil. *Comput. Geotech.* **2022**, *151*, 104949. [CrossRef]
8. Li, J.L.; Zhou, C.; Xin, G.F.; Long, G.X.; Zhang, W.L.; Li, C.; Zhuang, P.Z.; Yao, Z.Y. Study on reinforcement mechanism and reinforcement effect of saturated soil with a weak layer by DC. *Appl. Sci.* **2022**, *12*, 9770. [CrossRef]
9. Abedini, F.; Rafiee-Dehkharghani, R.; Laknejadi, K. Mitigation of vibrations caused by dynamic compaction considering soil nonlinearity. *Int. J. Civ. Eng.* **2022**, *20*, 809–826. [CrossRef]
10. Bradley, A.C.; Jaksa, M.B.; Kuo, Y.L. Finite element modelling of rolling dynamic compaction. *Comput. Geotech.* **2023**, *157*, 105275. [CrossRef]

11. Paulmichl, I.; Furtmüller, T.; Adam, C.; Adam, D. Numerical simulation of the compaction effect and the dynamic response of an oscillation roller based on a hypoplastic soil model. *Soil Dyn. Earthq. Eng.* **2020**, *132*, 106057. [CrossRef]
12. Chen, L.; Qiao, L.; Li, Q.W. Study on dynamic compaction characteristics of gravelly soils with crushing effect. *Soil Dyn. Earthq. Eng.* **2019**, *120*, 158–169. [CrossRef]
13. Yao, K.; Rong, Y.; Yao, Z.Y.; Shi, C.Y.; Yang, C.J.; Chen, L.C.; Zhang, B.S.; Jiang, H.G. Effect of water level on dynamic compaction in silty ground of Yellow River alluvial plain. *Arab. J. Geosci.* **2022**, *15*, 126. [CrossRef]
14. Sun, Y.W. Vertical additional dynamic stress propagation characteristics of silty foundation reinforced by dynamic compaction. *J. Transp. Sci. Eng.* **2023**, accepted.
15. Ma, Z.Y.; Dang, F.N.; Liao, H.J. Numerical study of the dynamic compaction of gravel soil ground using the discrete element method. *Granul. Matter* **2014**, *16*, 881–889. [CrossRef]
16. Li, Y.Q.; Ma, Z.Y.; Yang, F. Numerical study on micro-reinforcement mechanism and environmental control of gravel soil under dynamic compaction. *Arab. J. Geosci.* **2021**, *14*, 2682. [CrossRef]
17. Jia, M.C.; Yang, Y.; Liu, B.; Wu, S.H. PFC/FLAC coupled simulation of dynamic compaction in granular soils. *Granul. Matter* **2018**, *20*, 76. [CrossRef]
18. Wang, J.; Jiang, Y.; Ouyang, H.; Jiang, T.; Song, M.; Zhang, X. 3D continuum-discrete coupling modeling of soil-hammer interaction under dynamic compaction. *J. Vibroeng.* **2019**, *21*, 348–359. [CrossRef]
19. Jia, M.C.; Liu, B.; Xue, J.F.; Ma, G.Q. Coupled three-dimensional discrete element–finite difference simulation of dynamic compaction. *Acta Geotech.* **2021**, *16*, 731–747. [CrossRef]
20. Wang, W.; Wu, Y.J.; Wu, H.; Yang, C.Z.; Feng, Q.S. Numerical analysis of dynamic compaction using FEM-SPH coupling method. *Soil Dyn. Earthq. Eng.* **2021**, *140*, 106420. [CrossRef]
21. Feng, S.J.; Du, F.L.; Chen, H.X.; Mao, J.Z. Centrifuge modeling of preloading consolidation and dynamic compaction in treating dredged soil. *Eng. Geol.* **2017**, *226*, 161–171. [CrossRef]
22. Jia, M.C.; Cheng, J.X.; Liu, B.; Ma, G.Q. Model tests of the influence of ground water level on dynamic compaction. *Bull. Eng. Geol. Environ.* **2021**, *80*, 3065–3078. [CrossRef]
23. Li, P.X.; Sun, J.Y.; Ge, X.S.; Zhang, M.; Wang, J.Y. Parameters of dynamic compaction based on model test. *Soil Dyn. Earthq. Eng.* **2023**, *168*, 107853. [CrossRef]
24. Shen, M.F.; Martin, J.R.; Ku, C.S.; Lu, Y.C. A case study of the effect of dynamic compaction on liquefaction of reclaimed ground. *Eng. Geol.* **2018**, *240*, 48–61. [CrossRef]
25. Wu, S.F.; Wei, Y.Q.; Zhang, Y.Q.; Cai, H.; Du, J.F.; Wang, D.; Yan, J.; Xiao, J.Z. Dynamic compaction of a thick soil-stone fill: Dynamic response and strengthening mechanisms. *Soil Dyn. Earthq. Eng.* **2020**, *129*, 105499. [CrossRef]
26. Li, X.; Yang, H.; Zhang, J.Y.; Qian, G.P.; Yu, H.N.; Cai, J. Time-domain analysis of tamper displacement during dynamic compaction based on automatic control. *Coatings* **2021**, *11*, 1092. [CrossRef]
27. Wei, Y.J.; Yang, Y.Y.; Wang, J.T.; Liu, H.C.; Li, J.G.; Jie, Y.X. Performance evaluation of high energy dynamic compaction on soil-rock mixture geomaterials based on field test. *Case Stud. Constr. Mater.* **2023**, *18*, e01734. [CrossRef]
28. Wang, L.; Du, F.L.; Liang, Y.H.; Gao, W.S.; Zhang, G.Z.; Sheng, Z.Q.; Chen, X.S. A comprehensive in situ investigation on the reinforcement of high-filled red soil using the dynamic compaction method. *Sustainability* **2023**, *15*, 4706. [CrossRef]
29. Wang, G.B.; Yin, Y.; Wang, J.N. Vibration safety evaluation and vibration isolation control measures for buried oil pipelines under dynamic compaction: A case study. *Soil Dyn. Earthq. Eng.* **2023**, *167*, 107783. [CrossRef]
30. Alnaim, A.; AlQahtany, A.M.; Alshammari, M.S.; Al-Gehlani, W.A.G.; Alyami, S.H.; Aldossary, N.A.; Naseer, M.N. A systematic framework for evaluating the effectiveness of dynamic compaction (DC) technology for soil improvement projects using cone penetration test data. *Appl. Sci.* **2022**, *12*, 9686. [CrossRef]
31. Yao, J.K.; Yue, M.; Ma, H.S.; Yang, C.W. Wave propagation characteristics and compaction status of subgrade during vibratory compaction. *Sensors* **2023**, *23*, 2183. [CrossRef]
32. Gao, Q.Y.; Jin, Y.L.; Liu, Q.; Yan, P.; Zhang, H.Y.; Li, F.Y.; Wang, H. Monocular vision measurement technology applied in dynamic compaction ramming settlement monitoring. *Measurement* **2023**, *216*, 112941. [CrossRef]
33. Wu, Z.X.; Lei, J.J.; Ye, C.P.; Yu, C.; Zhao, J.L. Coupled FDM-DEM simulations of axial compression tests on FRP-confined concrete specimens. *Constr. Build. Mater.* **2022**, *351*, 128885. [CrossRef]
34. Zheng, Y.N.; Zheng, L.F.; Zhan, H.Y.; Huang, Q.F.; Jia, C.J.; Li, Z. Study on failure mechanism of soil–rock slope with FDM-DEM method. *Sustainability* **2022**, *14*, 17015. [CrossRef]
35. Huang, K.; Sun, Y.W.; Kuang, X.L.; Huang, X.Q.; Liu, R.N.; Wu, Q.J. Study on the restraint effect of isolation pile on surface settlement trough induced by shield tunnelling. *Appl. Sci.* **2022**, *12*, 4845. [CrossRef]
36. Huang, K.; Sun, Y.W.; Chen, X.S.; Deng, X.; Liu, R.N.; Wu, Q.J. Study on three-dimensional soil displacement characteristics in front of shield tunnel excavation face based on coupled FDM-DEM. *China J. Highw. Transp.* 2022; in press.
37. Huang, Z.K.; Argyroudis, S.; Zhang, D.M.; Pitilakis, K.; Huang, H.W.; Zhang, D.M. Time-dependent fragility functions for circular tunnels in soft soils. *ASCE-ASME J. Risk Uncertain. Eng. Syst. Part A Civ. Eng.* **2022**, *8*, 04022030. [CrossRef]
38. Huang, Z.K.; Zhang, D.M.; Pitilakis, K.; Tsinidis, G.; Huang, H.W.; Zhang, D.M.; Argyroudis, S. Resilience assessment of tunnels: Framework and application for tunnels in alluvial deposits exposed to seismic hazard. *Soil Dyn. Earthq. Eng.* **2022**, *162*, 107456. [CrossRef]

39. Potyondy, D.O. Simulating stress corrosion with a bonded-particle model for rock. *Int. J. Rock Mech. Min. Sci.* **2007**, *44*, 677–691. [CrossRef]
40. Feng, S.J.; Du, F.L.; Shi, Z.M.; Shui, W.H.; Tan, K. Field study on the reinforcement of collapsible loess using dynamic compaction. *Eng. Geol.* **2015**, *185*, 105–115. [CrossRef]

Disclaimer/Publisher's Note: The statements, opinions and data contained in all publications are solely those of the individual author(s) and contributor(s) and not of MDPI and/or the editor(s). MDPI and/or the editor(s) disclaim responsibility for any injury to people or property resulting from any ideas, methods, instructions or products referred to in the content.

Article

Numerical Investigation of Key Structural Parameters for Middle-Buried Rubber Waterstops

Yimin Wu [1], Haiping Wu [1], Chenjie Gong [1,*] and Le Huang [2]

[1] School of Civil Engineering, Central South University, Changsha 410075, China; wuyimin531@csu.edu.cn (Y.W.); 234801033@csu.edu.cn (H.W.)
[2] Hubei Provincial Communications Planning and Design Institute Co., Ltd., Wuhan 430050, China; lehuang@163.com
* Correspondence: gongcj@csu.edu.cn

Abstract: Leakage at the lining joints of mountain tunnels is frequent. According to the waterproofing mechanism of waterstops, it is known that the deformation of middle-buried rubber waterstops under stress in typical operating conditions determines their waterproof performance. In addition to the deformation of the adjacent lining concrete, the structural parameters of waterstops are the main factors influencing their deformation under stress. This study combines the common structural components of middle-buried waterstops and considers the bond strength between waterstops and the concrete. A localized numerical model of the lining joint is constructed to explore the impact of geometric parameters, such as hole size, number and position of waterstop ribs, and length and thickness of wing plates on the stress-induced deformation and waterproof performance of the waterstops. The effective mechanisms of different components are revealed, and recommended structural parameters are proposed to further optimize the design of middle-buried rubber waterstops.

Keywords: mountain tunnel; rubber waterstop; numerical investigation; structural optimization

MSC: 00A06

1. Introduction

Engineering practice shows that tunnel joint leakage problems are very serious [1]. As a waterproofing measure for joints in a tunnel, the waterproofing effect of the waterstop belt is not ideal. Water leakage will bring great difficulties and hidden dangers to tunnel construction, and it will also have adverse effects on the safety and durability of tunnel lining [2] and the life of facilities in the tunnel [3,4]. At the same time, water leakage will worsen the environment in the tunnel and seriously affect the traffic [5], which is one of the main factors leading to problems during the tunnel operation [6,7]. Therefore, it is very crucial to optimize the design of the existing waterstop belts, solve any tunnel leakage problems, and ensure the safety and long-term stability of tunnels.

Currently, there are various geometric configurations of waterstops available on the market, and different specifications provide differing requirements for waterstop structures. The Chinese national standard "Polymeric Waterproofing Materials Part 2: Waterstops" [8] and the "Technical Specification for Waterstops in Hydraulic Structures" [9] do not explicitly specify the specific dimensions of waterstops but provide corresponding geometric configurations. The railway standard "Waterproofing Materials for Railway Tunnels Part 2: Waterstops" [10] presents specific dimensions and corresponding geometric configurations of waterstops. However, the geometric configurations of waterstops are not explicitly defined in the highway tunnel specifications. Some geometric configurations of waterstops specified in various standards are shown in Figure 1.

Based on the current structural forms of waterstops, they can be divided into three parts: the center hole, the wing plate, and the rib (flat waterstops do not have a center hole), as shown in Figure 2.

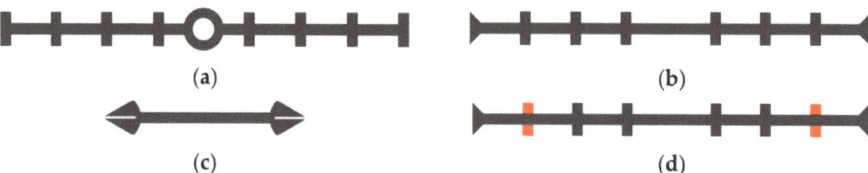

Figure 1. Waterstop structure diagram: (**a**) waterstop for expansion joints; (**b**) waterstop for construction joints; (**c**) waterstop combined with steel edge; and (**d**) waterstop combined with water-swelling rubber (The red part is the water swelling rubber).

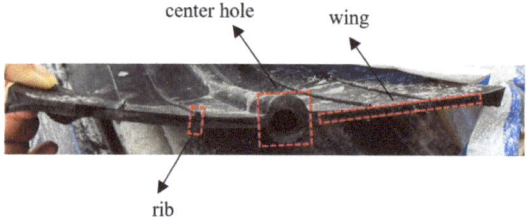

Figure 2. Schematic diagram of waterstop belt components.

Based on the above description, it can be concluded that the current specifications mostly specify the structural form of waterstops, but only the railway tunnel specification provides specific dimensions. In addition, the existing specifications do not provide the design principles for waterstops, making it difficult to determine whether the current geometric designs of waterstops are reasonable. Due to the frequent occurrence of tunnel leakage, and considering the close relationship between the geometric form of waterstops and their installation, waterproofing, and deformation behavior, many researchers have conducted studies on the geometric form of waterstops.

Some researchers [11,12] have studied the stress–strain characteristics of rubber waterstops in immersed tube tunnels and waveform waterstops in concrete dam panel joints using finite element simulation methods. Chen et al. [13] simulated the displacement, stretching, and compression of expansion joint waterstops and analyzed their deformation characteristics and stress distribution.

Lin et al. [14] simulated the deformation of expansion joint waterstops in utility tunnels and analyzed the stress characteristics of these waterstops under different conditions. Furthermore, they analyzed the deformation and stress characteristics of waterstops with different hole sizes and shapes and optimized the structure of existing waterstops.

Meng et al. and Li et al. [15,16] conducted simulations on the tensile and deformation behavior of rubber strips. They analyzed the stress characteristics of waterstops and further investigated the influence of waterstop thickness and the friction coefficient between rubber and concrete on stress distribution. They proposed that increasing the rubber thickness or the friction coefficient between rubber and concrete can effectively reduce the maximum stress in waterstops.

At present, using a numerical method is a popular way to calculate, but there is a need to pay attention to the accuracy of the numerical model [17–19]. The aforementioned analyses of rubber waterstops have certain limitations in terms of the contact between rubber and concrete. Scholars have only simply bound the waterstop under study to the concrete lining or applied friction between the waterstop and lining, without considering the adhesive force between the waterstop and concrete. Consequently, the analytical results may not accurately reflect the deformation and stress distribution of waterstops. Moreover, previous studies on waterstops have often focused on individual components and thus were lacking in depth, comprehensiveness, and systematic research.

In this study, we focused on the commonly used middle-buried rubber waterstops in engineering projects. Starting from the waterproofing mechanism of rubber waterstops, we considered the adhesion between waterstops and concrete in our finite element analysis. We conducted research on each component of waterstops and optimized the design based on the influence of the corresponding components on the deformation and stress distribution of waterstops. The aim was to overcome the traditional experience design, improve the rationality of the geometric structure of the waterstop belt, and enhance its waterproof performance.

2. Waterproofing Mechanism of Middle-Buried Rubber Waterstops

Based on previous research [20], it is known that the waterproofing ability of a middle-buried waterstop mainly depends on its water resistance and flow path. As shown in Figure 3, water resistance involves the contact pressure and adhesive force between the waterstop and concrete. Since the contact pressure is significantly smaller than the adhesive force, its influence on the deformation and stress of the waterstop can be disregarded during simulations. The flow path can dissipate hydraulic head pressure and increase the difficulty of groundwater seeping through tunnel joints.

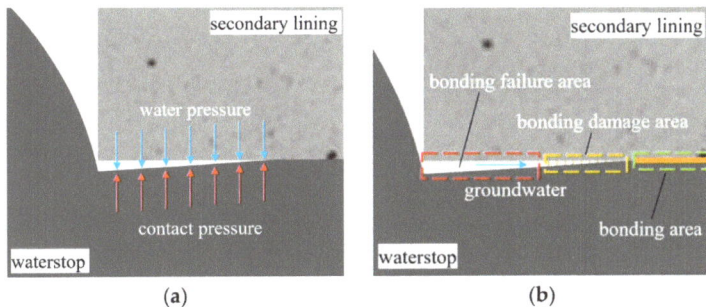

Figure 3. Waterstop waterproofing mechanism diagram: (**a**) water resistance through contact pressure; and (**b**) water resistance through adhesive force.

Meanwhile, due to the uncertainty of rock and soil, the tunnel lining will be deformed [21–23]. At this time, a waterstop is subjected to uneven settlement [24] or expansion due to the deformation of the lining. The maximum settlement can reach 30 mm, the maximum elongation is 20 mm, and the maximum compression is 10 mm. When deformation is significant, the stress on the waterstop may exceed the critical stress level. Prolonged exposure to high-stress levels can accelerate the deterioration of various mechanical properties of the waterstop and reduce its service life, leading to waterproofing failure before the expected service life is reached.

From this, it can be concluded that there are two main causes of failure for an embedded rubber waterstop: (1) water resistance that is lower than the groundwater pressure, and (2) excessive deformation stress on the waterstop. Therefore, to prevent waterproofing failure, it is necessary to ensure that the deformation stress on a waterstop is kept within a reasonable range while maintaining sufficient water resistance. According to relevant research reports, the stress level for synthetic rubber and other polymer materials should not exceed 20% of their tensile strength at fracture [25], which can result in a service life of over 100 years. Based on current specifications, the tensile strength of rubber waterstops is not less than 10 MPa, and a maximum allowable deformation stress of 2 MPa can be selected to ensure safety.

3. Numerical Model Setups

The real waterstop and concrete used in this study are shown in Figure 4. Based on this, a plane–strain finite element model of a waterstop in concrete lining was established according to the ABAQUS/Standard. Figure 5 shows a mesh diagram of the base model, along with the basic dimensions of the model.

Figure 4. Physical photo of the waterstop and concrete used in this study.

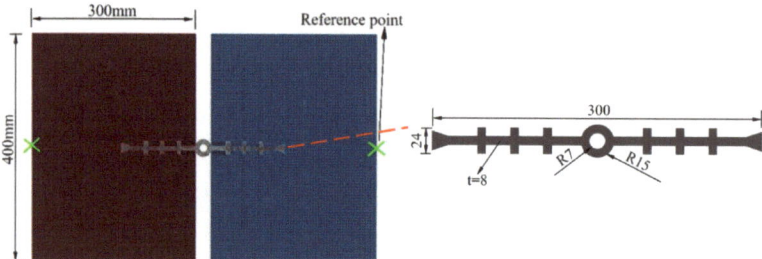

Figure 5. Finite element analysis model (unit: mm).

3.1. Constitutive Models of Materials
3.1.1. Constitutive Model of Concrete

The concrete lining strength is considered to be C30, with an elastic modulus (E_c) of 30 GPa and a Poisson's ratio (ν_c) of 0.2. The concrete damage plasticity model in ABAQUS is used to simulate the failure of the lining. For the damage plasticity parameters, the eccentricity (e_f), the ratio of biaxial to uniaxial compressive strength (f_{b0}/f_{c0}), and the coefficient (k) are set to the default values of 0.1, 1.16, and 0.667, respectively. The viscosity parameter (μ_c) is set to 0.005 for implicit solving in ABAQUS. The dilation angle (ψ) is taken as 30°. The stress–strain curves for uniaxial compression and the tension of concrete are referenced from the concrete design code [26], as shown in Table 1. Here, σ_c and σ_t represent compressive and tensile stresses, respectively, and ε_c^{in} and ε_t^{in} represent non-elastic strains and cracking strains, respectively.

Table 1. Uniaxial stress–strain relationship of concrete.

σ_c	ε_c^{in}	σ_t	ε_t^{in}
14.070	0	2.030	0
20.100	0.000802	2.010	0.000028
14.637	0.002456	1.232	0.000149
10.073	0.004080	0.849	0.000257
7.501	0.005638	0.661	0.000359
5.931	0.007162	0.548	0.000458
4.890	0.008668	0.473	0.000556
4.153	0.010165	0.419	0.000653
3.607	0.011655	0.378	0.000749
3.186	0.013141	0.346	0.000846

3.1.2. Constitutive Model of Rubber Waterstop

Rubber materials belong to hyperelastic materials, which exhibit significant deformations under certain loads and show dual nonlinearity in terms of material and geometry [27]. For numerical calculation, we need to determine the constitutive equation of the model used [28,29]. The constitutive modeling of rubber materials can be simulated using strain energy functions, including commonly used models such as the Mooney–Rivlin model, the Ogden model, and the Yeoh model [30–32] based on continuum mechanics, and the Arruda–Boyce model, Gent model, and Neo Hookean model [33–35] based on thermodynamic statistical theory. These models generally require the determination of parameters and model selection based on rubber testing data.

The selection of an appropriate constitutive model for hyperelastic materials is a fundamental issue. Scholars have compared [36] and modified existing models [37–39] based on experiments, theoretical analyses, and numerical simulations in order to obtain more accurate models. However, modified models are often specific and complex, making them difficult to apply widely. Some researchers argue that higher-order strain energy functions have limited value since the reproducibility of rubber-like materials is low, making it challenging to estimate a large number of parameters accurately [40]. Among the various constitutive models mentioned above, the Mooney–Rivlin model is the most widely used.

The Mooney–Rivlin model [41] is relatively simple compared to other models. It assumes that rubber materials, under a short period of time and constant temperature, behave as isotropic incompressible materials. The model parameters can be determined based on empirical formulas using rubber hardness [42]. It is widely accepted in the industry that the Mooney–Rivlin model can accurately simulate the mechanical properties of rubber and other hyperelastic materials when the strain does not exceed 150%, providing reasonable approximations compared to actual conditions.

In this study, the rubber waterstop was simulated using the dual-coefficient Mooney–Rivlin model in ABAQUS, and the strain energy function is defined as follows [43]:

$$W = C_{10}(I_1 - 3) + C_{01}(I_2 - 3) \tag{1}$$

In the equation, W represents the strain energy density, I_1 and I_2 are the strain tensor invariants, and C_{10} and C_{01} are the material mechanical property constants. Considering the incompressibility of rubber (Poisson's ratio $\mu = 0.5$), the relationship between the shear modulus G, the elastic modulus E_0, and the material constants can be derived as follows:

$$G = 2(C_{10} + C_{01}) \tag{2}$$

$$E_0 = 3G \tag{3}$$

$$E_0 = 6(C_{10} + C_{01}) \tag{4}$$

The elastic modulus E_0 of rubber can be determined based on the rubber hardness H_A, and the relationship is as follows:

$$E_0 = (15.75 + 2.15 H_A)/(100 - H_A) \tag{5}$$

According to current specification, the hardness of rubber waterstops for tunnel joints is 55~65. For this simulation, the intermediate value of 60 was chosen for calculation. Based on empirical data, a value of $C_{10}/C_{01} = 0.25$ can be used, which gives $C_{10} = 0.484$ MPa and $C_{01} = 0.121$ MPa.

3.2. Contact Model

For the interface issues of composite materials, it is a crucial problem to choose an appropriate constitutive model and utilize numerical computation methods to effectively predict the nonlinear behavior of the interface [44]. Currently, there is limited research on the bonding strength of rubber–concrete interfaces, both domestically and internationally. However, insights can be gained from studies on interface damage and cracking in other composite materials [45,46]. Among them, cohesive force models based on damage mechanics have significant advantages in addressing interface problems in composite materials, and the techniques for simulating interface damage and crack propagation under static loads are relatively well-developed.

Cohesive force represents the interaction forces between material molecules, and a cohesive force model is a simplified model used to describe the mechanical behavior of interfaces. By appropriately selecting parameters and defining the evolution of damage processes, it is possible to simulate interface cracking accurately. Interfaces in composite materials are held together by cohesive forces, which are related to the relative displacement between the interfaces. Currently, there are various cohesive force constitutive models available for simulation, as shown in Figure 6. Alfano G. conducted comparative calculations on multiple models and ultimately concluded that a bilinear model can meet the requirements of calculation accuracy and efficiency.

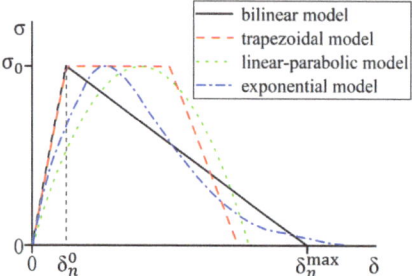

Figure 6. Cohesive damage constitutive models [47].

Generally, the relative displacement of an interface increases with an increase in external load. At this point, the cohesive force also increases. When the displacement reaches δ_n^0, the cohesive force reaches its maximum value σ_0. After reaching the maximum value, the cohesive force gradually decreases as the displacement continues to increase. When it decreases to zero, the relative displacement reaches its maximum value δ_n^{max}, indicating the failure of the bond at the interface of the composite material.

In order to determine the initiation displacement and failure displacement of damage, it is necessary to introduce damage initiation criteria and damage evolution criteria for research. Currently, there are four commonly used damage initiation criteria, which are as follows:

(1) Maximum nominal stress criterion:

$$\max\left\{<\sigma_n>/\sigma_n^0, \sigma_s/\sigma_s^0, \sigma_t/\sigma_t^0\right\}=1 \tag{6}$$

(2) Maximum nominal strain criterion:

$$\max\left\{<\delta_n>/\delta_n^0, \delta_s/\delta_s^0, \delta_t/\delta_t^0\right\}=1 \tag{7}$$

(3) Secondary nominal stress criterion:

$$\left\{<\sigma_n>/\sigma_n^0\right\}^2+\left\{\sigma_s/\sigma_s^0\right\}^2+\left\{\sigma_t/\sigma_t^0\right\}^2=1 \tag{8}$$

(4) Secondary nominal strain criterion:

$$\left\{<\delta_n>/\delta_n^0\right\}^2+\left\{\delta_s/\delta_s^0\right\}^2+\left\{\delta_t/\delta_t^0\right\}^2=1 \tag{9}$$

In the above equations, σ_n, σ_s, and σ_t represent the stresses in the normal and the two tangential directions; σ_n^0, σ_s^0, and σ_t^0 are the critical onset stresses for damage initiation in each direction; δ_n, δ_s, and δ_t are the strains in each direction; and δ_n^0, δ_s^0, and δ_t^0 are the critical onset strains for damage initiation in each direction.

The maximum nominal stress criterion and the maximum nominal strain criterion both indicate that the interface bond starts to undergo damage when the stress or strain in a particular direction reaches the critical onset value. On the other hand, the secondary nominal stress criterion and the secondary nominal strain criterion indicate that the interface bond starts to undergo damage when a certain value is reached by coupling the stresses or strains in all three directions.

As for damage evolution, it refers to the failure process of the interface bond after damage initiation. It is achieved by introducing a stiffness degradation parameter SDEG, which ranges from 0 to 1. When SDEG is 0, it indicates that the interface bond is intact, while a value of 1 indicates complete failure of the interface bond. For a bilinear constitutive model, the stiffness of the interface bond after damage initiation can be expressed as follows:

$$\text{SDEG} = \left[\delta_m^f\left(\delta_m^{max} - \delta_m^0\right)\right] / \left[\delta_m^{max}\left(\delta_m^f - \delta_m^0\right)\right] \quad (10)$$

$$K_i = K_i^0(1 - \text{SDEG}) \quad (11)$$

In Equation (10), δ_m^0 represents the displacement value at the node when the interface bond starts to undergo damage, δ_m^f represents the displacement value at the node when the interface bond completely fails, K_i^0 is the stiffness of the interface bond when it is intact, and K_i is the stiffness of the interface bond after damage initiation. Furthermore, to determine the value of the stiffness degradation parameter SDEG, it is necessary to introduce a damage evolution criterion. Commonly used damage evolution modes include those based on failure displacement or failure energy. Energy-based damage evolution criteria include the power criterion and B-K criterion, all of which can be directly selected in the ABAQUS 2021 finite element analysis software.

3.3. Element Types and Boundary Conditions

The concrete was simulated using CPE4 elements, while the rubber waterstop belt was simulated using CPE4RH elements. Coupling was applied to the concrete lining on both sides using the reference points. During simulation, deformations were applied to the reference points, with the other two directions being fixed when a single-direction deformation was applied.

4. Adhesive Force Test and Numerical Model Verification

4.1. Adhesive Force Test

In summary, in this study, a bilinear cohesive model was used to simulate the bonding interface between rubber and concrete. To obtain the required parameters for the model, rubber–concrete bond strength tests were conducted. The performance of concrete varies greatly with different mix ratio [48,49]. Due to the small size of the test specimens and the main bonding between concrete and rubber being the bonding between cement paste and rubber, cement blocks were used as a substitute for concrete to simulate the bond between concrete and rubber. Ordinary Portland cement with a compressive strength of 42.5 MPa (28 d) was used. The tensile bond strength and shear bond strength of rubber–cement were taken as the evaluation criteria. The rubber was cut into blocks with dimensions of 100 mm × 50 mm × 20 mm, and the cement blocks had the same dimensions as the rubber blocks. Good end surfaces were selected for pouring. After pouring, the specimens were cured in an environment with a temperature of 20 ± 2 °C and a relative humidity of over 95% for 28 days. The specimens were divided into two groups: tension and shear, with three specimens in each group. The test areas for tensile and shear bond strength were rectangular with dimensions of 50 mm × 20 mm and square with dimensions of 50 mm × 50 mm, respectively. The tensile and shear specimens are shown in Figure 7.

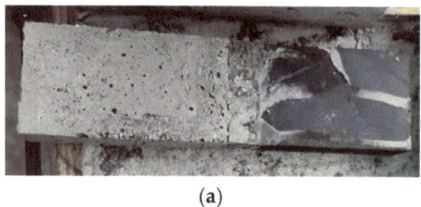 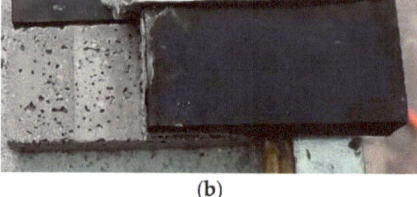

(a) (b)

Figure 7. Rubber–cement specimens: (**a**) tension specimen and (**b**) shear specimen.

The test equipment is shown in Figure 8. The tension machine consisted of four parts: a displacement measuring device, a loading apparatus, a tensiometer, and fixing installation. The measuring range of the tensiometer was 0~1000 N, and the accuracy was 1 N. The test loading took the displacement as the variable, and the accuracy of the loading device was 0.1 mm. Because the shape of the specimen used was rectangular, the adhesive force between rubber and concrete was small, and the bonding interface was brittle; the tensile speed of the selected loading device was 5 mm/min.

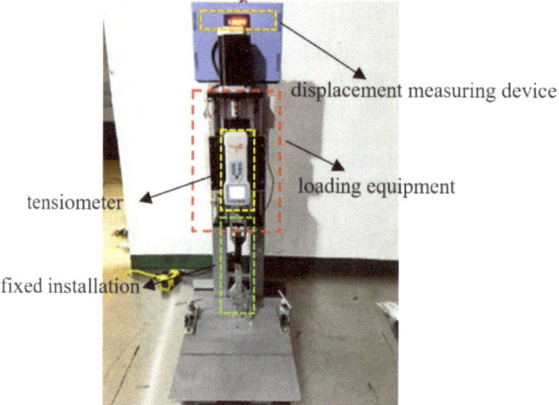

Figure 8. Tensile testing machine.

The maximum stress sustained by the rubber–cement specimens during the bonding failure caused by external forces is referred to as the tensile or shear strength. The average strength value of the three specimens in each group was taken as the measurement result, as shown in Table 2. Additionally, the deformation of the specimens during the testing process was recorded. The average deformation for the tensile specimens from start to finish was 7.7 mm, while the average deformation for the shear specimens was 5.9 mm.

Table 2. The bonding strength of rubber to concrete.

Conditions	1/MPa	2/MPa	3/MPa	Bonding Strength/MPa
Tensile specimen	0.414	0.387	0.356	0.386
Shear specimen	0.162	0.141	0.149	0.151

Therefore, the contact between rubber and concrete could be set as normal hard contact, while the tangential contact was implemented using the penalty function method with a friction coefficient of 0.3. Additionally, the bonding behavior was modeled as cohesive contact, with a normal stiffness of 3860 MPa/mm, a tangential stiffness of 1510 MPa/mm, a normal cohesive strength of 0.386 MPa, a tangential cohesive strength of 0.151 MPa, and a plastic displacement of 0.0009 mm.

4.2. Numerical Model Validation

To validate the rationality of the Mooney–Rivlin rubber constitutive model and the bilinear cohesive force model, a finite element model of rubber–concrete tension and shear was established using ABAQUS/Standard. The model is shown in Figure 9. The reference points were used to couple the concrete and rubber, with the concrete being fixed and displacement applied to the rubber reference points, while the reaction forces were recorded.

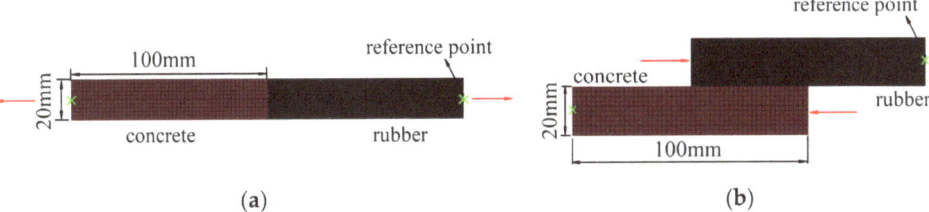

Figure 9. Rubber–concrete models: (**a**) tension model and (**b**) shear model.

The calculated results are shown in Figure 10, indicating that the bond strength and deformation obtained from the finite element analysis were slightly smaller than the measured values. The calculated tensile strength was 0.339 MPa, and the shear strength was 0.141 MPa, with differences of 12.2% and 6.6% from the measured values, respectively. The calculated tensile deformation was 7.45 mm, and the shear deformation was 5.2 mm, with differences of 3.2% and 11.9% from the measured values, respectively. The discrepancies may be attributed to the deformation of the rubber during simulation, but they were relatively small, and the simulated values were lower than the measured values. Therefore, it can be concluded that using the Mooney–Rivlin rubber constitutive model and the bilinear cohesive model to simulate the bond between rubber and concrete is reasonable.

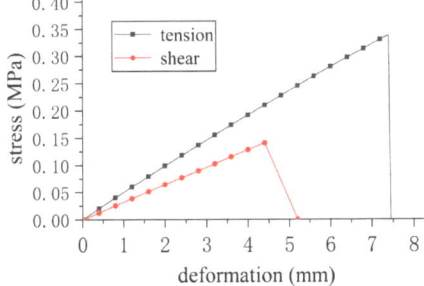

Figure 10. Simulation results for rubber–concrete bond failure.

5. Numerical Analysis of Key Structural Parameters

5.1. Different Parameters of Waterstop Center Hole

5.1.1. Fixed Outer Diameter of the Center Hole

By keeping the outer diameter of the center hole of the waterstop constant (r = 15), different inner diameters of the center hole were used to establish a 2D strain finite element model of buried waterstops in the concrete lining using ABAQUS/Standard, as shown in Figure 11. Tension, compression, and settlement deformations were applied with deformation magnitudes of 20 mm, 10 mm, and 30 mm, respectively.

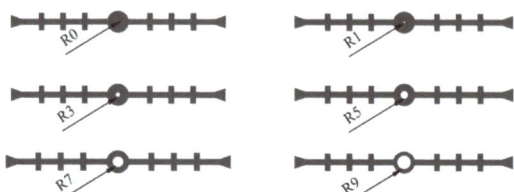

Figure 11. Models of waterstops with different inner diameters of the center hole (unit: mm).

The calculation results indicated that there was no damage to the concrete lining. The deformation stress of the waterstops is shown in Figure 12, revealing the following trends regarding the influence of the inner hole size:

(1) Under tensile deformation, the deformation stress initially increases and then decreases with an increase in the aperture size. The maximum stress occurs when the aperture size is R = 3 mm, possibly due to the aperture size being too small, thus resulting in stress concentration during deformation. The deformation stress in all scenarios remains below the critical stress value.

(2) During compressive deformation, the overall deformation stress decreases with an increase in the aperture size (though stress concentration may occur when $0 < R \leq 3$). However, when the aperture size is less than 5 mm, the deformation stress of the waterstop exceeds the critical stress value.

(3) During settlement deformation, the deformation stress initially decreases and then increases with an increase in the aperture size. The minimum stress occurs when the aperture size is R = 5 mm, and only in this case is the deformation stress below the critical stress.

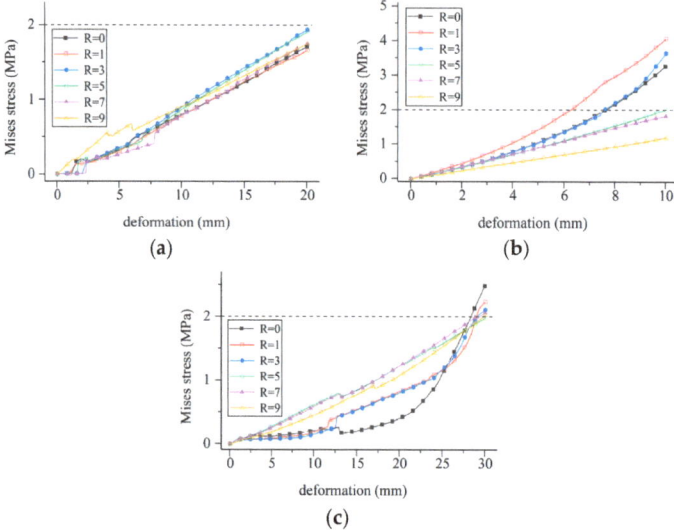

Figure 12. Deformation stress of waterstops with different inner diameters of the center hole: (**a**) tensile deformation; (**b**) compression deformation; and (**c**) settlement deformation. (The dashed line is the critical stress. All the pictures in this article are the same).

In summary, under the condition of a constant outer diameter of the waterstop aperture, increasing the inner diameter of the waterstop aperture primarily improves the stress distribution during compressive deformation. However, care should be taken to avoid having an excessively thin wall for the aperture, which could lead to tearing or puncturing of the waterstop. When designing a waterstop, an inner aperture diameter of R = 5 mm can be chosen.

Taking the tensile deformation of the simulated waterstops as an example, Figure 13 shows the region of bond failure between each waterstop and concrete after deformation for different inner hole diameters while keeping the outer hole diameter constant. Figure 14 shows the adhesive failure range of the waterstop belts with different inner diameters (single-side failure range of waterstops). It can be observed that the bond failure range of the waterstops is approximately the same for different inner hole diameters (the bond failure range for compression deformation and settlement deformation of the waterstops is similar). Therefore, it can be concluded that the inner hole diameter has little effect on the bond between a waterstop and concrete when the outer diameter of the waterstop's center hole is constant.

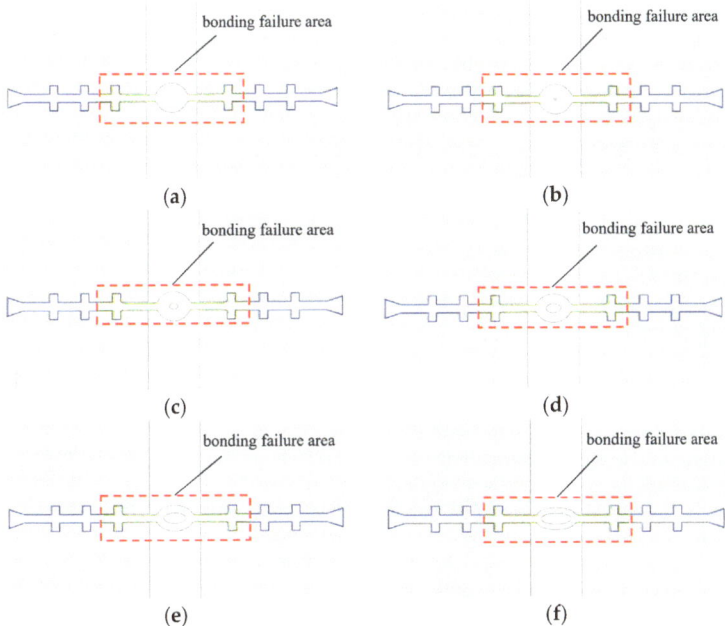

Figure 13. Debonding regions of waterstops with different inner hole diameters: (**a**) R = 0; (**b**) R = 1; (**c**) R = 3; (**d**) R = 5; (**e**) R = 7; and (**f**) R = 9.

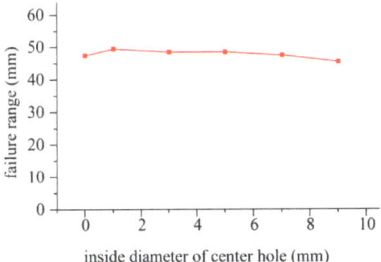

Figure 14. Adhesive failure range of different inner diameters of waterstop belts.

5.1.2. Fixed Inner Hole Diameter

Based on the above analysis, to avoid stress concentration in the inner hole of a waterstop, the inner hole diameter should be maintained at a certain size. By keeping the inner hole diameter of the waterstop constant (R = 7 mm), different outer hole diameters were used to establish a plane–strain finite element model of buried waterstops in the concrete lining using ABAQUS/Standard, as shown in Figure 15. The same deformations as mentioned earlier were applied.

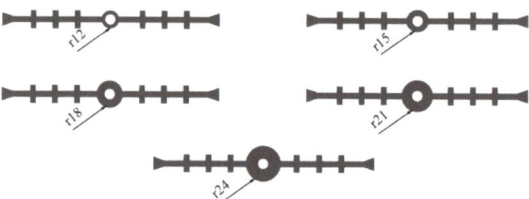

Figure 15. Models of waterstops with different outer hole diameters (unit: mm).

According to the calculation results, no damage was observed in the deformation of the concrete lining. The deformation stress of the waterstops is shown in Figure 16. With a constant inner hole diameter of the waterstops, the following could be observed:

(1) During tensile deformation, the deformation stress generally increases with an increase in the outer diameter. When the outer diameter of the aperture r > 21 mm, the deformation stress exceeds the critical stress threshold.
(2) During compressive deformation, the deformation stress initially increases and then decreases with an increase in the outer diameter of the aperture. The deformation stress in all scenarios remains below the critical stress level.
(3) During settlement deformation, the deformation stress shows a notable change with variations in the outer diameter of the aperture. It decreases as the outer diameter of the waterstop aperture increases. When the outer diameter r > 15 mm, the deformation stress is below the critical stress threshold.

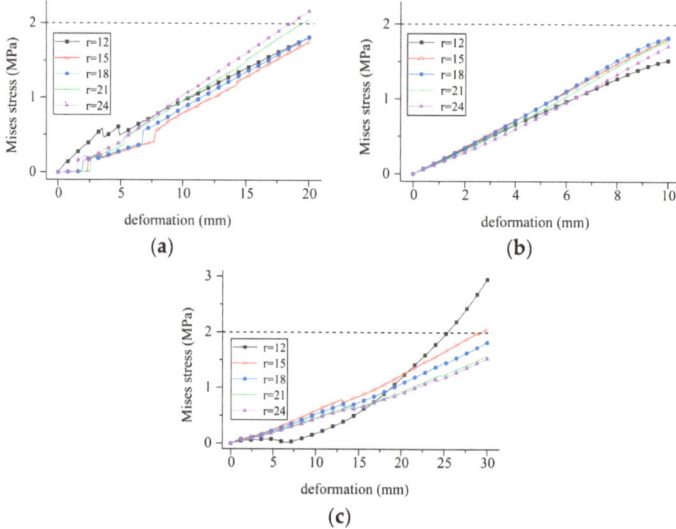

Figure 16. Deformation stress of waterstop with different outer diameters of the center hole: (**a**) tensile deformation; (**b**) compression deformation; and (**c**) settlement deformation.

In summary, under a constant inner diameter of the waterstop aperture, increasing the outer diameter of the aperture primarily serves to improve the stress distribution during settlement deformation. However, it is also important to prevent excessive tensile deformation stress. When designing a waterstop, an outer aperture diameter of r = 18 mm is recommended.

Similarly to the case of a constant outer hole diameter, when the inner hole diameter of the waterstop is fixed, the size of the outer hole has a minimal impact on the range of adhesive failure after the deformation of the waterstop.

5.1.3. Fixed Thickness of the Center Hole

The thickness of the center hole in the waterstop was kept constant at 8 mm. Different sizes of center holes were selected, and a 2D finite element model of the embedded waterstops in the concrete lining was established using ABAQUS/Standard, as shown in Figure 17. The simulation parameters were the same as described earlier.

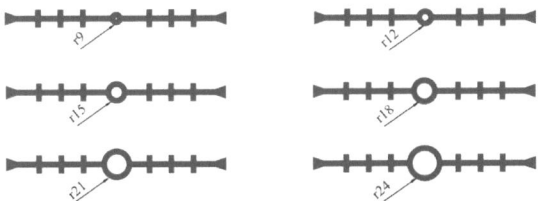

Figure 17. Waterstop models with different sizes of center holes (unit: mm).

The calculation results are shown in Figure 18. It can be observed from the results that, with a constant waterstop aperture wall thickness of 8 mm, the aperture size has a relatively minor effect on tensile deformation stress but a significant impact on compression and settlement deformation stress:

(1) During tensile deformation, the deformation stresses in all scenarios are below the critical stress value.
(2) During compression deformation, the deformation stress decreases with an increase in the aperture size. When the aperture outer diameter $r \geq 15$ mm, the deformation stress is below the critical stress value (at r = 9 mm, the deformation stress is excessively high, and the complete curve is not shown in the graph).
(3) During settlement deformation, the deformation stress decreases with an increase in the aperture size. When the aperture outer diameter r > 15 mm, the deformation stress is below the critical stress value.

In conclusion, under the condition of a constant waterstop aperture wall thickness, enlarging the waterstop aperture can effectively improve the stress distribution during waterstop deformation. It is recommended to choose an aperture size with r > 15 mm when designing a waterstop.

Similarly to the previous calculations, when the wall thickness of a waterstop's hole is constant, the size of the center hole has a minor influence on the range of bond failure after deformation.

5.2. Different Parameters of Waterstop Ribs

5.2.1. Number and Placement of Waterstop Ribs

To analyze the effect of the number and placement of waterstop ribs on the deformation and stress of waterstops, and taking the previous waterstop as an example, the distances from the waterstop ribs to the waterstop orifice and the spacing between the waterstop ribs are shown in Figure 19. The number of ribs on the waterstop was selectively reduced based on their positions, resulting in the creation of eight different waterstop models, as illustrated in Figure 20. ABAQUS/Standard was used to establish the plane–strain finite element models of the embedded waterstop in concrete lining, using the same simulation parameters as mentioned earlier.

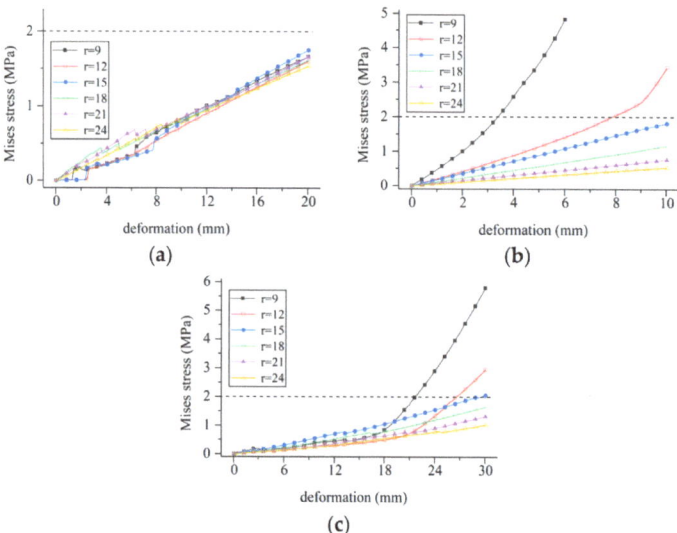

Figure 18. Deformation stress of waterstops with different sizes of the center hole: (**a**) tensile deformation; (**b**) compression deformation; and (**c**) settlement deformation.

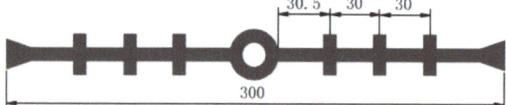

Figure 19. Illustration of waterstop rib positions (unit: mm).

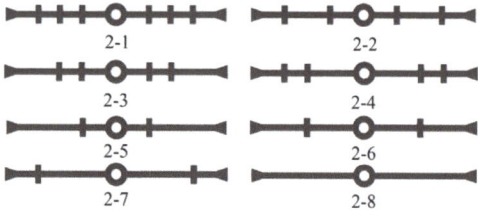

Figure 20. Waterstop models under different conditions.

Based on the calculation results, no damage was observed in the deformed concrete lining. The deformation stresses of the waterstop are shown in Figure 21. The following could be observed:

(1) Under tensile deformation, the stress values in all conditions are below the critical stress. Conditions 2-1, 2-2, 2-3, and 2-5 exhibit nearly identical deformation stresses, while conditions 2-4 and 2-6 also exhibit similar deformation stresses. The common factor among these pairs of waterstops with similar deformation stresses is that the position of the first waterstop rib on both sides is the same, with the difference being the number of ribs or the positions of the remaining ribs. Furthermore, conditions 2-5, 2-6, 2-7, and 2-8 demonstrate that as the distance between the first rib on both sides and the waterstop orifice increases, the tensile deformation stress of the waterstop decreases continuously. The difference between the maximum and minimum tensile deformation stresses can reach 233.5%.

(2) Under compressive deformation, the deformation stresses in all conditions are below the critical stress. Similarly to tensile deformation, the deformation stress of the waterstop is also primarily influenced by the distance between the first rib on both sides and the waterstop orifice.

(3) Under settlement deformation, when the distance between the first rib on both sides and the waterstop orifice exceeds 60 mm, the deformation stress is below the critical stress. The deformation stress of the waterstop under settlement deformation follows a similar pattern as described above.

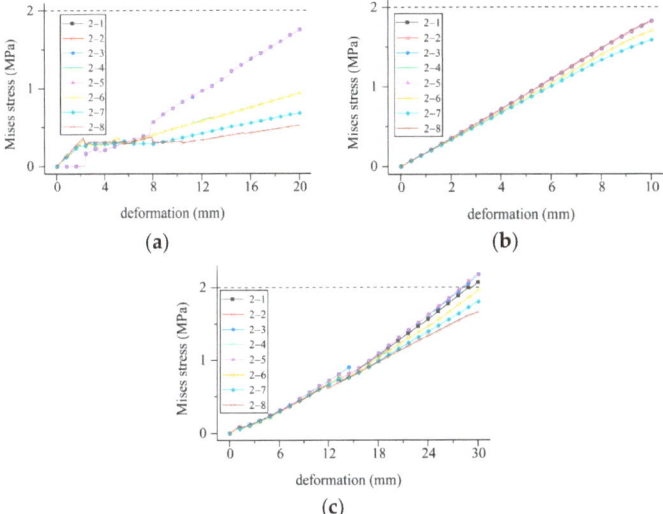

Figure 21. Deformation stresses of the waterstop under different conditions: (**a**) tensile deformation; (**b**) compression deformation; and (**c**) settlement deformation.

Based on the above analysis, it can be concluded that the deformation stress of the waterstop is independent of the number of ribs and is only related to the distance between the first rib on both sides of the waterstop and the hole. The farther the first rib is from the hole, the smaller the deformation stress of the waterstop. When the ribs of the waterstop are closer to the hole, the deformation stress may reach the critical stress. Therefore, when optimizing the design of a waterstop, it is advisable to increase the distance between the first rib on both sides of the waterstop and the hole.

Taking tensile deformation of the waterstop as an example, Figure 22 illustrates the zone of adhesive failure after deformation for different models with varying rib numbers and positions. Figure 23 shows the adhesive failure range of the waterstop belt under different conditions (single-side failure range of the waterstop). It can be observed that the adhesive failure range of the waterstop in each condition is only related to the position of the first rib on both sides of the waterstop. The farther the first rib is from the hole, the larger the range of adhesive failure after deformation. When there are no ribs on the waterstop, the adhesive failure area already includes almost the entire waterstop, indicating a nearly complete loss of adhesion between the waterstop and the concrete due to tensile deformation.

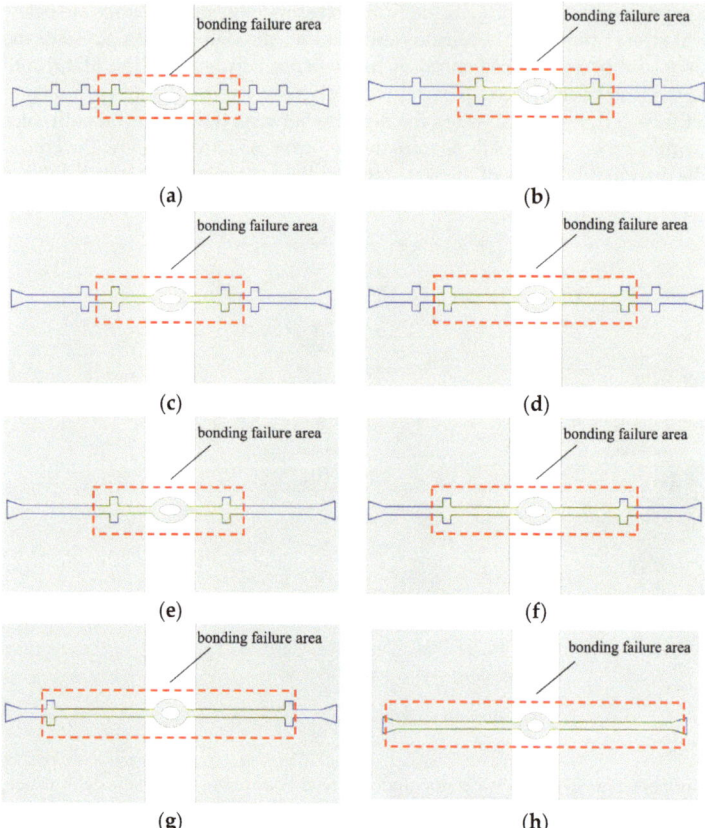

Figure 22. Adhesive failure zones of waterstop deformation under different conditions: (**a**) 2-1; (**b**) 2-2; (**c**) 2-3; (**d**) 2-4; (**e**) 2-5; (**f**) 2-6; (**g**) 2-7; and (**h**) 2-8.

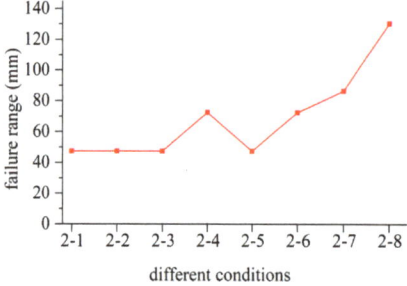

Figure 23. Adhesive failure range under different conditions.

Therefore, it can be concluded that the ribs of the waterstop can effectively prevent the adhesive failure between the concrete and the waterstop, and the failure range slightly exceeds the position of the first rib on both sides. To enhance the anchorage between the waterstop and the concrete and to ensure effective waterproofing, it is recommended to have at least one rib on the waterstop.

5.2.2. Spacing between Waterstop Ribs

When setting the spacing between waterstop ribs, the influence of coarse aggregate size in concrete should be considered. As shown in Figure 24, if the spacing between waterstop ribs is too small and it becomes difficult for coarse aggregates to penetrate, the quality of the concrete between waterstop ribs may be poor, resulting in lower strength and the formation of areas with quality defects. These areas can become weak points in waterproofing.

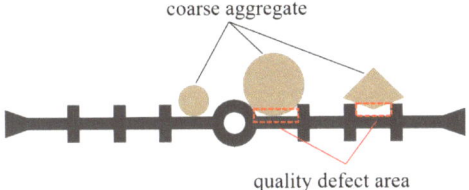

Figure 24. Schematic diagram of areas with quality defects.

According to the concrete mix design specifications, for pumped concrete, the minimum size of coarse aggregates should be greater than 5 mm. The maximum aggregate size, when pumping height is less than 50 m, should be less than one-third of the diameter of the conveying pipe, which is generally less than 40 mm. This indicates that the coarse aggregate size for pumped concrete should be between 5 mm and 40 mm. In tunnel construction, the typical gradation of coarse aggregates used is 5–10 mm and 10–25 mm. Therefore, to meet the requirements for concrete quality, it is recommended to set the distance between the ribs of the waterstop to the waterstop or the spacing between the ribs of the waterstop to be greater than 25 mm.

5.3. Different Parameters of Waterstop Wing

5.3.1. Wing Thickness

To investigate the influence of wing thickness on the performance of waterstops, while keeping other parameters constant, different wing thicknesses, denoted as t, were selected. As shown in Figure 25, finite element models of the embedded waterstop in concrete lining were established using ABAQUS/Standard, with the simulation parameters consistent with the previous analysis.

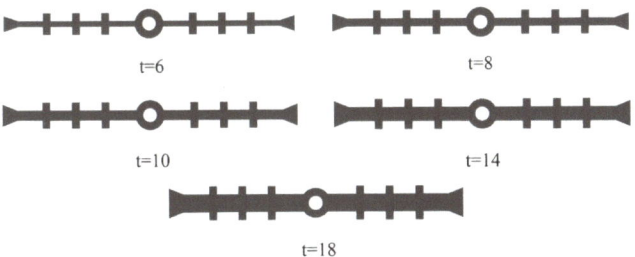

Figure 25. Models of waterstops with different wing thicknesses (unit: mm).

The calculation results are shown in Figure 26. It can be seen that the deformation stress of the waterstop belt increases with an increase in the thickness of the wing plate:

(1) During tensile deformation, when the thickness of the wing plate is greater than or equal to 14 mm, the tensile deformation stress is greater than the critical stress level.
(2) During compression deformation, when the flange thickness is greater than or equal to 14 mm, the compression deformation leads to tensile damage in the concrete lining (only partial curves are shown for the cases of t = 14 mm and t = 18 mm). The damage is due to the fact that when the other parameters of the waterstop belt remain

unchanged and the thickness of the wing plate increases, the outer contour of the hole in the waterstop belt decreases, the concrete lining joint narrows, and the compression deformation of the hole in the waterstop belt becomes increasingly intense with an increase in the thickness of the wing plate.

(3) During settlement deformation, the deformation stress for all cases exceeds the critical stress value.

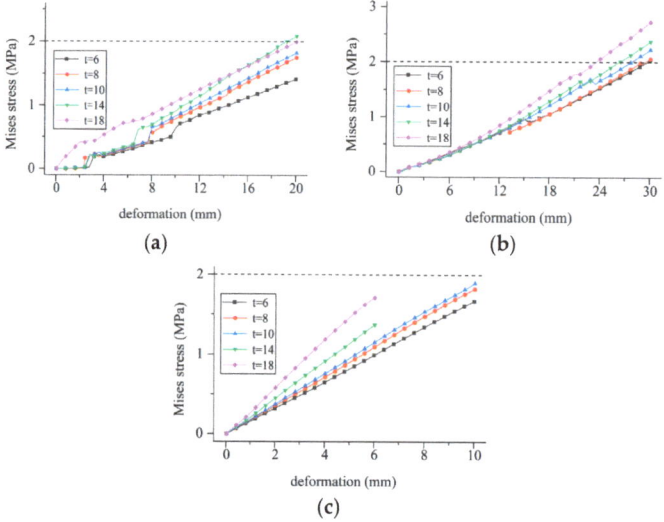

Figure 26. Deformation stress of waterstops under different wing thickness conditions: (**a**) tensile deformation; (**b**) compression deformation; and (**c**) settlement deformation.

In summary, to reduce the deformation stress of a waterstop and avoid damage to the concrete lining, it is necessary to control the thickness of the waterstop's flange. However, when the wing thickness is too small, there is a risk of tearing or puncturing the waterstop. According to the specifications for waterstops, the minimum thickness of waterstops should be 4 mm. From the perspectives of safety and waterproofing, it is recommended to design a waterstop with a wing thickness of 4–10 mm.

5.3.2. Wing Length

From the previous simulations, it can be observed that the deformation stress in a waterstop is mainly concentrated between the first pair of waterstop ribs on both sides. This indicates that increasing the length of the wing itself has a minimal impact on its deformation and stress state.

Considering the waterproofing mechanism of waterstops, it is known that a longer flow path can enhance the waterproofing reliability of the joint. The flow path length of the simulated embedded waterstop is determined by the length of the wing and the length of the waterstop ribs, as shown in Figure 27. Therefore, it can be inferred that increasing the length of the wing can result in a longer flow path, thereby improving the waterproofing reliability of the tunnel joint.

However, the embedded waterstop exhibits a cutting effect where the wing plates cut into the concrete lining. The cutting depth is equal to the length of the wing plates, resulting in a reduced integrity of the concrete lining. This creates a defect area that cannot be resolved through the construction process. The defect area is illustrated in Figure 28, showing a significant deficiency in the controllability of concrete quality in the arch area, with a risk of detachment at the ends. Particularly, when the positioning of the embedded waterstop is inaccurate or when deformation occurs, the uneven thickness of the cut concrete layers increases vulnerability to damage and detachment on the thinner side, thus compromising the reliability of the embedded connection between the waterstop and the concrete and leading to waterproofing failure. Moreover, longer wing plates exacerbate the cutting effect on the concrete lining. From this perspective, it is necessary to reduce the length of waterstop wing plates.

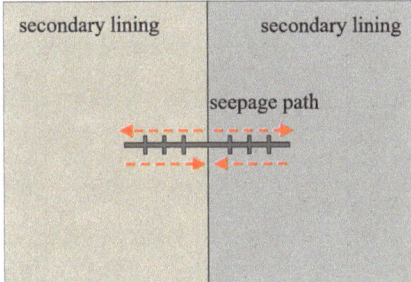

Figure 27. Waterstop flow path.

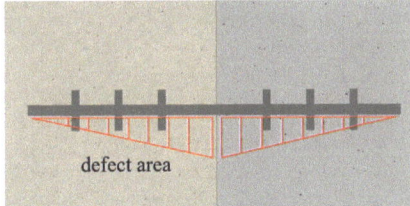

Figure 28. Defect area caused by cutting effect.

In summary, it is important to control the length of a waterstop's wing plates to minimize the impact of cutting on the concrete lining while maximizing the waterstop's flow path. However, the existing structure of the embedded waterstop makes it challenging to reconcile the contradiction between the flow path and the cutting effect. To address this issue, it may be necessary to explore alternative waterstop structures.

6. Conclusions

This paper is based on the waterproofing mechanism of an embedded rubber waterstop. It focuses on the structural characteristics of the waterstop and uses numerical methods to analyze the influence of the central hole, waterstop ribs, and wing on the stress and deformation characteristics of the waterstop. The effective mechanisms and the impact of key geometric parameters on the waterproofing performance are revealed, and recommended parameters for each component are proposed. Adopting the recommended parameters in the design of waterstops can reduce deformation stress, extend the service life of waterstops, and reduce the risk of waterproofing failure of waterstops. The main work and conclusions are as follows:

(1) The bond strength between rubber and concrete was tested, and the feasibility of using the Mooney–Rivlin model and bilinear cohesive force model to simulate the bonding between rubber and rubber–concrete interface was verified.
(2) The center hole of the waterstop primarily serves to accommodate the deformation of the joint and reduce the deformation stress. In the design of the center hole, increasing the outer diameter and reducing the wall thickness of the center hole can help mitigate excessive deformation stress.
(3) The waterstop ribs primarily enhance the anchorage between the waterstop and the concrete. As the deformation stress is mainly borne by the first ribs on both sides of

the waterstop, the deformation stress of the waterstop is independent of the number of ribs but depends on the distance between the first ribs and the center hole. A greater distance between the first ribs and the center hole results in lower deformation stress. To reduce the deformation stress of the waterstop, it is recommended to increase the distance between the ribs and the center hole, for example, increasing the spacing from 30 mm to over 35 mm. Additionally, to ensure the quality of the concrete between the ribs, it is suggested to have a rib spacing greater than 25 mm.

(4) The wing of the waterstop serves as a part that is embedded in the concrete to provide fixation. The thicker the wing, the greater the deformation stress. To avoid excessive deformation stress and reduce the risk of tearing or puncturing the waterstop, it is recommended to have a wing thickness of 4–10 mm. Moreover, the wing contributes to the leakage pathway, and a longer length of the wing enhances the waterproofing reliability of the waterstop. However, the wing cuts into the concrete, and the longer the flanges, the more severe the cutting effect on the concrete. The existing waterstop structure has difficulty reconciling the contradiction between the leakage pathway and the cutting effect, thus requiring the proposal of new waterstop structures to address this issue.

Author Contributions: Conceptualization, Y.W.; methodology, Y.W.; validation, H.W.; investigation, H.W.; resources, Y.W.; data curation, C.G.; writing—original draft preparation, H.W.; writing—review and editing, C.G.; visualization, L.H.; project administration, L.H. and C.G. All authors have read and agreed to the published version of the manuscript.

Funding: This research was funded by the Department of Transport of Hubei Province Science and Technology Project, grant number 2020-186-2-5.

Data Availability Statement: All data are available from the corresponding author upon request.

Conflicts of Interest: The authors declare no conflict of interest.

References

1. Gong, C.; Wang, Y.; Peng, Y.; Ding, W.; Lei, M.; Da, Z.; Shi, C. Three-Dimensional Coupled Hydromechanical Analysis of Localized Joint Leakage in Segmental Tunnel Linings. *Tunn. Undergr. Space Technol.* **2022**, *130*, 104726. [CrossRef]
2. Muhammad, N.Z.; Keyvanfar, A.; Majid, M.Z.A.; Shafaghat, A.; Mirza, J. Waterproof Performance of Concrete: A Critical Review on Implemented Approaches. *Constr. Build. Mater.* **2015**, *101*, 80–90. [CrossRef]
3. Zhou, Z.Q.; Li, S.C.; Li, L.P.; Shi, S.S.; Xu, Z.H. An Optimal Classification Method for Risk Assessment of Water Inrush in Karst Tunnels Based on Grey System Theory. *Geomech. Eng.* **2015**, *8*, 631–647. [CrossRef]
4. Sañudo, R.; Miranda, M.; García, C.; García-Sanchez, D. Drainage in Railways. *Constr. Build. Mater.* **2019**, *210*, 391–412. [CrossRef]
5. Yuan, Y.; Jiang, X.; Lee, C.F. Tunnel Waterproofing Practices in China. *Tunn. Undergr. Space Technol.* **2000**, *15*, 227–233. [CrossRef]
6. Peng, L.J. Existing Operational Railway Tunnel Water Leakage Causes and Remediation Technologies. In *Advanced Materials Research*; Trans Tech Publications Ltd.: Wollerau, Switzerland, 2014; Volume 1004, pp. 1444–1449.
7. Li, S.; Zhou, Z.; Li, L.; Xu, Z.; Zhang, Q.; Shi, S. Risk Assessment of Water Inrush in Karst Tunnels Based on Attribute Synthetic Evaluation System. *Tunn. Undergr. Space Technol.* **2013**, *38*, 50–58. [CrossRef]
8. GB 18173.2-2014; Polymeric Waterproofing Materials Part 2: Waterstops. Standards Press of China: Beijing, China, 2014.
9. DL/T 5215-2005; Technical Specification for Waterstops in Hydraulic Structures. China Electric Power Press: Beijing, China, 2005.
10. TB/T 3360.2-2014; Waterproofing Materials for Railway Tunnels Part 2: Waterstops. China Railway Publishing House: Beijing, China, 2015.
11. Luo, Y.; Feng, Z.; Liu, J.; He, B.; Guo, H. Research on Structure and Performance of Internal Rubber Waterstop. *Railw. Eng.* **2013**, 93–96.
12. Wang, W.; Luo, Y.; Kong, L.; Zhang, Y.; Chen, Y. Numerical Simulation and Experimental Study on Mechanical Properties of GINA Waterstop. *Mod. Tunn. Technol.* **2021**, *58*, 237–243. [CrossRef]
13. Chen, E.; Chen, K.; Ma, C.; Xin, Y. Finite Element Analysis of Rubber Waterstop Belt under Stress State. *World Rubber Ind.* **2010**, *37*, 15–19.
14. Lin, P.; Zhao, Z.; Fan, B.; Han, S.; Liu, G. Analysis of the Deformation Capacity and Size Optimization of Rubber Waterstop in the Deformation Joint of Utility Tunnel. *Bull. Sci. Technol.* **2020**, *36*, 57–63. [CrossRef]
15. Meng, C.; Li, R.; Liu, J.; Xu, Y.; Li, J.; Hao, J. Research on Internally-Side Attached Rubber Waterstop Belt: Part I Pull-out Tests of Rubber Strip and Its Numerical Simulation. *Water Power* **2021**, *47*, 69–72+95.
16. Li, R.; Meng, C.; Zhou, J.; Xu, Y.; Li, J.; Hao, J. Research on Interally-Side Attached Rubber Waterstop Belt: Part II Numerical Simulation on Waterstop Belt and Its Model Test. *Water Power* **2021**, *47*, 42–45.

17. Zhang, H.; Yang, X.; Tang, Q.; Xu, D. A Robust Error Analysis of the OSC Method for a Multi-Term Fourth-Order Sub-Diffusion Equation. *Comput. Math. Appl.* **2022**, *109*, 180–190. [CrossRef]
18. Yang, X.; Zhang, H.; Tang, J. The OSC Solver for the Fourth-Order Sub-Diffusion Equation with Weakly Singular Solutions. *Comput. Math. Appl.* **2021**, *82*, 1–12. [CrossRef]
19. Jiang, X.; Wang, J.; Wang, W.; Zhang, H. A Predictor-Corrector Compact Difference Scheme for a Nonlinear Fractional Differential Equation. *Fractal Fract.* **2023**, *7*, 521. [CrossRef]
20. Wu, Y.; Wu, H.; Chu, D.; Feng, S.; Zhang, J.; Wu, H. Failure Mechanism Analysis and Optimization Analysis of Tunnel Joint Waterstop Considering Bonding and Extrusion. *Appl. Sci.* **2022**, *12*, 5737. [CrossRef]
21. Ma, J.; Pei, H.; Zhu, H.; Shi, B.; Yin, J. A Review of Previous Studies on the Applications of Fiber Optic Sensing Technologies in Geotechnical Monitoring. *Rock Mech. Bull.* **2023**, *2*, 100021. [CrossRef]
22. Zhou, Z.; Zhang, J.; Gong, C. Hybrid Semantic Segmentation for Tunnel Lining Cracks Based on Swin Transformer and Convolutional Neural Network. *Comput.-Aided Civ. Infrastruct. Eng.* 2023. [CrossRef]
23. Zhang, L.; Wu, F.; Wei, X.; Yang, H.-Q.; Fu, S.; Huang, J.; Gao, L. Polynomial Chaos Surrogate and Bayesian Learning for Coupled Hydro-Mechanical Behavior of Soil Slope. *Rock Mech. Bull.* **2023**, *2*, 100023. [CrossRef]
24. Shen, Y.; Zhang, D.; Wang, R.; Li, J.; Huang, Z. SBD-K-Medoids-Based Long-Term Settlement Analysis of Shield Tunnel. *Transp. Geotech.* **2023**, *42*, 101053. [CrossRef]
25. Gu, G. *Mechanical Analysis of Rubber Waterstop Belt and Plastic Waterstop Belt*; Chinese Society of Hydroelectric Engineering: Beijing, China, 2004; pp. 399–406.
26. GB 50010-2010; Code for Design of Concrete Structures. China Building Industry press: Beijing, China, 2015.
27. Ponnamma, D.; Thomas, S. Origin of Nonlinear Viscoelasticity in Filled Rubbers: Theory and Practice. In *Non-Linear Viscoelasticity of Rubber Composites and Nanocomposites: Influence of Filler Geometry and Size in Different Length Scales*; Ponnamma, D., Thomas, S., Eds.; Springer-Verlag Berlin: Berlin, Germany, 2014; Volume 264, pp. 1–13; ISBN 978-3-319-08702-3.
28. Yang, X.; Wu, L.; Zhang, H. A Space-Time Spectral Order Sinc-Collocation Method for the Fourth-Order Nonlocal Heat Model Arising in Viscoelasticity. *Appl. Math. Comput.* **2023**, *457*, 128192. [CrossRef]
29. Tian, Q.; Yang, X.; Zhang, H.; Xu, D. An Implicit Robust Numerical Scheme with Graded Meshes for the Modified Burgers Model with Nonlocal Dynamic Properties. *Comput. Appl. Math.* **2023**, *42*, 246. [CrossRef]
30. Peng, X.; Han, L.; Li, L. A Consistently Compressible Mooney-Rivlin Model for the Vulcanized Rubber Based on the Penn's Experimental Data. *Polym. Eng. Sci.* **2021**, *61*, 2287–2294. [CrossRef]
31. Destrade, M.; Dorfmann, L.; Saccomandi, G. The Ogden Model of Rubber Mechanics: 50 Years of Impact on Nonlinear Elasticity. *Philos. Trans. R. Soc. A Math. Phys. Eng. Sci.* **2022**, *380*, 20210332. [CrossRef]
32. Gajewski, M.D.; Miecznikowski, M. Assessment of the Suitability of Elastomeric Bearings Modeling Using the Hyperelasticity and the Finite Element Method. *Materials* **2021**, *14*, 7665. [CrossRef] [PubMed]
33. Hossain, M.; Steinmann, P. Modelling and Simulation of the Curing Process of Polymers by a Modified Formulation of the Arruda-Boyce Model. *Arch. Mech.* **2011**, *63*, 621–633.
34. Yang, L.; Yang, L. Note on Gent's Hyperelastic Model. *Rubber Chem. Technol.* **2018**, *91*, 296–301. [CrossRef]
35. Kossa, A.; Valentine, M.T.T.; McMeeking, R.M.M. Analysis of the Compressible, Isotropic, Neo-Hookean Hyperelastic Model. *Meccanica* **2023**, *58*, 217–232. [CrossRef]
36. Nguyen, H.-D.; Huang, S.-C. The Uniaxial Stress-Strain Relationship of Hyperelastic Material Models of Rubber Cracks in the Platens of Papermaking Machines Based on Nonlinear Strain and Stress Measurements with the Finite Element Method. *Materials* **2021**, *14*, 7534. [CrossRef] [PubMed]
37. Rubin, M.B.; Ehret, A.E. An Invariant-Based Ogden-Type Model for Incompressible Isotropic Hyperelastic Materials. *J. Elast.* **2016**, *125*, 63–71. [CrossRef]
38. Melly, S.K.; Liu, L.; Liu, Y.; Leng, J. Modified Yeoh Model with Improved Equibiaxial Loading Predictions. *Acta Mech.* **2022**, *233*, 437–453. [CrossRef]
39. Zhou, L.; Wang, S.; Li, L.; Fu, Y. An Evaluation of the Gent and Gent-Gent Material Models Using Inflation of a Plane Membrane. *Int. J. Mech. Sci.* **2018**, *146*, 39–48. [CrossRef]
40. Gent, A.N. (Ed.) *Engineering with Rubber: How to Design Rubber Components*, 3rd ed.; Hanser Publishers: Munich, Germany; Cincinnati, OH, USA, 2012; ISBN 978-3-446-42764-8.
41. XiaoXiang, Y.; MingWang, F.; XiuRong, W.; XiaoYing, L. Nonlinear Finite Element Analysis of Crack Growth at the Interface of Rubber-like Bimaterials. *Sci. China Phys. Mech. Astron.* **2011**, *54*, 1866–1874. [CrossRef]
42. Gong, C.; Ding, W.; Soga, K.; Mosalam, K.M.; Tuo, Y. Sealant Behavior of Gasketed Segmental Joints in Shield Tunnels: An Experimental and Numerical Study. *Tunn. Undergr. Space Technol.* **2018**, *77*, 127–141. [CrossRef]
43. Ouyang, W. Mechanical Test and Numerical Analysis of Elastic Gaskets of Shield Tunnels. *Tunn. Constr.* **2013**, *33*, 933–936.
44. Lu, Z. A Simple Review for Cohesive Zone Models of Composite Interface and Their Applications. *Chin. J. Solid Mech.* **2015**, *36*, 85–94. [CrossRef]
45. Zhuo, X.R.; Ma, A. Molecular Dynamics-Based Cohesive Zone Model for Mg/Mg$_{17}$Al$_{12}$ Interface. *Metals* **2020**, *10*, 836. [CrossRef]
46. Barthel, E. Adhesive Contact: A Few Comments on Cohesive Zone Models and Self-Consistency. *J. Adhes.* **2012**, *88*, 55–69. [CrossRef]

47. Alfano, G. On the Influence of the Shape of the Interface Law on the Application of Cohesive-Zone Models. *Compos. Sci. Technol.* **2006**, *66*, 723–730. [CrossRef]
48. Gong, C.; Kang, L.; Zhou, W.; Liu, L.; Lei, M. Tensile Performance Test Research of Hybrid Steel Fiber—Reinforced Self-Compacting Concrete. *Materials* **2023**, *16*, 1114. [CrossRef]
49. Gong, C.; Kang, L.; Liu, L.; Lei, M.; Ding, W.; Yang, Z. A Novel Prediction Model of Packing Density for Single and Hybrid Steel Fiber-Aggregate Mixtures. *Powder Technol.* **2023**, *418*, 118295. [CrossRef]

Disclaimer/Publisher's Note: The statements, opinions and data contained in all publications are solely those of the individual author(s) and contributor(s) and not of MDPI and/or the editor(s). MDPI and/or the editor(s) disclaim responsibility for any injury to people or property resulting from any ideas, methods, instructions or products referred to in the content.

Article

Numerical Computing Research on Tunnel Structure Cracking Risk under the Influence of Multiple Factors in Urban Deep Aquifer Zones

Minglei Ma [1], Wei Wang [1,2,*], Jianqiu Wu [1], Lei Han [1], Min Sun [1] and Yonggang Zhang [1,3]

[1] China Construction Eighth Engineering Division Co., Ltd., Shanghai 200122, China
[2] State Key Laboratory of Ocean Engineering, Department of Civil Engineering, Shanghai Jiao Tong University, Shanghai 200240, China
[3] Key Laboratory of Geotechnical and Underground Engineering of Ministry of Education, Department of Geotechnical Engineering, Tongji University, Shanghai 200092, China
* Correspondence: ww096014@foxmail.com

Abstract: During the operation period of tunnels in urban deep aquifer zones, the geological environment around the tunnel is complex and the surrounding strata are rich in groundwater, which often poses a risk of structure cracking and groundwater leakage, seriously threatening the tunnel's safety. To reduce the risk of tunnel cracking, a theoretical calculation model and a three-dimensional concrete–soil interaction thermo-mechanical coupling numerical computing model was established to analyze the tunnel structure cracking risk under the influence of multiple factors in urban deep aquifer zones. The response mechanism of structural stress and deformation under the influence of the grade of rock and soil mass, overburden thickness, temperature difference, structure's length–height ratio, structure's thickness, and structure's elastic modulus was investigated, and the stress and deformation response characteristics of the structure with deformation joints were explored. The results show that the maximum longitudinal tensile stress of the structure increases with the increase in the grade of rock and soil mass, overburden thickness, temperature difference, structure's length–height ratio, and elastic modulus. The temperature difference has the most significant impact on the longitudinal tensile stress of the structure, with the maximum tensile stress of the structure increasing by 2.8 times. The tunnel deformation joints can effectively reduce the longitudinal tensile stress of the structure, and the reduction magnitude of the tensile stress is the largest at the deformation joints, which is 64.7%.

Keywords: maximum tensile stress; multiple factors influence; numerical computing model; tunnel structure cracking; urban deep aquifer zones

MSC: 74S20; 65Z99

1. Introduction

The deep groundwater environment in urban areas is relatively complex. During the operation period of tunnels in urban deep aquifer zones, the surrounding strata of the tunnel are rich in groundwater, and the tunnels are often exposed to the risk of groundwater leakage, resulting in deep and long cracks and large deformations in the tunnel concrete, which seriously threaten the tunnel's safety. Deformation joints are narrow gaps between various parts of concrete structures, including expansion joints and settlement joints, which can prevent uneven settlement and concrete shrinkage of open-cut cast-in situ concrete structures [1,2]. They are widely used in tunnels, multi-purpose utility tunnels, subway stations, and other engineering projects. However, as the weak part of the concrete structures, deformation joints increase the risk of water seepage. In deep aquifer zones, nearly 90% of subway stations have leakage problems, and nearly 30% of the leakage occurs at deformation joints [3,4]. Once water seepage occurs, it will not only reduce the strength of the concrete structure but also bring safety hazards to later operations. To ensure the safety of tunneling operations, a new numerical analysis is required, by means of which the influence of multiple factors in urban deep aquifer zones and deformation joints on structure cracking risk can be reasonably researched.

At present, various methods, namely empirical methods, analytical methods, numerical methods, and model test methods have made great accomplishments in the study of tunnel cracking risk. Liu et al. [5] analyzed 109 tunnels with lining cracks and found that the main influencing factors for tunnel lining cracking are bias pressure, concrete shrinkage, back cavities, landslides, and relaxation pressure. Li et al. [6] found that temperature and concrete shrinkage were important reasons for concrete cracking in multi-purpose utility tunnels. These studies obtained the influencing factors of cracking based on empirical statistics, but cannot quantitatively analyze these factors. Based on double K theory [7–9], damage mechanics theory [10], and linear elastic fracture mechanics [11], some researchers have studied the propagation mechanism and theoretical model of concrete cracks from the concrete material itself. The model test method can truly reflect the cracking situation of the structure, but the testing process is relatively complex [12,13]. Liu et al. [14,15] carried out a series of model tests on structure cracking. Numerical simulation can consider tunnel cross-section shapes, geological properties, complex construction processes, and the coupling interaction between surrounding rock and tunnel structures [16–18]. It is currently a commonly used method for studying structure cracking risk. Based on the load-structure method, the effect of strata on the structure is simplified as the load acting on the structure [19,20]. Huang et al. [21] established a numerical model to analyze the influence mechanism of geological factors and temperature factors, and determined that concrete cracking depends on the maximum tensile stress of the structure. He et al. [22], Liu et al. [23], and Li et al. [24] also investigated the impact of different influencing factors on structure cracking based on the load-structure method. For the abovementioned studies, nevertheless, existing studies have generally focused on the effects of a single influencing factor, such as geological conditions [25], temperature [26,27], etc. on structure cracking risk, and lack of comprehensive analysis under the influence of multiple factors. At the same time, the load-structure method analyzes the concrete structure as a plate [28,29], ignoring the interaction between the concrete structure and the surrounding soil, which is not consistent with the actual engineering situation and results in inaccurate calculation results.

Based on the above shortcomings, a theoretical calculation model and a three-dimensional concrete–soil interaction thermo-mechanical coupling model was established and the maximum tensile stress of the tunnel structure was analyzed in this paper. Furthermore, the response mechanism of structural stress and deformation under the influence of the grade of rock and soil mass, overburden thickness, temperature difference, structure's length–height ratio, structure's thickness, and structure's elastic modulus was investigated, and the stress and deformation response characteristics of the structure with deformation joints were explored. The research results can provide important technical guidance for the cracking risk of tunnel structure under the influence of multiple factors in urban deep aquifer zones and for reducing the risk and cost of engineering construction.

2. Theoretical Model

The deformation of a concrete structure is constrained by the foundation. Based on this, a concrete wall model on an elastic foundation is established, as shown in Figure 1. It is assumed that the concrete wall and the foundation are deformable elastic structures, and the constraints between them can be reflected by the relationship between stress and deformation [30,31].

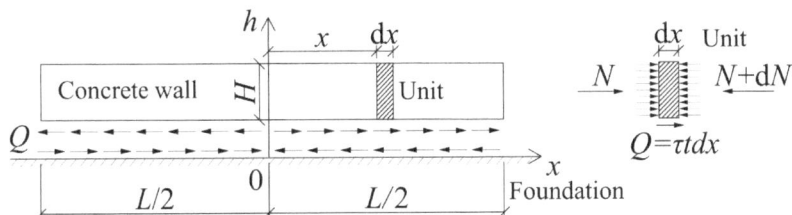

Figure 1. Schematic diagram of stress analysis of concrete wall.

Assume that the horizontal shear stress is linear with the horizontal displacement:

$$\tau = -C_x u \qquad (1)$$

where τ is the shear stress on the interface between the concrete wall and foundation, u is the horizontal displacement of the foundation, and C_x expresses the horizontal resistance coefficient of the foundation.

Taking a unit at x point of the structure for stress analysis, the balance equation can be expressed as

$$N + dN - N + Q = 0 \qquad (2)$$

$$Htd\sigma_x + \tau t dx = 0 \qquad (3)$$

$$\frac{d\sigma_x}{dx} + \frac{\tau}{H} = 0 \qquad (4)$$

where N is the internal force of the unit, Q represents the shear stress of the foundation to the unit, σ_x is the internal stress of the unit, and H and t are the height and width of the unit, respectively.

The displacement at any point of the structure is composed of constrained displacement and free displacement:

$$u = u_\sigma + \alpha T x \qquad (5)$$

where u_σ is the constrained displacement, α is the linear expansion coefficient of concrete, and T is the temperature difference.

According to the generalized Hooke's law [32], the stress-strain relationship of the structure can be expressed as:

$$\sigma_x = E\frac{du_\sigma}{dx} = E\frac{du}{dx} - E\alpha T \qquad (6)$$

$$\frac{d\sigma_x}{dx} = E\frac{d^2 u_\sigma}{dx^2} = E\frac{d^2 u}{dx^2} \qquad (7)$$

where E is the elastic modulus of concrete.

Substituting Equations (1) and (7) into Equation (4) gives

$$E\frac{d^2 u}{dx^2} - \frac{C_x u}{H} = 0 \qquad (8)$$

If $\beta = \sqrt{\frac{C_x}{HE}}$, then Equation (8) can be changed to

$$\frac{d^2 u}{dx^2} - \beta^2 u = 0 \qquad (9)$$

The general solution of Equation (9) is

$$u = A\cosh\beta x + B\sinh\beta x \qquad (10)$$

where A and B are obtained by boundary conditions. At the 0 point, $u = 0$. At the $L/2$ point, $\sigma_x = 0$. L is the length of the concrete wall.

Then Equation (10) can be given as

$$A = 0, B = \frac{\alpha T}{\beta \cosh \beta \frac{L}{2}} \tag{11}$$

Substituting Equation (11) into Equation (10) obtains

$$u = \frac{\alpha T}{\beta \cosh \beta \frac{L}{2}} \sinh \beta x \tag{12}$$

Then the horizontal stress of the concrete wall can be obtained:

$$\sigma_x = -E\alpha T \left(1 - \frac{\cosh \beta x}{\cosh \beta \frac{L}{2}}\right) \tag{13}$$

According to Equation (13) and the symmetry of the structure, the maximum horizontal stress of the concrete wall is

$$\sigma_{x\max} = -E\alpha T \left(1 - \frac{1}{\cosh \beta \frac{L}{2}}\right) \tag{14}$$

3. Numerical Simulation Model

3.1. Engineering Background

Hangzhou Road multi-purpose utility tunnel is located in Hangzhou Road, High-tech Industrial Development Zone, Liaocheng City (Figure 2). The utility tunnel starts from Guangyue Road in the west and ends at Lushan Road in the east. The Hangzhou Road multi-purpose utility tunnel has a total length of 3162.7 m, with a single-cabin rectangular section and cast-in-site reinforced concrete structure. About 30 m of the tunnel is divided into one construction section, and deformation joints are set in two adjacent sections. The main structure concrete of the utility tunnel adopts self-waterproof C35 concrete. The Quaternary geomorphic units along the proposed tunnel belong to the central part of the Yellow River alluvial plain, with relatively flat terrain and low terrain. The strata are mainly composed of silty clay, silt, and sand.

Liaocheng's river systems mainly belong to the Yellow River and the Haihe River, each with numerous tributaries. The types of groundwater in Liaocheng City are relatively complex. According to the occurrence conditions of groundwater, the water-bearing rock groups are divided into rock groups bearing loose rock pore water, and rock groups bearing carbonate-rock-like fissure karst water. The loose rock pore water aquifers can be divided into shallow unconfined aquifers, intermediate confined water aquifers, and deep confined water aquifers.

3.2. Numerical Model

To further study the stress and displacement characteristics of the tunnel, the simulation software of FLAC3D is applied in this study for further numerical work. FLAC3D is a commercial finite difference numerical simulation software that includes 18 elastic and plastic constitutive models, five calculation modes, and various modes that can be coupled with each other. Compared with other software, FLAC3D has the advantages of fast solving speed and accurate calculation results and can simulate complex geotechnical problems, and has been widely used in the field of geotechnical engineering [33–36]. Wang [37] et al. carried out a FLAC3D numerical simulation study of the deformation of a coal mine's deep buried track, and the calculation results are consistent with the field measurement results, with a small error (within 5%). Unlu and Gercek [38] employed FLAC3D software to calculate the radial boundary displacement along the longitudinal direction of a circular tunnel. Through the built-in Fish programming language, batch modeling was carried out and structured hexahedral-only volume meshes were created in this study.

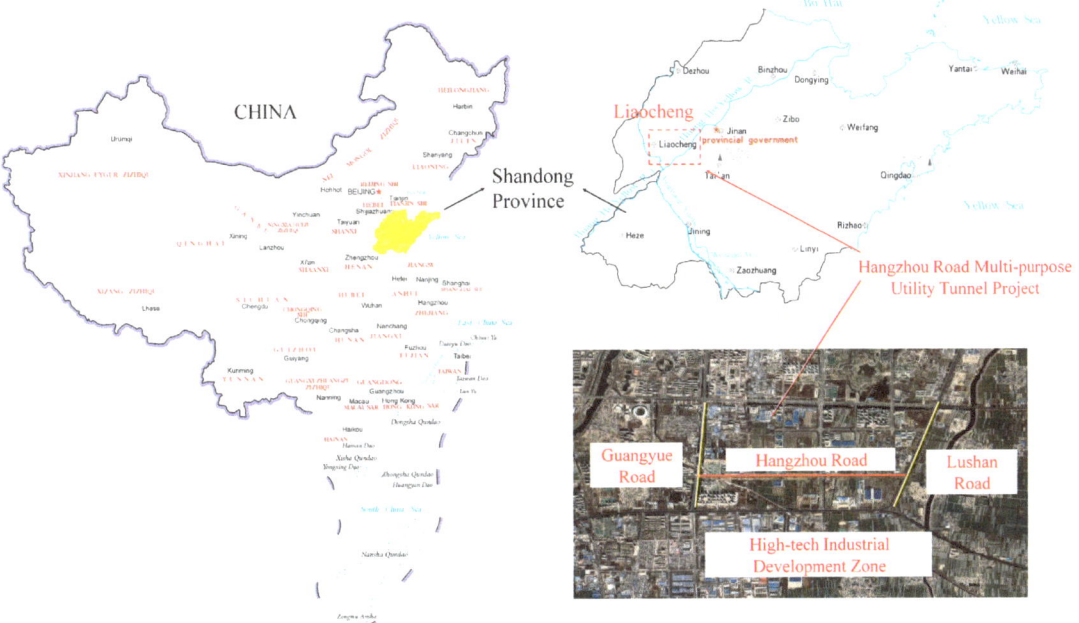

Figure 2. Location of the research area.

3.2.1. Model Validation

Model validation is an important step to ensure appropriate and acceptable results of computational simulation, which is usually carried out by comparing model simulation data with independent experimental or field datasets [39–41]. In Huang [42], the vertical displacement of a utility tunnel project in Chongqing was measured. Based on this reference, the same numerical model was established to simulate the tunnel displacements. The length of the tunnel is 8.9 m, the width is 3.9 m, and the buried depth is 4.2 m. The thickness of the tunnel is 0.4 m, the total length is 30 m, the entire model size is 64 m × 30 m × 20 m. Eight-node brick elements are used to simulate the soil and concrete. Figure 3 shows the simulation and measured results of the maximum vertical displacement of the top and bottom of the structure. The error of the maximum vertical displacement between the numerical result and the actual measured value is small, which is less than 10%. Therefore, the numerical model is reliable.

3.2.2. Three-Dimensional Numerical Model

The schematic diagram of the numerical model is shown in Figure 4. Based on the project design drawings, the cross-section of the concrete structure is a rectangle, L = 10 m, h = 4 m, and w = 30 m. The thickness of the structure is D = 0.5 m, buried depth is 5 m. According to Saint Venant's principle [43], the whole model size is 70 m × 21 m × 30 m, which is composed of 32,860 grid points and 29,640 zones. Eight-node brick elements are used to simulate the soil and concrete. All tunnel meshes established in the study adopt the same size. The mesh is divided into 1 m in the longitudinal direction of the tunnel, 0.5 m in the length and height directions, and 0.2 m in the thickness direction.

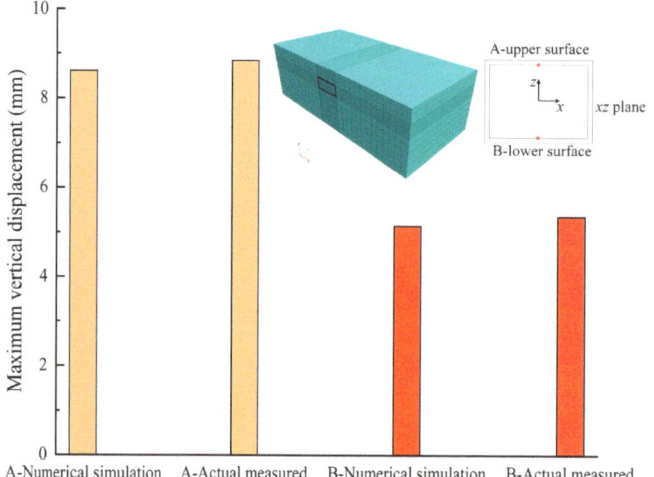

Figure 3. Maximum vertical displacement of example.

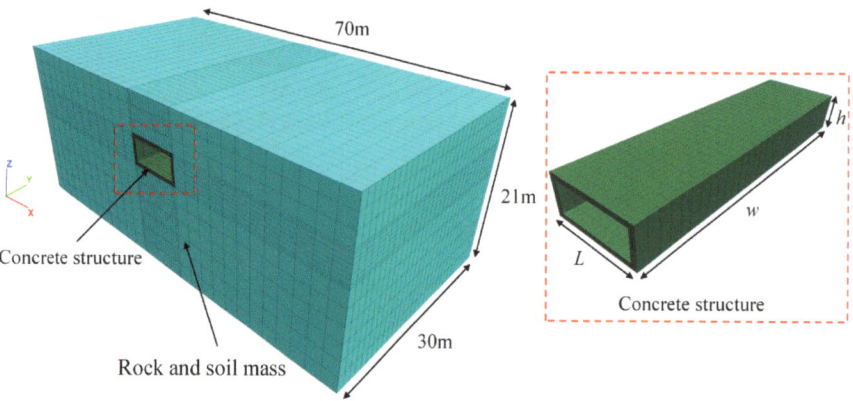

Figure 4. Schematic diagram of the numerical model.

The deformation joints are mainly connected by waterstops, and the liner structural element is used to simulate the deformation joints. The deformation joints are set in the middle of the structure, as shown in Figure 5, with a width of 30 mm and an elastic modulus of 2.6 MPa [44,45]. The mechanical behavior of concrete is described through the elastic constitutive model, and the rock and soil mass's behavior is simulated with the Mohr–Coulomb constitutive model. The structure adopts C35 concrete, and the surrounding soil adopts Grade IV rock and soil mass for calculation. Related physical and mechanical parameters are listed in Table 1 [46,47]. The surface between the structure and the soil is simulated by the interface element, and the friction angle is 15° [48]. Assume that the temperature of the structure decreases gradually from outside to inside, and the temperature difference is taken as 5 °C [49].

For the whole model, the soil is homogeneous, continuous, and isotropic, regardless of groundwater. The top surface of the model is set as a free boundary, the bottom of the model is a fixed boundary, and normal constraint is applied to the rest of the surfaces. The isotropic conduction model is used in the thermo-mechanical coupling calculation, the internal and external temperatures of the structure are fixed, and adiabatic boundaries are prescribed around the model surfaces.

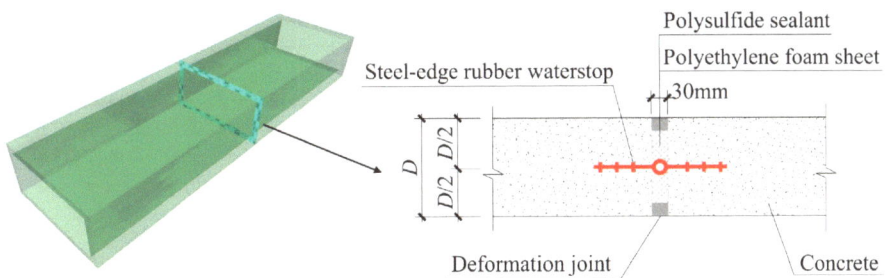

Figure 5. Schematic diagram of deformation joints.

Table 1. Model material parameters.

Model Material	Elastic Modulus/GPa	Density/(kN/m³)	Poisson's Ration	Cohesion/MPa	Friction Angle/°	Linear Expansion Coefficient	Thermal Conductivity/ kJ·(m·h·°C)⁻¹	Specific Heat /kJ·(kg·°C)⁻¹
C35 concrete	31.5	23	0.20	—	—	1.0×10^{-5}	10.6	0.96
Grade IV rock and soil mass	1.3	20	0.35	0.5	18	0.8×10^{-5}	8.4	1.44

3.3. Numerical Simulation Result

After the casting and backfilling of the open-cut cast-in situ concrete structure, the longitudinal stress and deformation of the structure are shown in Figure 6.

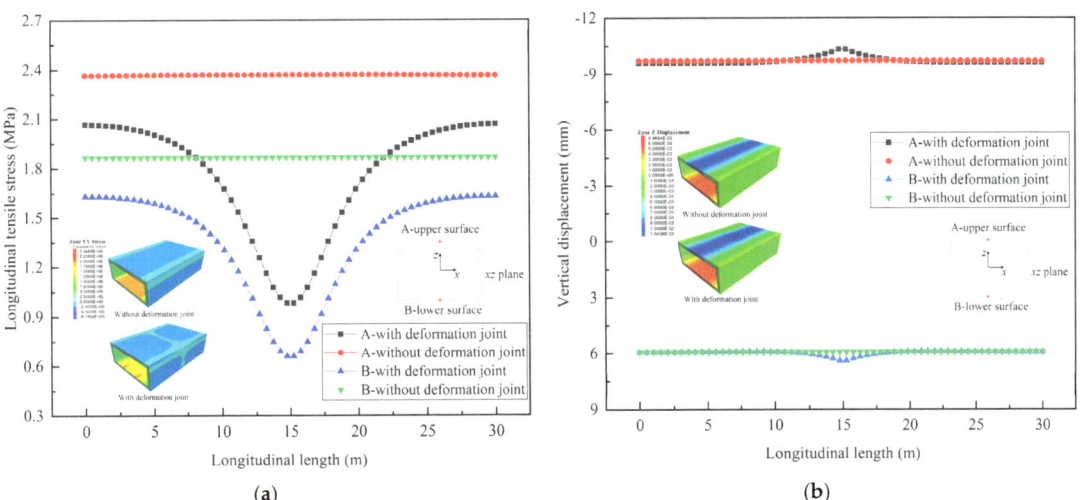

Figure 6. Stress and displacement of concrete structure. (**a**) Longitudinal tensile stress. (**b**) Vertical displacement.

As seen in Figure 6a, the maximum longitudinal stress is concentrated at the top and bottom of the structure, and the top and bottom are in tension on the inside and compression on the outside. When the structure has no deformation joints, the maximum tensile stress of the upper surface is 2.37 MPa, which is greater than that of the lower surface of 1.87 MPa. With deformation joints, the tensile stress is distributed in a V-shaped curve along the Y direction of the structure, the minimum tensile stress appears at the deformation joint, and the maximum tensile stress appears at both ends of the model. This kind of distribution characteristic of tensile stress was also reported by Zhuo et al. [20]. The maximum tensile stress of the upper surface is 2.07 MPa, which is greater than that of the lower surface of 1.63 MPa. Compared with no deformation joints, the maximum tensile stress of the upper and lower surface is reduced by 12.7% and 12.8%, respectively, and the tensile stress at the deformation joints of the upper and lower surface is reduced by 58.6% and 64.7%, respectively. Taking the horizontal resistance coefficient C_x as $1.0\ \text{N/mm}^3$ [50], calculating the maximum tensile stress of the lower surface using Equation (14) gives 1.50 MPa, which is slightly smaller than the numerical simulation result, with an error of 8.0%, and the theoretical calculation value is relatively safe.

As shown in Figure 6b, the maximum vertical displacement is concentrated at the top and bottom of the structure; the top of the structure subsides, and the bottom of the structure uplifts. When the structure has no deformation joints, the maximum vertical displacement of the upper surface is 9.75 mm, which is greater than that of the lower surface of 5.94 mm. With deformation joints, the vertical displacement changes greatly at the deformation joints, and the maximum vertical displacement of the upper surface is 10.44 mm, which is greater than that of the lower surface of 6.38 mm. Compared with no deformation joints, the maximum vertical displacement of the upper and lower surface increases by 7.1% and 7.4%, respectively.

Since the structural strength at the deformation joints is smaller than that of the concrete on both sides, the stress is released at the deformation joints, and the tensile stress of the structure is significantly reduced, while the deformation at the deformation joints increases. The increase in the deformation at the deformation joints will further cause stress release in the structure, leading to a decrease in stress at the deformation joints. The deformation joints can effectively reduce the longitudinal tensile stress of the structure. This conclusion is basically in agreement with previous research [21–24]. However, they did not consider the influence of multiple factors on the stress and deformation of the structure.

4. Effect of External Environment

4.1. Rock and Soil Properties Effect

Based on the "Specifications for design of highway tunnels" (JTG 3370-2018) in China, the rock and soil mass can be divided into four grades (III, IV, V, VI) according to the strength from strong to weak [47]. The physical and mechanical parameters of different grades of rock and soil mass are shown in Table 2.

Table 2. Physical and mechanical parameters of rock and soil mass.

Rock and Soil Mass Grade	Elastic Modulus/GPa	Density/(kN/m^3)	Poisson's Ratio	Cohesion/MPa	Friction Angle/°
III	6.0	23	0.30	1.0	21
IV	1.3	20	0.35	0.5	18
V	1.0	17	0.40	0.2	15
VI	0.5	15	0.45	0.1	12

Figure 7 shows the longitudinal tensile stresses of the structure under different rock and soil mass grades. The density of the rock and soil mass directly affects the load of the overlying soil on the structure. At the same time, the better the strength of the rock and soil, the stronger the self-stabilization ability of the rock and soil, and the smaller the additional stress of the overlying soil on the structure. Therefore, as the rock and soil mass grade increases, the maximum longitudinal tensile stress of the structure gradually increases, and the risk of structural cracking increases. The properties of the rock and soil mass around the structure are directly related to the structural stress, which is consistent with the results of Weng et al. [12] and Huang et al. [21]. Without deformation joints, the maximum longitudinal tensile stress under grade VI rock and soil mass is 3.00 MPa, which is 36.4% higher than that under grade III rock and soil mass of 2.20 MPa. With deformation joints, the maximum longitudinal tensile stress under grade III rock and soil mass is reduced to

1.92 MPa, which is a reduction of 12.7%. The maximum longitudinal tensile stress under grade VI rock and soil mass is reduced to 2.63 MPa, which is a reduction of 12.3%.

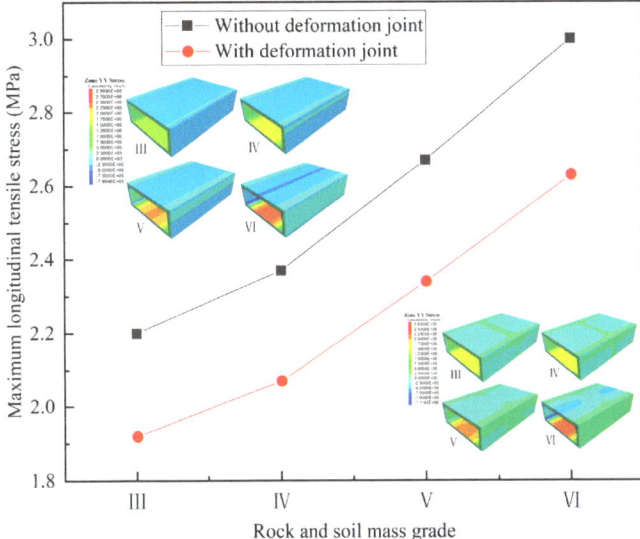

Figure 7. Longitudinal tensile stresses under different rock and soil mass grades.

The settlement displacements under different rock and soil mass grades are shown in Figure 8. The same as the influence law of the maximum tensile stress of the structure, the rock and soil mass grades increase, and the maximum settlement displacement of the structure increases. Therefore, by improving the strength properties of the soil around the structure, the settlement displacements can be effectively reduced, and this result is consistent with that of Wang et al. [50] and Tan et al. [51]. Without deformation joints, the maximum settlement value under grade VI rock and soil mass is −13.50 mm, which is 89.3% higher than that under grade III rock and soil mass of −7.13 mm. The deformation growth is relatively obvious. With deformation joints, the maximum settlement value increases by 10.1% under grade III rock and soil mass. The growth magnitude of the maximum settlement value gradually decreases while the rock and soil mass grade increases.

4.2. Overburden Thickness Effect

In previous numerical studies [19–24], there have been few studies on the impact of overburden thicknesses on the structural cracking risk. Figure 9 shows the longitudinal tensile stresses of the structure under different overburden thicknesses when the grade of rock and soil mass is IV. The overburden thickness directly affects the load of the upper soil on the structure, so as the overburden thickness increases, the longitudinal tensile stress of the structure increases, and the risk of structural cracking increases. Without deformation joints, the maximum longitudinal tensile stress increases by 13.1% as the overburden thickness increases from 5 m to 20 m, which indicates that overburden thicknesses have a relatively small influence on structural cracking. With deformation joints, the maximum longitudinal tensile stress is reduced by 12.7% under an overburden thickness of 5 m. The decreased magnitude of longitudinal tensile stress gradually decreases as the overburden thickness increases.

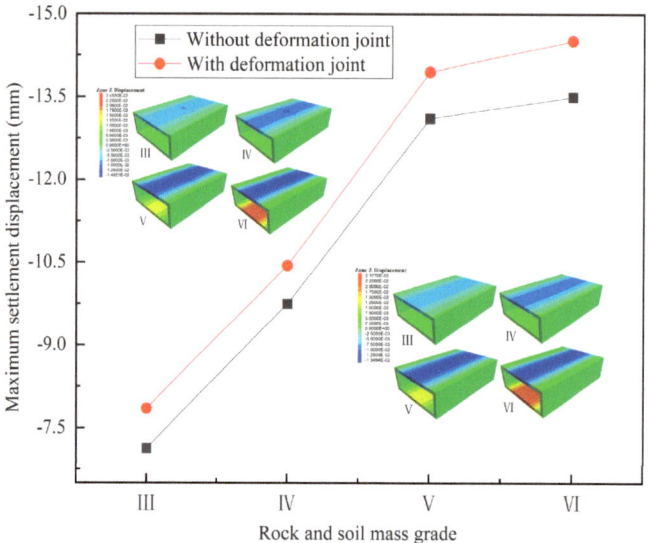

Figure 8. Settlement displacements under different rock and soil mass grades.

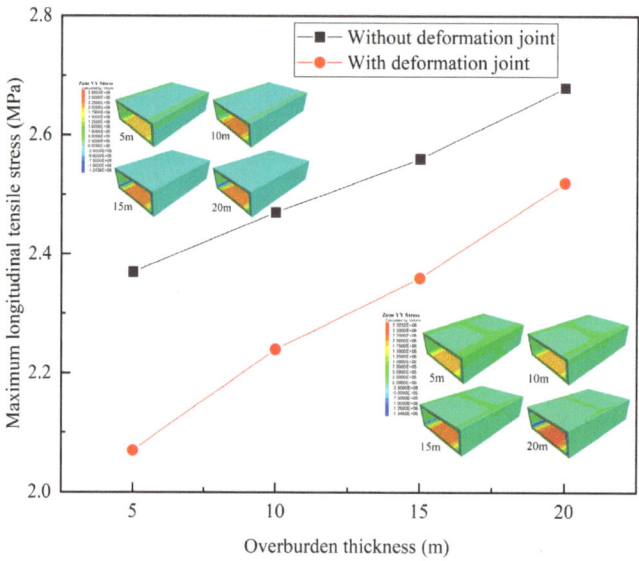

Figure 9. Longitudinal tensile stresses under different overburden thicknesses.

Figure 10 shows the settlement displacements of the structure under different overburden thicknesses. Without deformation joints, the maximum settlement displacement of the structure increases by 60.6% as the overburden thickness increases from 5 m to 20 m. With deformation joints, the maximum settlement displacement increases. As the overburden thickness increases, the growing magnitude of the maximum settlement displacement decreases.

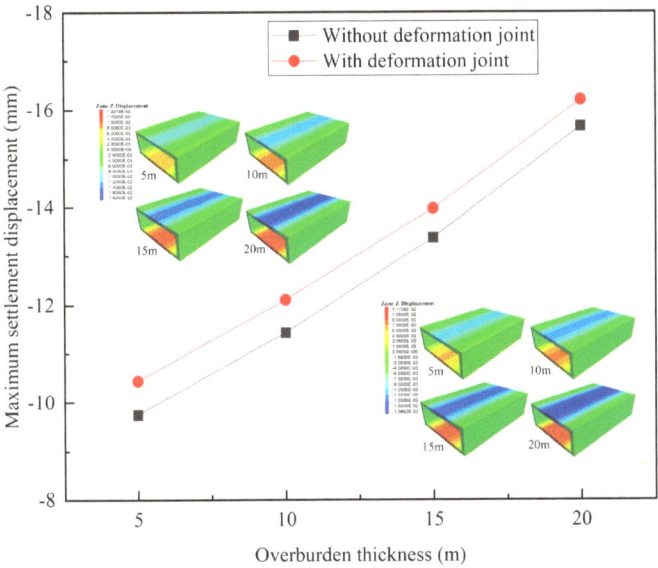

Figure 10. Settlement displacements under different overburden thicknesses.

4.3. Temperature Difference Effect

Figure 11 shows the longitudinal tensile stresses of the structure under different temperature differences when the grade of rock and soil mass is IV and the overburden thickness is 5 m. The longitudinal tensile stress of the structure increases with the increase in temperature difference. Without deformation joints, the maximum longitudinal tensile stress is 0.82 MPa under a temperature difference of 0 °C, and the maximum longitudinal tensile stress is 3.14 MPa under a temperature difference of 7.5 °C. The maximum longitudinal tensile stress of the structure increases by 2.8 times. The temperature difference has a significant impact on the tensile stress of the structure, so the change in temperature difference is the main factor leading to structural cracking. The observed influence law of temperature differences in this study is similar to that reported by Liu et al. [5] and Li et al. [6], but the results obtained through numerical calculations in this article are more intuitive and obvious. Based on the works of Huang et al. [21], Wang [30], and De Schutter [31], the phenomenon above can be attributed to the expansion deformation of concrete structures and the increase in temperature stress. Meanwhile, it can be seen from Equation (14) that the maximum tensile stress of the structure is linearly related to the temperature difference, and the numerical simulation results are consistent with the theoretical calculation results.

With deformation joints, the maximum longitudinal tensile stress of the structure increases by 2.35 times as the temperature difference increases from 0 °C to 7.5 °C. The deformation joints can effectively reduce the influence of temperature differences on the structural tensile stress, which is consistent with the results of Dong et al. [1]. Compared with no deformation joints, the maximum longitudinal tensile stress is reduced by 2.4% under a temperature difference of 0 °C, and 14.6% under a temperature difference of 7.5 °C. The greater the temperature difference, the greater the reduction magnitude of the longitudinal tensile stress, and the more significant the effect of deformation joints.

Figure 12 shows the settlement displacements of the structure under different temperature differences. Without deformation joints, as the temperature difference increases from 0 °C to 7.5 °C, the maximum settlement displacement of the structure increases by 1.7%, and temperature difference has little effect on structural settlement displacement, and this result is consistent with that of Huang et al. [21]. With deformation joints, the maximum settlement value of the structure increases by 10.4% as the temperature difference increases from 0 °C to 7.5 °C. Compared with no deformation joints, the larger the temperature difference, the greater the growth magnitude of structural deformation.

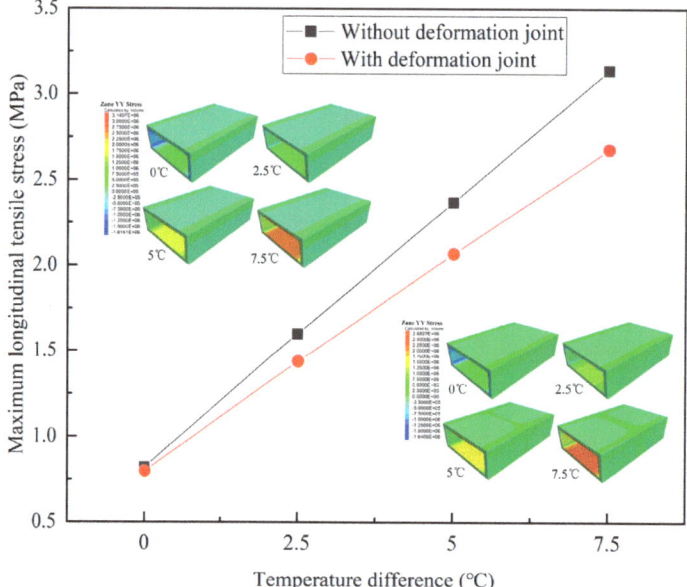

Figure 11. Longitudinal tensile stresses under different temperature differences.

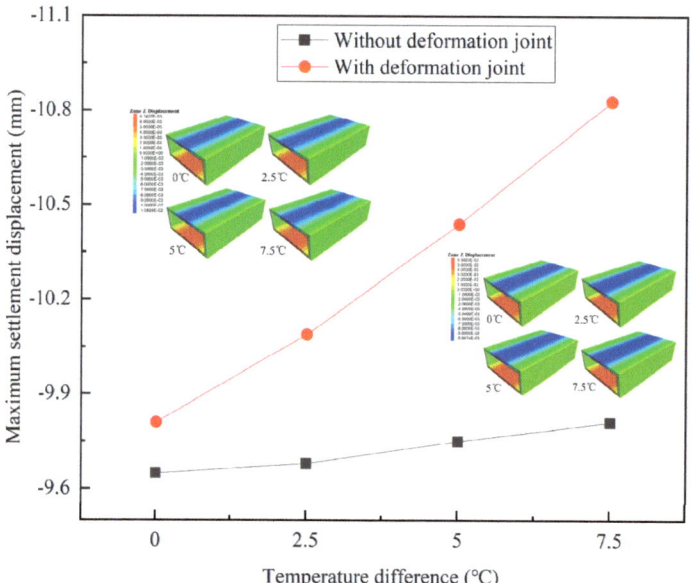

Figure 12. Settlement displacements under different temperature differences.

5. Effect of Structural Parameters

5.1. Length–Height Ratio Effect

Figure 13 shows the longitudinal tensile stresses of the structure under different length–height ratios when the height of the structure is 4 m. With the increase in the length–height ratio, the longitudinal tensile stress of the structure increases, and the risk of structural cracking increases, which is consistent with the influence law presented in He et al. [22]. However, in his research, there was no quantitative analysis of the influence degree of structural length–height ratios. Without deformation joints, the maximum longitudinal tensile stress of the structure increases by 43.9% as the length–height ratio increases from 1.5 to 3. With deformation joints, the maximum longitudinal tensile stress is reduced by 16.0% under a length–height ratio of 3. As the length–height ratio increases, the decreased magnitude of longitudinal tensile stress increases gradually.

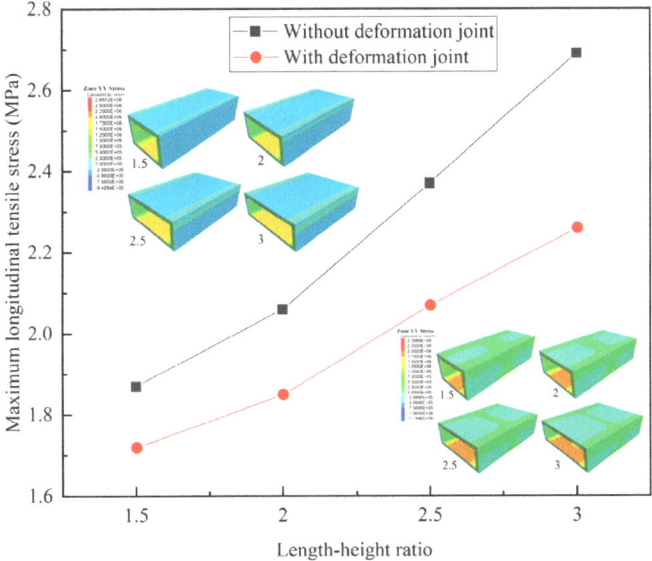

Figure 13. Longitudinal tensile stresses under different length–height ratios.

In Figure 14, with the increase in the length–height ratio of the structure, the settlement displacement increases from −0.80 mm to −19.97 mm, and the increment is very significant. With deformation joints, the maximum settlement displacement increases. The larger the length–height ratio, the smaller the deformation growth rate.

5.2. Structure Thickness Effect

Figure 15 shows the longitudinal tensile stresses under different structure thicknesses when the length–height ratio of the structure is 2.5. The greater the structure thickness, the smaller the longitudinal tensile stress of the structure, which is consistent with the influence law presented by Equation (14) and Liu et al. [23]. Without deformation joints, the maximum longitudinal tensile stress of the structure decreases by 14.9% as the structure thickness increases from 0.3 m to 0.6 m. With deformation joints, the maximum longitudinal tensile stress is reduced by 14.4% under a structure thickness of 0.6 m. The greater the thickness of the structure, the greater the reduction magnitude of the longitudinal tensile stress.

In Figure 16, when without deformation joints, the ability of the structure to resist deformation increases as the structure thickness increases [22,23]. The maximum settlement displacement of the structure decreases by 66.0% as the structure thickness increases from

0.3 m to 0.6 m, with a significant change. With deformation joints, the maximum settlement displacement increases by 9.9% under a structure thickness of 0.6 m. The change magnitude of the maximum settlement displacement increases with the increase in structure thickness.

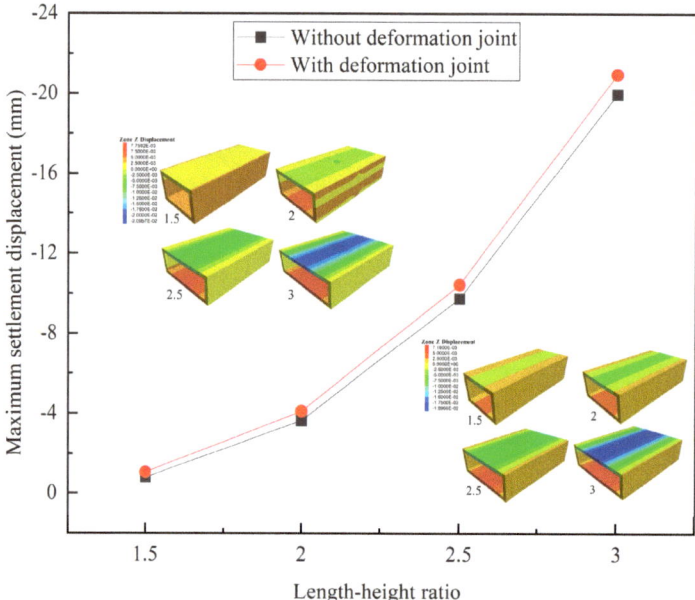

Figure 14. Settlement displacements under different length–height ratios.

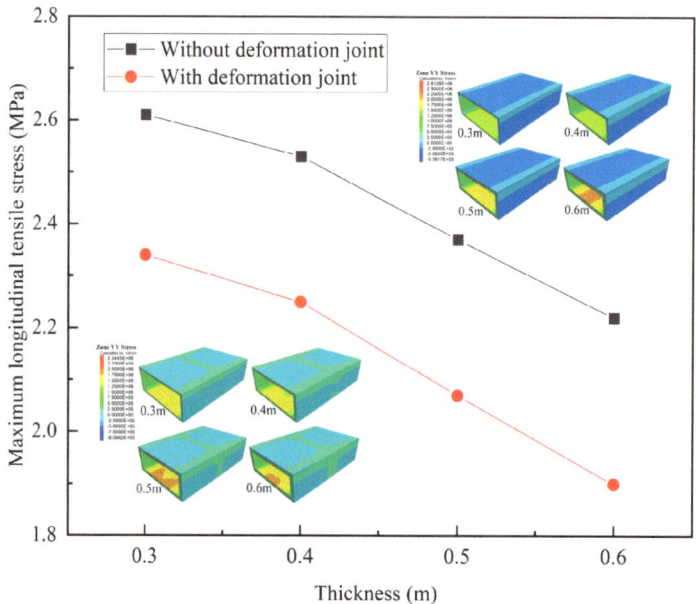

Figure 15. Longitudinal tensile stresses under different structure thicknesses.

Figure 17 shows the the longitudinal tensile stresses under different concretes when the length–height ratio of the structure is 2.5 and the structure thickness is 0.5 m. With the increase in the elastic modulus, the longitudinal tensile stress of the structure increases, mainly because the elastic modulus is positively correlated with the temperature stress of concrete [26,27]. Without deformation joints, the maximum longitudinal tensile stress of the structure increases by 7.1% as the elastic modulus increases from 28 GPa to 32.5 GPa. With deformation joints, the maximum longitudinal tensile stress is reduced by 12.8% under an elastic modulus of 28 GPa, and 12.4% under an elastic modulus of 32.5 GPa.

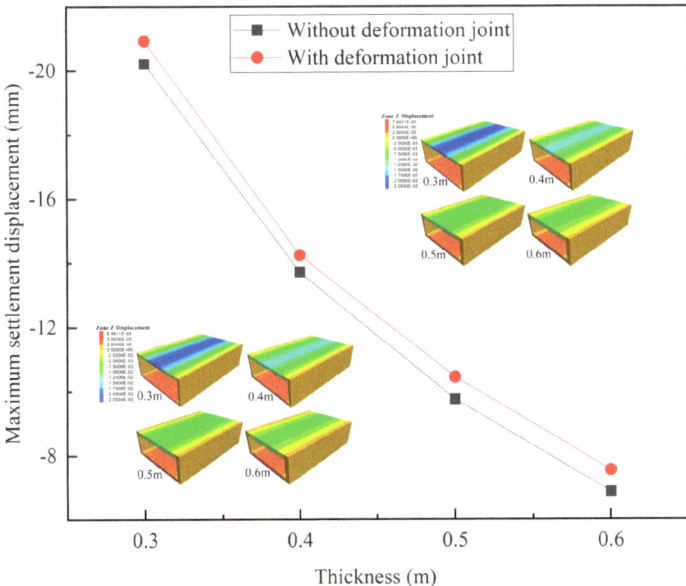

Figure 16. Settlement displacements under different structure thicknesses.

5.3. Structure Material Effect

The main difference between different concrete materials is the elastic modulus, and the elastic moduli of different concretes are shown in Table 3.

Table 3. Elastic moduli of different concretes.

Concrete	C25	C30	C35	C40
Elastic modulus/GPa	28.0	30.0	31.5	32.5

In Figure 18, when without deformation joints, the elastic modulus of the structure increases, and the ability of the structure to resist deformation increases. The maximum settlement displacement of the structure decreases by 5.1% as the elastic modulus increases from 28 GPa to 32.5 GPa. With deformation joints, the maximum settlement displacement increases by 7.2% under an elastic modulus of 32.5 GPa. The growth magnitude of the maximum settlement displacement increases with the increase in the elastic modulus.

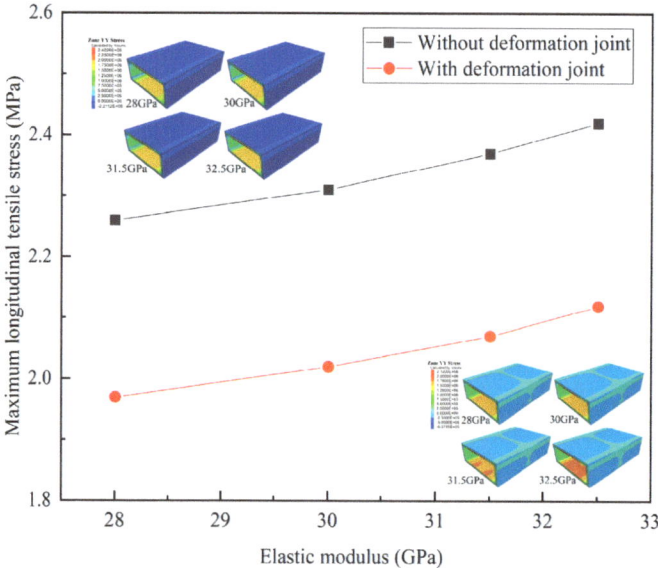

Figure 17. Longitudinal tensile stresses under different structure materials.

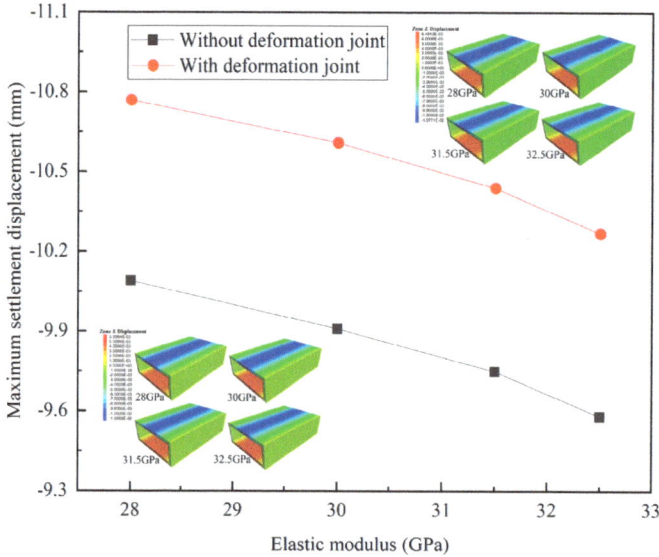

Figure 18. Settlement displacements under different structure materials.

6. Conclusions

(1) After the casting and backfilling of the open-cut cast-in situ concrete structure, the maximum longitudinal stress and vertical displacement are concentrated at the top and bottom of the structure. The maximum longitudinal tensile stress and vertical displacement of the upper surface are greater than those of the lower surface.

(2) The maximum longitudinal tensile stress, settlement displacement, and the cracking risk of the structure increase with the increase in the grade of rock and soil mass, overburden thickness, temperature difference, and the structure's length–height ratio, while decreasing

with the increase in the structure's thickness. With the increase in the concrete's elastic modulus, the maximum longitudinal tensile stress increases, and the maximum settlement displacement decreases. The effect of temperature difference on longitudinal tensile stress is the most significant, with the maximum tensile stress of the structure increasing by 2.8 times.

(3) When with deformation joints, the tensile stress is distributed in a V-shaped curve along the Y-direction of the structure, with the minimum tensile stress occurring at the deformation joint and the maximum tensile stress occurring at both ends of the model. The deformation joints can effectively reduce the longitudinal tensile stress of the structure, and the reduction magnitude of the tensile stress is the largest at the deformation joints, which is 64.7%. The vertical displacement of the structure changes abruptly at the deformation joints, and the maximum vertical displacements at the top and bottom of the structure increase to a certain extent compared with a structure with no deformation joints.

Author Contributions: Conceptualization, M.M. and W.W.; methodology, W.W. and J.W.; software, W.W.; validation, L.H. and M.S.; formal analysis, M.M.; resources, J.W.; data curation, W.W.; writing—original draft preparation, M.M. and W.W.; writing—review and editing, L.H., Y.Z. and M.S.; supervision, L.H. and M.S.; project administration, W.W. and J.W.; funding acquisition, M.M. and W.W. All authors have read and agreed to the published version of the manuscript.

Funding: This research was funded by China Construction Eighth Engineering Division Co., Ltd., grant number 2020-3-43.

Data Availability Statement: All data have been included in the article.

Conflicts of Interest: The authors declare no conflict of interest.

References

1. Dong, H.; Wu, Y.; Zhao, Y.; Liu, J. Behavior of deformation joints of RC utility tunnels considering multi-hazard conditions. *Case Stud. Constr. Mater.* **2022**, *17*, e01522. [CrossRef]
2. Han, L.; Liu, H.; Zhang, W.; Ding, X.; Chen, Z.; Feng, L.; Wang, Z. Seismic behaviors of utility tunnel-soil system: With and without joint connections. *Undergr. Space* **2022**, *7*, 798–811. [CrossRef]
3. Yuan, Y.; Jiang, X.; Lee, C.F. Tunnel waterproofing practices in China. *Tunn. Undergr. Space Technol.* **2000**, *15*, 227–233. [CrossRef]
4. Mao, Z.; Wang, X.; An, N.; Li, X.; Wei, R.; Wang, Y.; Wu, H. Water leakage susceptible areas in loess multi-arch tunnel operation under the lateral recharge conditions. *Environ. Earth Sci.* **2020**, *79*, 368. [CrossRef]
5. Liu, D.; Huang, H.; Yue, Q.; Xue, Y.; Zhang, M.; Xu, Q. Study on cracking mechanism and rapid repair method for tensile cracks of tunnel lining. *China Civ. Eng. J.* **2015**, *48*, 236–243.
6. Li, M.; Song, J.; Zhang, Y. Review of the causes of utility tunnel concrete cracking during construction. *Concrete* **2019**, *7*, 157–160.
7. Xu, S.; Reinhardt, H.W. Determination of double-Determination of double-K criterion for crack propagation in quasi-brittle fracture Part I: Experimental investigation of crack propagation. *Int. J. Fract.* **1999**, *98*, 111–149. [CrossRef]
8. Xu, S.; Reinhardt, H.W. Determination of double-K criterion for crack propagation in quasi-brittle fracture, Part II: Analytical evaluating and practical measuring methods for three-point bending notched beams. *Int. J. Fract.* **1999**, *98*, 151–177. [CrossRef]
9. Xu, S.; Reinhardt, H.W. Determination of double-K criterion for crack propagation in quasi-brittle fracture, Part III: Compact tension specimens and wedge splitting specimens. *Int. J. Fract.* **1999**, *98*, 179–193. [CrossRef]
10. Amorim, D.L.N.d.F.; Proença, S.P.B.; Flórez-López, J. Simplified modeling of cracking in concrete: Application in tunnel linings. *Eng. Struct.* **2014**, *70*, 23–35. [CrossRef]
11. Judt, P.O.; Ricoeur, A. Crack growth simulation of multiple cracks systems applying remote contour interaction integrals. *Theor. Appl. Fract. Mech.* **2015**, *75*, 78–88. [CrossRef]
12. Weng, X.; Hu, J.; Mu, X.; Niu, H.; Huang, X. Model test study on the influence of the collapsibility of loess stratum on an urban utility tunnel. *Environ. Earth Sci.* **2023**, *82*, 32. [CrossRef]
13. Xu, Q.; Bai, C.; Peng, J.; Lu, Q.; Zhao, J. Model test of prefabricated underground utility tunnel crossing active ground fissures. *Tunn. Undergr. Space Technol.* **2023**, *140*, 105279. [CrossRef]
14. Liu, X.; Guo, B.; Li, X.; Sang, Y. Model experiment study on effect of deformation joints on road tunnel resisting destruction by thrust fault stick-slip dislocation. *Chin. J. Rock Mech. Eng.* **2015**, *34*, 3837–3843.
15. Liu, X.; Zhang, P.; Zhou, M. Analysis of effect of longitudinal cracks on bearing capacity of tunnel lining. *Chin. J. Rock Mech. Eng.* **2012**, *31*, 2096–2102.
16. Ammarullah, M.I.; Afif, I.Y.; Maula, M.I.; Winarni, T.I.; Tauviqirrahman, M.; Akbar, I.; Basri, H.; van der Heide, E.; Jamari, J. Tresca Stress Simulation of Metal-on-Metal Total Hip Arthroplasty during Normal Walking Activity. *Materials* **2021**, *14*, 7554. [CrossRef]

17. Ammarullah, M.I.; Hartono, R.; Supriyono, T.; Santoso, G.; Sugiharto, S.; Permana, M.S. Polycrystalline Diamond as a Potential Material for the Hard-on-Hard Bearing of Total Hip Prosthesis: Von Mises Stress Analysis. *Biomedicines* **2023**, *11*, 951. [CrossRef]
18. Ammarullah, M.I.; Santoso, G.; Sugiharto, S.; Supriyono, T.; Kurdi, O.; Tauviqirrahman, M.; Winarni, T.I.; Jamari, J. Tresca stress study of CoCrMo-on-CoCrMo bearings based on body mass index using 2D computational model. *J. Tribol.* **2022**, *33*, 31–38.
19. Shen, Y.; Zhang, D.; Wang, R.; Li, J.; Huang, Z. SBD-K-medoids-based long-term settlement analysis of shield tunnel. *Transp. Geotech.* **2023**, *42*, 101053. [CrossRef]
20. Zhuo, Y.; Zou, C.; Yan, Z. Long highway tunnel experimental study on the abolition of deformation joint. *Strateg. Study CAE* **2009**, *11*, 59–65.
21. Huang, M.; Xiong, H.; Shen, Q.; Zhou, Y.; Tan, Z. Influencing factors and optimization of deformation joint set in Gongbei Tunnel open excavation section. *China J. Highw. Transp.* **2016**, *29*, 124–133.
22. He, X.; Luo, C.; Tang, X.; Kong, Y.; Huang, Z.; Li, S.; Xu, C. Analysis and optimization of the influencing factors of the deformation joints in the middle section of the Aixi Lake open-cut tunnel in Nanchang. *Bull. Sci. Technol.* **2022**, *38*, 109–117.
23. Liu, D.; Zhang, M.; Wang, Y.; Liang, B. Optimization of deformation joint spacing and waterproof structure of comprehensive pipe gallery in water-rich and weak stratum near the sea. *J. Henan Univ. Sci.* **2021**, *51*, 496–504.
24. Li, X.; Dai, Z.; Gu, X.; Cao, Z. Influence of deformation joint spacing on internal force of tunnel under active fault movement. *Tunn. Constr.* **2014**, *34*, 237–242.
25. Winkler, E.M. Frost damage to stone and concrete: Geological considerations. *Eng. Geol.* **1968**, *2*, 315–323. [CrossRef]
26. Malik, M.; Bhattacharyya, S.K.; Barai, S.V. Thermal and mechanical properties of concrete and its constituents at elevated temperatures: A review. *Constr. Build. Mater.* **2021**, *270*, 121398. [CrossRef]
27. Ma, Q.; Guo, R.; Zhao, Z.; Lin, Z.; He, K. Mechanical properties of concrete at high temperature—A review. *Constr. Build. Mater.* **2015**, *93*, 371–383. [CrossRef]
28. Liu, Q.; Peng, Y.; Tan, Z.; Li, Z.; Cheng, Z. Optimization of the deformation joint distance in tunnel open excavation section. *J. Beijing Jiaotong Univ.* **2015**, *39*, 88–95.
29. Ma, D.; Zhai, C.; Zhang, G.; Tu, X.; Li, C. Setting spacing optimizing of deformation joints in cast-in-situ concrete utility tunnel. *Tunn. Constr.* **2019**, *39*, 301–307.
30. Wang, T. Comprehensive method for cracking-control in structure. *Constr. Technol.* **2000**, *29*, 5–9.
31. De Schutter, G. Finite element simulation of thermal cracking in massive hardening concrete elements using degree of hydration based material laws. *Comput. Struct.* **2002**, *80*, 2035–2042. [CrossRef]
32. Li, L.C.; Liu, H.H. A numerical study of the mechanical response to excavation and ventilation around tunnels in clay rocks. *Int. J. Rock Mech. Min. Sci.* **2013**, *59*, 22–32. [CrossRef]
33. Bai, Y.; Li, X.; Yang, W.; Xu, Z.; Lv, M. Multiscale analysis of tunnel surrounding rock disturbance: A PFC3D-FLAC3D coupling algorithm with the overlapping domain method. *Comput. Geotech.* **2022**, *147*, 104752. [CrossRef]
34. Sitharam, T.G.; Maji, V.B.; Verma, A.K. Practical Equivalent Continuum Model for Simulation of Jointed Rock Mass Using FLAC3D. *Int. J. Geomech.* **2007**, *7*, 389–395. [CrossRef]
35. Wang, H.; Wu, Y.; Tian, Y.; Li, X.; Yang, Z.; He, L. Numerical Simulation of Subdam Settlement in Ash Disposal Based on CGSW Optimization. *Appl. Sci.* **2023**, *13*, 8370. [CrossRef]
36. Chen, J.; Wang, S.; Zhao, Y.; Liu, K.; Skrzypkowski, K.; Zagórski, K.; Zagórska, A. Influence of Grout Properties on the Tensile Performance of Rockbolts Based on Modified Cable Elements. *Materials* **2023**, *16*, 5362. [CrossRef]
37. Wang, R.; Li, X.; Xu, J.; Pan, L. Development and verification of large deformation model considering stiffness deterioration and shear dilation effect in FLAC3D. *Int. J. Min. Sci. Technol.* **2018**, *28*, 959–967. [CrossRef]
38. Unlu, T.; Gercek, H. Effect of Poisson's ratio on the normalized radial displacements occurring around the face of a circular tunnel. *Tunn. Undergr. Space Technol.* **2003**, *18*, 547–553. [CrossRef]
39. Danny Pratama Lamura, M.; Imam Ammarullah, M.; Hidayat, T.; Izzur Maula, M.; Jamari, J.; Bayuseno, A.P. Diameter ratio and friction coefficient effect on equivalent plastic strain (PEEQ) during contact between two brass solids. *Cogent Eng.* **2023**, *10*, 2218691. [CrossRef]
40. Ammarullah, M.I.; Santoso, G.; Sugiharto, S.; Supriyono, T.; Wibowo, D.B.; Kurdi, O.; Tauviqirrahman, M.; Jamari, J. Minimizing Risk of Failure from Ceramic-on-Ceramic Total Hip Prosthesis by Selecting Ceramic Materials Based on Tresca Stress. *Sustainability* **2022**, *14*, 13413. [CrossRef]
41. Lamura, M.D.P.; Hidayat, T.; Ammarullah, M.I.; Bayuseno, A.P.; Jamari, J. Study of contact mechanics between two brass solids in various diameter ratios and friction coefficient. *Proc. Inst. Mech. Eng. Part J J. Eng. Tribol.* **2023**, *237*, 1613–1619. [CrossRef]
42. Huang, L. Study on the Settlement Characteristics and Calculating Methods of Utility Tunnels in Mountain City. Master's Thesis, Chongqing University, Chongqing, China, 2021.
43. Do, N.-A.; Dias, D.; Oreste, P.; Djeran-Maigre, I. Three-dimensional numerical simulation of a mechanized twin tunnels in soft ground. *Tunn. Undergr. Space Technol.* **2014**, *42*, 40–51. [CrossRef]
44. Zhao, J.; Tan, Z.; Zhou, Z. Discussion on the waterproof and drainage system of the coastal tunnel and analysis of water pressure law outside lining: A case study of the Gongbei Tunnel. *Adv. Civ. Eng.* **2021**, *2021*, 6610601. [CrossRef]
45. Glerum, A. Developments in immersed tunnelling in Holland. *Tunn. Undergr. Space Technol.* **1995**, *10*, 455–462. [CrossRef]
46. *GB 50010-2010*; Code for Design of Concrete Structures. China Architecture & Building Press: Beijing, China, 2010.
47. *JTG 3370-2018*; Specifications for Design of Highway Tunnels. China Communications Press: Beijing, China, 2018.

48. Yin, Z.; Zhu, H.; Xu, G. A study of deformation in the interface between soil and concrete. *Comput. Geotech.* **1995**, *17*, 75–92.
49. Zhao, P.; Chen, J.; Luo, Y.; Li, Y.; Chen, L.; Wang, C.; Hu, T. Field measurement of air temperature in a cold region tunnel in northeast China. *Cold Reg. Sci. Technol.* **2020**, *171*, 102957. [CrossRef]
50. Wang, X.; Tan, Z.; Dai, Y.; Huang, M.; Zhao, J. Proper spacing of the deformation joints of a bored section of the Gongbei Tunnel. *Mod. Tunn. Technol.* **2018**, *55*, 27–35.
51. Tan, Y.; Lu, Y.; Wang, D. Practical Solutions for Concurrent Excavation of Neighboring Mega Basements Closely Surrounded by Utility Tunnels in Shanghai Hongqiao CBD. *Pract. Period. Struct. Des. Constr.* **2019**, *24*, 05019005. [CrossRef]

Disclaimer/Publisher's Note: The statements, opinions and data contained in all publications are solely those of the individual author(s) and contributor(s) and not of MDPI and/or the editor(s). MDPI and/or the editor(s) disclaim responsibility for any injury to people or property resulting from any ideas, methods, instructions or products referred to in the content.

Article

The Effect of Asynchronous Grouting Pressure Distribution on Ultra-Large-Diameter Shield Tunnel Segmental Response

Chen Wang [1], Ming Song [2,3], Min Zhu [1,*], Xiangsheng Chen [1] and Xiaohua Bao [1]

- [1] School of Civil and Transportation Engineering, Shenzhen University, Shenzhen 518061, China; wangchen2021@email.szu.edu.cn (C.W.)
- [2] China Communications Construction Company Second Highway Consultant Co., Ltd., Wuhan 430056, China
- [3] Research and Development Center on Tunnel and Underground Space Technology, China Communications Construction Company, Wuhan 430056, China
- * Correspondence: zhuminfnf@szu.edu.cn

Abstract: The complex distribution of synchronous grouting pressure results in excessive tunnel deformation and various structural diseases, especially for ultra-large-diameter shield tunnels. In this study, to reduce the risk of tunnel failure, a three-dimensional refined finite element model was established for the Wuhan Lianghu highway tunnel project, taking into account the non-uniform distribution of synchronous grouting pressure. This study focuses on investigating the development patterns of internal forces, deformations, and damages in segment structures under varying grouting pressure ratios. The results indicate that the primary failure mode of a segment is tensile failure occurring at the outer edge of the arch. Moreover, an increased ratio of grouting pressure between the arch bottom and top leads to a higher positive bending moment value and greater tensile damage at the arch waist. The tunnel ring gradually exhibits distinct "horizontal duck egg" shape deformation. When the grouting pressure ratio is 2.8, there is a risk of tensile cracking at the outer edge of the arch waist. At this time, the segment convergence deformation is 39.71 mm, and the overall floating amount reaches 43.12 mm. This research offers engineering reference for the prediction of internal forces and deformations in ultra-large-diameter shield tunnels during grouting construction, thereby facilitating their application in the development of resilient cities.

Keywords: numerical model; ultra-large-diameter shield tunnel; synchronous grouting; grouting pressure ratio; tunnel convergence; tensile damage

MSC: 74S05; 65Z05; 00A06

1. Introduction

With the continuous advancement of tunnel construction equipment and technology, ultra-large-diameter shield tunnels have become an influential development trend [1–3]. During the shield tunneling process, it is necessary to fill the gap between the segment ring and the surrounding strata by synchronous grouting. When the synchrotron grout pressure is not properly controlled, large upheavals may occur, especially for ultra-large-diameter shield tunnels, which can cause serious structural diseases, including segment cracks, misalignment, damage, and leakage [4–7].

The pressure profile of synchronous grouting has been extensively studied by scholars around the world. Regarding the theoretical model, in order to calculate the grout filling pressure and diffusion distance, Li et al. [8] developed a compound diffusion model on a semi-elliptic surface without predetermined flow channels. Ye et al. [9] developed a hemispherical diffusion model that takes into account the percolation effect of synchronous grouting in shield tunnel construction. In addition to theoretical models that reveal the distribution of synchronous grouting pressure along the segment rings [10], physical model testing, as an intuitive and direct experimental method, also plays a crucial role in scientific research. In practical engineering, maximum synchronous grouting pressure can be solved by testing the control of tunnel displacement and deformation [11,12]. The distribution and long-term evolution of grouting pressure can also be obtained through on-site monitoring [13]. For example, Hashimoto et al. [14] outlined the development of tunnel grouting pressure during construction and long-term grouting, and the resulting lining bending moments. Talmon et al. [15] analyzed the grouting consolidation and formation process of the Groene Hart tunnel under field conditions. More importantly, the theoretical models can be verified by the physical model tests. Assuming that the grouting pressure varies as a power function with time, Zhao et al. [16] proposed a simulation framework to explain the observations in the model tests. Based on the existing theoretical models and physical model tests, most of the research on synchronous grouting pressure has been focused on conventional subway shield tunnels, while less work has been done on the synchronous grouting pressure distribution patterns in ultra-large-diameter shield tunnels.

In addition, with the rapid development of computers, the effect of synchronous grouting on the stress and deformation of the lining structure has also been studied through numerical simulations. Lavasan et al. [17,18] considered three different variants of simulated synchronous grouting to study the impact of synchronous grouting on the tunnel excavation process. In variant I, the slurry is regarded as a distributed load applied on the soil. Due to its simplicity and computational ease, this numerical simulation method is currently used in most studies [19]. On this basis, numerous scholars have also studied the influence of grouting pressure changes on the deformation and mechanical properties of foundation pits and tunnels [20,21]. With the increasing size of modern tunnels, research on large-diameter tunnels and even ultra-large-diameter tunnels is becoming more and more significant [22]. For an ultra-large-diameter shield tunnel, the grout pressure difference between the vaults is larger due to the influence of the grout self-weight during the synchronous grouting process, and the segment is divided into multiple blocks with complex structures. Therefore, the stress and deformation patterns of the lining structure are also complex, but there are few relevant studies.

In this study, to investigate the mechanical response of ultra-large-diameter tunnels under asynchronous grouting pressure more clearly, a three-dimensional refined finite element model was established based on the engineering case of the Wuhan Lianghu highway tunnel. The deformation and damage properties of the tunnel segment were studied for different grout pressure ratios, and the weak position of the segment was determined. The results provide theoretical support for the scientific control of the synchrotron grouting pressure in ultra-large-diameter tunnels.

2. Engineering Background
2.1. Project Overview

The Wuhan Lianghu highway tunnel is the largest double-layer, ultra-large-diameter shield tunnel in China. The project is situated in the southern region of Wuhan City, which serves as the capital of Hubei Province in China. Its primary objective is to facilitate direct connectivity between the northern and southern sectors of Wuchang District, thereby enhancing the overall road network within this district. The Lianghu Tunnel project spans a total distance of 19.25 km, encompassing both the East Lake and South Lake sections. The total length of the shielding section is 13.3 km. The diameter of the shield machine is 16.2 m, the outer diameter of the segment ring is 15.5 m, and the thickness of the segment is 0.65 m. The surrounding environment of the tunnel is complex, passing numerous existing roads, Metro lines 4 and 8, and multiple underground pipelines. As shown in Figure 1, the section of the Lianghu tunnel under the Wuxian railway was chosen for analysis in this study. The radius of curvature of the tunnel is 700 m, the longitudinal slope is 0.5%, and the buried depth is 16.5 m (1.02 D). The angle between Lianghu tunnel and Wuxian railway is about 65°.

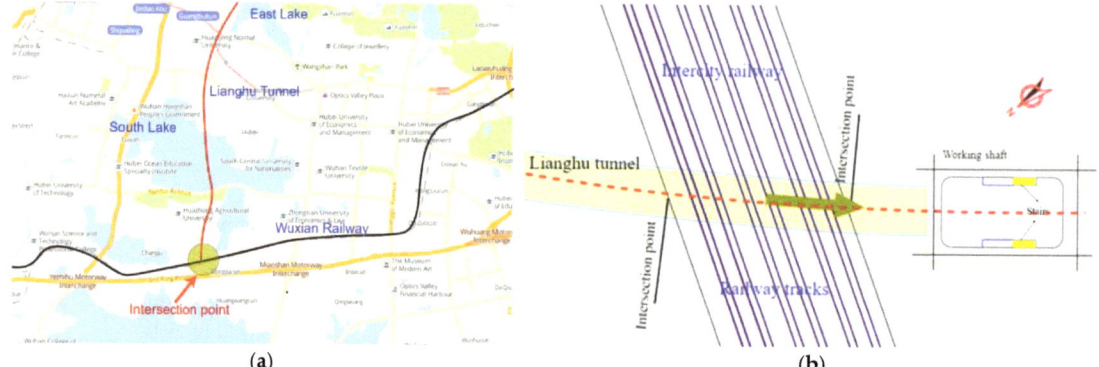

Figure 1. Lianghu Tunnel and Wuxian Intercity Railway. (**a**) Location map and (**b**) Intersection plan.

2.2. Geological Conditions

Figure 2 shows the longitudinal geological profile. The overlying soil layer of the shield tunnel is a sequence of plain fill, gravel, mudstone, and mudstone greywacke. The average thickness of the plain fill and gravel soil is about 0.5 m and 4.5 m, respectively. The inference of the formation beneath the intercity railway is based on the geological borehole adjacent to the railway, as drilling is not feasible within the railway area. In accordance with the geotechnical engineering geological investigation report, Table 1 presents the corresponding geological attributes.

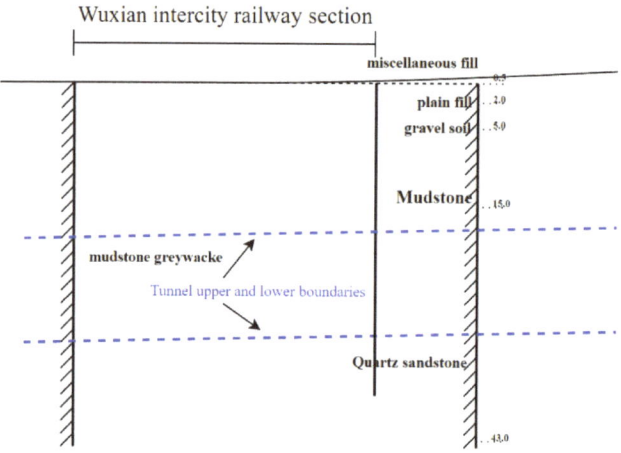

Figure 2. Geological profile.

Table 1. Physical and mechanical parameters of the stratum.

Stratum	γ (kg/m^3)	$E_{S0.1-0.2}$ (MPa)	ν	φ (°)	c (kPa)
Plain fill	19.2	3.8	0.40	13	10
Gravel soil	19.5	25	0.29	27	10
Mudstone	23.5	60	0.36	28	150
Mudstone greywacke	25.6	90	0.35	29	200

3. Establishment of the Finite Element Model

3.1. Overview

The numerical model of the shield tunnel segment is shown in Figure 3. The segmented ring has an outer diameter of 1550 mm, a thickness of 650 mm, and a width of 2000 mm. As shown in Figure 3a, the lining ring is composed of 10 prefabricated reinforced concrete segments, including 1 capping block (F), 2 adjacent blocks (L1 and L2) and 7 standard blocks (B1, B2, B3, B4, B5, B6, and B7). The segments are connected by 30 oblique bolts with a diameter of 36 mm and a length of 740 mm, which is shown in Figure 3b. The mesh of both the segments and the bolts adopts hexahedral grids, and the element type is eight-node linear element C3D8R. The finite element model of the whole segment ring is shown in Figure 4.

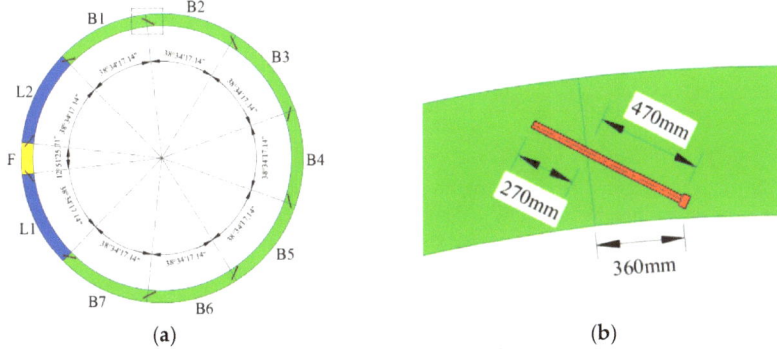

Figure 3. Schematic diagram of (**a**) segment block and (**b**) bolt structure.

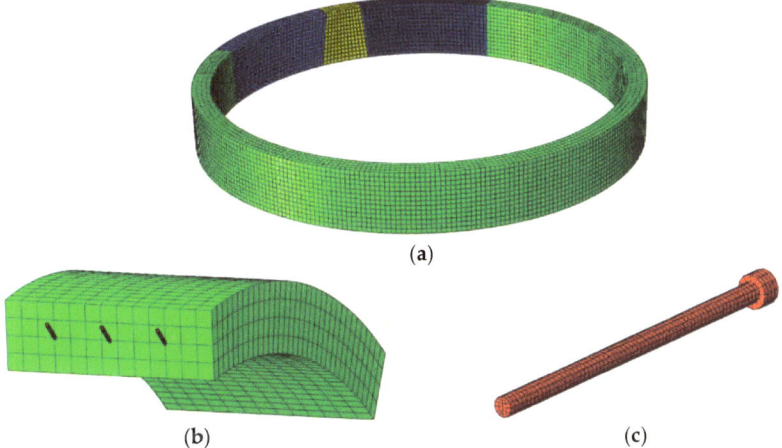

Figure 4. (**a**) Integral ring, (**b**) segment, and (**c**) bolt.

3.2. Material Parameters

The strength grade of precast concrete used in the segment is C60, and the parameters of its compression and tension damage characteristics are determined by the "Code for Design of Concrete Structures" (GB50010-2010) [23]. Table 2 shows the parameters of the plastic damage model for C60 concrete. The bolts adopt the elastic–plastic constitutive model, with elastic modulus $E = 200$ GPa, Poisson's ratio $\mu = 0.3$, yield strength

f_y = 640 MPa, and ultimate strength f = 800 MPa. When the bolt stress reaches the yield stress, the modulus of elasticity decreases to 1/100 of its previous value.

Table 2. C60 concrete plastic damage model parameters.

Parameter	Value
ρ (kg/m³)	2500
E (GPa)	36
ν	0.2
ψ (°)	40
ϵ	0.1
f_{b0}/f_{c0}	1.16
K_c	0.66667
μ	0.0005
σ_{cf} (MPa)	38.5
ε_{c0}	0.00177
σ_{tf} (MPa)	2.85
ε_{t0}	0.00011

3.3. Boundary Conditions and Interactions

The model of the load-structure method is developed for the calculations. As shown in Figure 5, the interaction between the soil and the segmented lining is simulated by ground springs arranged around the segmented ring, which can accurately reflect the resistance generated by the stratum [24]. The ground springs consist of one normal spring and two tangential springs (shown in Figure 6). The normal spring is only under compression but not tension, and the parameters can be obtained by multiplying the bed coefficient of the stratum by the unit area. In the calculated example, the bed coefficient is 5 kN/m³. According to the results of Koyama [25] and Wang [26], the parameters of a tangential spring are 1/3 of those of a normal spring.

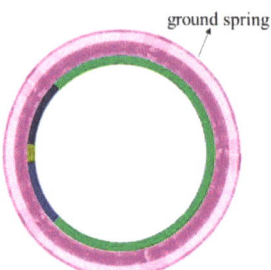

Figure 5. Boundary conditions.

Figure 7 shows the contact setting method for segment–segment and segment–bolt. The contacts between adjacent segments are modeled by surface-to-surface contacts. Finite slip tracking and face-to-face discretization methods were used in the analysis. Finite slip tracking is the most general tracking method, allowing for arbitrary relatively separated, sliding, and rotating contact surfaces, and is suitable for relatively large slides. Face-to-face discretization can better solve the problem of primary surface nodes penetrating the secondary surface. The tangential mechanical properties and normal mechanical properties of the contact obey the penalty function and rough contact, respectively, and the friction coefficient is 0.5 [27]. The accuracy of the calculation results of the local structure in the model is directly influenced by the level of refinement in this part during numerical simulation calculations. However, the focus of this study is not to study the specific analysis of the bolt joint, so the contact between the segment and the bolt is simulated by embedding.

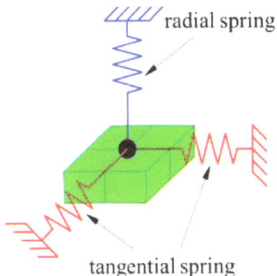

Figure 6. Ground springs schematic.

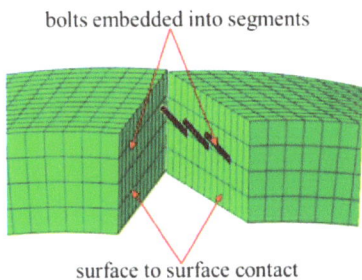

Figure 7. Schematic diagram of the seam contact simulation setup.

3.4. Grouting Pressure Distribution

The grouting pressure is applied to the tunnel segment as an isotropic hydrostatic pressure, and its magnitude and distribution have a strong influence on the results of the calculation of the overall deformation of the tunnel segment. Using the non-uniform grouting pressure distribution model that considers the self-weight of the grout, the upper half ring adopts uniform pressure distribution, and the lower half ring increases linearly according to the pressure difference between the top and the bottom of the tunnel (Figure 8), which is consistent with the distribution form of grouting pressure proposed in the literature [17,28]. The pressure at the vault was determined from the pressure at the excavation face, and the static earth pressure at the tunnel axis was 421.66 kPa. Therefore, the grouting pressure of the vault is selected as 420 kPa, and the pressure ratio of the vault bottom and the vault is set to 1.0, 2.0, 2.4, 2.6, and 2.8, for a total of five groups (respectively, working conditions ① to ⑤).

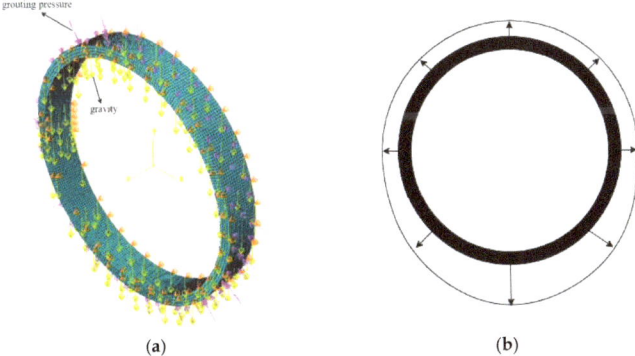

Figure 8. (**a**) Schematic diagram of pipe ring stress; (**b**) grouting pressure distribution pattern.

4. Calculation Results Analysis

4.1. Damage Evolution of Tunnel Segment

Figures 9 and 10, respectively, show the tensile and compressive damage cloud diagrams of the shield tunnel concrete segments for different grouting pressure distribution forms, where the deformation display is enlarged by 20 times. As can be seen from Figure 9, the concrete is in a fully elastic state until the tunnel segment grouting pressure ratio is 1:2.4. As the segmental arch bottom grouting pressure increases, the concrete tensile damage factor gradually increases and is mostly distributed at the arch waist edge position. And when the grouting pressure ratio of the segment vault bottom and the vault reaches 1:2.8, the tensile damage factor of the concrete reaches 0.87 and there is a risk of cracking. Since the compressive strength of concrete is much greater than the tensile strength, the compressive damage of concrete tunnel segments under different grouting pressure distribution forms is significantly smaller than the tensile damage.

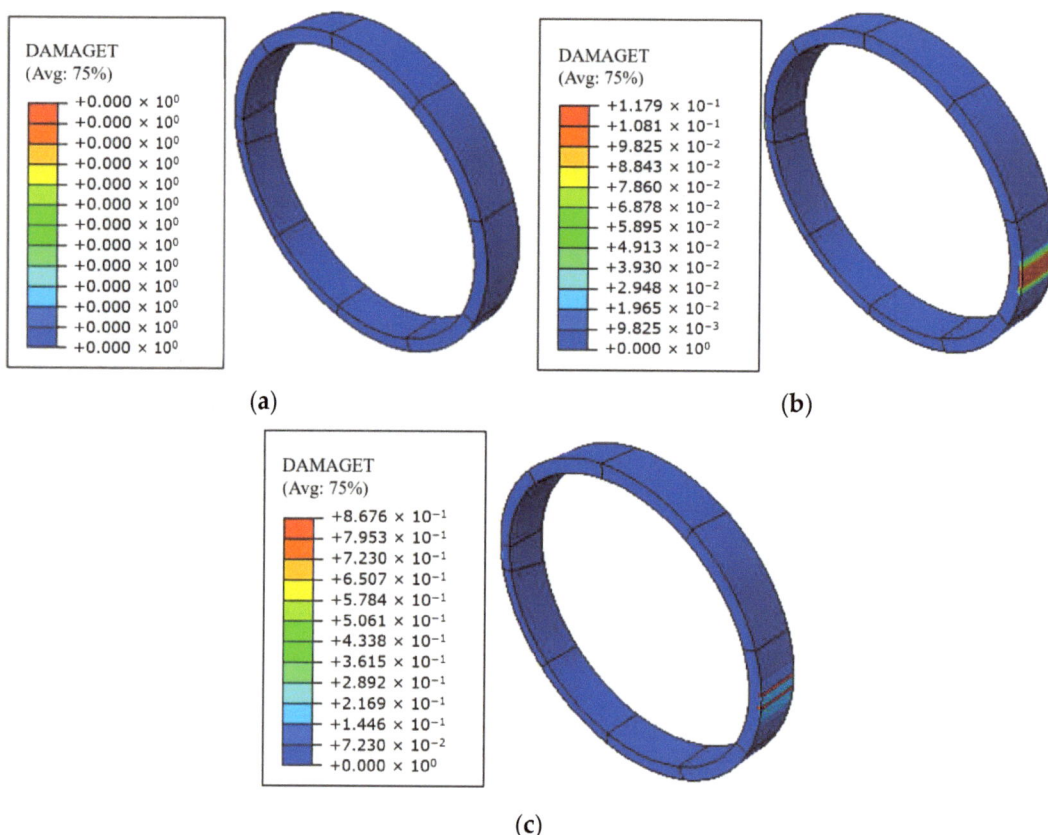

Figure 9. Cloud diagram of tunnel segment tensile damage under different grouting pressure distribution forms: (**a**) working conditions ①~③; (**b**) working condition ④; (**c**) working condition ⑤.

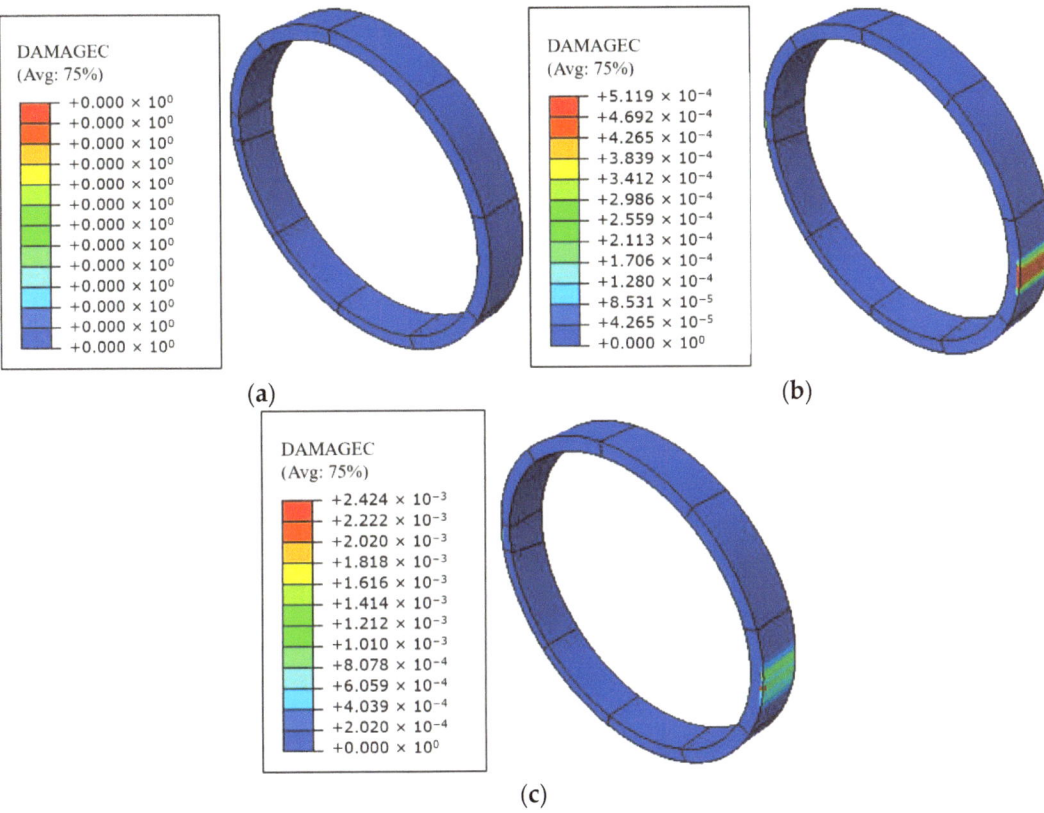

Figure 10. Cloud diagram of tunnel segment pressure damage under different grouting pressure distribution forms: (**a**) working conditions ①~③; (**b**) working condition ④; (**c**) working condition ⑤.

4.2. Internal Force and Stress

Figure 11 shows the bending moment distribution curves of the shield tunnel segment rings for different grouting pressures, and Table 3 lists the bending moments of the tunnel segment rings at the vault, waist, and bottom of the tunnel for the five operating conditions. During homogeneous grouting, the bending moments at different positions of the tunnel segment ring differ by a small amount. As the grout pressure is increased, the bending moment at the vault decreases significantly, while the bending moment at the waist of the arch gradually increases. When the grouting pressure ratio is 2.8, the bending moments of the vault and arch waist are −1320 kN·m and 1760 kN·m, respectively, and the difference between them reaches 3080 kN·m. In addition, the absolute value of the maximum bending moment of the whole ring appears at the waist of the arch under the action of the non-uniformly distributed grout pressure. As the grouting pressure ratio gradually increases, the absolute value difference between the arch waist and the arch crown also increases gradually, reaching a maximum of 440 kN·m. From this, it follows that the distribution of the grouting pressure has a large influence on the internal forces of the segment rings, and that the position of the arch waist is the weak position.

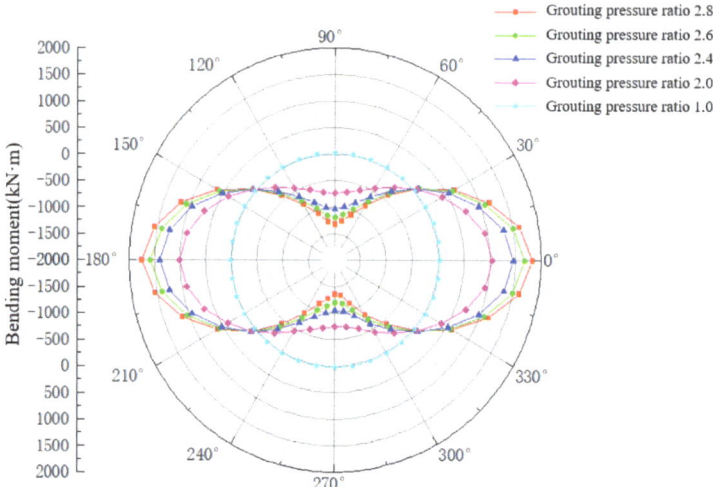

Figure 11. Bending moment distribution of the tunnel segment ring under different grouting pressures.

Table 3. Bending moments at different positions of the segment ring under 5 working conditions.

Working Condition	Grouting Pressure Ratio	Position	Bending Moment/(kN·m)
1	1.0	arch crown (90°) arch waist (180°) arch soffit (270°)	25.3 25.9 24.5
2	2.0	arch crown (90°) arch waist (180°) arch soffit (270°)	−739 1020 −742
3	2.4	arch crown (90°) arch waist (180°) arch soffit (270°)	−1040 1400 −1050
4	2.6	arch crown (90°) arch waist (180°) arch soffit (270°)	−1190 1600 −1210
5	2.8	arch crown (90°) arch waist (180°) arch soffit (270°)	−1320 1760 −1360

Figures 12 and 13 show, respectively, the maximum and minimum principal stress cloud diagrams for the shield tunnel segments at a grouting pressure ratio of 2.8 for the pipe rings and bolts. It can be seen from Figure 12 that the outer edge of the waist of the arch and the inner edge of the vault of the segment bear a large main tensile stress. Moreover, the principal tensile stress is greater at the outer edge of the arch waist than at the inner edge of the vault, while the inner edge of the arch waist bears a larger principal compressive stress. The maximum principal tensile stress of the pipe ring is 2.87 MPa, which appears at the outer edge of the arch waist, and the maximum principal compressive stress is 21.99 MPa, which appears at the inner edge of the arch waist. It can be seen from Figure 13 that the maximum principal tensile stress of the bolts in the tunnel segment ring is 337.1 MPa, which is less than the yield strength of 640 MPa, and none of the bolt yields.

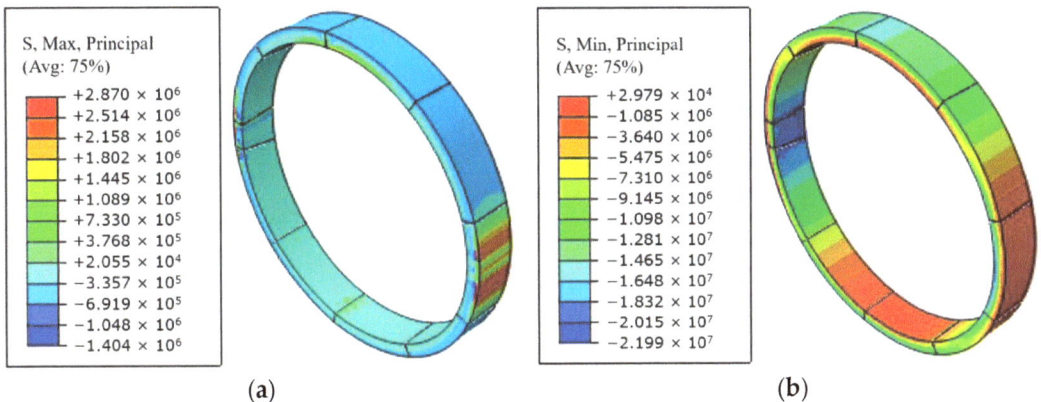

Figure 12. (a) Maximum and (b) minimum principal stress nephograms of tunnel segment rings in working condition ⑤.

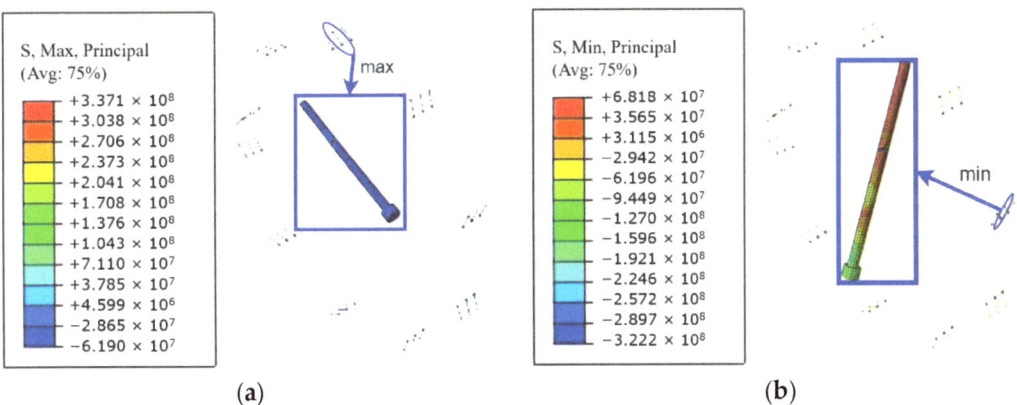

Figure 13. (a) Maximum and (b) minimum principal stress nephograms of tunnel bolts in working condition ⑤.

4.3. Shield Tunnel Deformation

Figure 14 shows the horizontal and vertical displacement contours of the tunnel segment ring at a maximum grouting pressure ratio of 2.8, where the deformation amplification ratio is 20. It can be clearly seen from the figure that the segment ring exhibits a large horizontal displacement outward at the arch waist, while in terms of vertical displacement, the segment ring as a whole is in a floating state, and the floating displacement increases with the increase in the buried depth. At this point, with a grouting pressure ratio of 2.8, the converged deformation of the segment ring waist reaches 39.71 mm and the overall floating value of the tunnel ring reaches 43.12 mm.

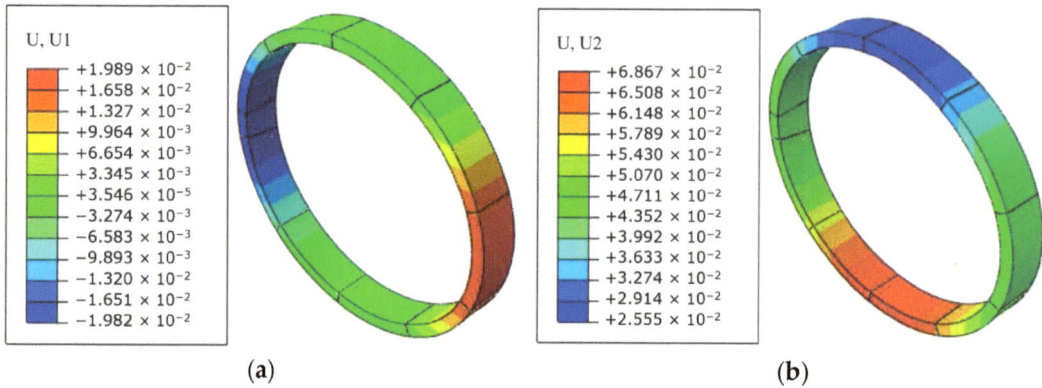

Figure 14. (a) Horizontal and (b) vertical displacement nephograms of segment rings in working condition ⑤.

Table 4 shows the segment ring convergence deformations and the overall floating values for the five different grouting pressure ratios. As can be seen from the table, the distribution of displacements at different positions of the pipe ring is consistent, except for the uniform grouting. And with the increase in the grouting pressure ratio, the convergence deformation and the overall floating value of the waist of the tunnel pipe ring also increase, and the pipe ring as a whole presents a "horizontal duck egg" shape. Combined with Table 3, it can be seen that in the case of uneven grouting, there is a large positive bending moment at the waist of the arch and its transverse displacement value expands outward, which also explains the deformed shape of the pipe ring mentioned above. Second, there is a large negative bending moment at the bottom of the vault, but the grouting pressure at the bottom of the vault is greater than that at the top of the vault, so the overall floating value of the segment ring increases with the increase in the grouting pressure.

Table 4. Segment ring convergence deformation and overall floating value in working condition ⑤.

Grouting Pressure Ratio	Lateral Displacement Value of Left Arch Waist (mm)	Lateral Displacement Value of Right Arch Waist (mm)	Waist Convergence Deformation (mm)	Arch Crown Floating Value (mm)	Arch Bottom Floating Value (mm)	Overall Floating Value of Tunnel Pipe Ring (mm)
1.0	0.99	−0.98	1.97	−5.12	−3.15	1.97
2.0	−1.03	1.03	2.06	12.09	36.59	24.50
2.4	−1.49	1.49	2.98	18.91	52.57	33.66
2.6	−1.73	1.72	3.45	22.28	60.59	38.31
2.8	−1.98	1.99	3.97	25.55	68.67	43.12

The present study conducts a comprehensive numerical simulation analysis on an ultra-large-diameter shield tunnel subjected to asynchronous grouting, serving as a valuable reference for the design and construction of increasingly larger tunnels, including ultra-large-diameter ones. The working conditions adopted in this study are commonly encountered in practical engineering projects, and are specifically based on the Wuhan Lianghu ultra-large-diameter highway tunnel project. To address this issue, most researchers employ numerical methods and field monitoring tests to predict the impact of grouting on tunnel deformation and internal forces. In addition, the presence of joints and cracks in the rock surrounding the tunnel segments may induce variations in grout pressure [29]. An emphasis on analyzing this aspect should be prioritized in future research. Moreover, this study primarily focuses on the overall mechanical and deformation properties of the tunnel segment, while the localized connection between bolts and segments remains to be explored.

5. Conclusions

In this study, based on the Wuhan Lianghu ultra-large-diameter highway tunnel project, we developed a three-dimensional finite element model using Abaqus, analyzed and discussed the damage evolution, overall floating, converging deformation, and stress of the lining structure during the synchronous grouting process during the construction of a shield tunnel, and can draw the following conclusions:

(1) The failure mode of a segment under non-uniform synchronous grouting pressure is characterized by tensile failure at the outer edge of the arch waist. Elastic deformation occurs in the segmental concrete of shield tunnels when the grouting pressure ratio between the bottom and top of the vault is less than or equal to 2.4, with increasing tensile damage as this ratio increases. When the grouting pressure ratio is 2.8, the tensile damage to the concrete reaches 0.867.

(2) The higher the grouting pressure ratio, the greater the positive bending moment value of the segmental arch waist, and the greater the negative bending moment value of both the arch top and bottom. In the case of uneven grouting, a higher principal tensile stress is experienced at the outer edge of the segmental arch waist and inner edge of the vault. Additionally, the outer edge of the arch bears a greater principal tensile stress than the inner edge of the vault, while the inner edge of the arch bears a larger principal compressive stress.

(3) With the increase in the grouting pressure ratio, the tunnel ring undergoes a distinct "horizontal ellipse" deformation, and there is also a corresponding increase in convergent deformation at the waist of the tunnel pipe ring and overall floating value. At a grouting pressure ratio of 2.8, the converged deformation at the waist measures 39.71 mm, while the overall floating value of the pipe ring reaches 43.12 mm.

Author Contributions: Conceptualization, M.Z.; methodology, M.Z.; software, C.W.; data curation, C.W.; writing—original draft, C.W.; supervision, X.C. and X.B.; funding acquisition, M.S. and X.C. All authors have read and agreed to the published version of the manuscript.

Funding: The research is supported by the National Natural Science Foundation of the People's Republic of China (52008263).

Data Availability Statement: Not applicable.

Conflicts of Interest: The authors declare no conflict of interest.

References

1. Gan, X.; Yu, J.; Gong, X.; Zhu, M. Characteristics and countermeasures of tunnel heave due to large-diameter shield tunneling underneath. *J. Perform. Constr. Facil.* **2020**, *34*, 04019081. [CrossRef]
2. Zhang, D.M.; Chen, S.; Wang, R.C.; Zhang, D.M.; Li, B.J. Behaviour of a large-diameter shield tunnel through multi-layered strata. *Tunn. Undergr. Space Technol.* **2021**, *116*, 104062. [CrossRef]
3. Xie, X.; Yang, Y.; Ji, M. Analysis of ground surface settlement induced by the construction of a large-diameter shield-driven tunnel in Shanghai, China. *Tunn. Undergr. Space Technol.* **2016**, *51*, 120–132. [CrossRef]
4. Tan, Z.; Li, Z.; Tang, W.; Chen, X.; Duan, J. Research on stress characteristics of segment structure during the construction of the large-diameter shield tunnel and cross-passage. *Symmetry* **2020**, *12*, 1246. [CrossRef]
5. Avgerinos, V.; Potts, D.M.; Standing, J.R. Numerical investigation of the effects of tunnelling on existing tunnels. *Géotechnique* **2017**, *67*, 808–822. [CrossRef]
6. Shen, Y.; Zhang, D.; Wang, R.; Li, J.; Huang, Z. SBD-K-medoids-based long-term settlement analysis of shield tunnel. *Transp. Geotech.* **2023**, *42*, 101053. [CrossRef]
7. Jin, D.; Yuan, D.; Li, X.; Zheng, H. An in-tunnel grouting protection method for excavating twin tunnels beneath an existing tunnel. *Tunn. Undergr. Space Technol.* **2018**, *71*, 27–35. [CrossRef]
8. Li, P.; Liu, J.; Shi, L.; Zhai, Y.; Huang, D.; Fan, J. A semi-elliptical surface compound diffusion model for synchronous grouting filling stage in specially shaped shield tunnelling. *Int. J. Numer. Anal. Methods Geomech.* **2022**, *46*, 272–296. [CrossRef]

9. Ye, F.; Yang, T.; Mao, J.; Qin, X.Z.; Zhao, R.L. Half-spherical surface diffusion model of shield tunnel back-fill grouting based on infiltration effect. *Tunn. Undergr. Space Technol.* **2019**, *83*, 274–281. [CrossRef]
10. Liang, Y.; Huang, X.; Gao, S.; Yin, Y. Study on the Floating of Large Diameter Underwater Shield Tunnel Caused by Synchronous Grouting. *Geofluids* **2022**, *2022*, 2041924. [CrossRef]
11. Ding, W.; Duan, C.; Zhu, Y.; Zhao, T.; Huang, D.; Li, P. The behavior of synchronous grouting in a quasi-rectangular shield tunnel based on a large visualized model test. *Tunn. Undergr. Space Technol.* **2019**, *83*, 409–424. [CrossRef]
12. Zou, J.; Zuo, S. Similarity solution for the synchronous grouting of shield tunnel under the vertical non-axisymmetric displacement boundary condition. *Adv. Appl. Math. Mech.* **2017**, *9*, 205–232. [CrossRef]
13. Bezuijen, A.; Talmon, A.M.; Kaalberg, F.J.; Plugge, R. Field measurements of grout pressures during tunnelling of the Sophia Rail Tunnel. *Soils Found.* **2004**, *44*, 39–48. [CrossRef]
14. Hashimoto, T.; Brinkman, J.; Konda, T.; Kano, Y.; Feddema, A. Simultaneous backfill grouting, pressure development in construction phase and in the long-term. *Tunnelling. A Decade Prog. GeoDelft* **1995**, *2005*, 101–107.
15. Talmon, A.M.; Bezuijen, A. Simulating the consolidation of TBM grout at Noordplaspolder. *Tunn. Undergr. Space Technol.* **2009**, *24*, 493–499. [CrossRef]
16. Zhao, T.; Ding, W.; Qiao, Y.; Duan, C. A large-scale synchronous grouting test for a quasi-rectangular shield tunnel: Observation, analysis and interpretation. *Tunn. Undergr. Space Technol.* **2019**, *91*, 103018. [CrossRef]
17. Lavasan, A.A.; Schanz, T. Numerical investigation of hydromechanical interactions at the tail void of bored tunnels due to grouting. In *Geotechnical Aspects of Underground Construction in Soft Ground*; CRC Press: Boca Raton, FL, USA, 2017; pp. 161–169.
18. Shah, R.; Lavasan, A.A.; Peila, D.; Todaro, C.; Luciani, A.; Schanz, T. Numerical study on backfilling the tail void using a two-component grout. *J. Mater. Civ. Eng.* **2018**, *30*, 04018003.
19. Lavasan, A.A.; Zhao, C.; Barciaga, T.; Schaufler, A.; Steeb, H.; Schanz, T. Numerical investigation of tunneling in saturated soil: The role of construction and operation periods. *Acta Geotech.* **2018**, *13*, 671–691.
20. Lou, P.; Li, Y.; Lu, S.; Xiao, H.; Zhang, Z. Deformation and Mechanical Characteristics of Existing Foundation Pit and Tunnel Itself Caused by Shield Tunnel Undercrossing. *Symmetry* **2022**, *14*, 263. [CrossRef]
21. Liang, Y.; Zhang, J.; Lai, Z.S.; Huang, Q.Y.; Huang, L.C. Temporal and spatial distribution of the grout pressure and its effects on lining segments during synchronous grouting in shield tunnelling. *Eur. J. Environ. Civ. Eng.* **2020**, *24*, 79–96. [CrossRef]
22. Gan, X.; Yu, J.; Gong, X.; Hou, Y.; Liu, N.; Zhu, M. Response of operating metro tunnels to compensation grouting of an underlying large-diameter shield tunnel: A case study in Hangzhou. *Undergr. Space* **2022**, *7*, 219–232.
23. *GB 50010-2010*; Code for Design of Concrete Structures. China Standard Press: Beijing, China, 2010.
24. Su, D.; Chen, W.; Wang, X.; Huang, M.; Pang, X.; Chen, X. Numerical study on transverse deformation characteristics of shield tunnel subject to local soil loosening. *Undergr. Space* **2022**, *7*, 106–121.
25. Koyama, Y. Present status and technology of shield tunneling method in Japan. *Tunn. Undergr. Space Technol.* **2003**, *18*, 145–159.
26. Wang, F.; Zhang, D.M.; Zhu, H.H.; Huang, H.W.; Yin, J.H. Impact of overhead excavation on an existing shield tunnel: Field monitoring and a full 3D finite element analysis. *Comput. Mater. Contin.* **2013**, *34*, 63–81.
27. Zhou, L.; Zhu, H.H.; Shen, Y.; Yan, Z.; Guan, L. Stress and deformation properties of shield segmental linings under internal water pressures. *Chin. J. Geotech. Eng.* **2023**, *45*, 1763–1772. (In Chinese)
28. Fu, Y.B.; Zhao, J.; Wu, X.; Zhong, J.Y. Back-fill pressure model research of simultaneous grouting for shield tunnel. *J. Disaster Prev. Mitig. Eng.* **2016**, *36*, 107–113. (In Chinese)
29. Shahsavar, J.; Johari, A.; Binesh, S. Stochastic analysis of rock slope stability considering cracked rock masses. In Proceedings of the International Conference on Civil Engineering: Modern and Practical Findings, Shiraz, Iran, 15 December 2021.

Disclaimer/Publisher's Note: The statements, opinions and data contained in all publications are solely those of the individual author(s) and contributor(s) and not of MDPI and/or the editor(s). MDPI and/or the editor(s) disclaim responsibility for any injury to people or property resulting from any ideas, methods, instructions or products referred to in the content.

MDPI AG
Grosspeteranlage 5
4052 Basel
Switzerland
Tel.: +41 61 683 77 34

Mathematics Editorial Office
E-mail: mathematics@mdpi.com
www.mdpi.com/journal/mathematics

Disclaimer/Publisher's Note: The title and front matter of this reprint are at the discretion of the Guest Editors. The publisher is not responsible for their content or any associated concerns. The statements, opinions and data contained in all individual articles are solely those of the individual Editors and contributors and not of MDPI. MDPI disclaims responsibility for any injury to people or property resulting from any ideas, methods, instructions or products referred to in the content.

www.ingramcontent.com/pod-product-compliance
Lightning Source LLC
LaVergne TN
LVHW072351090526
838202LV00019B/2524